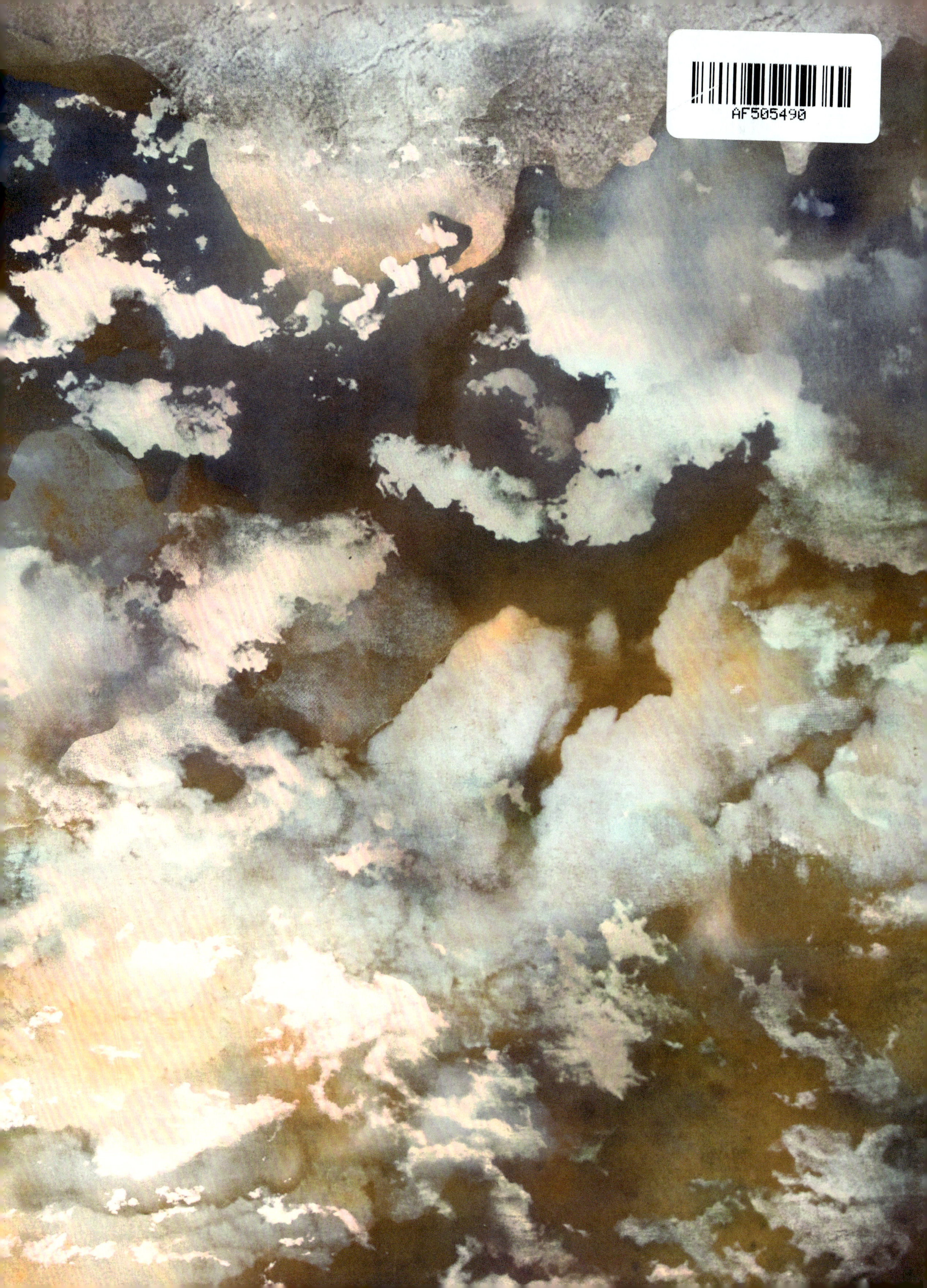
AF505490

Jay Heikes

Jay Heikes

Edited by
Jenelle Porter

Contributions by
Jay Heikes, Sarah Lehrer-Graiwer, Jenelle Porter,
Philippe Vergne, and Hamza Walker

Marianne Boesky Gallery
Gregory R. Miller & Co.

Contents

Outside World

Jenelle Porter

Jay Heikes cut a hole in the wall of an art gallery and titled it *Outside World*. The notched rectangle was centered at eye level and spanned by parallel white bars to conjure the grill of a Mack truck.[1] Beyond the grill all there was to see was a defiantly unglorious view of the adjacent asphalted parking lot. Less straightforward than this description sounds, the hole/whole was low-key in affect and forceful in effect. I can't verify what the titular words describe or depict: the M-shaped frame, the cut hole, the view through it, a phenomenological exchange? Perhaps the artist was performing the magician's misdirection. While Heikes points to the intimidating or malevolent forces of the world—like coming face-to-grill with a truck—he beckons the external world to infiltrate, contaminate, and dynamize the rarified air of art.[2]

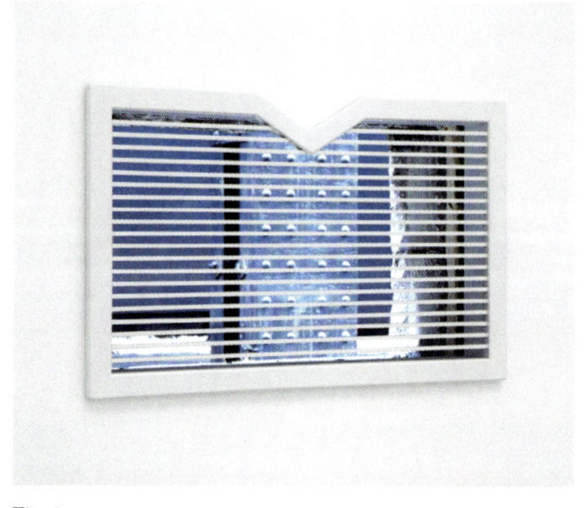

Fig. 1
Outside World, 2010
Enamel on wood
18 ¾ × 29 ¼ × 3 ½ inches, 47.6 × 74.3 × 8.9 cm

The exchange of art and the world was not merely metaphorical: in the dead-end room the flow of air animated pieces of silvery material scattered across the floor. Resembling shredded sheets of thin aluminum, *Molting* (2010) is the outcome of a congealed mixture of gelatin, water, and metallic pigment being poured over forms and peeled away to become what Heikes describes as "cosmic skin." The formal qualities may echo the anti-form pours and scatters of 1960s postminimalists but in fact emerge from the artist's self-assigned study of the properties of various materials that can constitute form. Heikes often uses materials that reify states of transformation—better living through chemistry. For *Molting*, the primary material is gelatin, an atypical sculptural medium that Heikes tracked from the capsule he swallowed to alleviate a headache to its animal carcass source. In other words, while we might swallow the pill and go on with our day, Heikes mulled over the expressive potential of rigidified biological tissue reconfigured as a medicinal delivery system. The artist's primary impulse was "the idea of reconstituting death through sculpture"—a kind of reverse transubstantiation.[3] Indeed, the exhibition that included *Molting* was titled *Inanimate Life*.

Mounted in 2010, *Inanimate Life* demonstrated the range of Heikes's material and formal inquiries, from sculptures, paintings or painted objects, and photography to the site-specific intervention *Outside World*. Passage through the exhibition, which flowed through three rooms, was hindered by threatening objects in the form of driftwood poles rising straight up from the floor and pierced by hundreds of colorfully dyed porcupine quills.[4] With titles such as *Prickly*, *Ickly*, and *Creeply* (all 2010), the cactus-like sculptures mimicked the bendy trees and funky, repetitive word play of Dr. Seuss stories. Indeed, just as many children's books teach us life lessons through allegory, Heikes goes literal: he describes these sculptures as "raw emotions." Like *Molting*, they are repellent, awkward, and a little humorous.

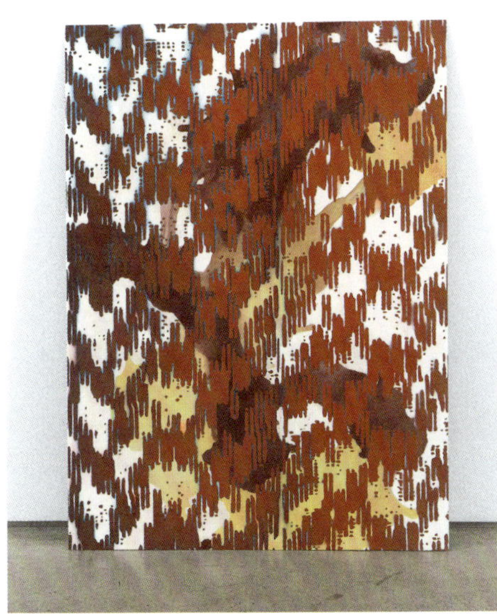

Fig. 2
Conversations with a Bitter Pill, 2010
Sprayed enamel and pigment on steel
62 × 46 inches, 157.5 × 116.8 cm

The main room of the exhibition included, alongside *Molting*, painted rectangular and square steel panels that Heikes calls "fallen" paintings, which rest on the floor and lean against the wall.[5] Unlike the literal opening of *Outside World*, the fallen paintings felt like so many closed windows, albeit slightly cracked by Heikes's distinctive narrative titling: *Conversations with a Bitter Pill* and *Negative Approach* (both 2010). They are spray painted with enamel and pigment in patterns of multicolored zigzags that look like television screen noise, or static. Where the steel is unpainted, rust and oxidation set in, and will, over time, alter the work's surface as well as its physical structure. (Rust erodes; oxidation coats.) Corrosion is also central to a large sculpture made of iron and bronze—materials that when alloyed are compositionally akin to a corroding battery—cast from conjoined driftwood and rope: *Heartless Ascension* (2010) twisted on the floor and arced into space like a line drawing or a whip. These works in metal—the sculptures and the paintings—enact the paradoxical simultaneity of stasis and entropy.

Inanimate Life was Heikes's spillover event of 2010.[6] From this point on, his work displayed ever more ambitious material and formal experimentation. Most significantly, it was the artist's first foray into the pragmatics and poetics of alchemy. Mining the magical thinking at alchemy's core (base metals become noble), he began to deploy what he considers impossible materials. Not only can they be difficult to acquire and manipulate, these materials often point beyond the cloister of art. However, Heikes declines to signal topical or social practice modes with his choice of materials (the works are not about, for example, destructive mining industries), but he also won't go out of his way to refute the associations and histories we viewers bring to them. For instance, if the decomposition of fugitive materials reminds us that we inhabit bodies with expiration dates, so be it. *Inanimate Life* was exhibition as life cycle. The point to consider, once we're invited inside, is why these materials are put together, what they do to each other, *and* what they do to the visitor. If rust and corrosion are materials (but also tools, something we will return to), why and how are they being used—as content, form, image, performance?

Career Ender, or the Infinity Problem

*Do I always have to search for unexplored possibilities or can I just present a kind of
deadpan futility that acts as satire? Maybe I'm just an existentialist in denial.*[7]
  —JAY HEIKES

The fallen paintings and composite metal sculptures included in *Inanimate Life*
were the final elements in Heikes's first major body of work, a series that began
in 2005 with a joke—of all ideas!—at its conceptual center. This joke is about a
pirate who tries to teach his new parrot to speak. "Polly wanna cracker?" coaxes the
pirate. "Fuck you, one-eye!" the parrot replies. The pirate's repeated attempts to
train the bird to speak are fruitless, a never-ending loop of command and affront.
The exasperated pirate finally locks the parrot in the freezer. The next morning, he
finds the parrot dead, its frozen wing flipping the bird: a definitive "statement." Is
this joke funny? Depends on your sense of humor, which is contingent, contextual,
historical, and experiential as much as temperamental. Does it matter if it's funny?
For Heikes, the joke's magnitude resides in its pathetic loop, whose correlative
artistic sentiment of futility might be "All the good ideas have been used up." To
his ear, one can swap "pirate and parrot" with "artist and artwork" to summarize
the creative endeavor. But since the way out is often through, it also presents a
road map for making art. Heikes explains: "The artwork refuses to behave, and
my work emerges from a refusal of mimicry. The joke symbolized that not only
could an artwork be wild, out of your control, but that I could attempt an artistic
practice in which I would let the artwork rebel against me. That's when I became
anti-illustration. And that meant that the artwork might not be what I wanted it
to be. That's why I made the video of the joke."

The video recording of Heikes performing the joke, with longish hair
brushed forward over his face and tucked under his eyeglasses, was the first work in
what would become a series presented as "retellings." From one seemingly humble
source, the work spins off in myriad directions, many of which were stimulated by
the artist's reading of Arte Povera's foregrounding of symbolism, transformation,
contingency, and a nonhierarchical engagement of everyday, or "poor," materials. (The pirate joke itself might be said to be in "poor" taste.) By using the joke
as *prima materia*, both reducing and enlarging it, Heikes amplified the feedback
loop—a twist on minimalism's repetitive strategies—until the original source (the
joke, the video) was so degraded, or distilled, as to become something new.

The drawing installations that emerged from video stills expanded
into sculpture and painting, and all these modes were exhibited together in

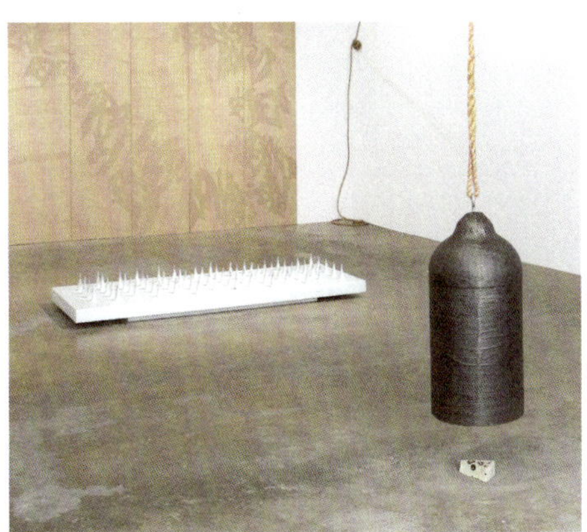

Fig. 3
Installation view, *Jay Heikes*, Institute of Contemporary Art,
University of Pennsylvania, Philadelphia, 2007

metaphor-probing installations. Video stills were printed, photocopied, collaged, drawn and painted over, and splotched with blobs and drips that obliterate the image, evoking both an abstract expressionist gesture and the residue of a juicy tomato lobbed at a lousy performer. Heikes's investigations led to explorations of staging, performance, and theater. *New Heaven Hook* (2005), a seven-foot cast aluminum hook, was hung from the Whitney Museum's iconic concrete ceiling grid like a cane for pulling a comedian (or, the institution?) off-stage to cut a wretched routine. At the Walker Art Center in 2006, the installation *So There's This Pirate . . . Live from Minneapolis* included objects resembling theatrical props and band gear, painted stage black, and incorporated facile visual gags: a black-painted light bulb in a cast-iron pan (deadpan), a walker with an attached dildo (getting it up—and keeping it up). In one "retelling," installed in 2007 concurrently at the Institute of Contemporary Art in Philadelphia and Marianne Boesky Gallery in New York, Heikes incorporated works that adapt motifs from Jean-Paul Sartre's plays. The stasis of a locked room in the existentialist's *No Exit* inspired a number of symbolic objects: a bed of spikes in *The Soft Pillow* (2007) representing sleeplessness; a cuckoo clock, fleeting time; a dome-shaped hanging rat trap, futility; and a curtained box, the opportunity to "change." Other lodestones include Andy Kaufman's off-kilter, absurdist performances (in which no jokes were *delivered*) and Lee Lozano's *Dropout Piece* (about 1970), a deadpan life-art action in which the artist "dropped out" of her insular art community.

The pirate joke (the material) was a battery forced to rust, which in turn led to the use of literally corrosive materials—a transfer of concept to form. What Heikes did in this body of work was to isolate the potential energy of a closed system—the joke, the battery—and in doing so perverted it beyond all narrative. I consider this idea as being like a parasite that annihilates its host. The distillation is a corruption so profound as to be either a wellspring or a career ender, or both. This line of inquiry begs the question, When does appropriation metamorphose into originality? Repetition as infinitude? Let's put a pin in that.

The Material Mine

Heikes engages materials that literally continue developing long after he stops manipulating them. The corrosion that results from mixing iron and bronze is one example. The same proposition defines the fallen paintings, that is, rust invades and animates the painted static. As Heikes began his tireless experimentation with materials' transmutative capacities—like an escalating sequence of dares— the concept and practice of alchemy became central to his work. I confess to a fascination with the principle of magical ideation that surrounds alchemy, and this is a facet of Heikes's work I find particularly engaging. To my eye, his work has the fervor of devotion written all over it, however often he points to his actual *dis*belief in belief (in the sense of phony spiritualism, "new age stuff," hocus-pocus—he is the son of a chemist, after all). Jay is the consummate skeptic.

The exploration and exploitation of the dualities intrinsic to alchemy, including the reconciliation of opposites, are fundamental to Heikes's work. We see many of the same premises in the work of Sigmar Polke, one of Heikes's principal guides in matters conceptual, philosophical, and material. I draw your attention to the specifics of Polke's solo representation of West Germany at the 1986 Venice Biennale, which drew supple connections among the Roman and Byzantine Empire's harvesting of sea mollusks for a purple pigment that would come to represent nobility and power, the diabolical ends to which the Nazis implemented science, and the alchemist's furnace from which the exhibition took its title, *Athanor*.[8] Among Polke's works on view, in many media, was *Purple (Purpur)* (1986), a swatch of pale silk stained with a Tyrian purple dye. Blotches and doodles of color give this ten-foot-long textile the appearance of a map, an abstract petroglyph, or, unsettlingly, evidence of the messy extermination required to produce the pigment, conducted in Polke's kitchen and disclosed in accompanying photographs and a film.[9] Alchemy is not always benevolent.

Central to *Athanor* is the Mediterranean region, which Heikes explored during an extended stay in Rome in 2011. Away from his regular materials and tools (and the equilibrium of home), Heikes made a body of work that mined the region's histories, myths, and materials. The resulting exhibition at Federica Schiavo Gallery, *The Material Mine*, included works informed by alchemical legacies and chemical reactions. *Fields* (2011) is two sheets of purple linen laid flat on the floor, anchored at its four corners by aluminum sulfate crystals. The sculpture evokes Mike Kelley's floor-bound installations of knitted afghans and found objects, not only formally but also in its shared allusion to art as a therapeutic enterprise, heightened by the presence of crystals. *Fields* is rooted in New Age,

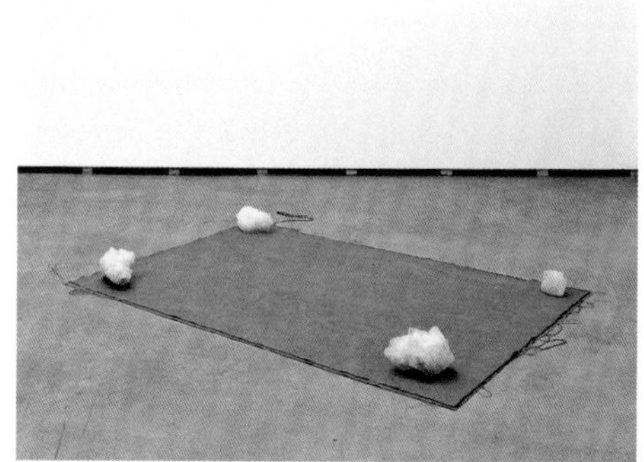

Fig. 4
Fields, 2011
Purpurissum pigment on linen and aluminum sulfate crystals
4 ¾ × 38 ⅝ × 50 ⅜ inches, 12 × 98 × 128 cm

alchemy, and Polke's use of crystals and quicksilver, arsenic and mercury. Heikes dyed the linen with Purpurissum, a synthetic purple derived from the carnivorous mollusk whose secretions were used by the ancients. He grew the crystals from aluminum sulfate, a material that is used as a mordant in dyeing as well as in the production of electronics. Symbolically, then, the field becomes a magnetic plain, or an archaic receiver. For Heikes, always the contrarian, the sculpture allegorizes and critiques "the new age stuff I don't believe in."

Heikes's selection of materials is always directed by an exhaustive research approach. *Salamander's Wool* (2011), for example, is titled after an antiquated name for asbestos, which was "discovered" in China by Italian explorer Marco Polo. The history (and myth) of the material includes accounts of soldiers setting their asbestos-coated garments aflame to intimidate their enemies. On learning of this history, or I should say this story, Heikes procured raw silk from China, combined it with carbon-saturated concrete, and poured the mixture into rect-angular molds. The resulting bas-relief works illustrate the structure and color of chrysotile asbestos, but they're imposters: approximations of one substance are transmuted into another to create a kind of proxy.

The proxy is a central theme in Heikes's work. We see it in Civilians (2008–10), a photographic series showing desiccated scarecrow-like figures with stick bones protruding here and there. They wear round metal-frame eyeglasses on their hornet-nest heads, channeling Eisenstein's *Battleship Potemkin* as quoted by Francis Bacon, and a nineties-era grunge uniform of flannel shirt and 501s. Their hands and feet are cast from the artist's own. Parenthetical subtitles bespeak desperate or altered states: *howling, hopeless, drunk*. The photos are palladium prints, which result from a labor-intensive process that creates a more painterly effect than the silver gelatin prints that materially connect to *Molting*. To make a palladium print, you sensitize a sheet of paper by painting it with liquid metal, transfer an image onto its surface by exposing a negative just above it to ultra-violet light, add some color tinting, perhaps, and you've got a permanent photograph.[10]

The horror-movie vibe of these images goes beyond film; as noted in the shorthand title of the series, it references the innumerable civilian casualties of the post-9/11 American-led invasions of Afghanistan and Iraq. It was the grotesque image of the burned corpses of four war contractors hanging from the trusses of a bridge in Fallujah, looking like so much charred wood, that impelled Heikes to make this work and, more broadly, to narratively explore topical events involving the destruction of bodies and civilizations. (The straw man here is built and then destroyed, destroyed and then built; the straw man is the fallacy that leads to end-less war.) The construction of a creature calls to mind two points of comparison.

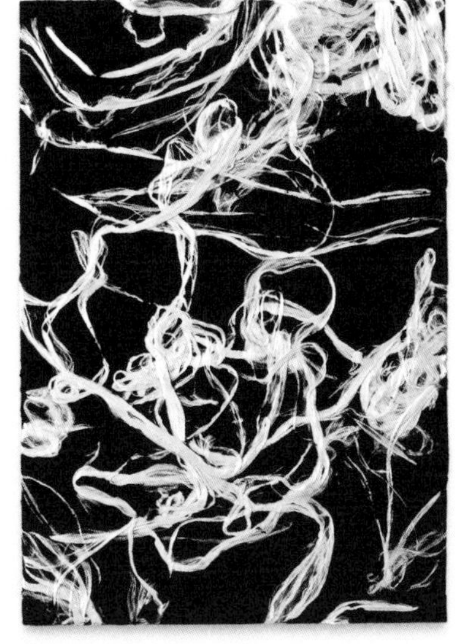

Fig. 5
Salamander's Wool, 2011
Silk, concrete and carbon pigment
26 × 18 1/8 × 1 1/2 inches, 66 × 46 × 3.8 cm

First, the pinhole-camera photographs Hirsh Perlman made from 1998 to 2001 of cardboard assemblages with humanoid features.[11] Perlman's date-stamped prints chart the hours devoted to combating the futility, loneliness, and dead ends of work in the studio. Second, the hubris of creation central to Mary Shelley's nineteenth-century allegorical tale *Frankenstein; or, the Modern Prometheus*. ("I saw the pale student of unhallowed arts kneeling beside the thing he had put together," Shelley explained of her novel.[12])

The proxy—one thing substituting for another—is repeatedly rehearsed by Heikes, and it informs a series of exhibitions he organized in the mid-2010s. His first curatorial foray, *Trieste*, comprised three sequential exhibitions at affiliating galleries in Rome (2012), New York (2013), and Amsterdam (2014).[13] Including works by nine artists (Heikes included), each iteration of the exhibition was an effort to "present a perfect fragment" of their thought, process, inspiration, and conversation.[14] The comprehensive catalogue published in 2014 includes installation documentation and conversations between Heikes and each of the artists: Huma Bhabha, Isa Newby Gagarin, Jessica Jackson Hutchins, Matthew Day Jackson, Lisa Lapinski, Karthik Pandian, Erin Shirreff, and Johannes VanDerBeek.

In 2015 Heikes organized *Consequences* for the Fondazione Giuliani per l'arte contemporanea in Rome. The artworks on view—by Felix Culpa, Jessica Jackson Hutchins, Ari Marcopolous, Josiah McElheny, Todd Norsten, Conny Purtill, Justin Schlepp, Gedi Sibony, Michael Stickrod, The Unknown Artist, and the ghost of Lee Lozano—were created collaboratively, or to be precise, in the manner of the surrealist game exquisite corpse (itself derived from a period word game called Consequences). Heikes has explained the impetus for this approach as the need to rescue his work from what he considered a self-obsessed path "hopelessly leading to a strategic type of branding my soul couldn't entertain."[15]

Using collectivity and collaboration as vehicles with which to explore authority, authorship, and agency, Heikes invited his fellow artists to respond to his selection of a particular material or object. He sent Hutchins a picnic table; Schlepp, psychic transmissions; Sibony, a box of dyed plywood scraps; and so on. Does this sound convoluted? That's the idea. Heikes included work of his own, including a monstrous ruin titled *Our Frankenstein* (2015). Acknowledging pop culture's revival of a novel about isolation into a metaphor for just about any awkward mixture—from Dr. Frankenstein the creator to Frankenstein the monster—*Our Frankenstein* is a chaotic mash-up: a mannequin severed at the waist is clothed with garments belonging to the invited artists and fitted with Heikes's cast cement hands and feet and a *Creature from the Black Lagoon* mask.[16] This apparition is loaded with so many symbols, ideas, and metaphors that it short-circuits.

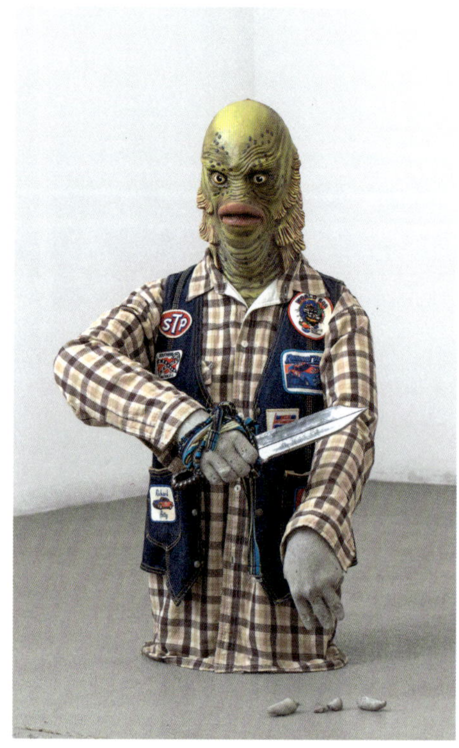

Fig. 6
Our Frankenstein, 2015 (top)
Concrete, steel, plastic, and fabric
37 3/8 × 17 3/4 × 23 5/8 inches, 95 × 45 × 60 cm

Generational Anxiety

My goal is not to turn lesser metal into gold but to show that art is magic and realism is a naïve melody worth humming along to.[17]
—JAY HEIKES

The Material Mine concluded the most intensive phase of Heikes's involvement in material conduction. At this point, 2012 or so, his inquiry into repetition as a form of erasure and ultimately genesis had acquired a sense of inevitability. "I got to the point where I needed to start again," he has said. "I'd taken my work so far in this material direction that I had to now make the tools, too. If you want to reinvent the language you have to reinvent the tools. This felt like a breakthrough." We generally consider breakthroughs to be positive, but let's take a moment to appreciate the term. It's a rupture. Heikes sometimes describes himself as being in a kind of survivor mode during this period, a state of mind that can provoke extreme actions. In the process of rewinding your practice to its zero point, you'll suffer self-imposed isolation and alienation. Imagine: If your task is to create a new language, you must render yourself mute. It's just you and the walls, so to speak. In many ways, this is the artist's studio.

A recalibration needs a mission statement. Heikes, adopting the zeal as well as the organ of the twentieth-century avant-garde—the futurists, Dadaists, Gutai Group, situationists, actionists, Valerie Solanas, Dogme 95—writes a manifesto. Typewritten on a yellowing piece of paper, "Manifesto for the anti social" proclaims: "We lead healthy lives to keep filthy minds." (Typical Jay. Funny, rebellious, contrarian, poignant, absurd, stupidly sincere.) Is the healthy life led inside or outside the studio? In the sweet spot between those worlds? And, now, in 2020, what is a healthy life during a pandemic? What is a healthy life if you're Black in America? (Does Heikes's manifesto now read as prescient or retrograde?) Is the only way we get through the extraordinary crisis of 2020 to wallow in the filth until it's spread so thin we surface with a new skin? Does the filth harden into a tool that pries us from this mess? With a gimlet eye and modest ego, Heikes hastens to state that "the manifesto is a changeable, slight exercise meant only to inspire transformation."[18]

What followed on the heels of the manifesto was a series of small, enigmatic objects that resemble amulets, relics, and ancient implements that might be useful in terms of "I could draw/douse/poke a hole/fasten with that." Heikes cobbled together a bricoleur's workbench of eccentric utensils made from studio detritus, found objects—especially from nature—and straight-up trash, which temporarily replaced traditional studio devices. At the same time, the artist made what he calls Cave paintings. Why? Ancient cave paintings are thought to be incantatory renderings for desired outcomes. In this sense, painting is prophecy, and Heikes needed to make work that might predict (or at least hint at) new directions. The Cave paintings are objects that hover on the wall like acid-hued auras. Titles such as *Ear of Dionysius* (2011) and *Bell Witch* (2012) are the names of actual caves.[19] A layer of papier-mâché is applied to expanded aluminum and wood, then covered in gesso that is sanded and pigmented. The object resembles a plaster tablet, a kind of receiving surface. Inked leather hides are pressed into the surface to create an allover design with the texture of skin. You may recognize connections to the ways Yves Klein, Ana Mendieta, David Hammons, and others employed bodies, their own or others, as brushes or stamps. Handprints—indexes of the imprinting process—disrupt the picture plane, the visual effect of which is very cave-painting-meets-frottage-meets-bloody-handprint, horror-movie-poster-meets-birth-announcement. The Cave paintings, then, are beginning (predictive) and end (recording), a loop.

While there are myriad cave metaphors to plumb, the connection of the so-called sacred space of art, the white cube, to Paleolithic caves is extraordinarily summarized by Thomas McEvilley. As in the art gallery, prehistoric paintings and sculptures were located "in a setting deliberately set off from the outside world and difficult to access." He goes on: "Such ritual spaces are symbolic reestablishments of the ancient umbilicus which, in myths worldwide, once connected heaven and earth. . . . Since this is a space where access to higher metaphysical realms is made to seem available, it must be sheltered from the appearance of change and time."[20] The relevance of McEvilley's words to Heikes's engagement with paradox, stasis, and entropy, staggers. "The construction of a supposedly unchanging space, then, or a space where the effects of change are deliberately disguised and hidden, is sympathetic magic to promote unchangingness in the real or non-ritual world; it is an attempt to cast an appearance of eternity over the status quo in terms of social values and also, in our modern instance, artistic values."[21]

As the Cave paintings progressed, the tool objects asserted their autonomy. Their utilitarian assembly on the studio wall looked to Heikes like a painting, with each tool serving as a mark. The first instantiation of this was the manifesto-derived *We lead healthy lives to keep filthy minds* (2013). Composed of fourteen objects hung in two rows of seven, the work resembles an anthropological display. There is a wand-like stick with copper wires gathered at one end, a red waxy orb, a comb-like device, and other oddball bits. The conceptual evolution from

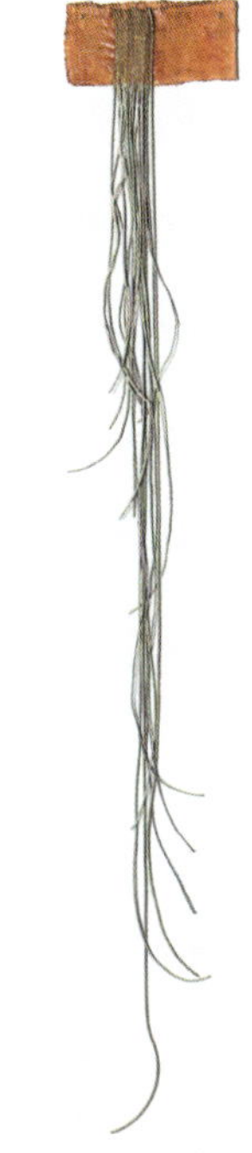

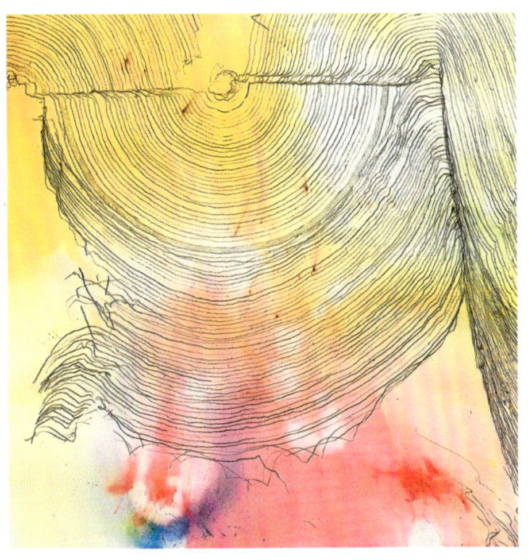

Fig. 7 (top)
Eva Hesse, *Test Piece*, 1967–68
Natural rubber on cloth and opaque (rubber?) tubing
78 × 5 inches, 198.1 × 12.7 cm
UC Berkeley Art Museum & Pacific Film Archive (BAMPFA),
Gift of Mrs. Helen Hesse Charash, 1979

Fig. 8 (bottom)
Music for Minor Planets (Oz), 2015 (detail)
Graphite and pigment on dyed and bleached paper
50 1/8 × 86 inches, 127.3 × 218.4 cm

making tools to paint with to making paintings out of tools emerged from the artist's desire for the instruments to be more than bit players in the existential drama of painting. In describing one object that could be used as a stamp, Heikes has said, "I concluded that the stamp was the content instead of the mark it had made because my focus from the beginning was how to challenge the structure of language at its most primitive starting point."[22]

Conceptually akin to Heikes's tools are Eva Hesse's so-called "studio-work," or test pieces.[23] Neither finished nor unfinished, not quite merely provisional but not fully complete either, their awkward standing makes their interpretation a provocative line of inquiry, one that will continue to metamorphose along with the sensibilities of art historians. In these small works, Hesse could experiment with fugitive materials, clocking the material transformations of, say, latex. Their existence points to the ever-expanding list of questions (often without answers) that arise in relation to an artist's process: When is the artwork finished? When does the work *make* a work? What is a creation and what is an experiment? How does an artwork change when it travels from the studio to public or private display? And what of an artwork that will change over time?

As Heikes's tools became "less tool-like and more autonomous as wall sculptures that seem more direct and symbolic, like a dirty palette instead of a table of curious elements," he doubled back.[24] He returned to using the tools to make artworks. For the series Music for Minor Planets, Heikes dragged a "pencil rake" over large horizontal sheets of paper stained with colored dye. The rake is a device he made that secures together all the pencils he found lying around the studio one day and is capable of drawing sixty-five parallel lines simultaneously.[25] Visually recalling seismograms, the lines swoop, swivel, and pinch tight at right angles. They start and end outside the paper's edge, side to side, as if the sheet were only a section of a larger expanse. To my eye, it is as though Heikes had transformed the musical staff into the music itself, with splotches of pigment reading as so many notes, or as planets in a solar system—hence the title. "They're spacey and psychedelic and owe a lot to David Reed, John Cage, and the Japanese avant-garde of the 1960s," the artist explains.[26] The coloring is either subtle and ethereal, or as dramatic as a solar flare. The technique for making these drawings was anticipated by the rake, or "developer," devised by Jack Whitten for his "slab" paintings, Rosemarie Trockel's *Painting Machine*, made from the hair of fellow artists, and other devices artists have developed to effect a simultaneity of gesture and, just as importantly, a means to distance the hand from the unique mark. The goal is not quite authorlessness, but there is a notable quarrying of the logic of mechanical production. For many years, Heikes's drawings functioned as something like the studio soundtrack to the works he exhibited publicly: he made them, but he didn't exhibit them. (Later, they would serve as quasi-blueprints for three-dimensional sculptures.)

The parenthetical titles of the works in the Music for Minor Planets series reveal my favorite aspects of Heikes as an artist, among them the dazzling maker mixed with the smart-ass satirist, as well as the stuff he thinks about as he works, whether art, television, world events, chemical admixtures, music, aspirations, or magic: *Polke*; *Piccard*; *Picasso the Asshole*; *The Next Kurt Cobain*. This is not the text that will search Heikes's biography to speculate on his reasons for becoming an artist or to suggest what triggered this work or that. But there is one event that, because of its lingering and pervasive aura, bears discussion. On several occasions, Heikes has relayed the impact of installing, as part of a temporary crew, a historical survey of Arte Povera at the Walker Art Center in the fall of 2001. He was at work on September 11. I don't want to project, so I'll share only my own experience of that day and those that followed. I recall the fear, grief, and uncertainty of those weeks, how the ground shifted under my feet. I can't help but compare those feelings to those aroused right now, with this pandemic, these protests, this economic collapse, this flailing democracy. My point is this: Extraordinary crises expose vulnerabilities. And yet, as all hell breaks loose outside the museum walls, your job might be planting cactus for a Janis Kounellis sculpture or unpacking the aluminum coils of Marisa Merz's *Untitled (Living sculpture)* (1966), and these activities might reside vividly in your head and your body; years later, you might make *Molting*. "It was [the] moment in which I shifted my thinking from image culture to material culture," the artist explained to me. "I saw this whole other world that lacked any reference but the material it used. The bronze didn't relate to anything but bronze. At that point, as a young artist, it seemed so freeing." I would put it this way: When you install artworks, your eyes and hands are all over them (gloved, of course); you're up close, nearer than museum visitors are allowed; you carry the artwork, experiencing its weight and its smell, unpack it, assemble it, recreate it from instructions. When you spend time installing art, you learn many things about how and why people make it.

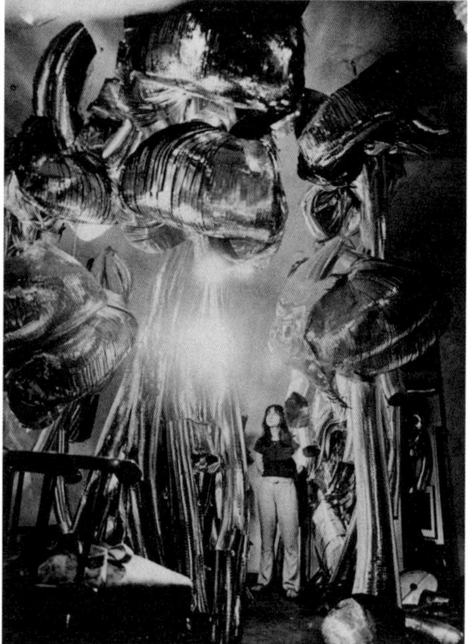

Fig. 9
Marisa Merz with her *Untitled (Living Sculpture)*, Turin, 1966

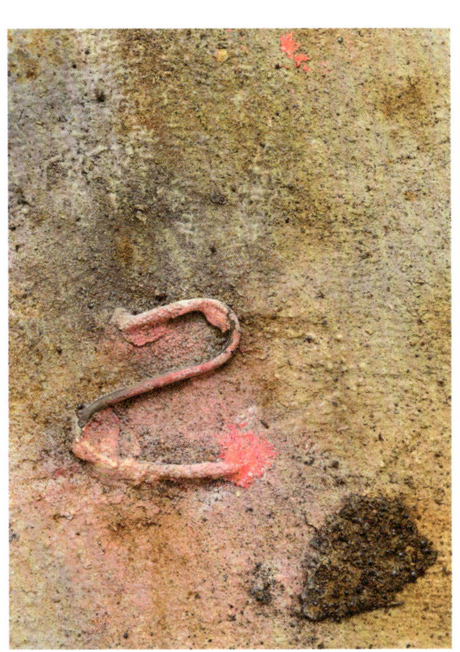

Fig. 10
Zs, 2016 (detail)
Pigmented mortar, dyed burlap, salt, steel slag, copper wire,
enamel, and wood
40 ⅛ × 30 ¾ × 2 inches, 102 × 78 × 5 cm

Before Common Era

*I want to present an atmosphere—an ambience—which is so peaceful that you're
shattered when you leave.*[27]
　　　　—PAUL THEK

Heikes began a series of paintings in 2017 whose title, Mother Sky, is swiped
from a song by Krautrock band CAN that was soundtracking his work in the
studio one day. That day Heikes decided to just . . . paint . . . the . . . sky. He may
have had this impulse because in January 2017 people with brains didn't think it
could get any worse: a lying, cheating, sexually harassing, racist malignancy was
inaugurated as president of the United States. We stand corrected. It's gotten so
much more abject: he's murdering us with lies and propaganda and ignorance
and race-baiting. Throughout 2016, Heikes made works that now jangle with an
unsettling clairvoyance.

　　　In the grip of midlife and world-events-induced sleep deprivation, Heikes
asked himself, as one might, Where do we go when we sleep? Where is our consciousness when we're unconscious? These monkey-brain ramblings and a story
shared by a friend about an art exhibition so lackluster that she scribed "ZZZ" in
the gallery register led Heikes down meandering paths: so-called boring content;
consequential versus inconsequential images; the slow-burn "sleeper" hit. Z. It's
the last letter, the end of language, the contents of a comic-strip bubble above a
sleeper. First, Heikes made a series of Z drawings and prints with asphaltum, a tar-
like material (also called bitumen) that is put to many uses, including the ancient
practice of embalming. He then made easel-scale paintings/objects composed of
dyed, pigmented, and/or burned burlap wrapped around mortared stretchers, the
surfaces of which were incised with Zs or pierced by bent copper Zs. Rather than
a retreat from the devastating and corrupted 2016 election, Heikes's response
was elegiac. The Z paintings were "like the inside of my brain. . . . As much as I
wanted to board up the windows, the world was coming in through the cracks."
One 2017 work was constructed with a Z-shaped reinforcement like that of barn
doors or windows, its vertical wooden planks oozing salt and pigment.

　　　In a series of sculptures called Minor Planets, Heikes marshaled his facil-
ity with anomalous art materials to create hand-scaled orbs composed of bismuth,
copper, steel slag, Gladstone ore, lignum vitae, bronze, leather, glue, clay, Kevlar,
and, in one case, a geode. The orbs allude to the splotches on the Music for Minor
Planets drawings made the same year, works that, as previously mentioned, were
realized in 2017 as three-dimensional metal sculptures inspired by the barbed

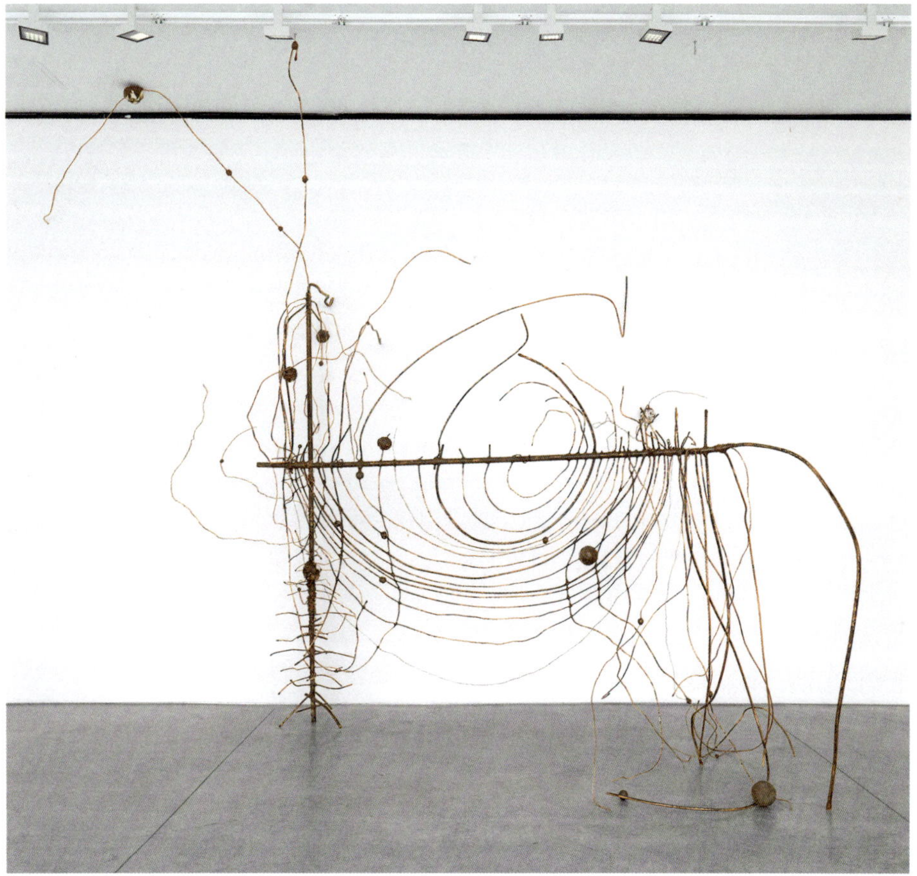

wire fences and tumbleweeds of the Texas prairie (where Heikes, in early 2017, participated in a Chinati Foundation residency) and science museum solar system models. The three-dimensional orbs, scattered on the floor at the foot of the wire sculptures, embody thoughts so fully formed they drop like overripe fruit. In 2018, *Music for Minor Planets* was "played" as a score by musicians.

"This era has made me think of all the accepted things I've thought of as unchangeable," Heikes told me by way of explaining the transformations in his work of the last few years. He thought most about the view from the Z-planked window, and what he wanted it to be: majestic skies. Heikes asked himself, If cave paintings are predictive tools, why can't we deploy that sympathetic magic right now? The Mother Sky canvases show clouds, or more specifically, distortions of found and photographed images. Heikes describes the works as "soft fantasies, stained, screened and dabbed into existence with equal parts Morris Louis, Bob Ross and Andy Warhol." He'll throw in Gerhard Richter and Polke, too. Heikes's unpublished 2019 text about these works, "I Wavereth," is worthy of lengthy quotation:

> At times it feels like I am playing God with these landscapes, imagining an atmosphere from above that has finally freed itself of all human trivialities. I was supposed to pick up the mantle of activism and help answer the people's cries but instead I became more distant, even hidden, while creating these representational moods of the soul. Did I really think I could control the weather? Or at least my weather? Obviously no, but as our world descended and still lurches into a convenient relationship between the always impending apocalypse and the shirking of responsibility to do anything about it because of a never-ending list of preordained prophecies, I am left with the difficult question of where do I stand? And what do I want to look at while I can still see? I for one am at my wit's end and have come to the conclusion that when I die I'd like to be cremated and then have my ashes be used in a glaze to coat a ball of fired clay. That way close friends and relatives would be able to not only roll me around while I achieve my ultimate goal of being an inanimate object, but also see the true palette of my being. I can only imagine it being a dull gray with a hint of yellow. Or maybe pink.

The cloud imagery is composited from disparate sources to underscore its unworldliness. There is no up or down. Even if the images are meteorologically possible, the colors aren't. As the series has progressed, the clouds have become images of smoke from, for example, the 2019 Australian wildfires and Notre Dame's conflagration. Nature is burning and so are the churches. Heikes can't help himself: even his longing for beautiful skies has yielded to the intrusion of ominous human-caused plumes. As escapist as it may at first seem, the rendering of heavenly phenomena has long carried meaning deeper than mere cloud identification. Heikes's work asks, What if the horizon shifts entirely? What if the clouds go vertical? I'd add, What if the clouds are collected grief? What if the clouds are an airborne toxic event? Zadie Smith writes, "The art of mid-life is surely always cloudier than the art of youth, as life itself gets cloudier."[28]

Now, Stuplimity

Stuplimity is a neologism merging *stupefaction* and *sublimity*. Emerging from affect theory, the word describes a condition of "numbness and hyper-attentiveness, boredom and awe, nonchalance and monotony in the face of the overwhelming." That's about how now, this unprecedented now, feels to me. Other words and phrases that swirl in the present atmosphere like objects in a tornado: self-isolation, cautious optimism, contact-free, social distance, pause, new normal, systemic racism, whiteness, deconstruct, defund, cancel, abolish. I write and edit this essay during the spring and summer of 2020. In the last few months, the coronavirus pandemic has spread around the world and stolen the lives of hundreds of thousands, the livelihoods of millions. So far. The social and economic repercussions are catastrophic and will undoubtedly transform society and the course of history. In the last weeks, protests stemming from the police lynching of George Floyd have broadened into a reckoning with systemic racism and social and economic injustice that will, quite possibly (please please please) lead to revolutionary change. So many ifs. I attempt to describe and contextualize these current events not because they're current but because they reflect a pervasive and toxic norm. It is impossible to do cultural work without writing about culture, and art is culture's most versatile and profound manifestation. Art is a magnifying glass and a mirror, a quiet cave, a frontline, a flash point, a unifier, and a disrupter; it is a virus and a vaccine. Heikes's work, despite its purported "anti social" stance, is as vital and nourishing as ever. Its very operation—conducted through his curious, "filthy" mind and dogged material experimentation—is a model of devotion. It points us back at ourselves, our own minds, as an amulet against the world outside.

One last artwork before we go. The 2013 series fragment from the Theory of Everything is constituted of wall-hung objects—latticed branches wrapped with horsehair and wax. To me, they resemble Micronesian stick charts, archaic navigational tools that map ocean swells and currents, atolls and islands, compelling and elegant objects that were so individualized they could be read only by their makers. And the artist's poetic title? If the "Theory of Everything" pertains to the scientific quest to link every physical aspect of the universe, then isn't a fragment just too pathetic? The theory, vast in its ambitions, "relates to our ideas about God, and how life is one long stakeout, with, to prove the case, circumstantial evidence at best," the artist explains. "We're presented with fragments that don't fit together. Belief systems are coping strategies we use to shield ourselves from what's behind the curtain—something which most of us cannot bear to witness." Heikes did not have maps or unified theory in mind when he made these works, but rather the

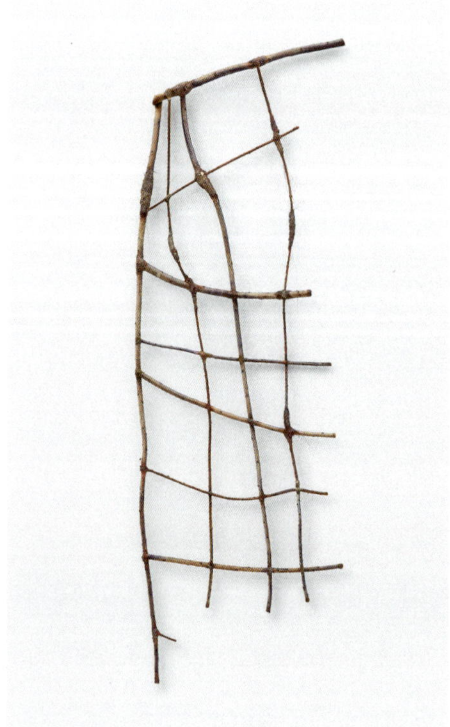

Fig. 12
fragment from the Theory of Everything, 2013
Wax, wood, horsehair, ink, and steel wire
73 ⅝ × 29 ⅛ × 4 ¾ inches, 187 × 74 × 12 cm

desire, once again, to bring his work back to a zero degree by literally stripping the canvas from the support, physically and metaphorically exposing what's underneath the surface. This is the skeleton of the painting, skin flayed, framing nothing, presenting nothing. Total exposure; willful vulnerability. The painting is no longer a window out but a window in. Or it may be neither, only a void as unlocatable as *Outside World*.

1. The Mack truck grill, the artist explained to me, also references Stephen King's 1986 B-movie *Maximum Overdrive*, wherein previously inanimate objects exact revenge on stupid humans.

2. In another work related to the interpenetration of interior and exterior realms, *Storytelling* (2013), Heikes exposed a sensitized piece of fabric to light by opening the door to the darkened studio, inviting the outside world to impress itself on the latent artwork. The resulting overexposed "image" is of nothing or perhaps an unseeable everything, a wry commentary on the romanticization of creativity in the studio. On the mid-twentieth-century fascination with the artist's studio that this calls to mind for me, the scouring of the "debris" visible in documentary photographs for insight into the creative process, see Briony Fer, *Eva Hesse: Studiowork* (Edinburgh: Fruitmarket Gallery, 2009), 33.

3. Unless otherwise noted, all quotations by the artist are from a two-part interview with the author conducted in Los Angeles on January 9 and 10, 2020.

4. When Heikes queried the seller about the source of the quills, concerned that they might have been poached, he was told they were "found."

5. Heikes has noted that his inspiration for the nickname "fallen" paintings was a passage in Douglas Coupland's 1998 novel *Girlfriend in a Coma* in which, during the year after the end of the world, "ten million pictures fall from ten million walls." Douglas Coupland, *Girlfriend in a Coma* (New York: HarperCollins, 1998), 5.

6. A spillover event occurs when a pathogen is transferred from one species to another.

7. Bartholomew Ryan, "A Table of Curious Elements: Jay Heikes on *Filthy Minds*," Walker Art Center, July 3, 2013, https://walkerart.org/magazine/a-table-of-curious-elements-jay-heikes-on-filthy-minds.

8. See Lanka Tattersal, "Eight Days a Week," in *Alibis: Sigmar Polke, 1963–2010*, ed. Kathy Halbreich (New York: Museum of Modern Art, 2014).

9. The overall theme of the 1986 Venice Biennale was "Art and Science" and the largest section of its thematic subheadings was "Art and Alchemy." Polke won the Golden Lion award that year.

10. Being impervious to chemical changes, palladium prints are extremely durable. "Scarce, expensive noble metals, like gold, platinum, and palladium, combine with nearly nothing in nature." Alan Weisman, *The World Without Us* (New York: St. Martin's Press, 2007), 246.

11. Heikes studied with Hirsh Perlman at the Yale School of Art, New Haven, Connecticut, from 2003 to 2005.

12. Quoted in *The New Yorker*, February 12, 2018, https://www.newyorker.com/magazine/2018/02/12/the-strange-and-twisted-life-of-frankenstein.

13. Federica Schiavo Gallery, Rome (2012), Marianne Boesky Gallery, New York (2013), and Grimm Gallery, Amsterdam (2014).

14. Jay Heikes, *Trieste* (Rome: Federica Schiavo Gallery; New York: Marianne Boesky Gallery; Amsterdam: Grimm Gallery, 2014), 7.

15. Heikes, *Consequences* (Rome: CURA.BOOKS, 2016), 7.

16. The latex *Creature from the Black Lagoon* mask resembles those designed by Ray Heikes, a sculptor who lived outside Detroit. Jay discovered these facts during an Internet search of his own name. The proximity of their full names—differing by only one letter—Ray's profession, and the fact that he died on Jay's day of birth, January 14, were generative coincidences.

17. Jay Heikes, quoted in *Jay Heikes: Walkabout* press release, Marianne Boesky Gallery, New York, 2013.

18. Jay Heikes, "Manifesto," *Art in America* 101, no. 2 (February 2013), 40–41.

19. The caves are located in Syracuse, Italy, and Adams, Tennessee, respectively.

20. Thomas McEvilley, introduction to *Inside the White Cube: The Ideology of the Gallery Space*, by Brian O'Doherty (Berkeley and Los Angeles: University of California Press, 1999), 8.

21. Ibid., 9.

22. Heikes, quoted in Ryan, "A Table of Curious Elements."

23. See Fer, *Eva Hesse*, 19.

24. Heikes, quoted in Ryan, "A Table of Curious Elements."

25. For a compelling confluence of manifesto and music, see Charles Gaines's installation *Manifestos* (2008), for which the artist scored the texts of social manifestos including those of the Zapatistas and the Black Panthers.

26. Heikes, quoted in Ryan, "A Table of Curious Elements."

27. Richard Flood, "Paul Thek: Real Misunderstanding," in *Notes from the Playground* (London: Ridinghouse, 2017), 26.

28. Zadie Smith, "On Optimism and Despair," in *Feel Free: Essays* (New York: Penguin Random House, 2018), 37–38.

Kill Yr Idols . . . Part III, 2002 (still)
Digital video transferred to DVD, color, silent, 115:00 minutes

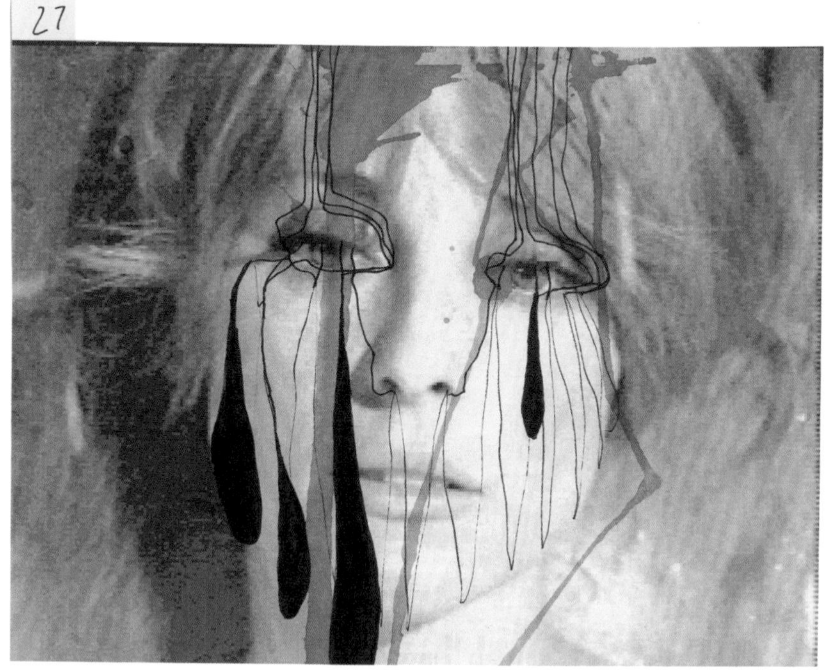

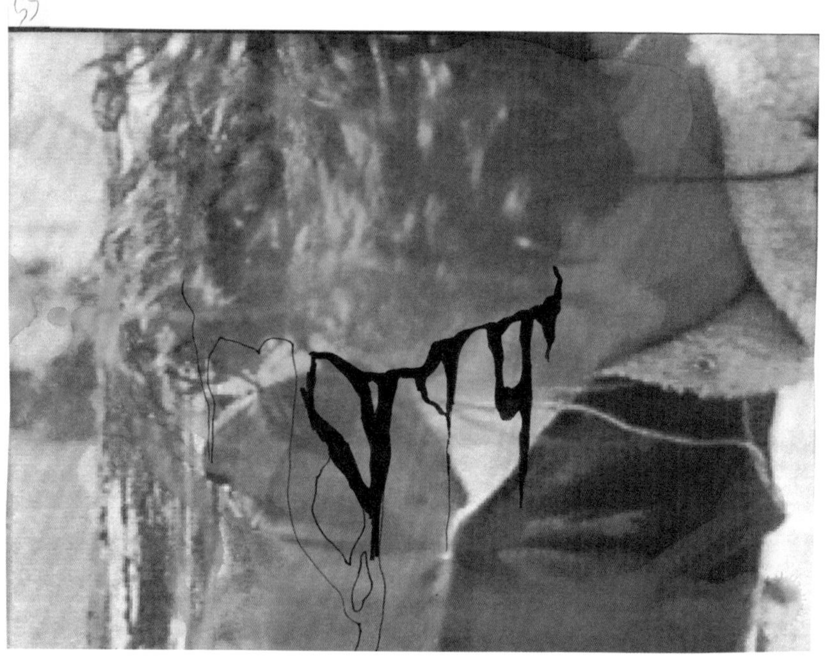

Kill Yr Idols . . . Part II (Still 27), 2002
Gouache and marker on inkjet print, 7 × 8 ½ inches, 17.8 × 21.6 cm

Kill Yr Idols . . . Part II (Still 55), 2002
Gouache and marker on inkjet print, 7 × 8 ½ inches, 17.8 × 21.6 cm

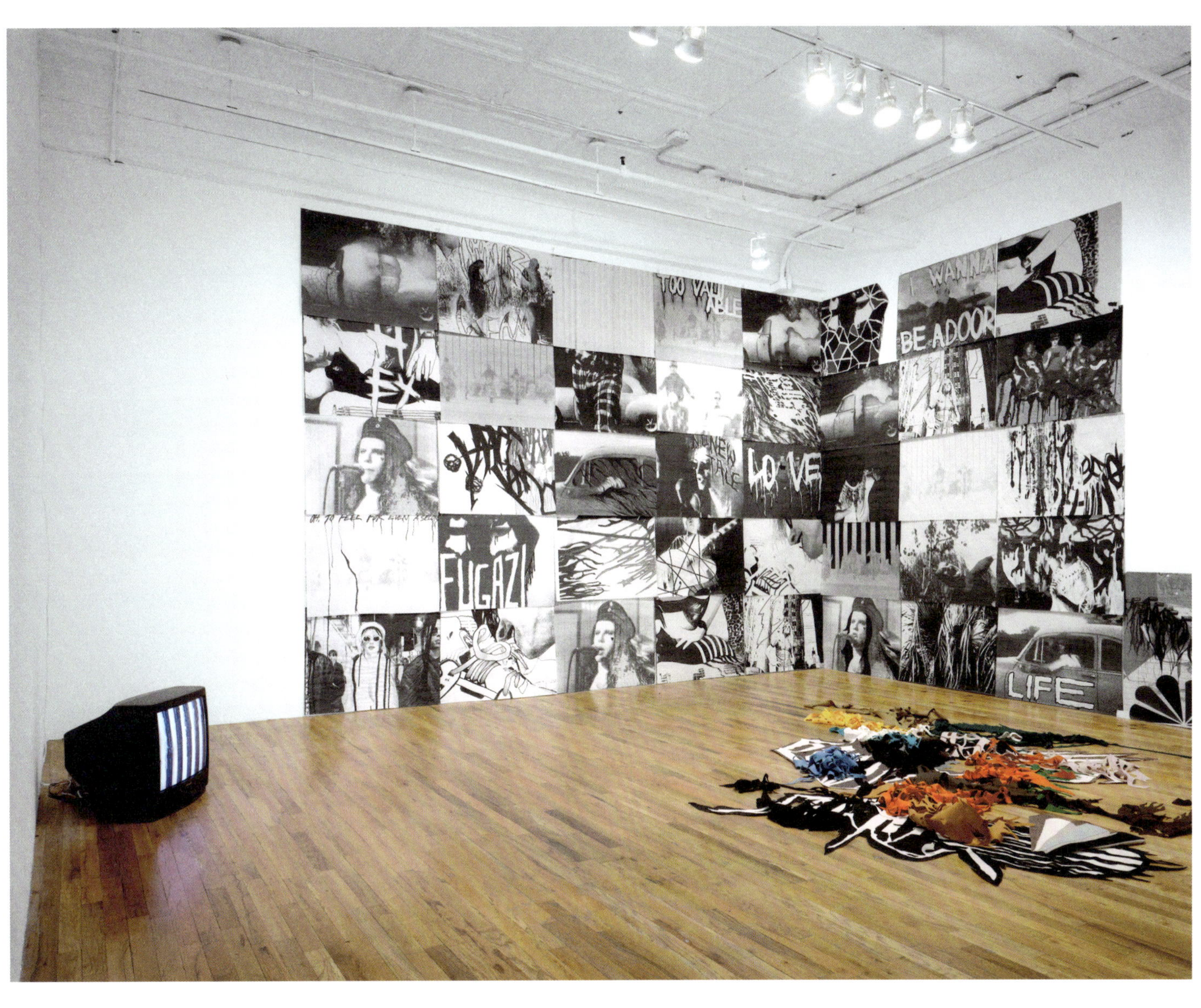

Installation view:

Kill Yr Idols, Artists Space, New York, 2003

Left to right:

Kill Yr Idols . . . Part III, 2002; *White Light (stills)*, 2003; *Kill Yr Idols . . . Part I*, 2003

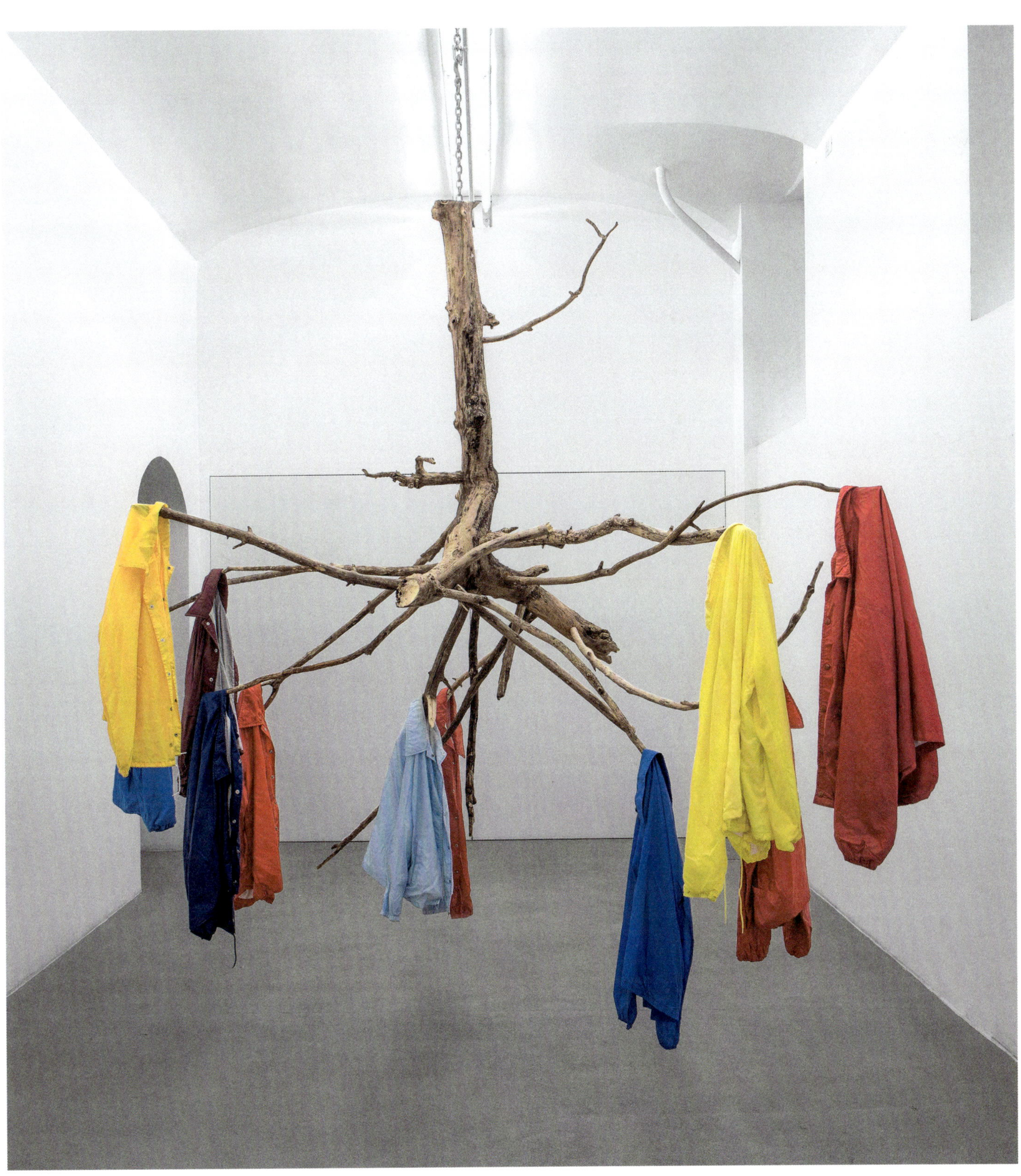

The Family Tree, 2003
Driftwood, nylon jackets, and steel hardware, 132 × 108 × 144 inches, 335.3 × 274.3 × 365.8 cm

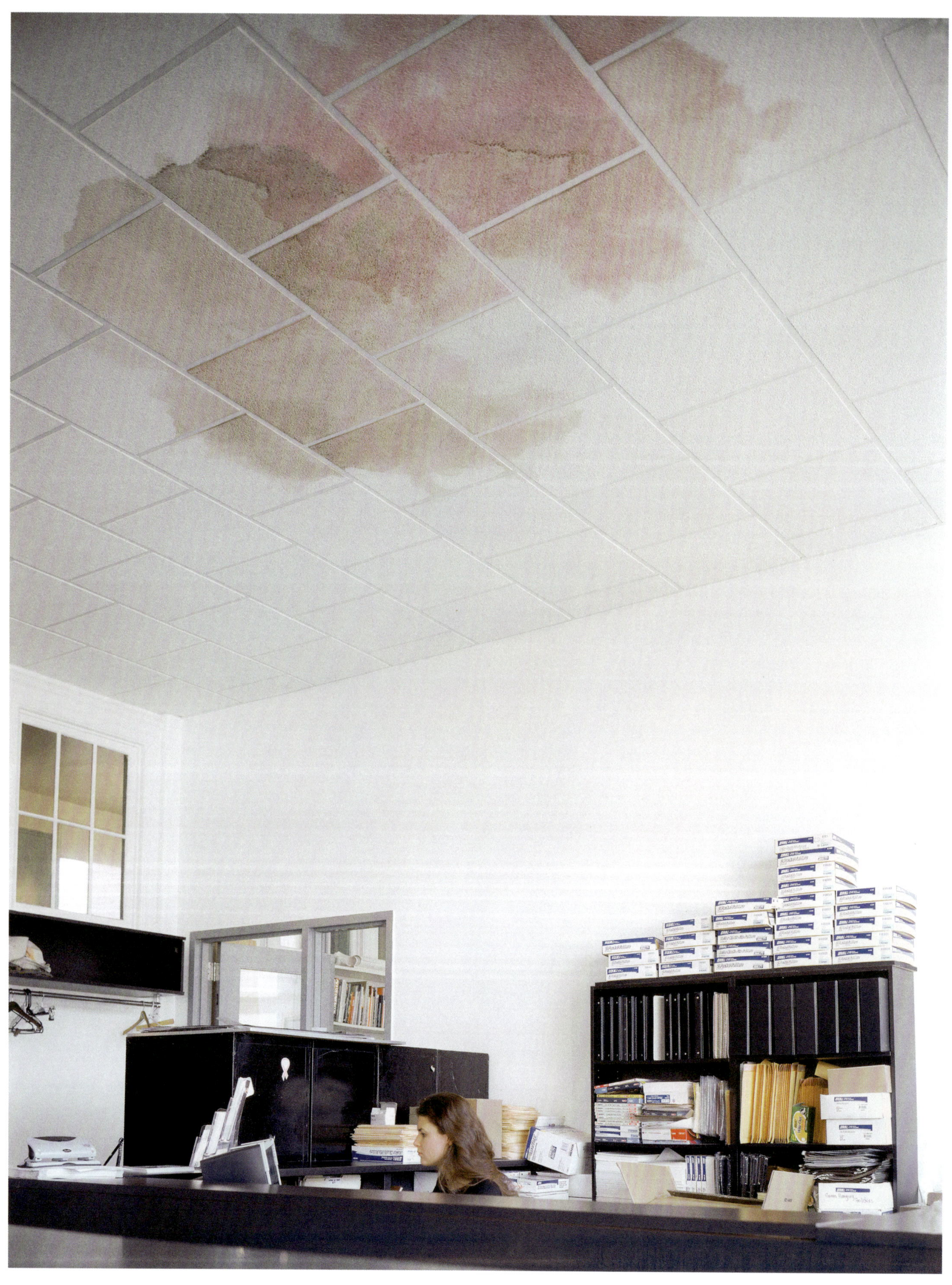

The Hill Upstairs, 2005
Beet juice and coffee on acoustical ceiling tiles, dimensions variable
Installation view, P.S.1 Contemporary Art Center, Long Island City, NY, 2005–07

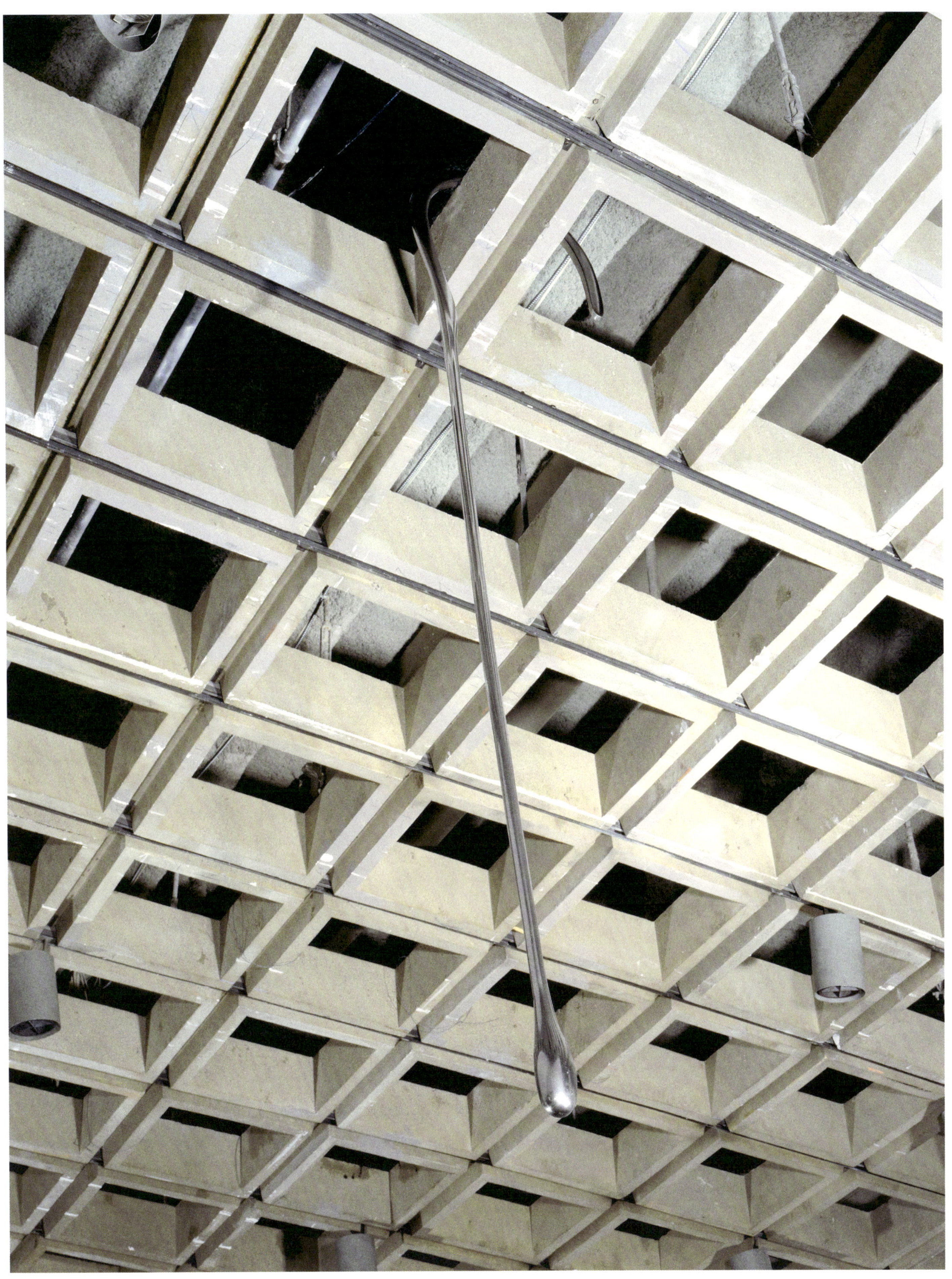

New Heaven Hook, 2005
Cast aluminum, 83 × 17 ½ × 2 inches, 210.8 × 44.5 × 5.1 cm. Walker Art Center, Minneapolis, Butler Family Fund, 2006
Installation view, *Whitney Biennial 2006: Day for Night*, Whitney Museum of American Art, New York

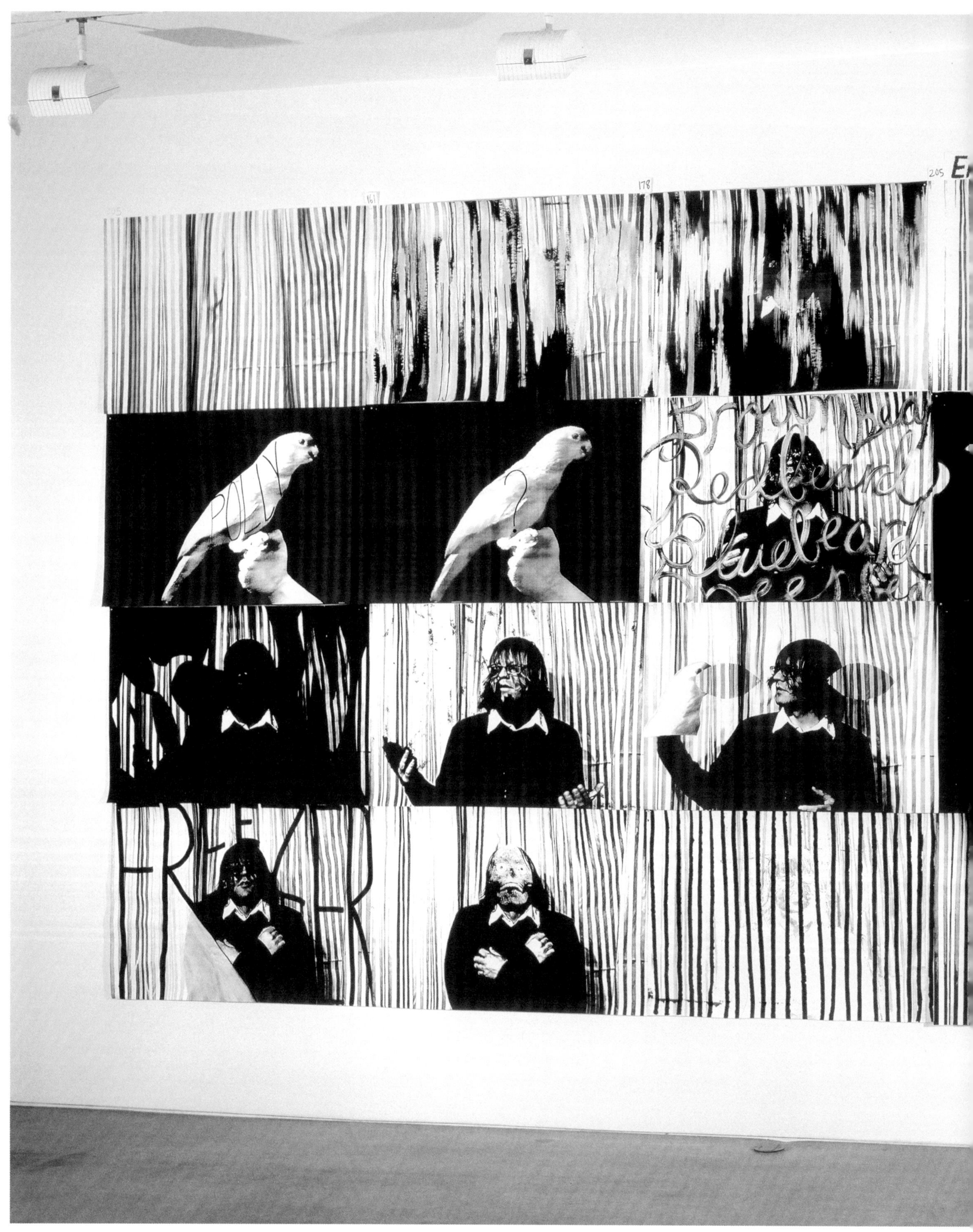

So There's This Pirate . . . , 2005
Tempera, marker, and pencil on photocopy, overall: 114 × 240 ⅛ inches, 289.6 × 610 cm
Hood Museum of Art, Dartmouth College: Anonymous Gift, 2018

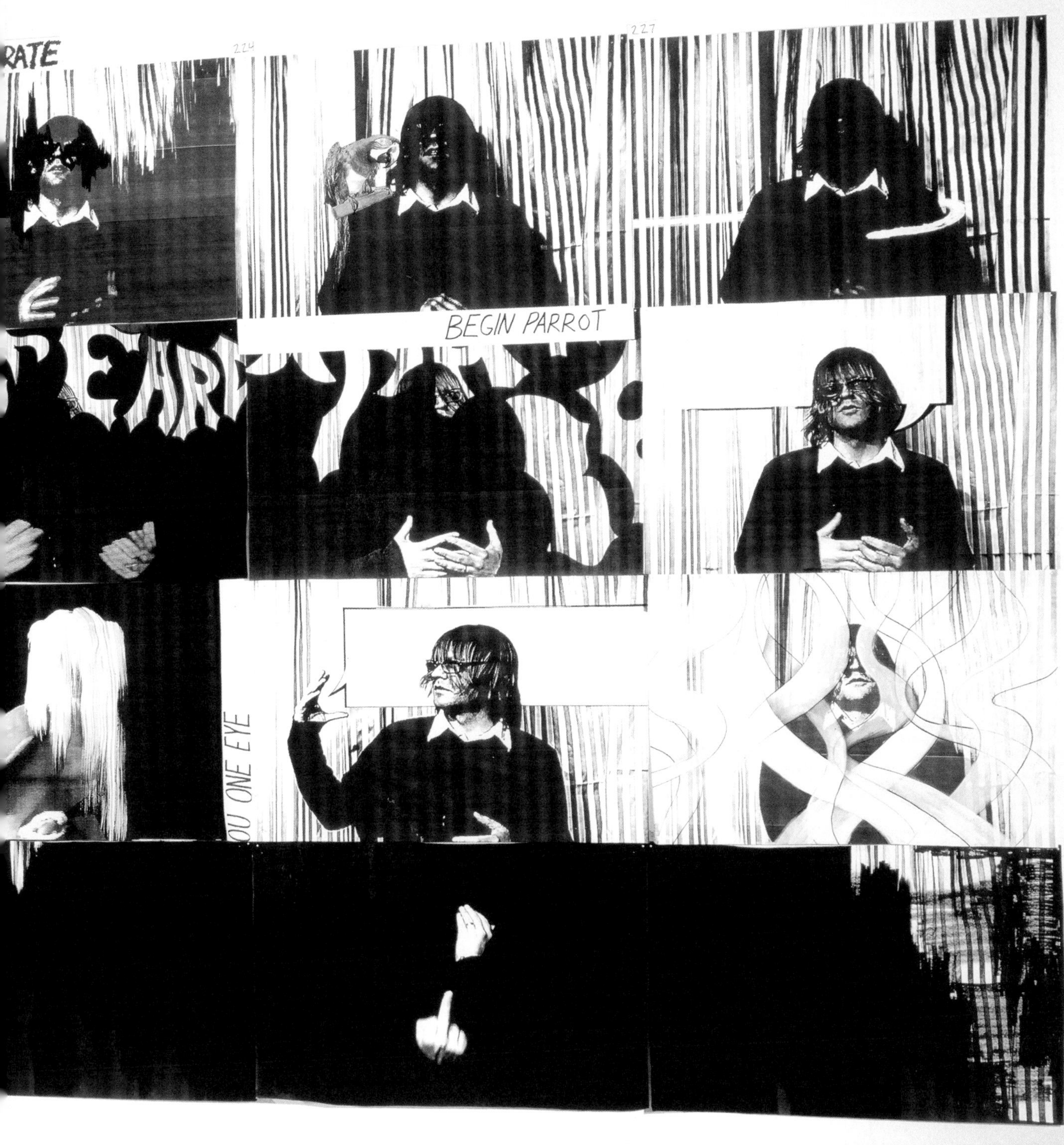
RATE
BEGIN PARROT
OU ONE EYE
227

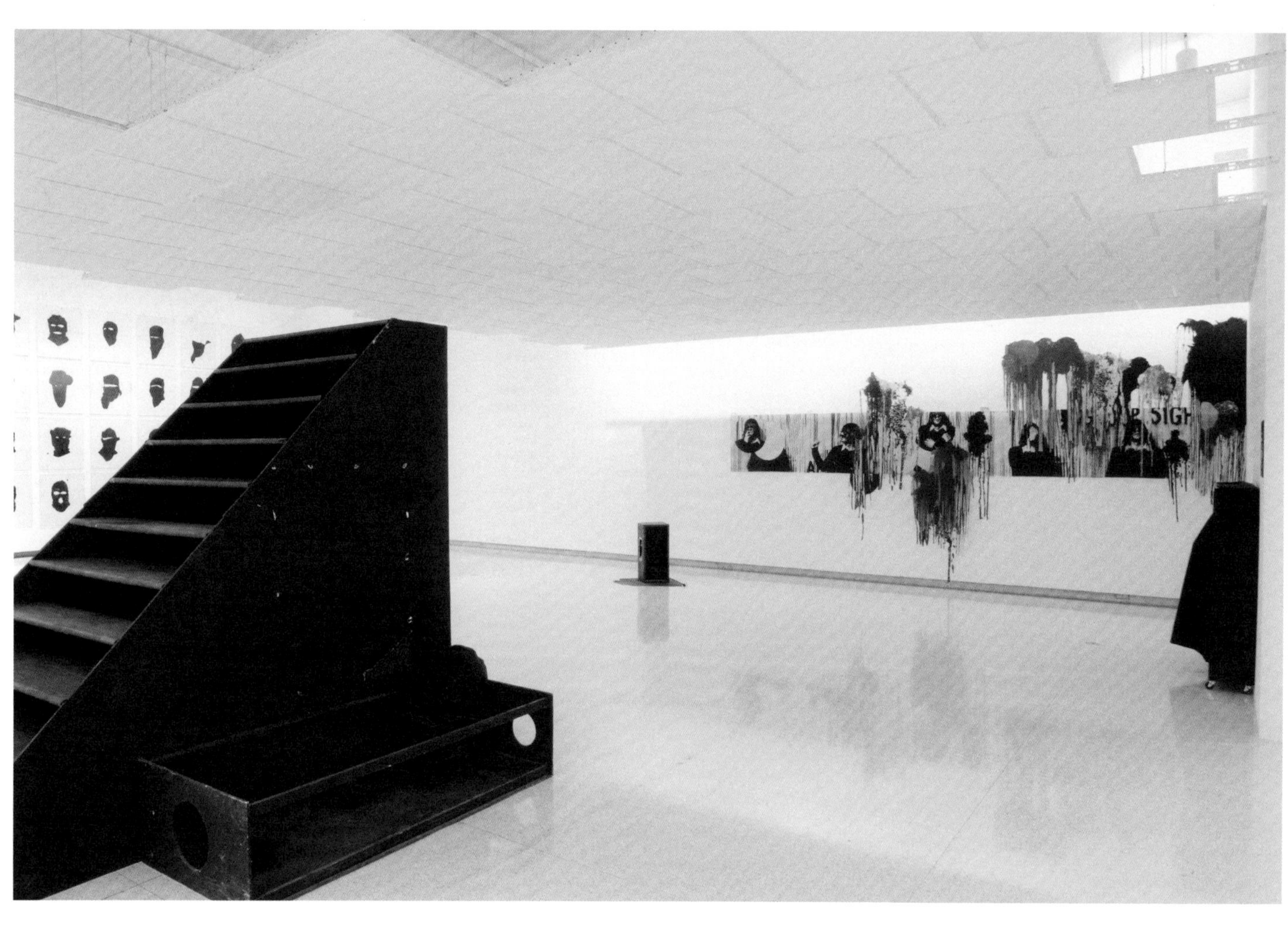

Installation view:

Ordinary Culture: Heikes/Helms/McMillian, Walker Art Center, Minneapolis, 2006

Left to right:

*Roadgear (Staircase, Severing Box, Beach Ball, Milk Crate, Extension Cord, Frying Pan and Light Bulb,
Bocce Ball, Clock, Giant Toblerone, Rain Stick, Duffle Bag Box)*, 2006; *Roadgear (Speaker and Paper)*, 2006;
So There's This Pirate . . . Live from Minneapolis, 2006; *Roadgear (Dildo Walker and Closet)*, 2006;
far left, on wall: Adam Helms, *Untitled (48 Portraits)*, 2006

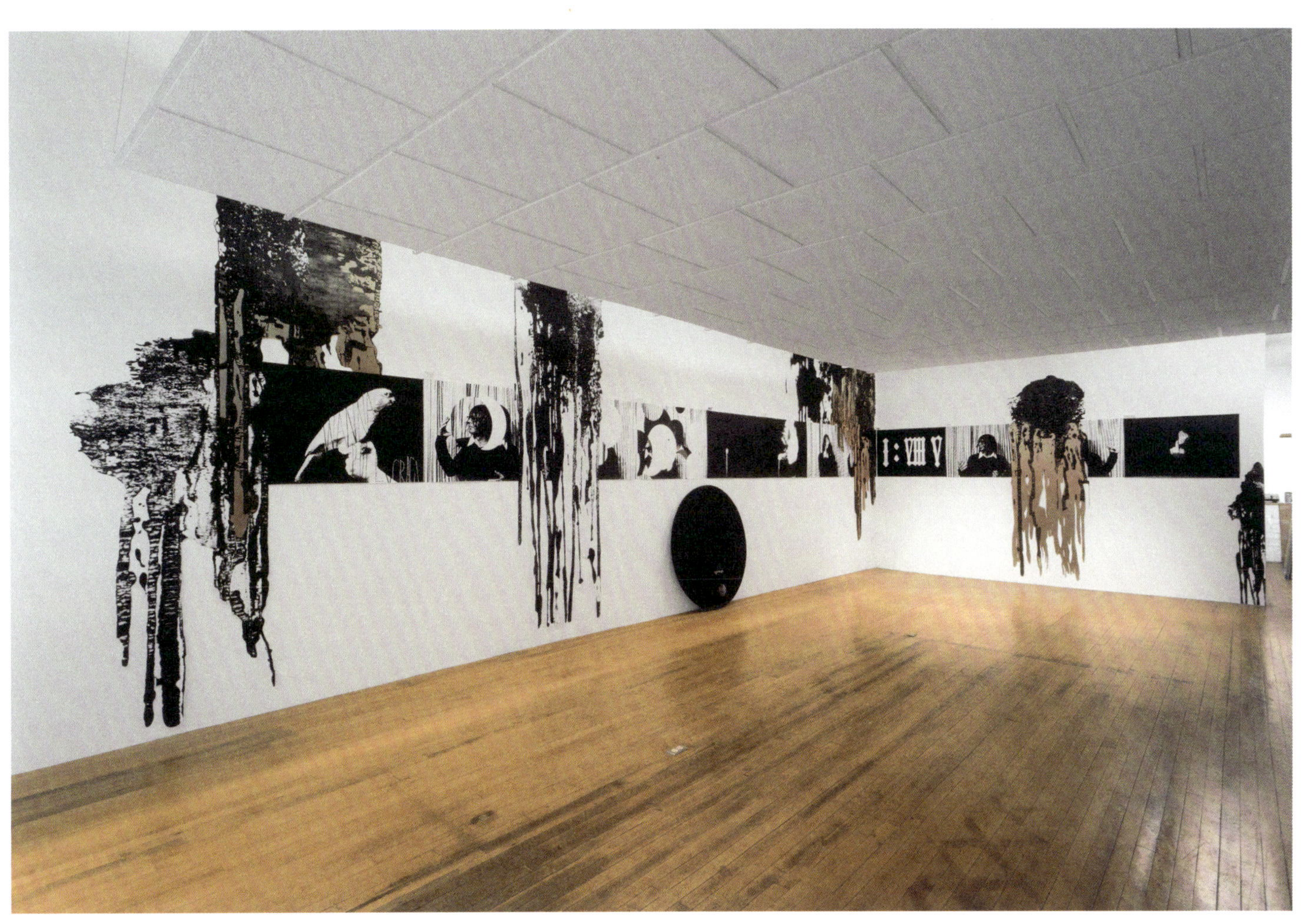

Installation view:

The Sixth Retelling, Shane Campbell Gallery, Chicago, 2006

Left to right:

The Sixth Retelling, 2006; *Roadgear (Clock)*, 2006

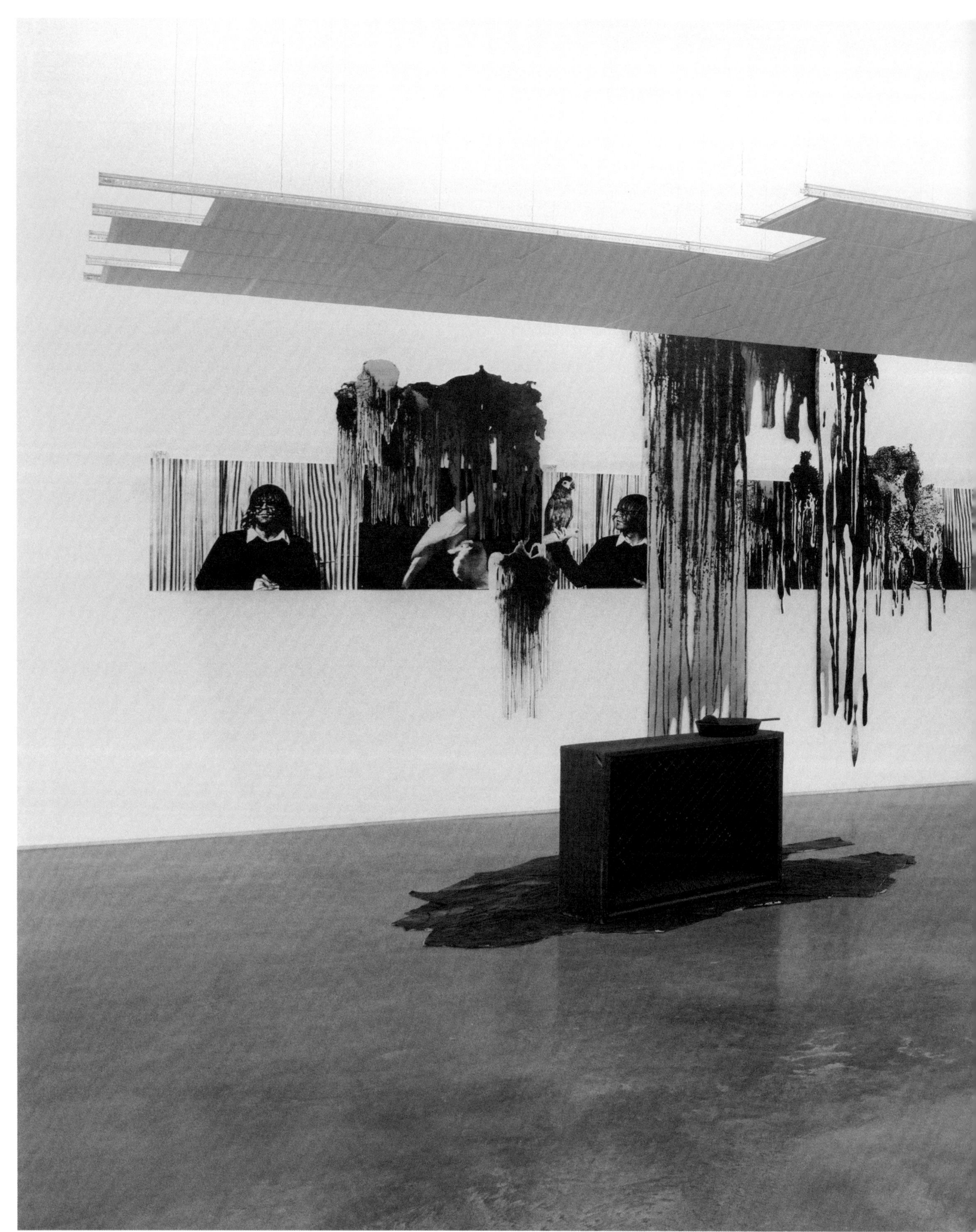

Installation view:

 Joe Deutch, Jay Heikes, Chris Moukarbel, Kianja Strobert, Jeffrey Wells, Marianne Boesky Gallery, New York, 2006

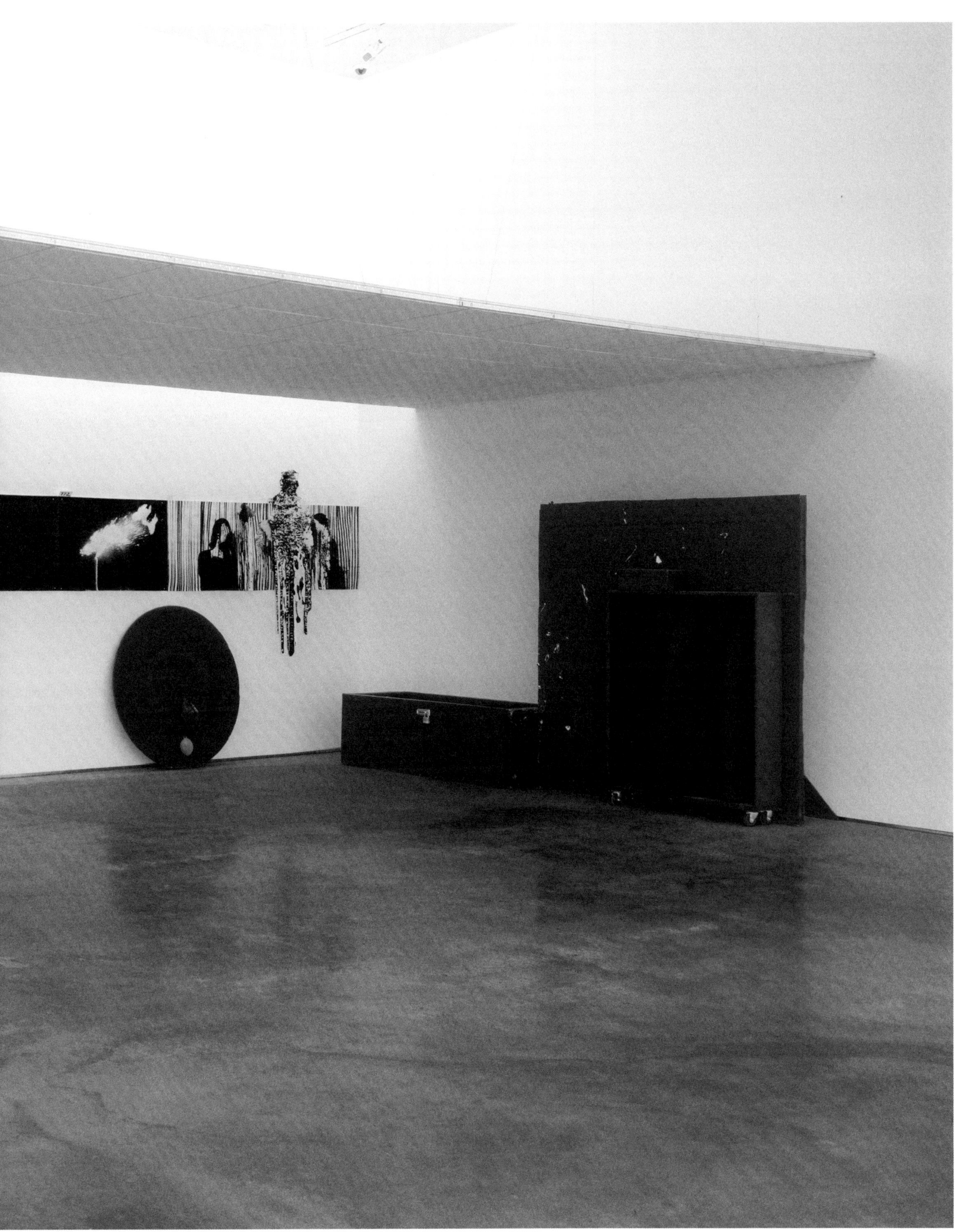

Left to right:
Left for Dead in New York, 2006; *Roadgear (Speaker, Paper, Frying Pan and Lightbulb)*, 2006; *Roadgear (Clock)*, 2006; *Roadgear (Abstract Sculpture in Severing Box)*, 2006; *Roadgear (Dildo Walker and Closet)*, 2006; *Roadgear (Shoebox)*, 2006; *Roadgear (Square Staircase)*, 2006

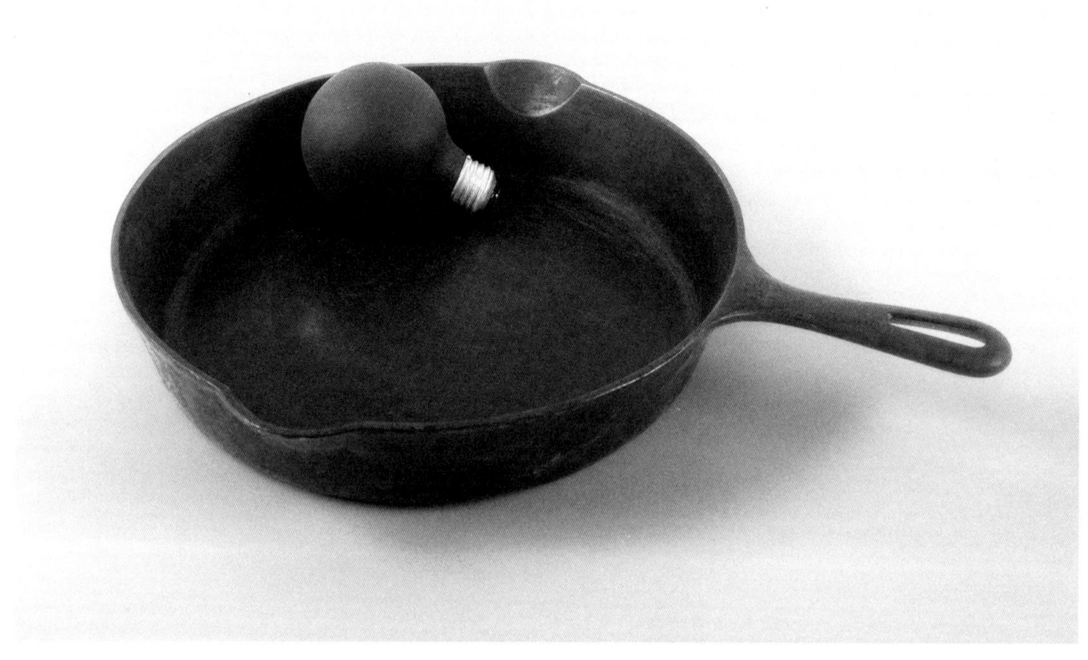

Roadgear (Frying Pan and Lightbulb), 2006
Painted lightbulb and cast iron frying pan, 3 × 16 × 11 inches, 7.6 × 40.6 × 27.9 cm

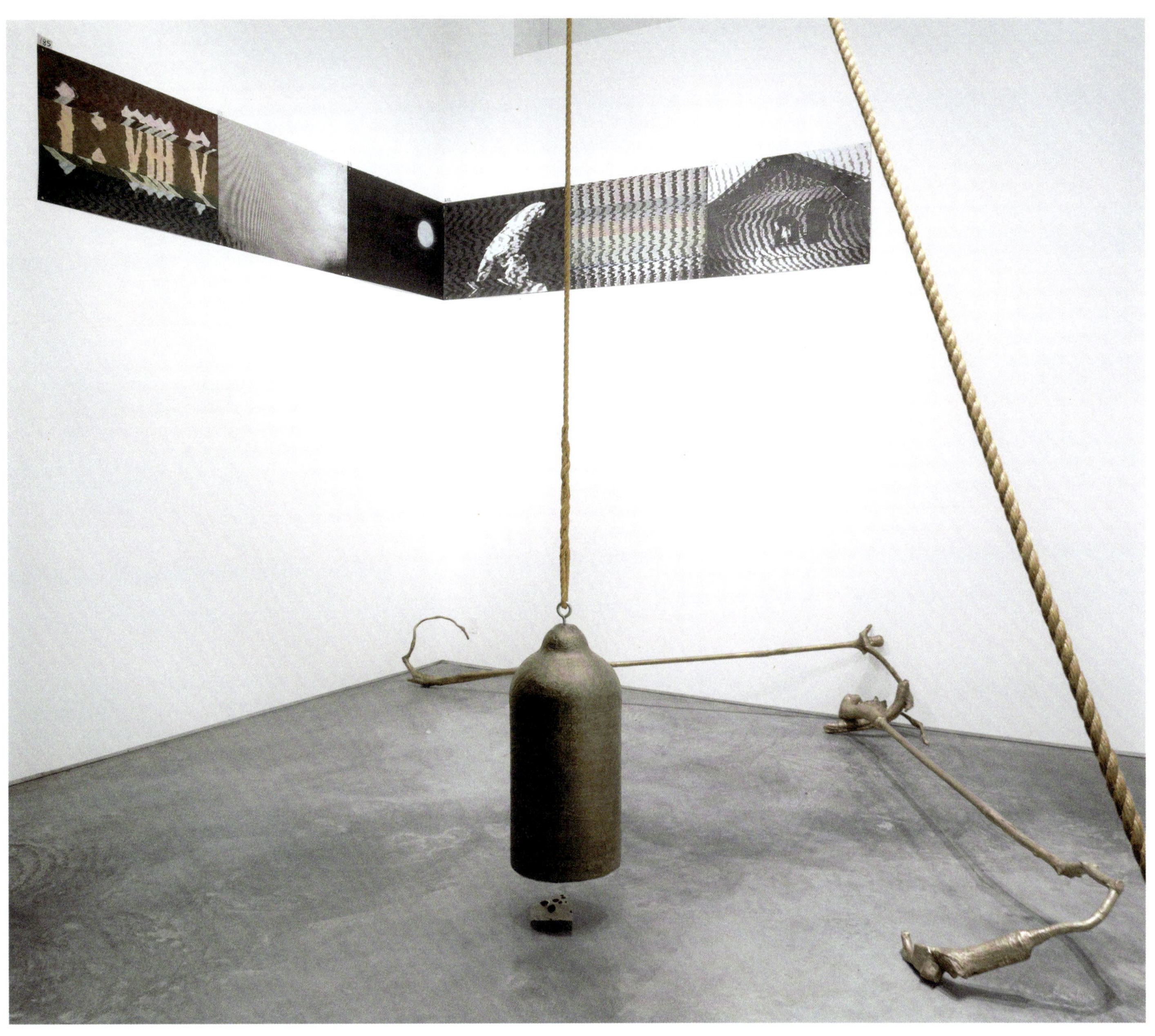

Installation view:

The Seventh Retelling, Marianne Boesky Gallery, New York, 2007

Left to right:

I:VIII V, 2007; *Broken Record*, 2007; *The Rules of Attraction*, 2007

Installation view:

Jay Heikes, Institute of Contemporary Art, University of Pennsylvania, Philadelphia, 2007

Top to bottom:

6:30 Today, tomorrow, and the day after that, 2007; *The Soft Pillow*, 2007 (detail)

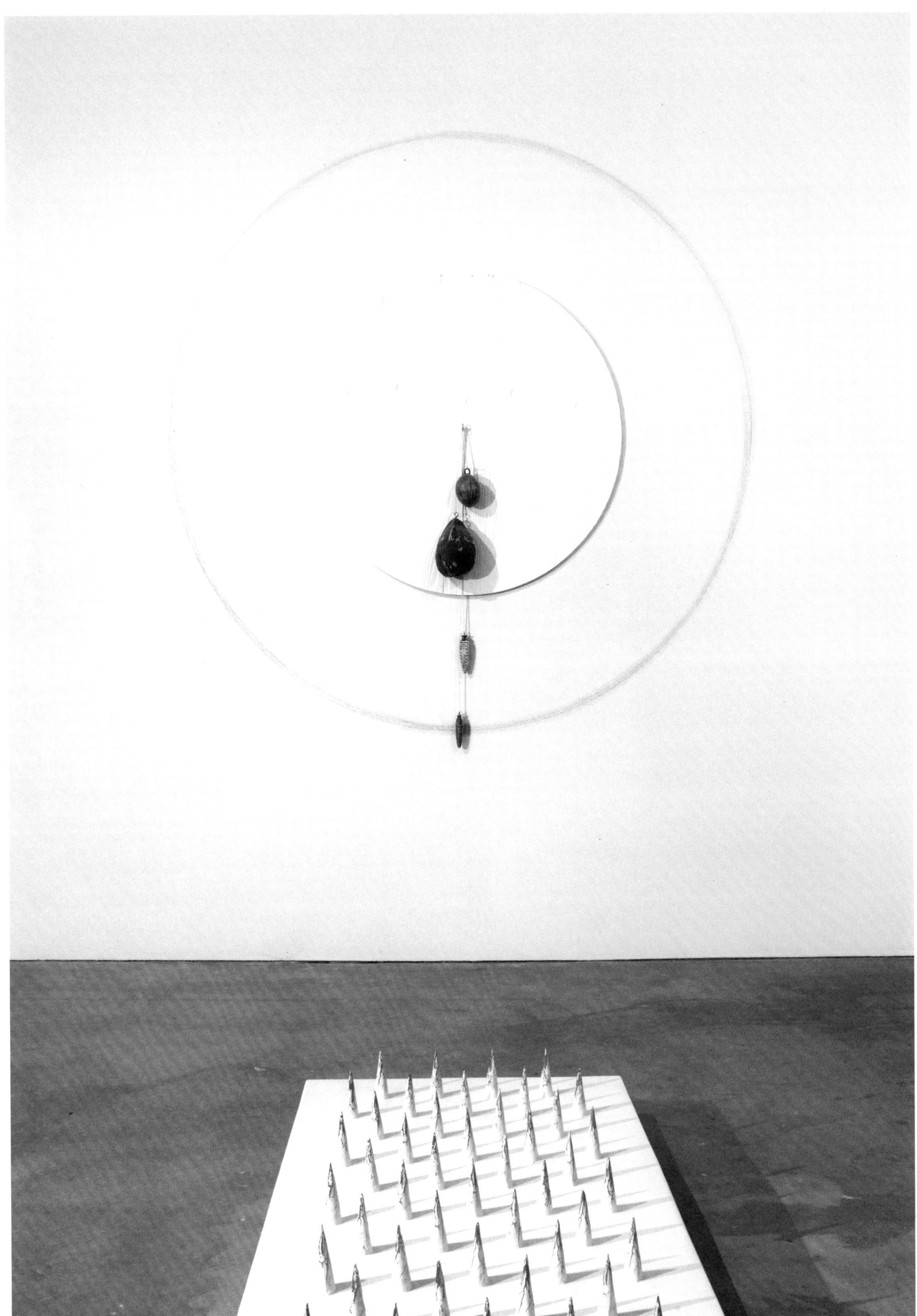

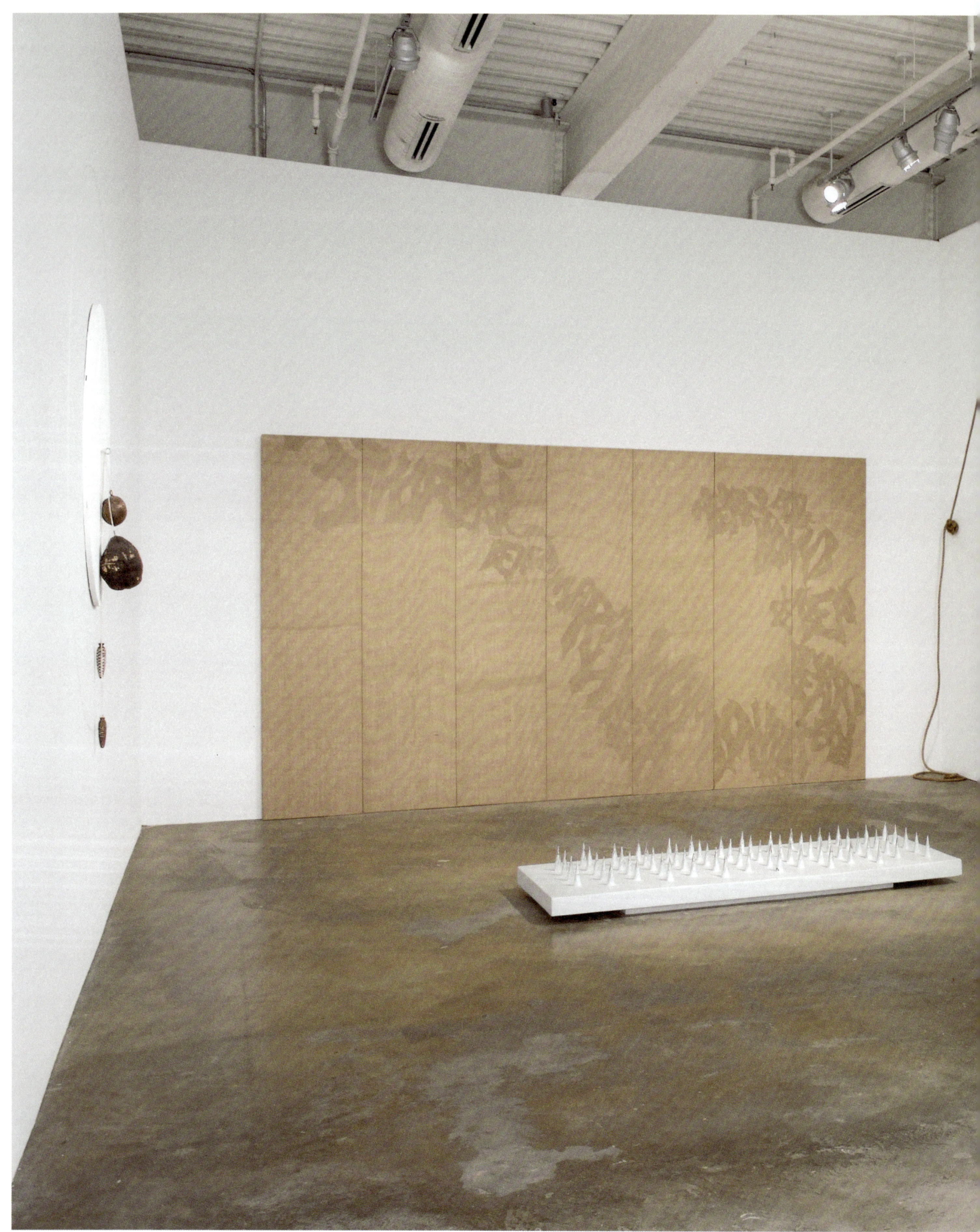

Installation view:
Jay Heikes, Institute of Contemporary Art, University of Pennsylvania, Philadelphia, 2007

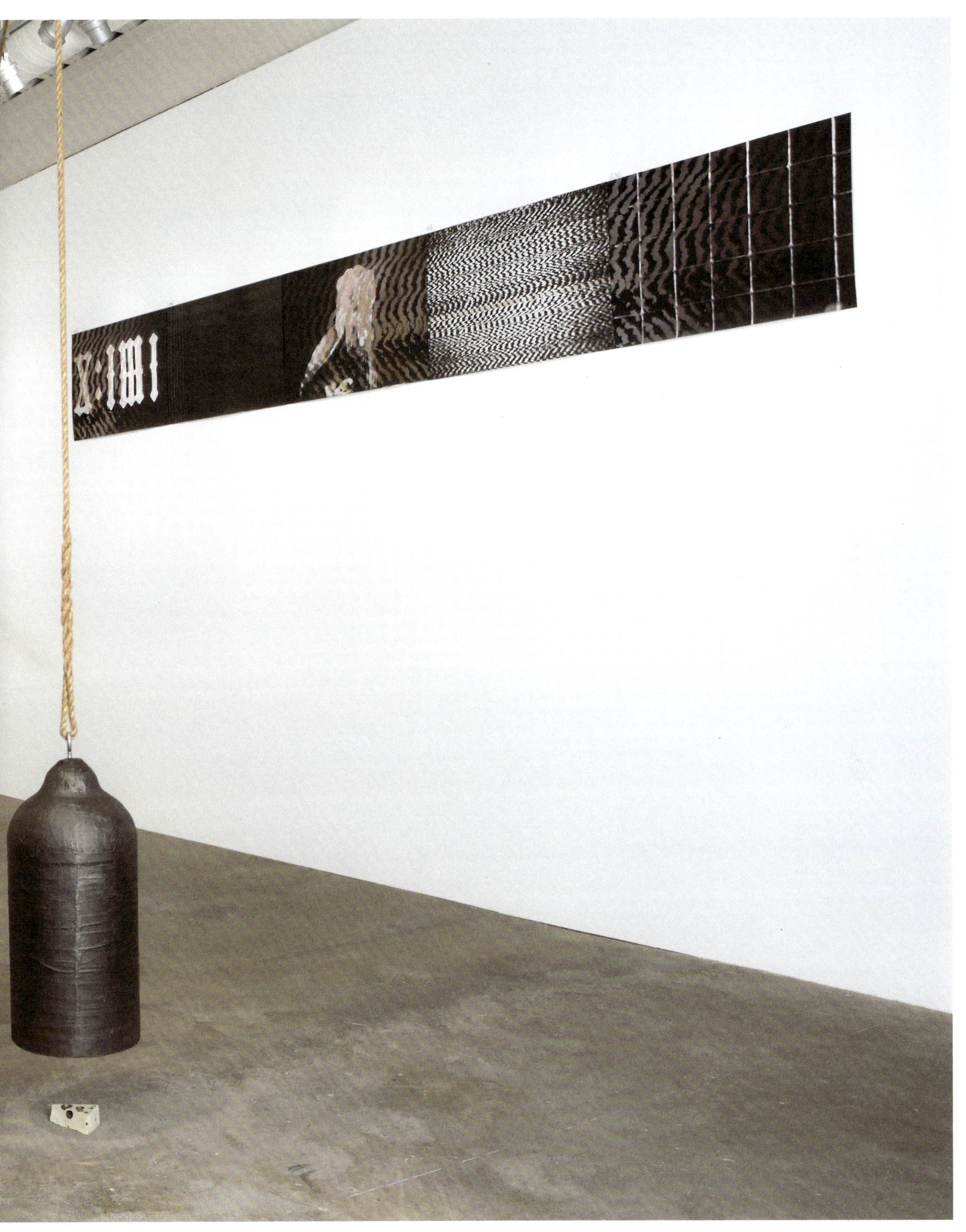

Left to right:

6:30 Today, tomorrow, and the day after that, 2007; *In the Belly of a Basking Shark*, 2007; *The Soft Pillow*, 2007; *The Rules of Attraction*, 2007; *X:I III I*, 2007

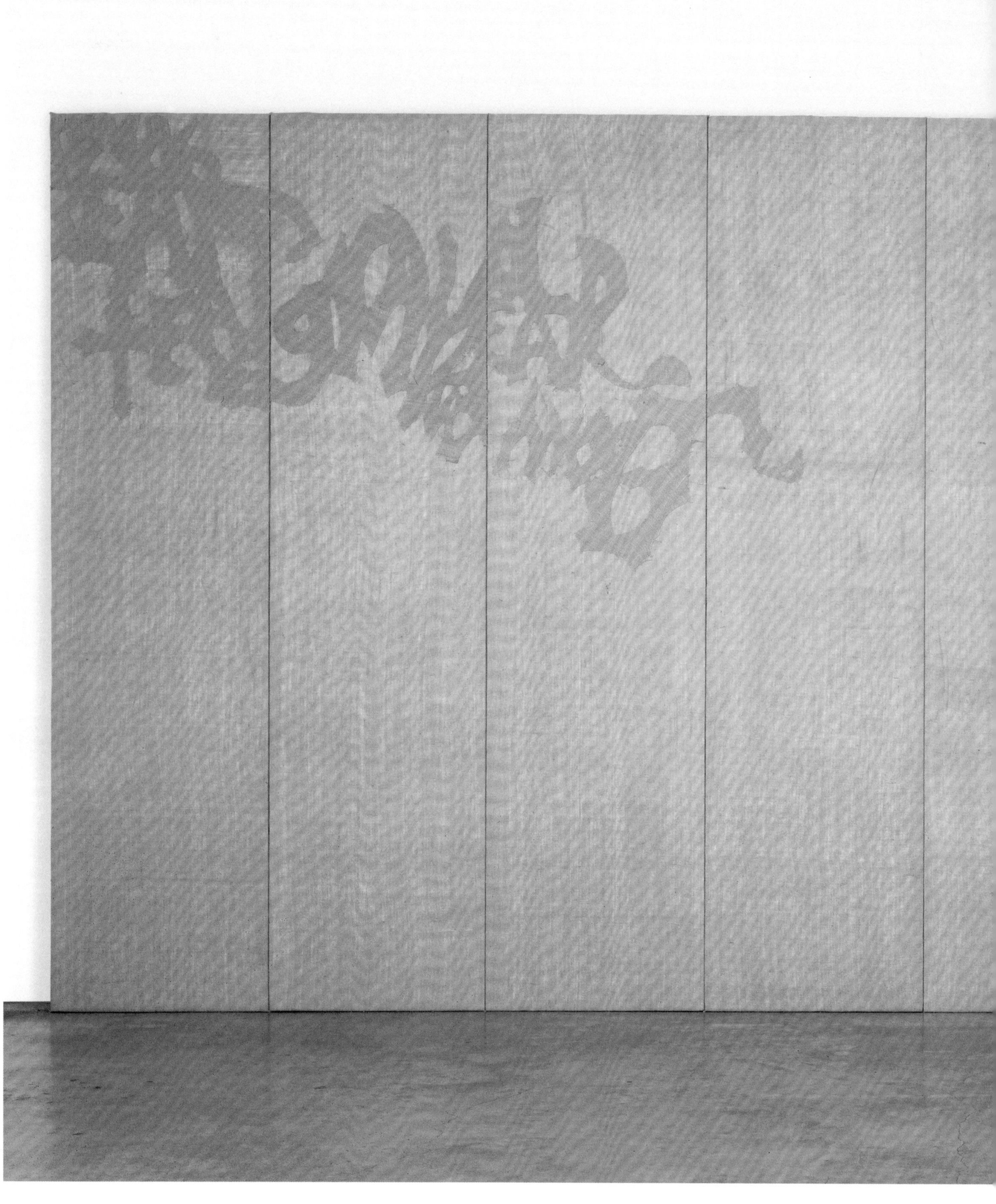

In the Belly of a Whale Shark, 2007
Burlap, foam, dry adhesive, and upholstery tacks, nine panels, overall: 96 × 216 × 2 inches, 243.8 × 548.6 × 5.1 cm

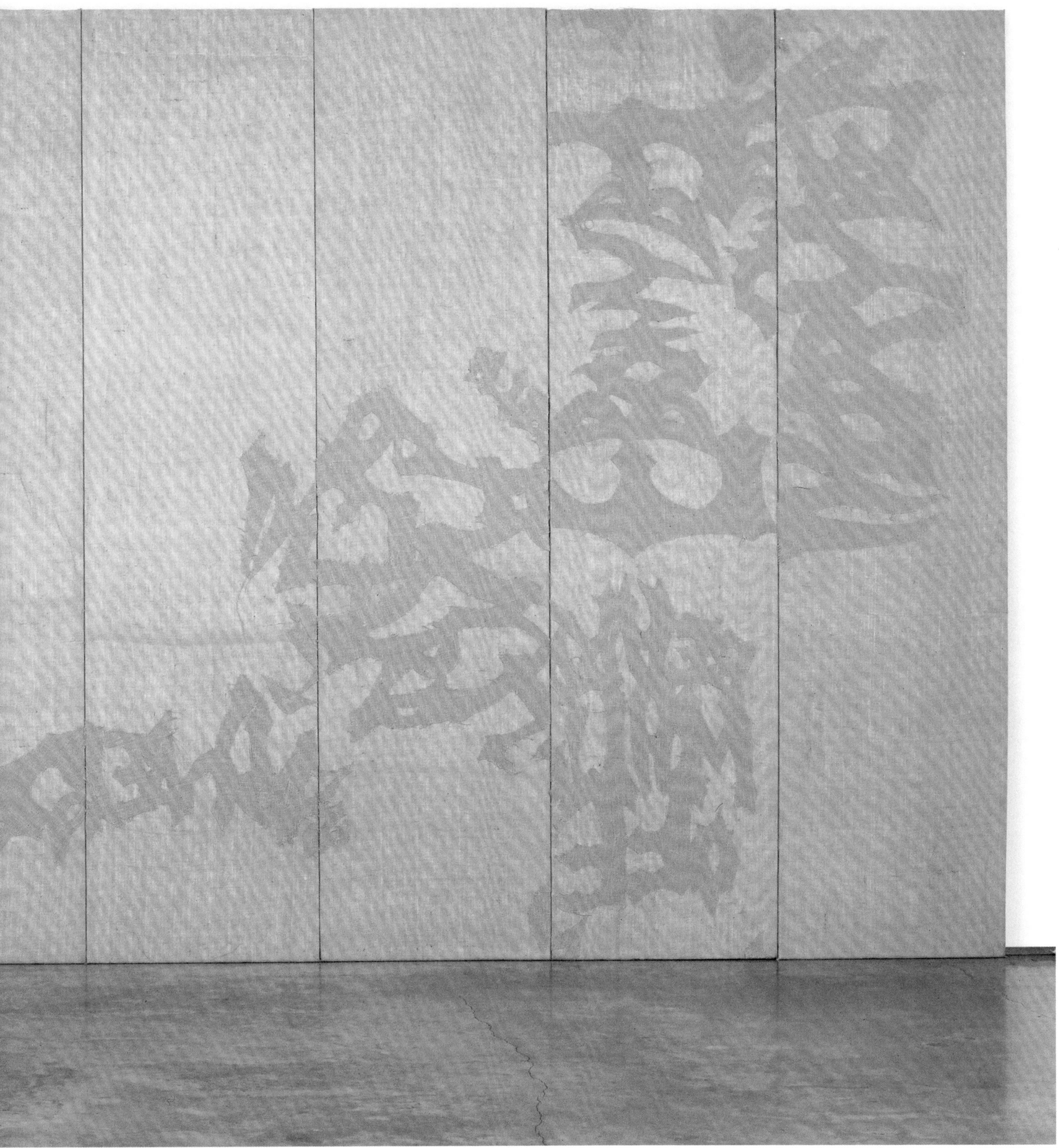

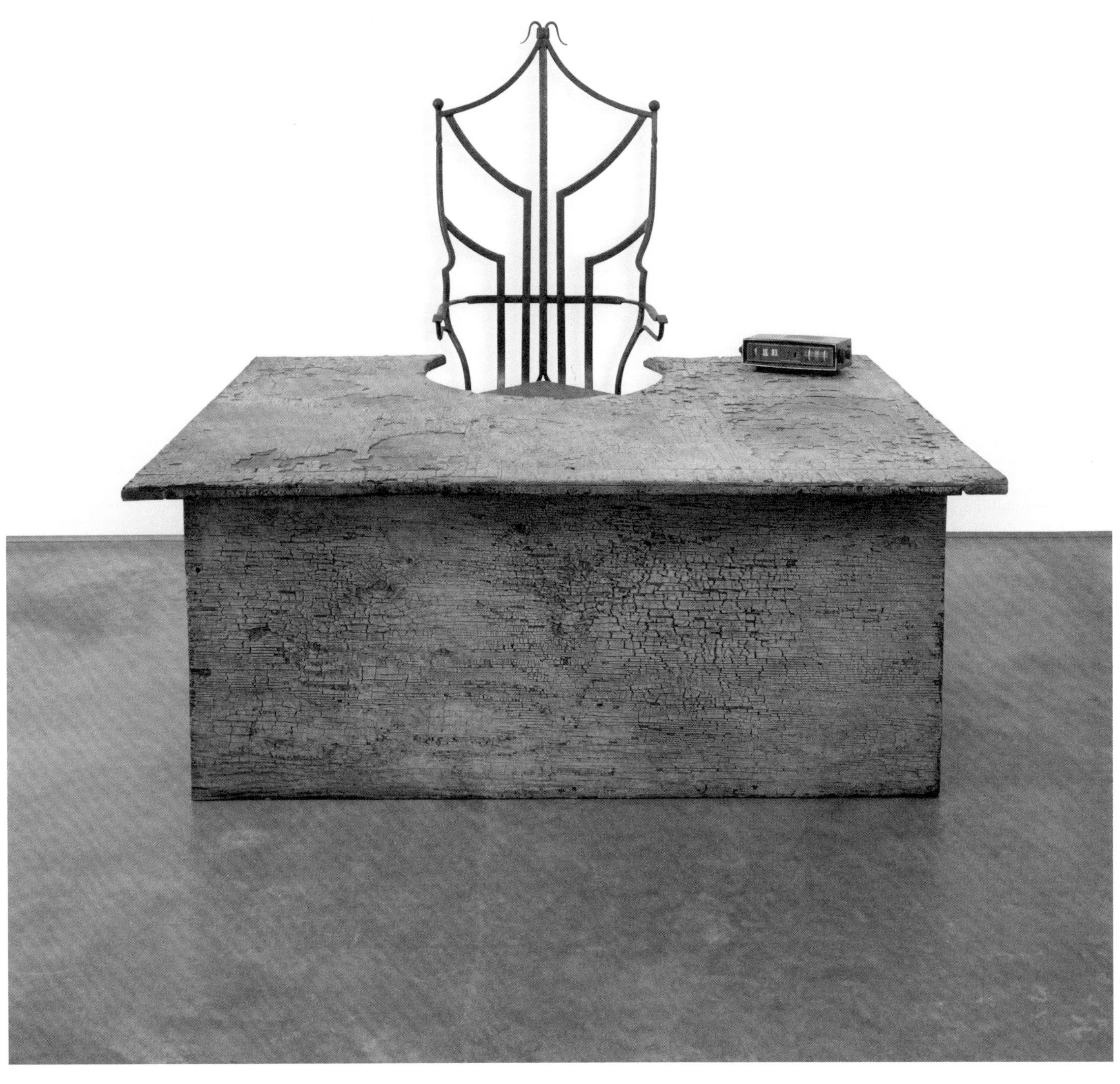

Private Hell, 2008
Burned wood, wrought iron, enamel, wax, stone, and electric clock, 67 × 56 × 72 inches, 170.2 × 142.2 × 182.9 cm

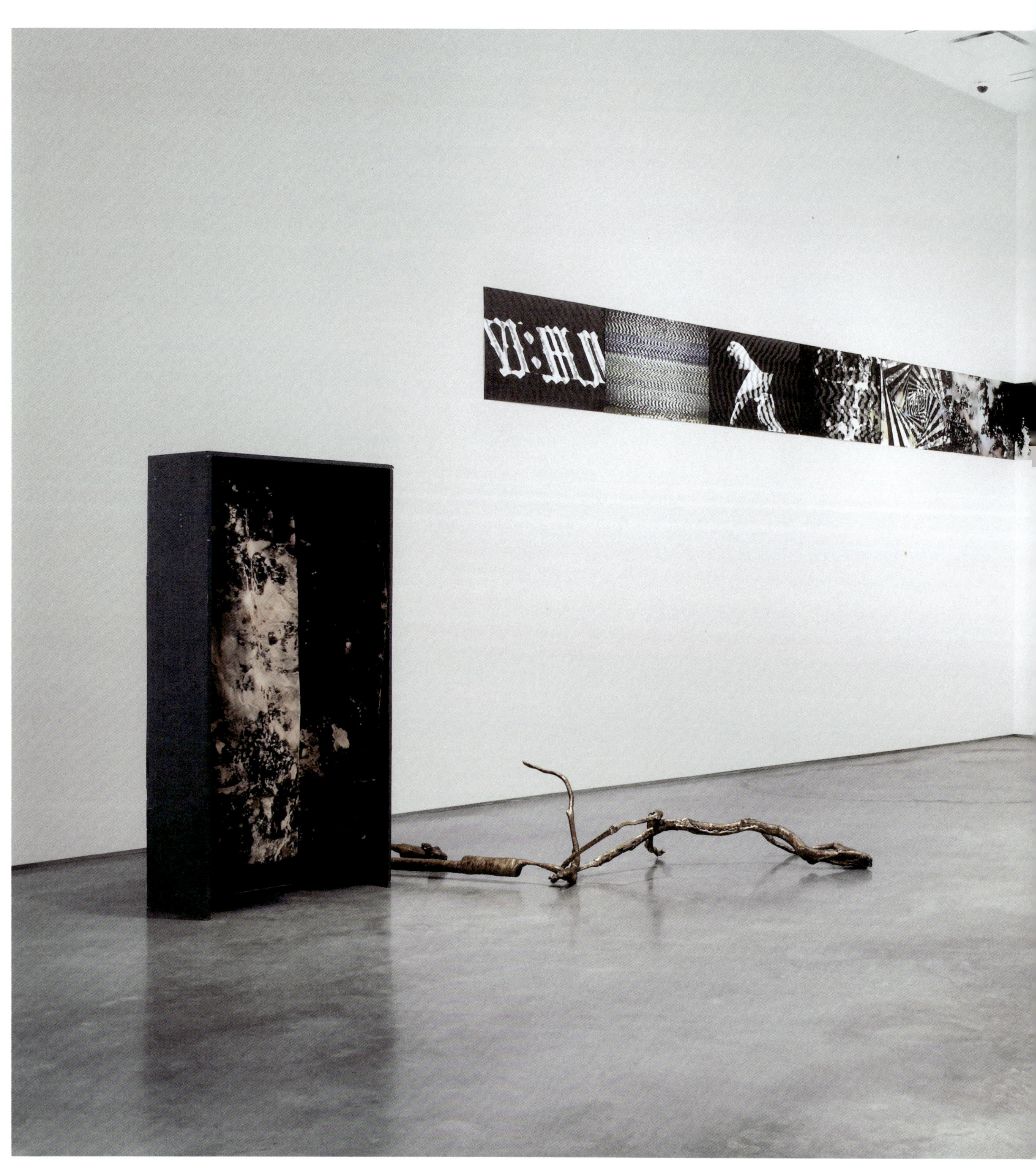

Installation view:
Like a Broken Record, Marianne Boesky Gallery, New York, 2007

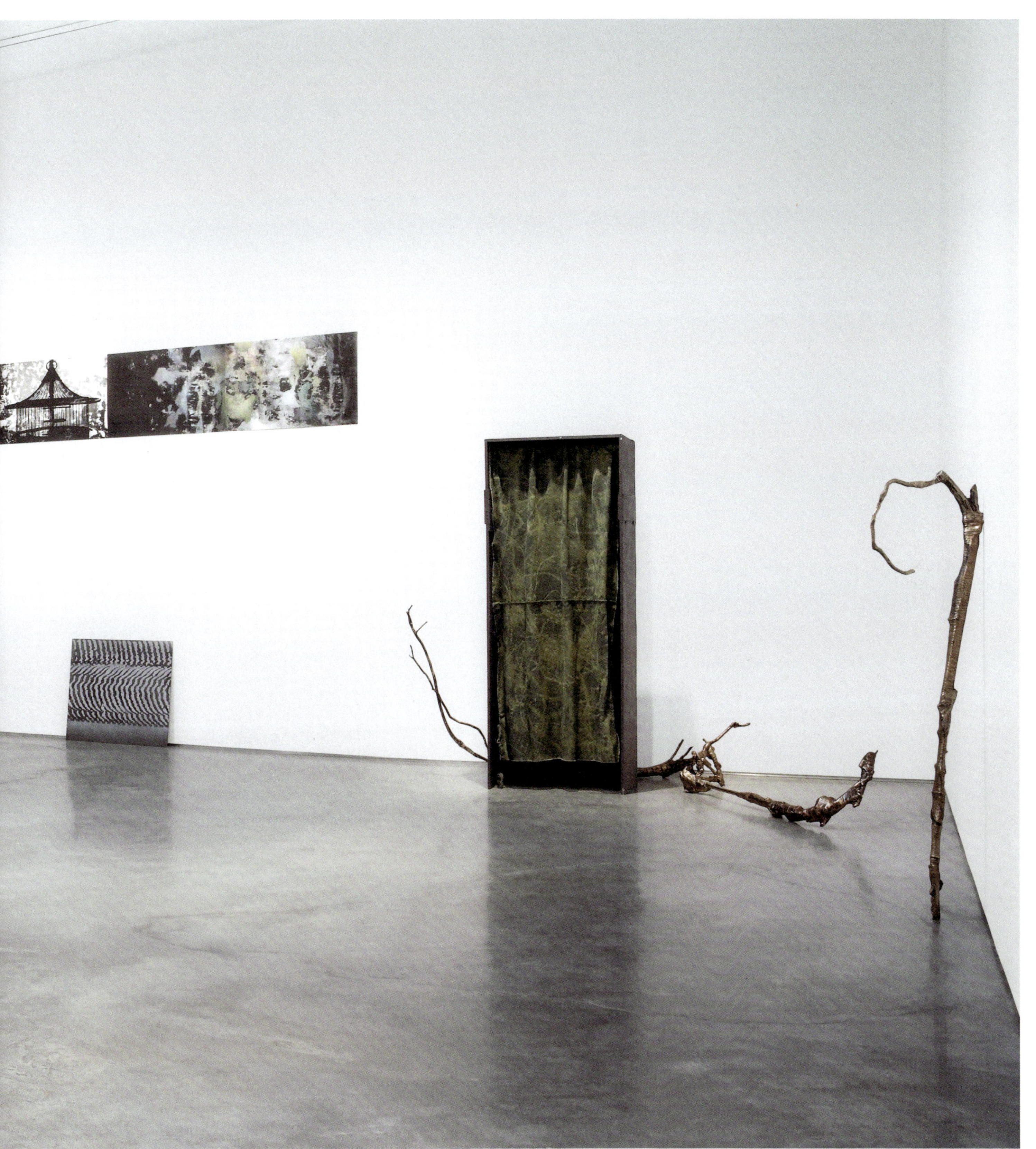

Left to right:

A Broken Record Not a Broken Record, 2007; *VI: III II*, 2007; *Everything All at Once (Channel 4)*, 2007;
A Broken Record Not a Broken Record Just a Sound, 2007; *Ninth Retelling*, 2007

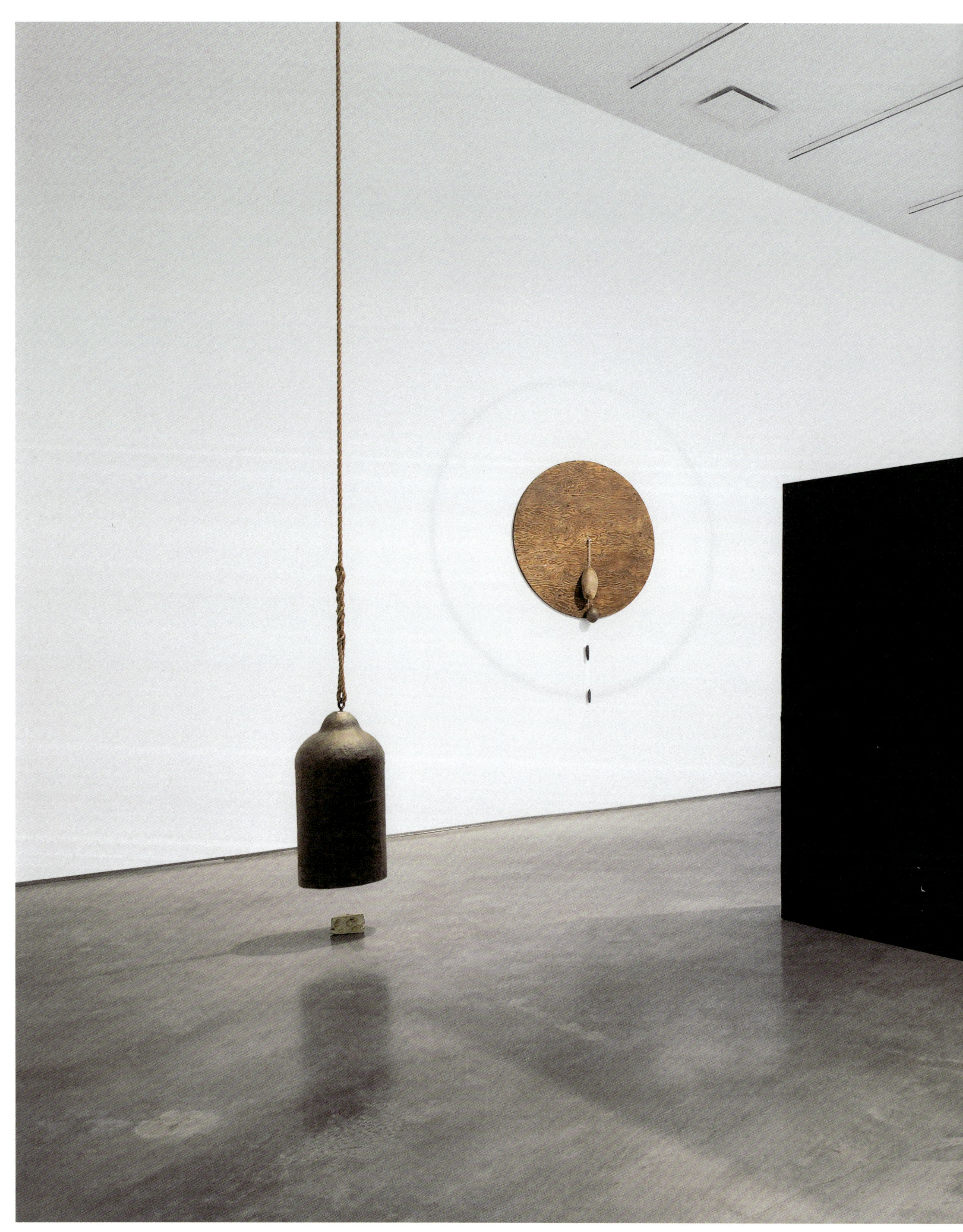

Installation view:
Like a Broken Record, Marianne Boesky Gallery, New York, 2007

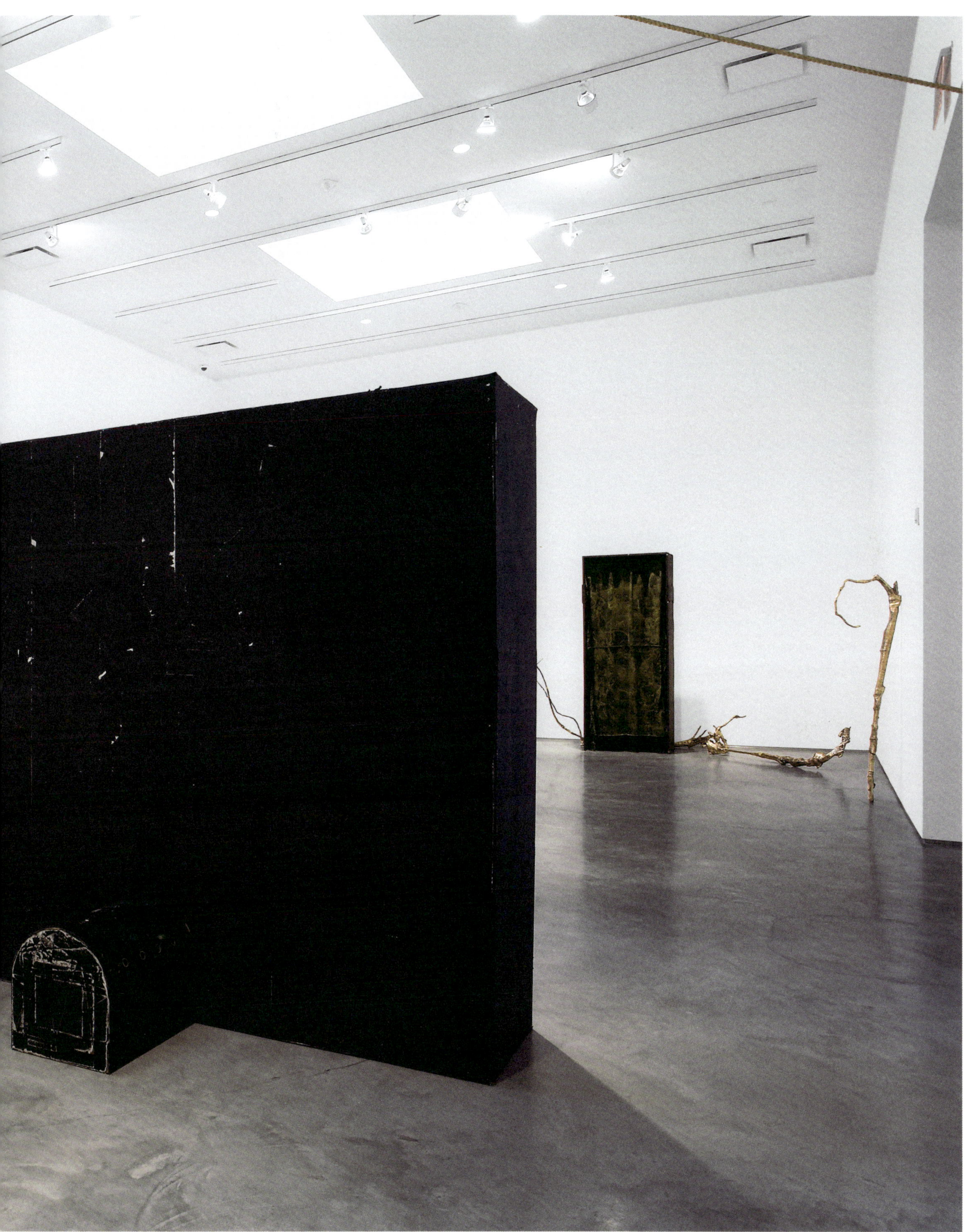

Left to right:
The Rules of Attraction, 2007; *6:30 Tonight, tomorrow, and the next day*, 2007; *The Tomb*, 2007;
Theater of the Mind, 2007; *A Broken Record Not a Broken Record Just a Sound*, 2007; *Ninth Retelling*, 2007

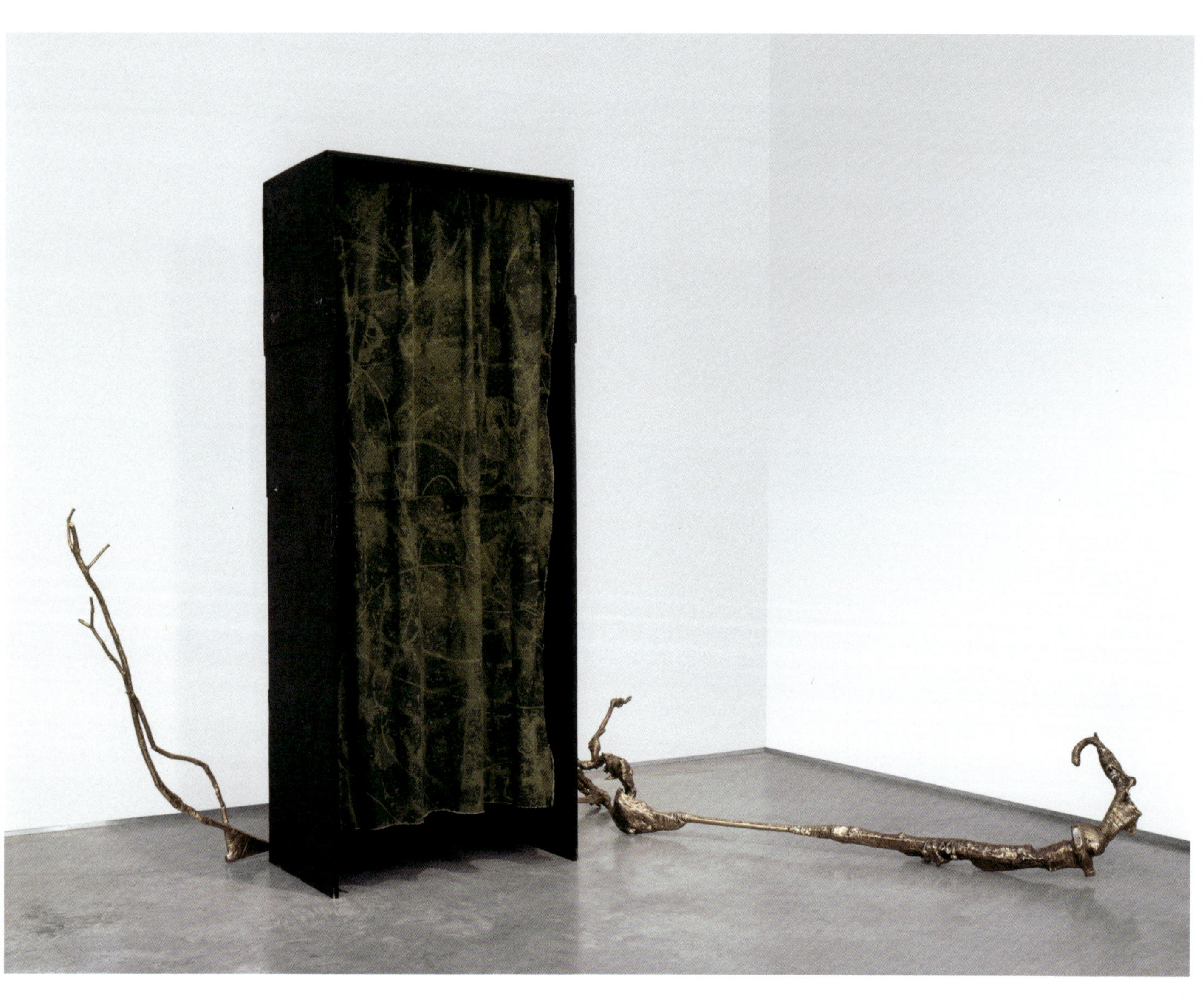

A Broken Record Not a Broken Record Just a Sound, 2007
Cast bronze, bleached cotton, wood, steel, paper, and latex, 92 × 130 × 92 inches, 233.7 × 330.2 × 233.7 cm

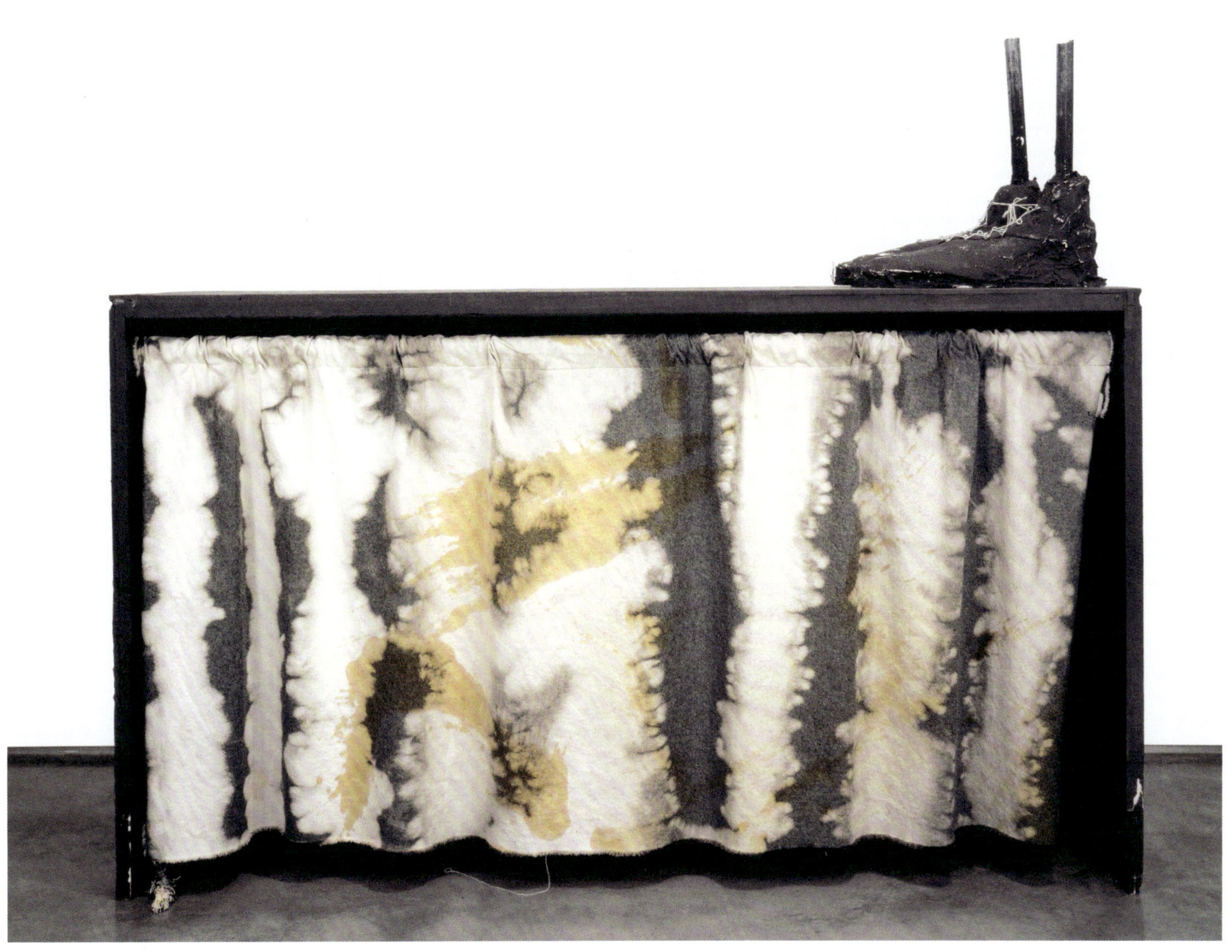

Tongue Tied Theater, 2007
Hydrocal, burlap, steel pipe, bleached and stained cotton, eyehooks, and string, 67 ¾ × 18 ½ × 81 inches, 172.1 × 47 × 205.7 cm

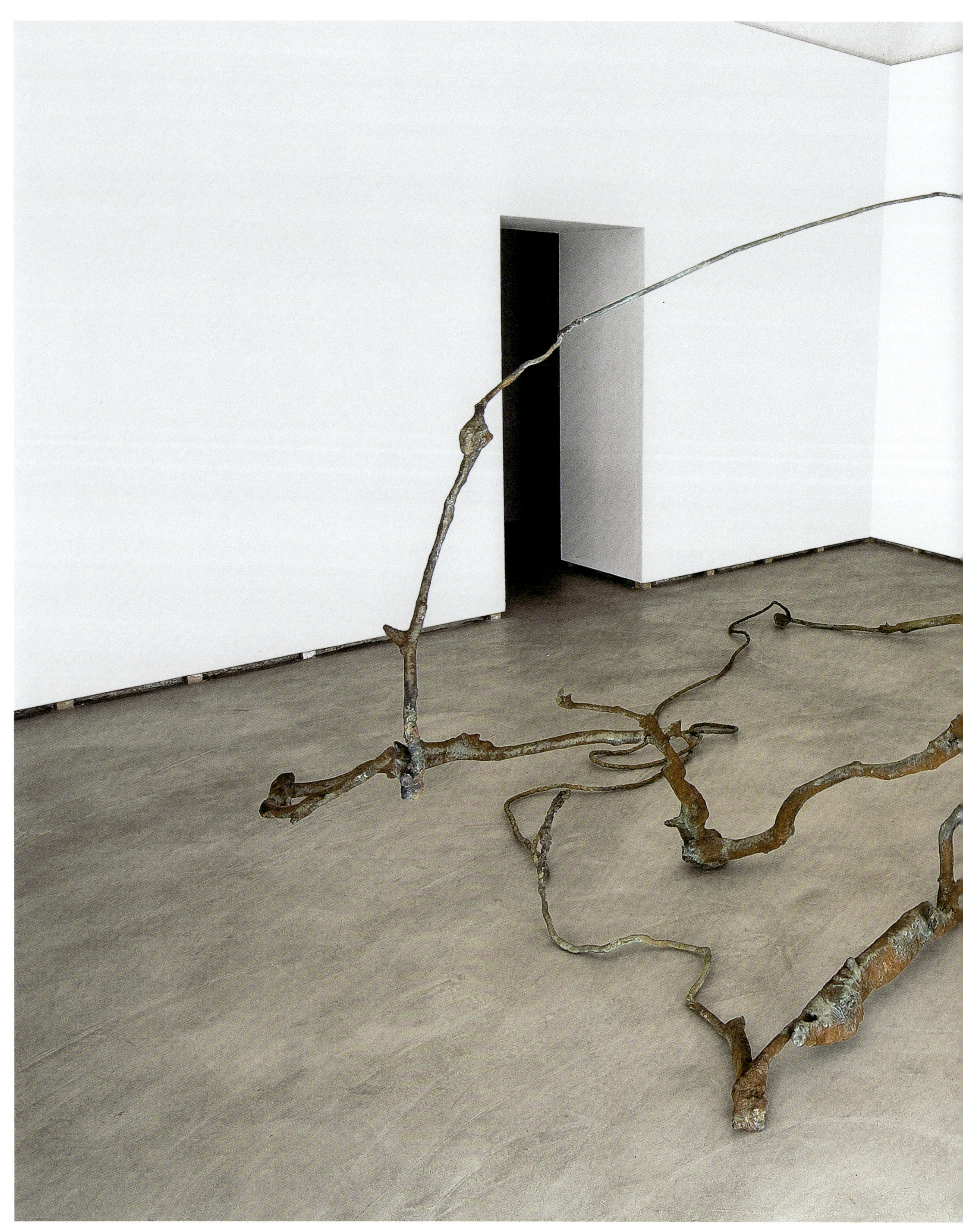

Vertigo Revisited, 2011
Cast bronze, iron, and rust, 72 × 152 ⅜ × 167 inches, 183 × 387 × 424 cm

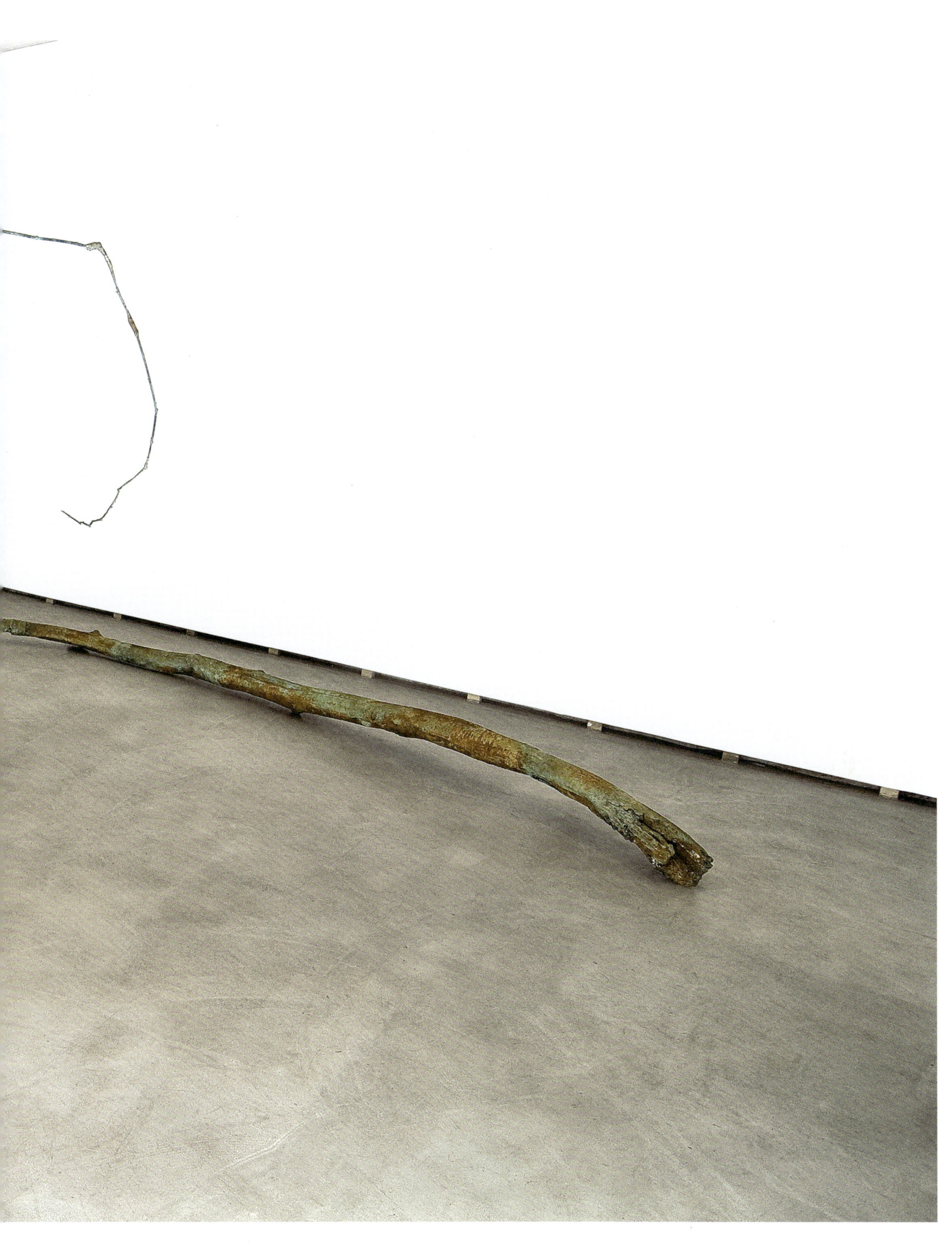

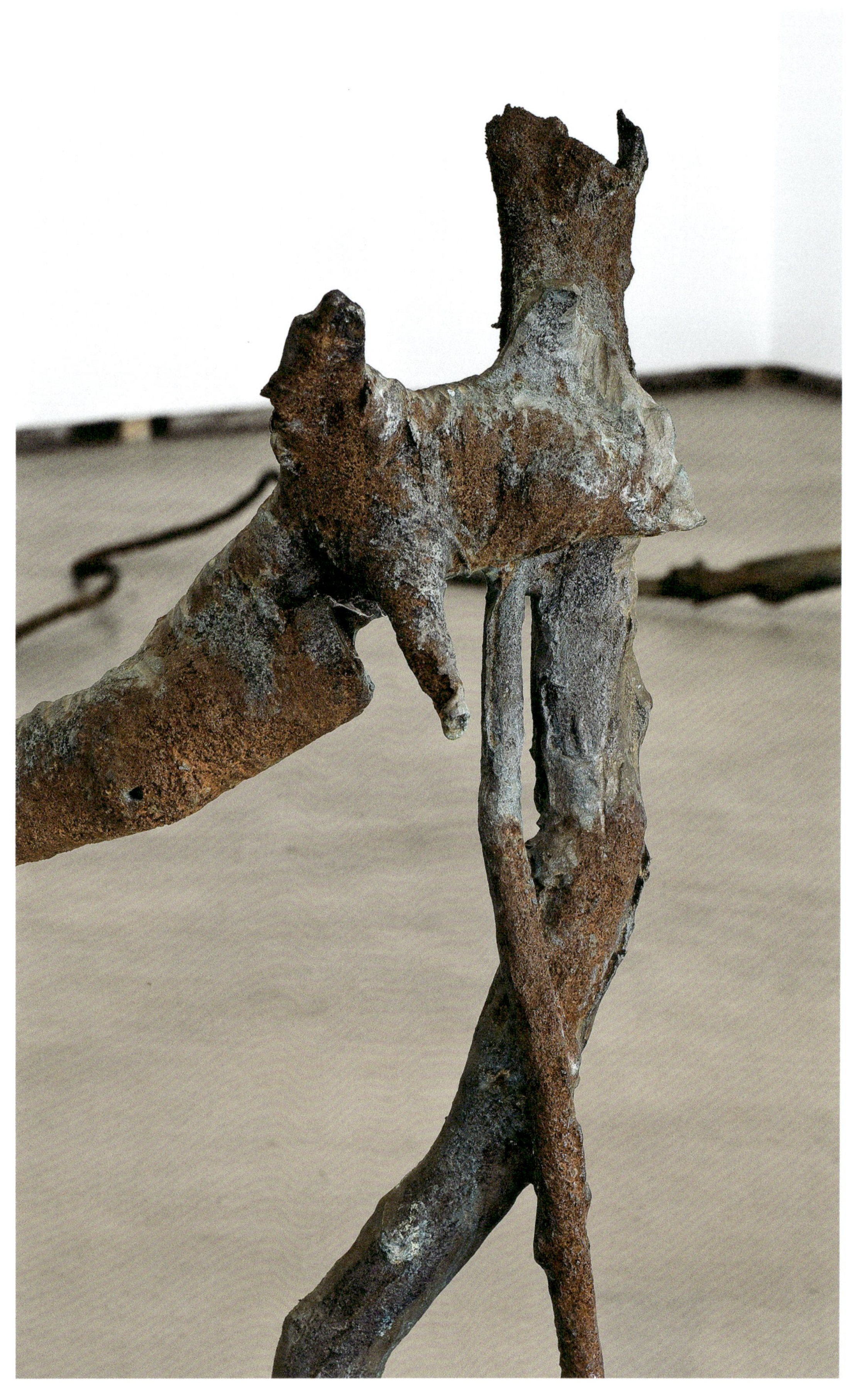

Vertigo Revisited, 2011 (detail)

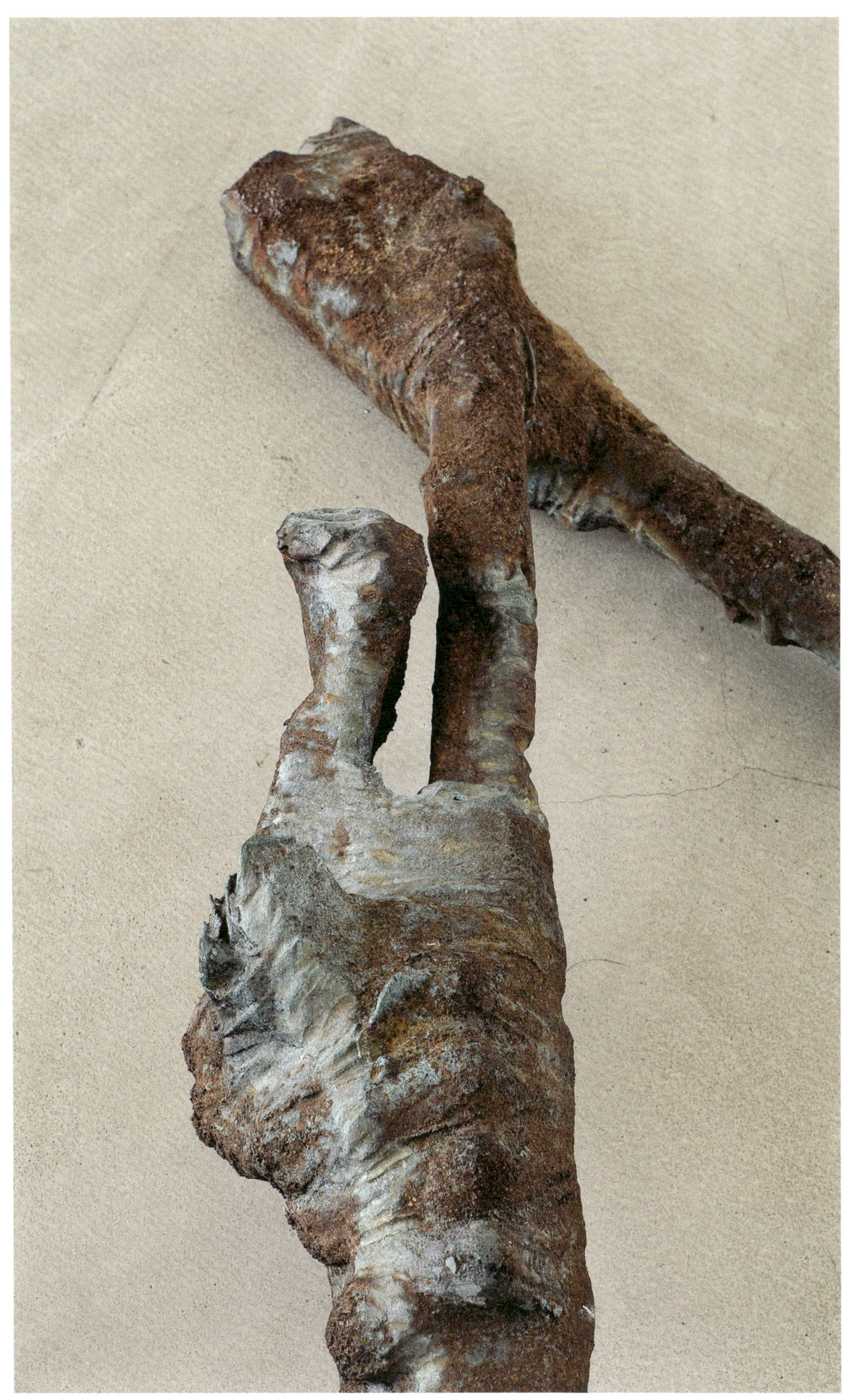

Vertigo Revisited, 2011 (detail)

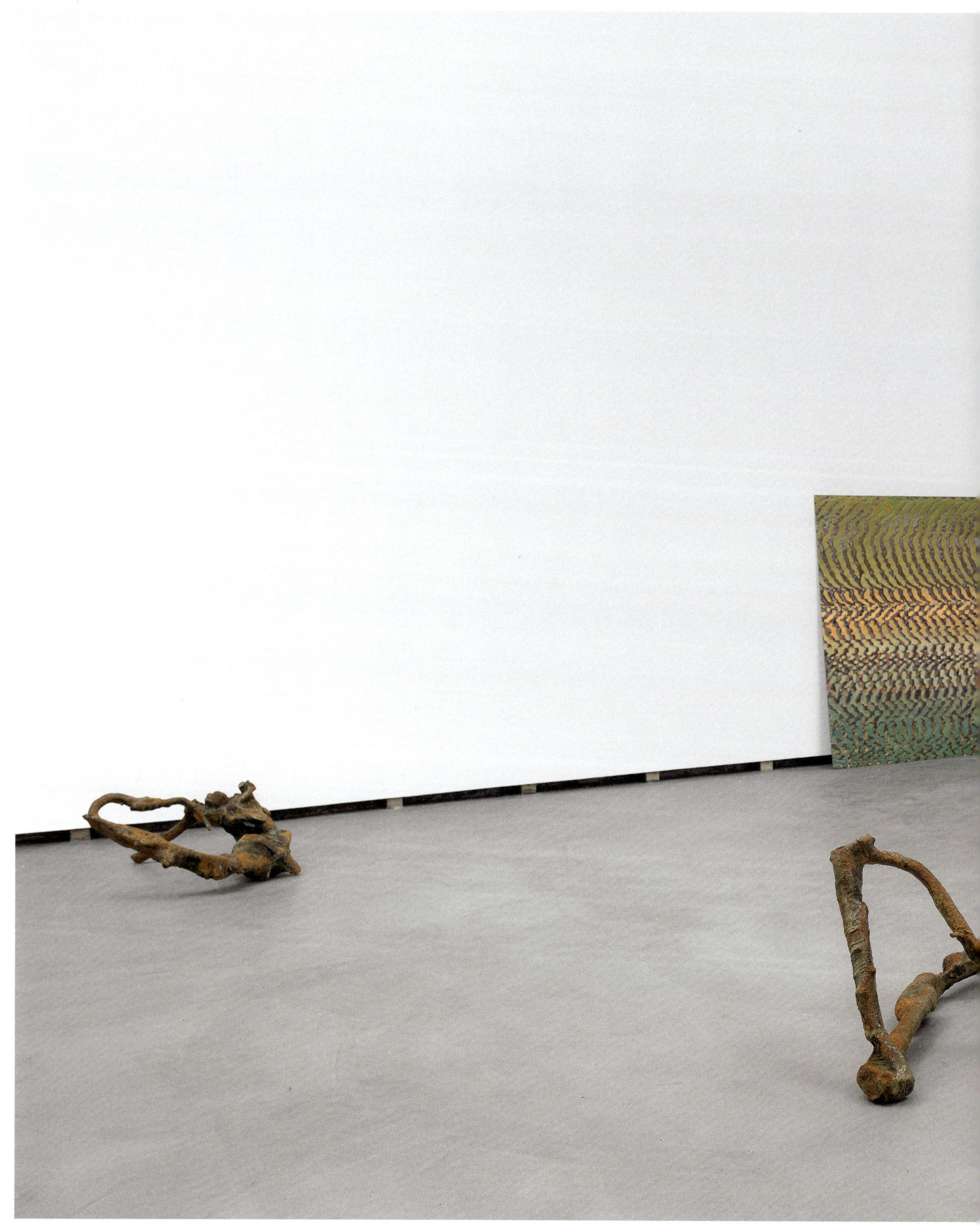

Installation view:
Eroding Rainbow, Schiavo Mazzonis Gallery, Rome, 2009

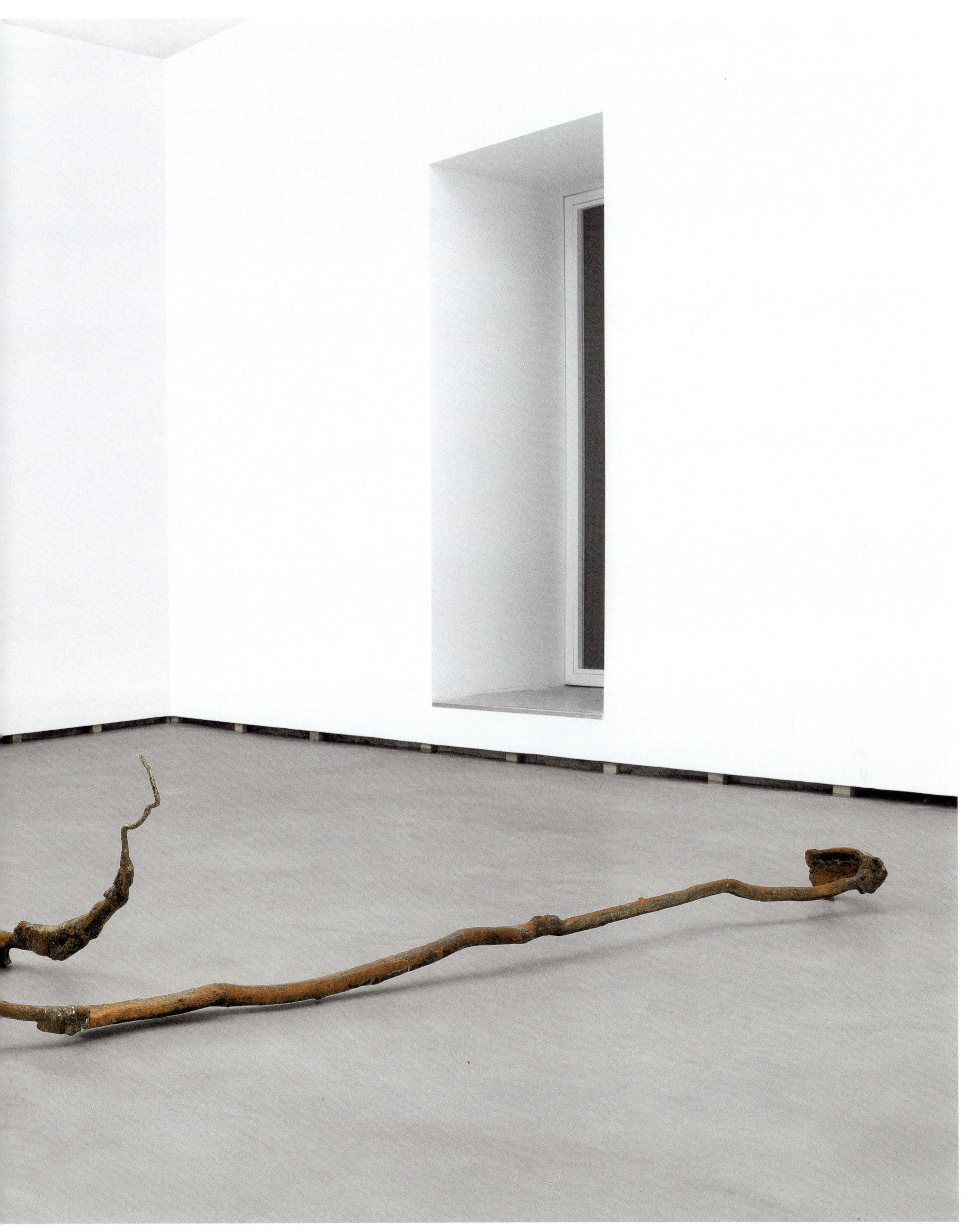

Left to right:
Sinking Feeling, 2008; *Caustic Afternoon*, 2008; *Dead Air*, 2008

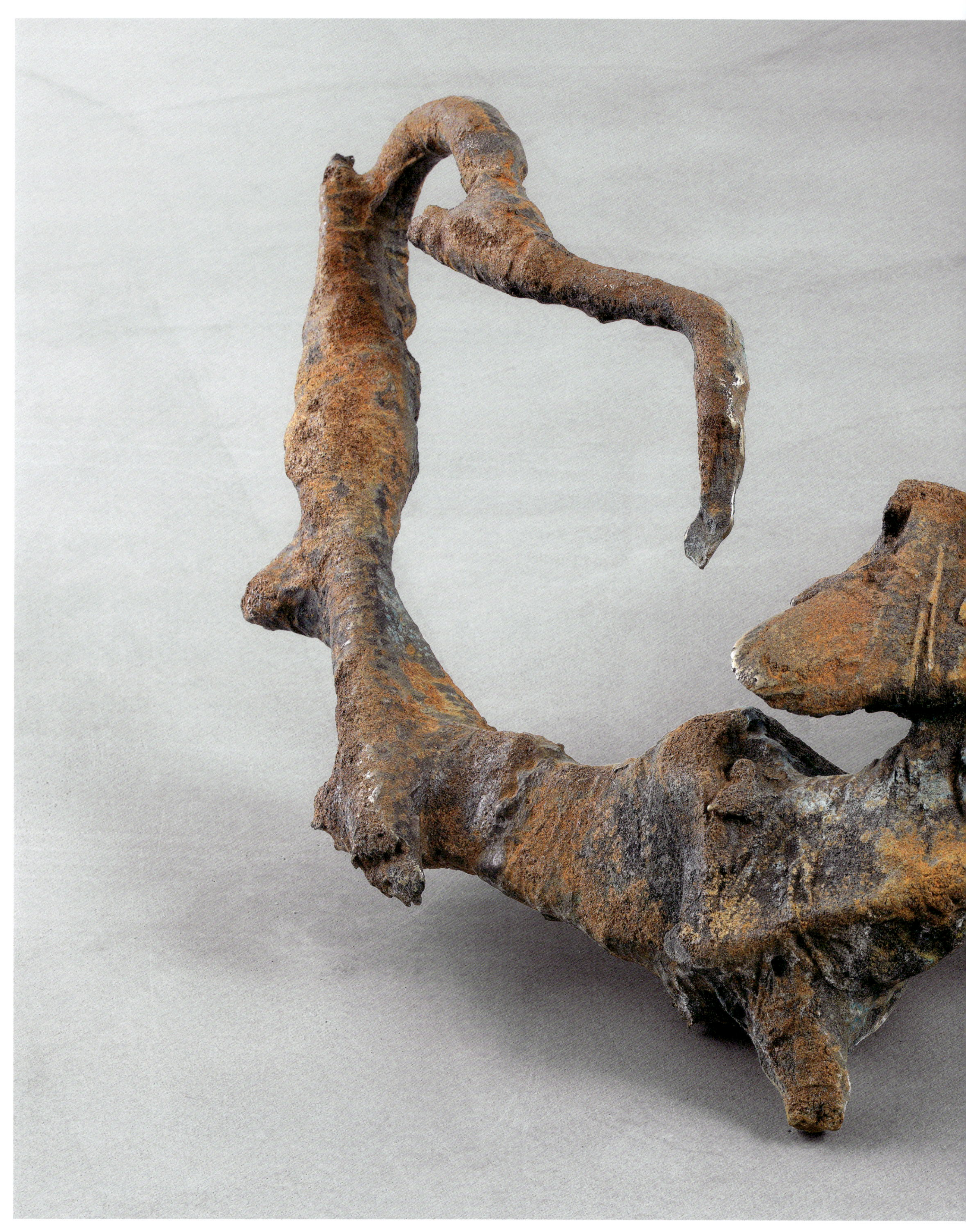

Sinking Feeling, 2008
Cast bronze, iron, and rust, 11 × 29 × 27 inches, 27.9 × 73.7 × 68.6 cm

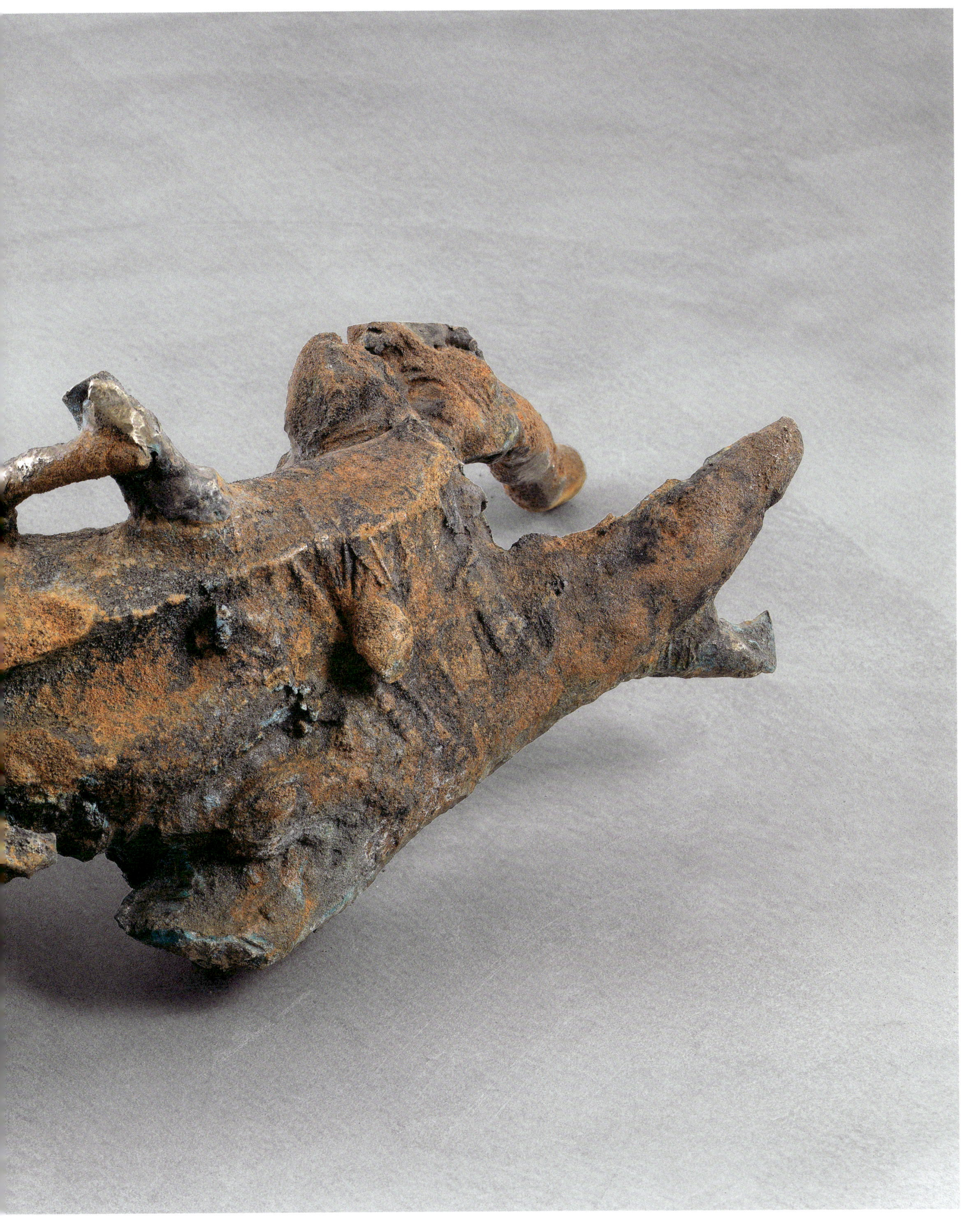

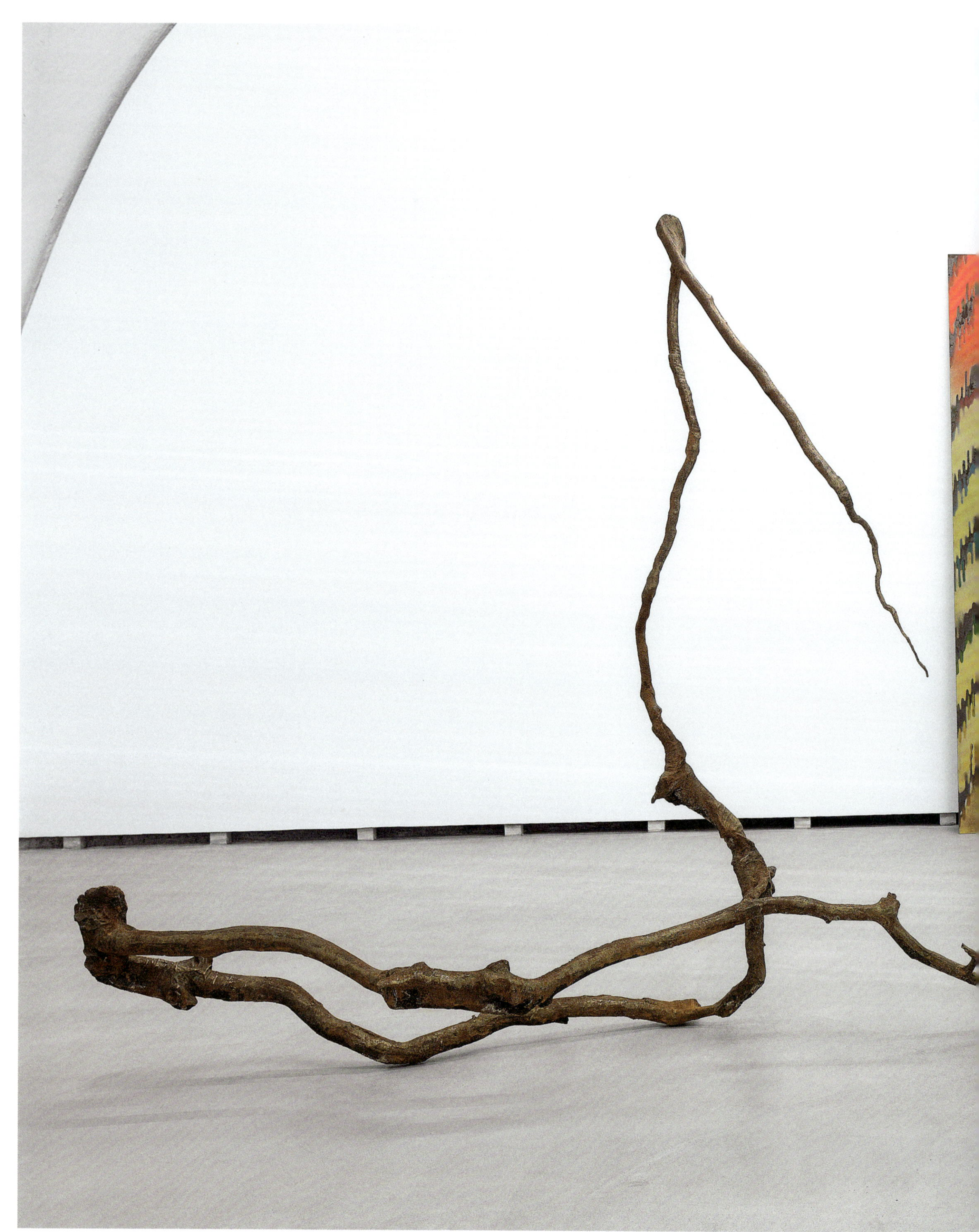

Installation view:

Eroding Rainbow, Schiavo Mazzonis Gallery, Rome, 2009

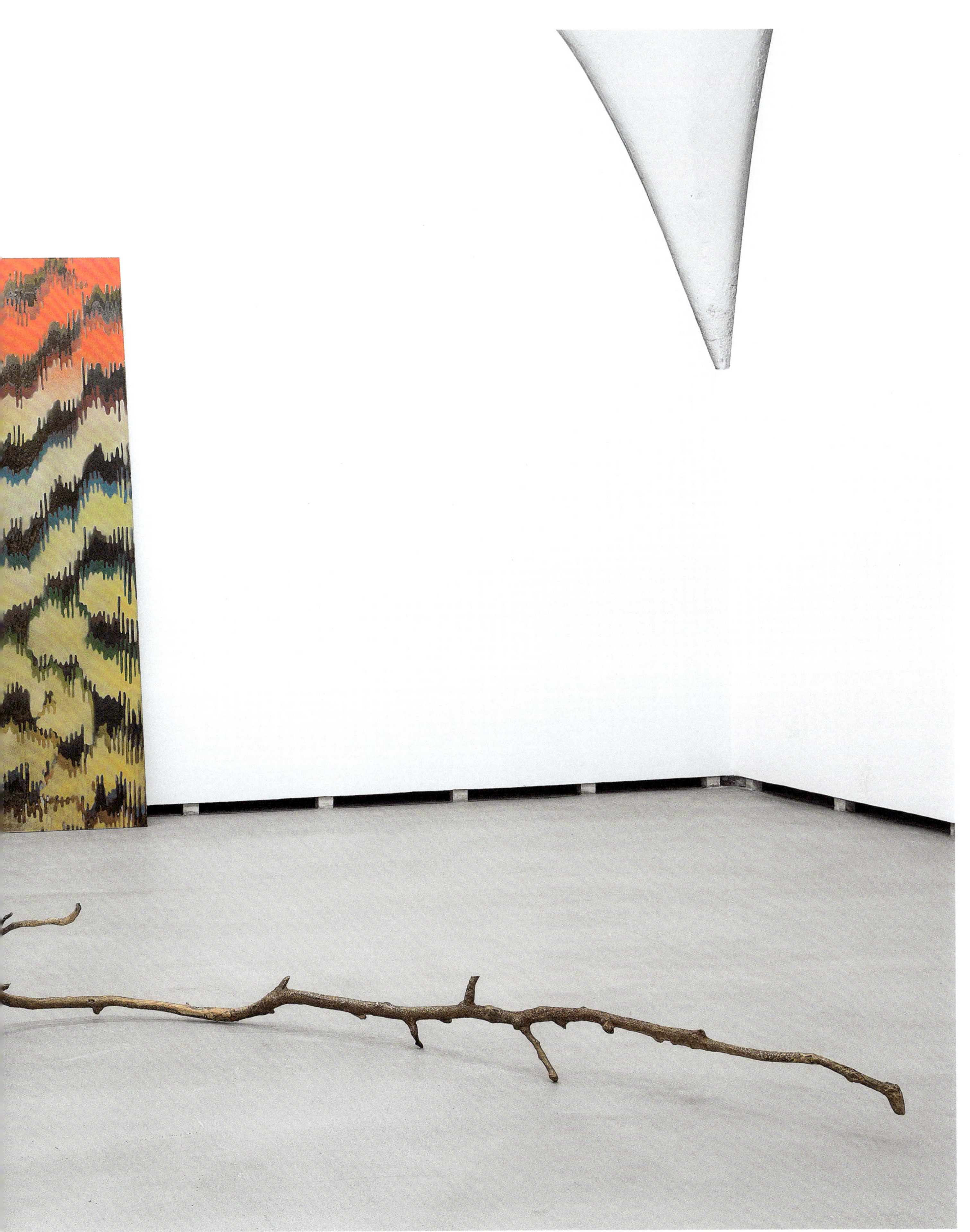

Left to right:
River's Edge, 2008; Here on Earth, 2008

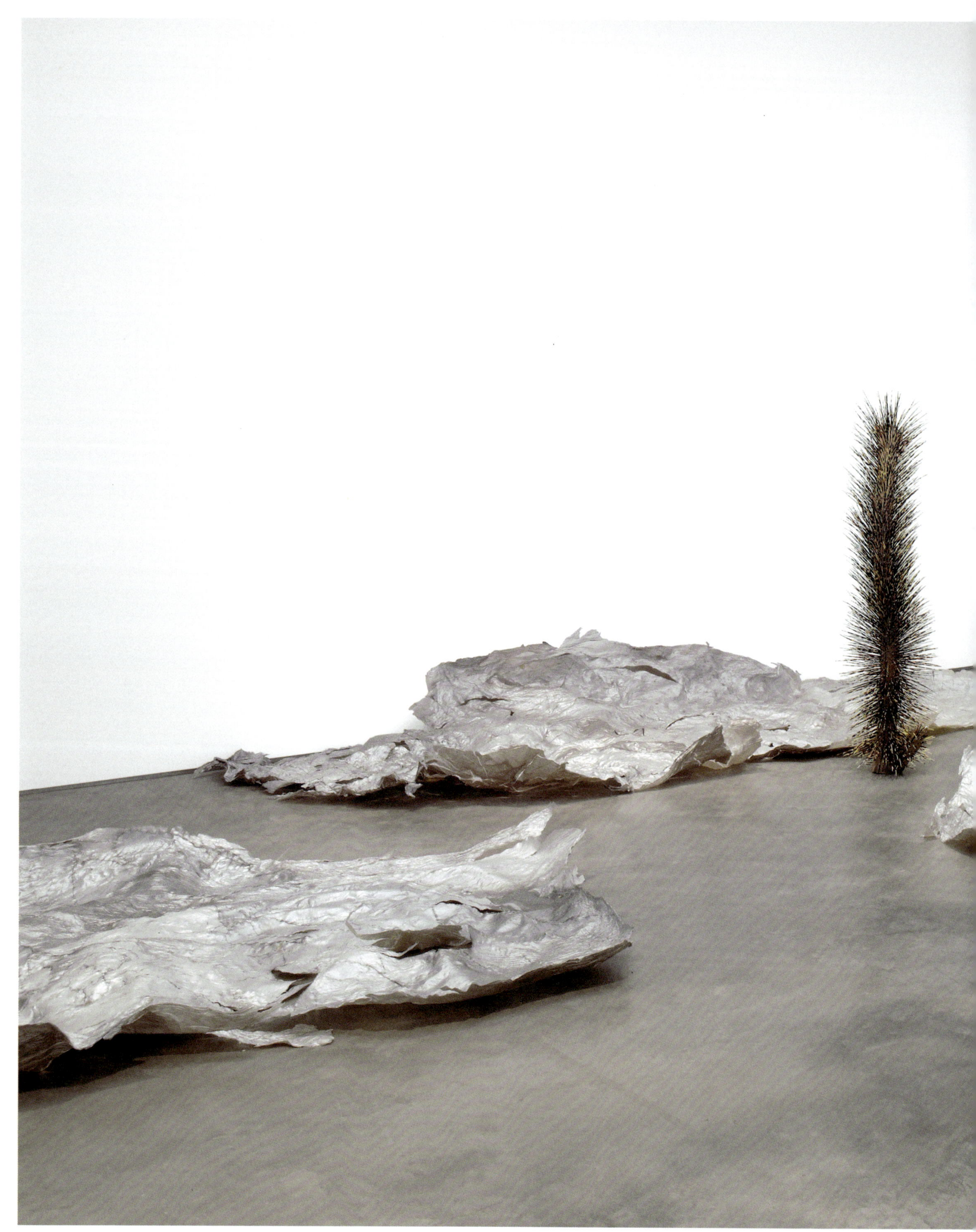

Installation view:
Inanimate Life, Marianne Boesky Gallery, New York, 2010

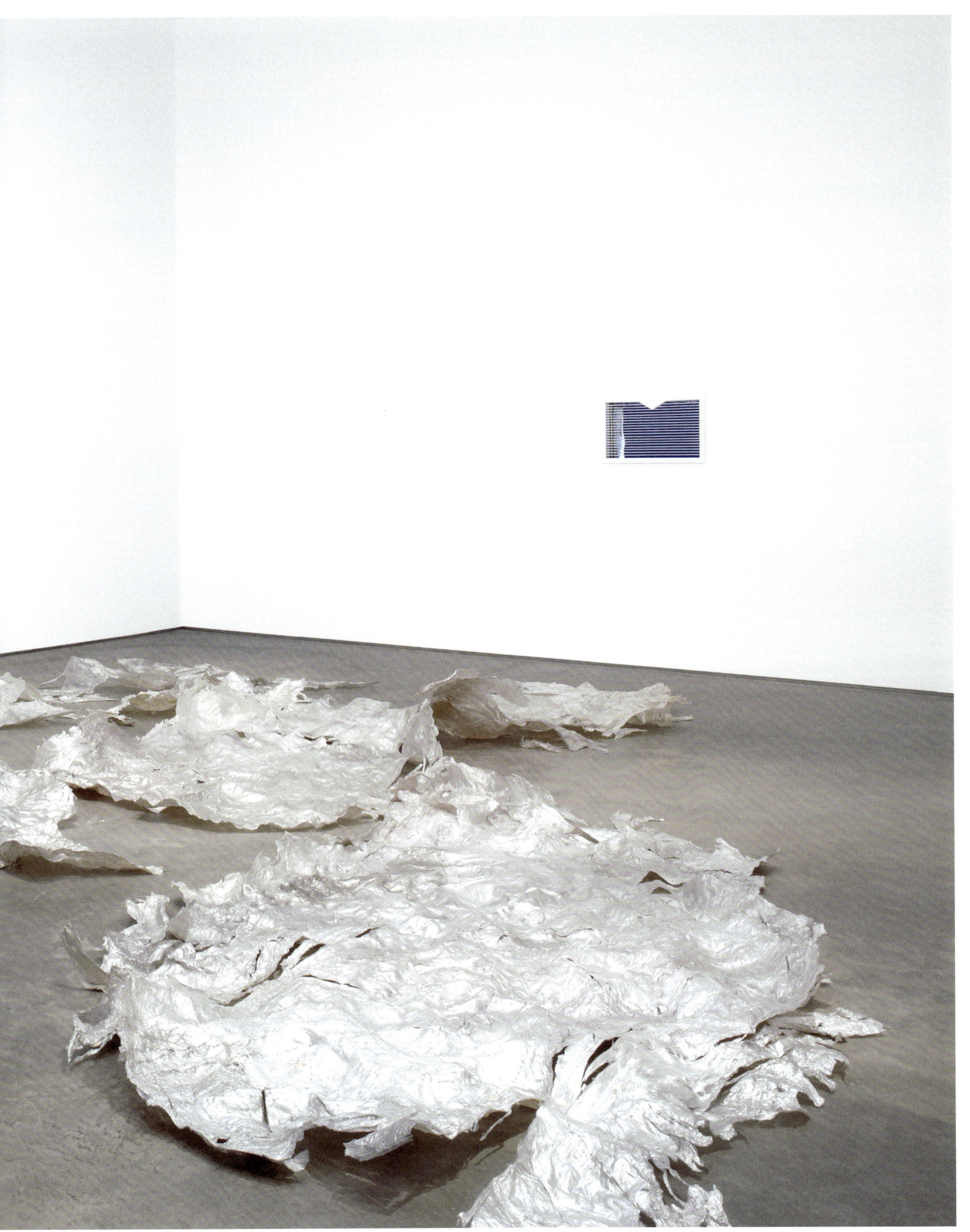

Left to right:
Molting, 2010; Thickly, 2010; Outside World, 2010

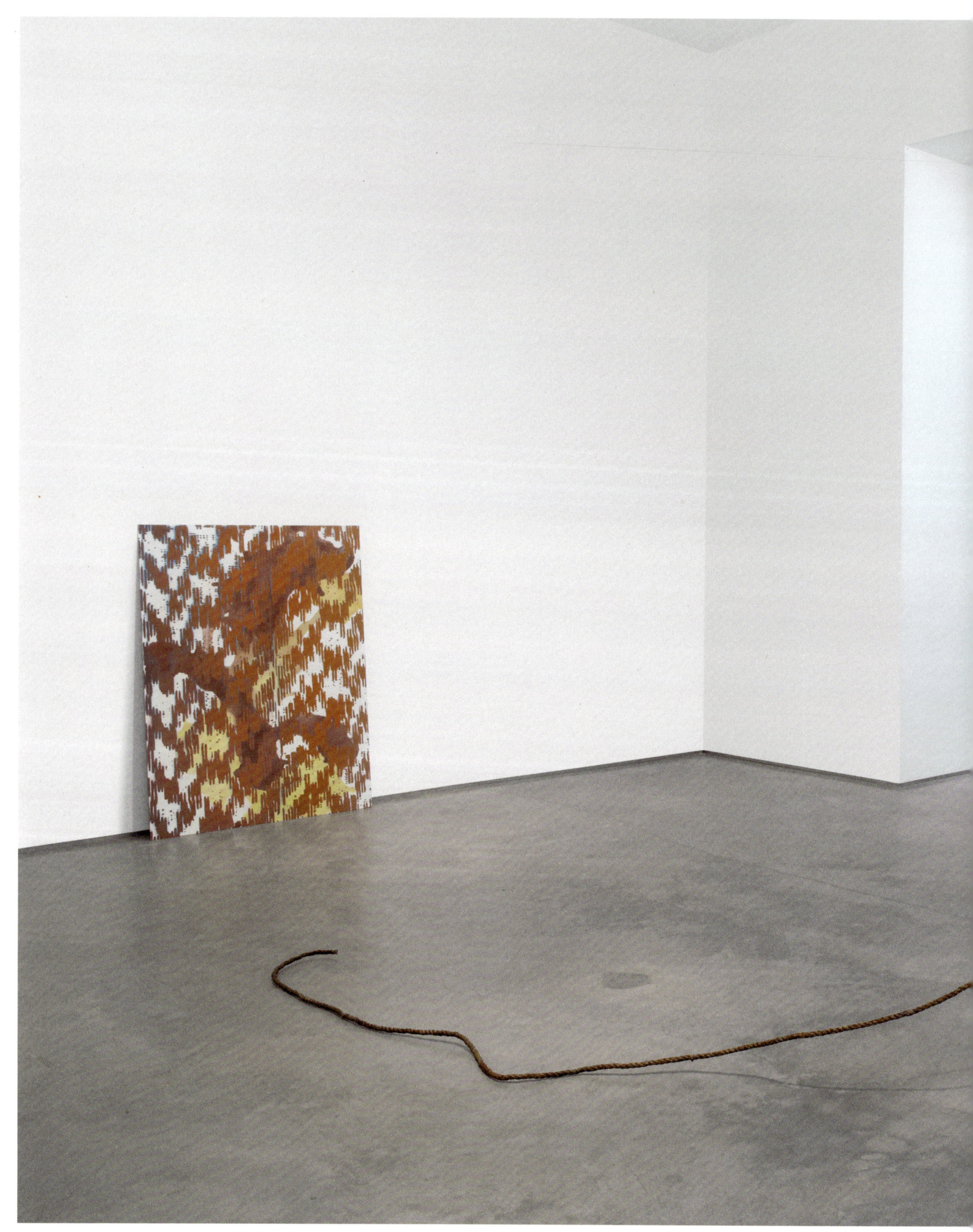

Installation view:
Inanimate Life, Marianne Boesky Gallery, New York, 2010

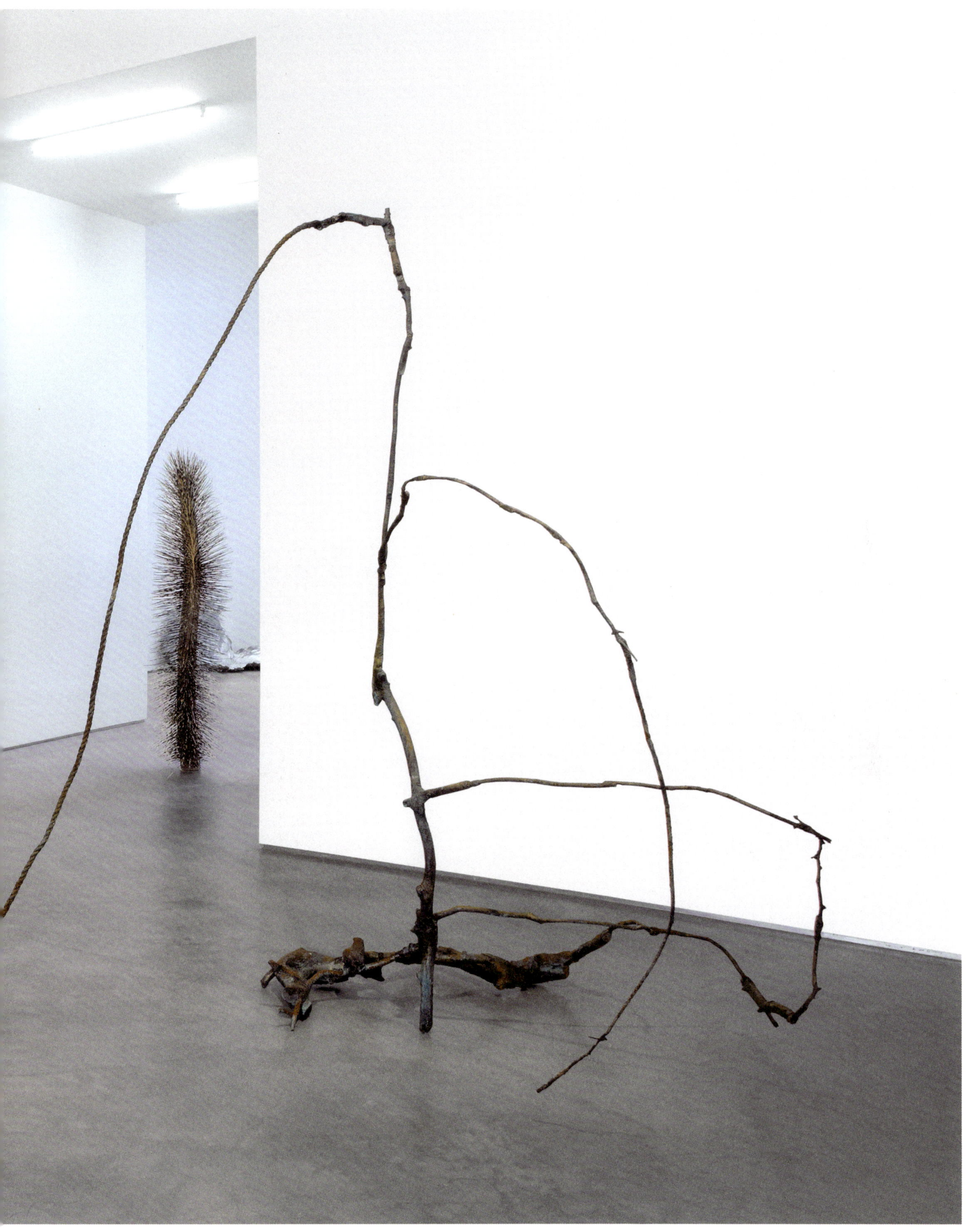

Left to right:

Conversations with a Bitter Pill, 2010; *Heartless Ascension*, 2010; *Prickly*, 2010

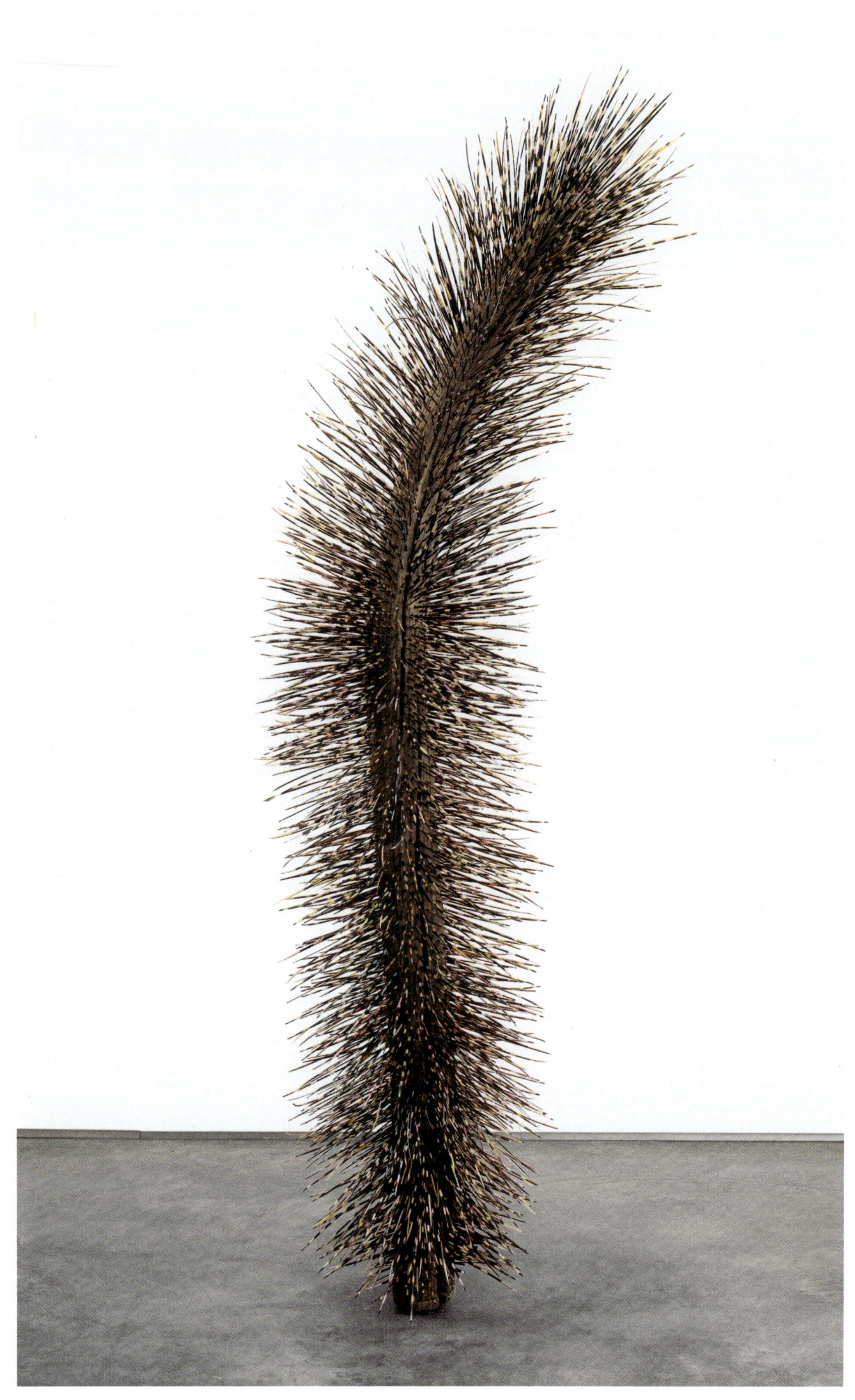

Prickly, 2010
Dyed porcupine quills, driftwood, and steel, 82 ½ × 38 × 21 inches, 209.6 × 96.5 × 53.3 cm

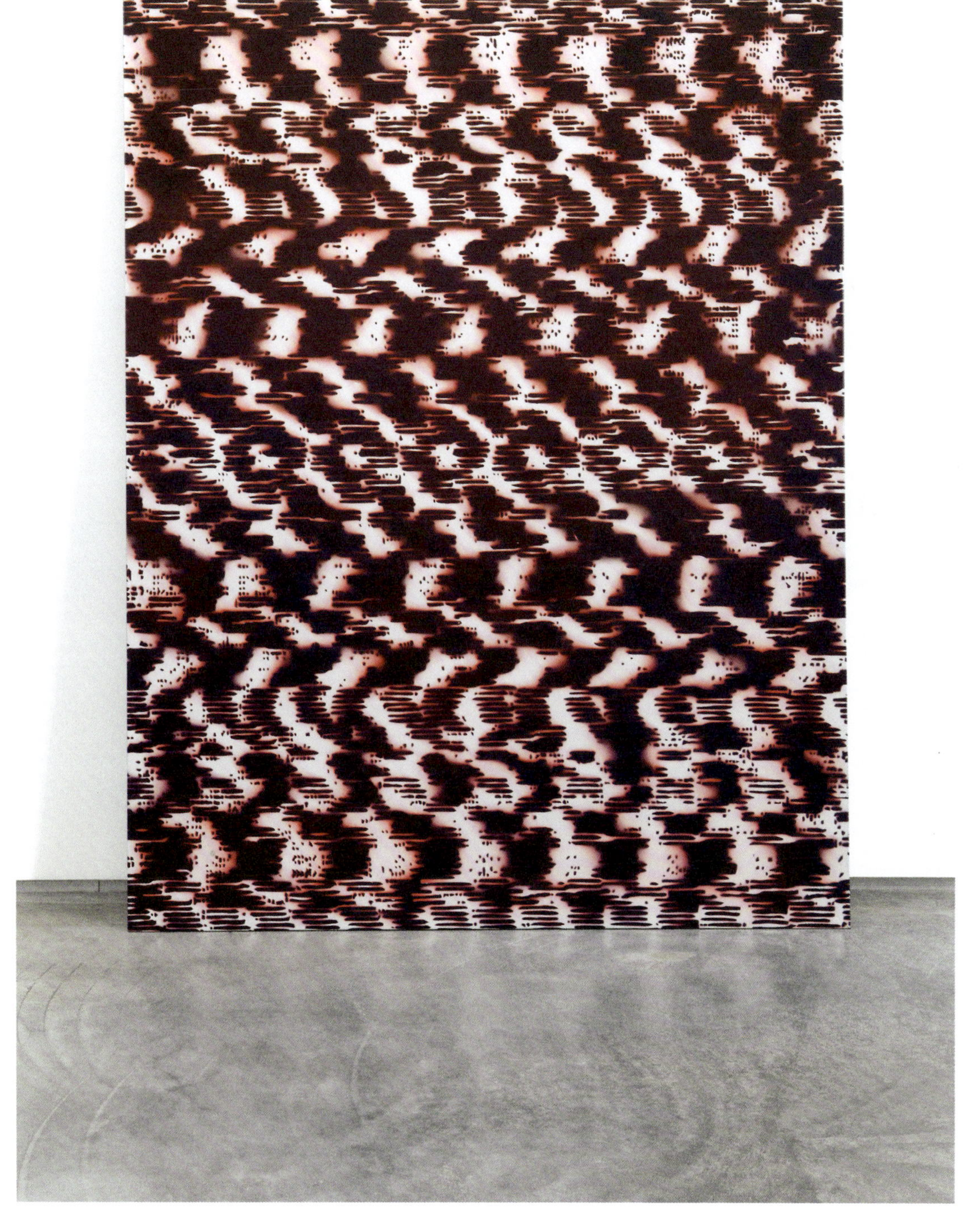

Negative Approach, 2010
Sprayed enamel on steel, 52 × 41 inches, 132.1 × 104.1 cm

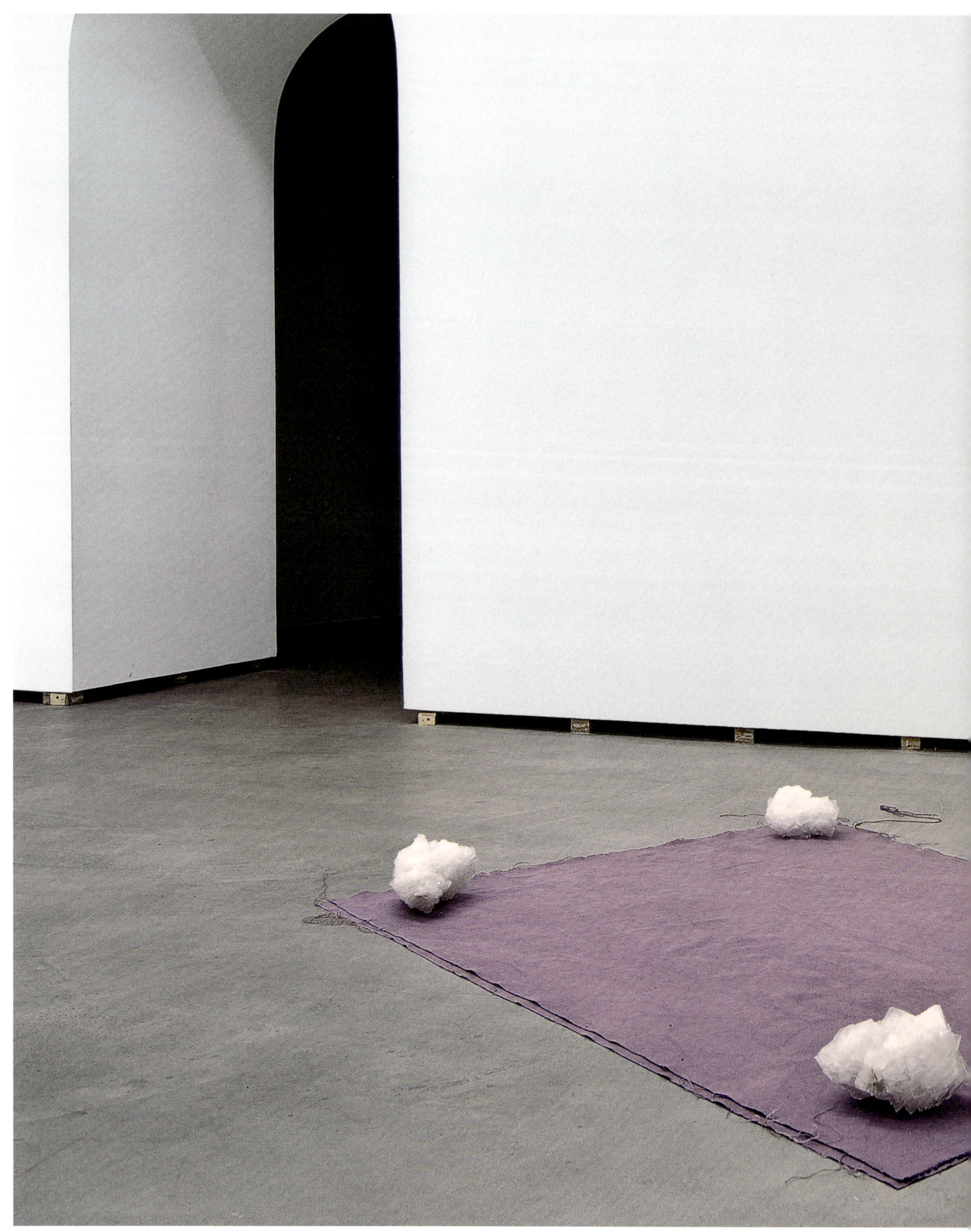

Fields, 2011

Purpurissum pigment on linen and aluminum sulfate crystals, overall: 4 ¾ × 38 ⅝ × 50 ⅜ inches, 12 × 98 × 128 cm

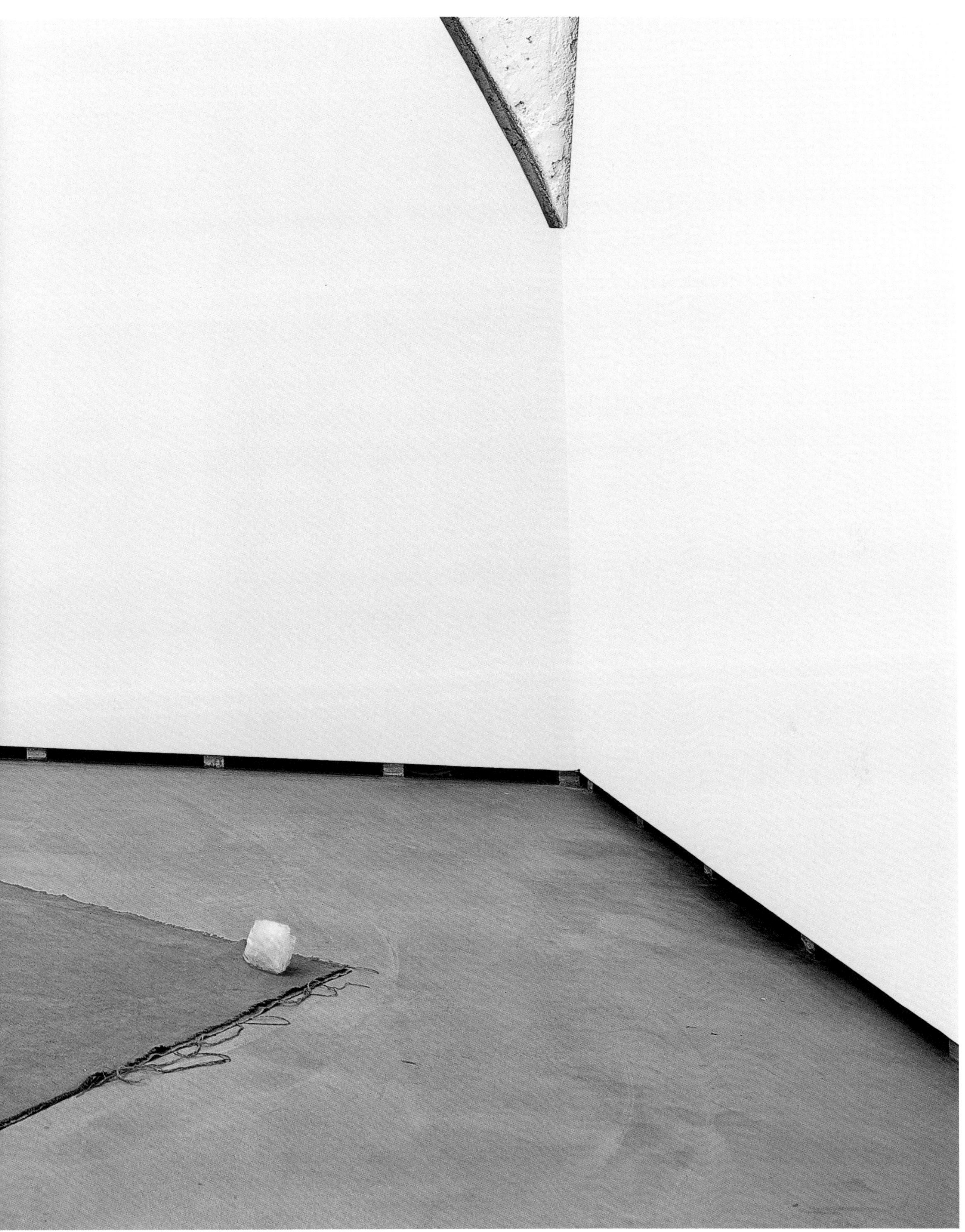

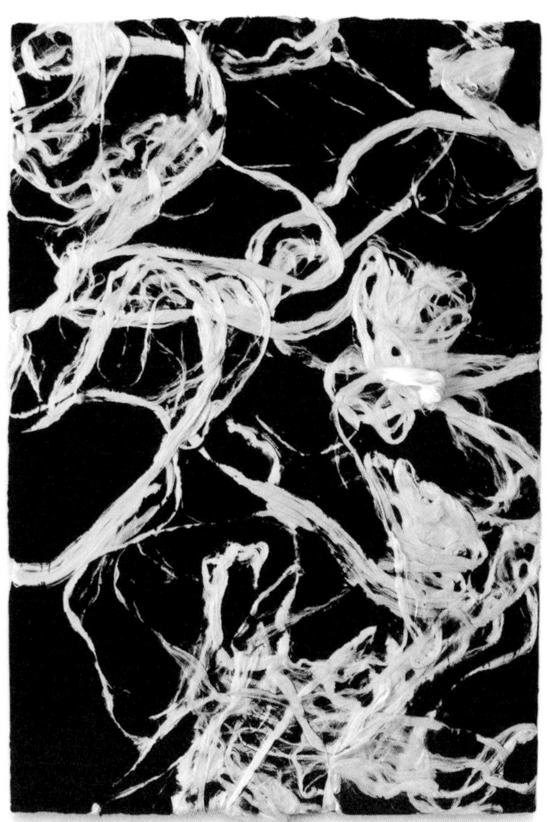
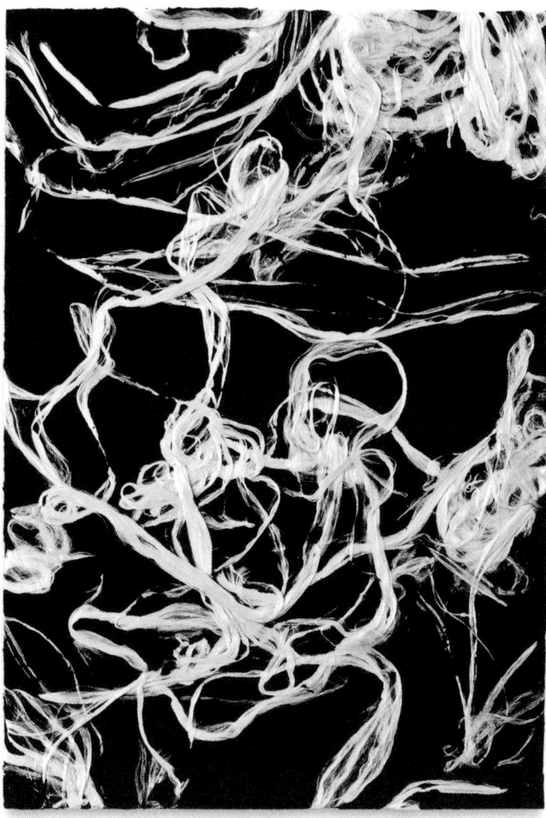
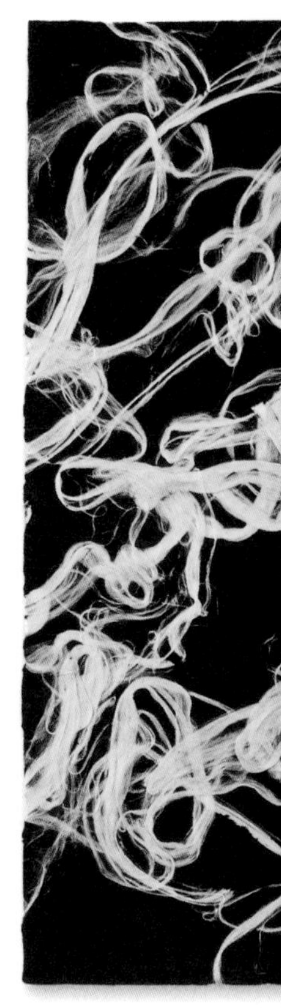

Salamander's Wool, 2011

70   Silk, concrete, and carbon pigment, each: 26 × 18 ⅛ × 1 ½ inches, 66 × 46 × 3.8 cm

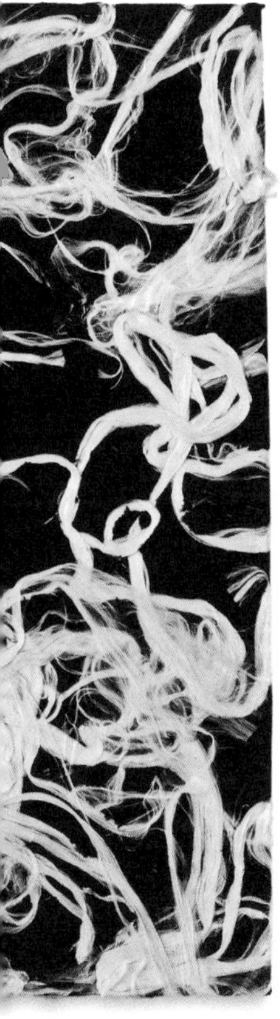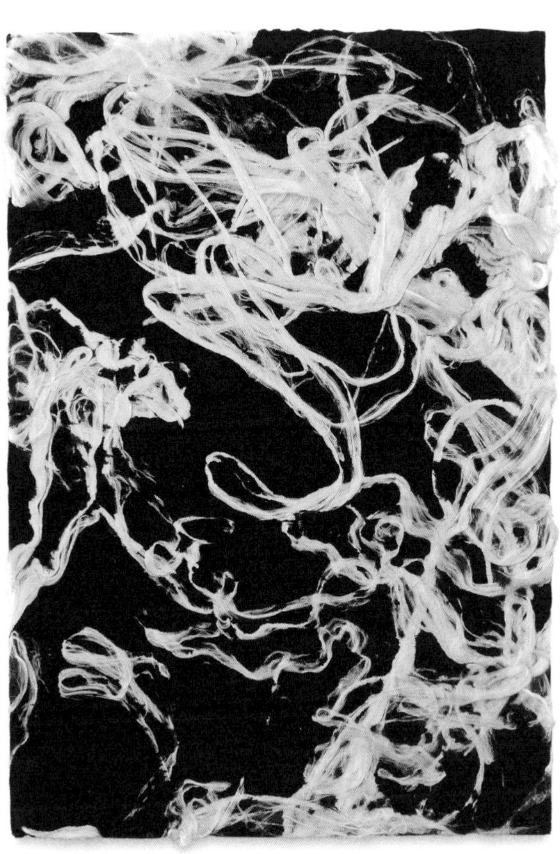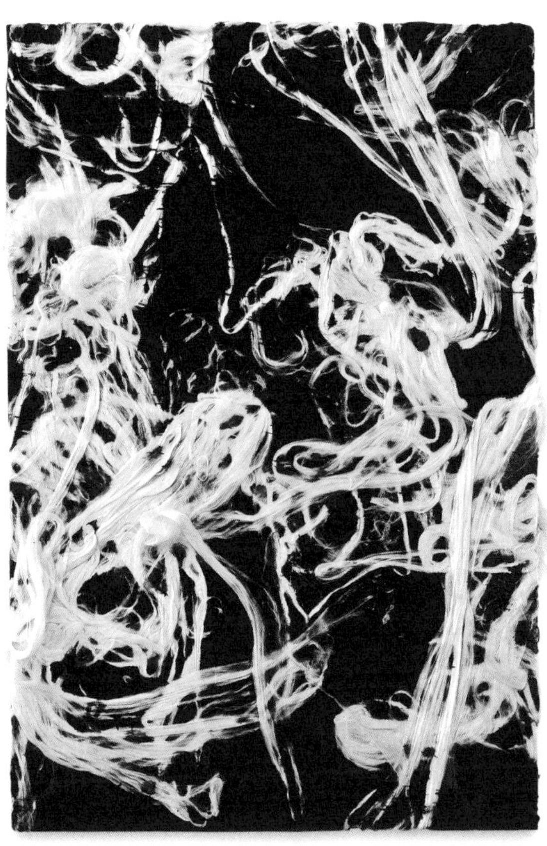

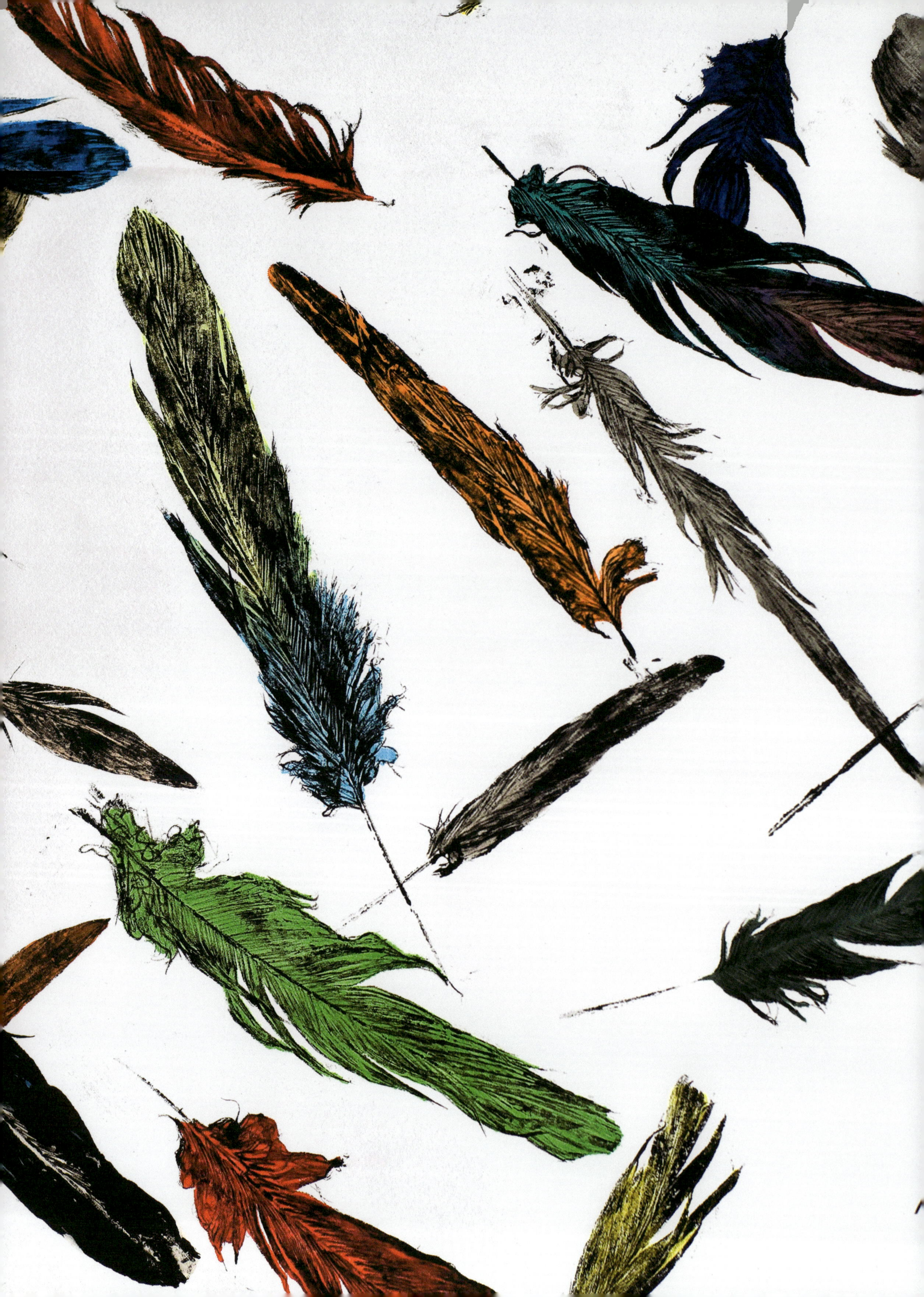

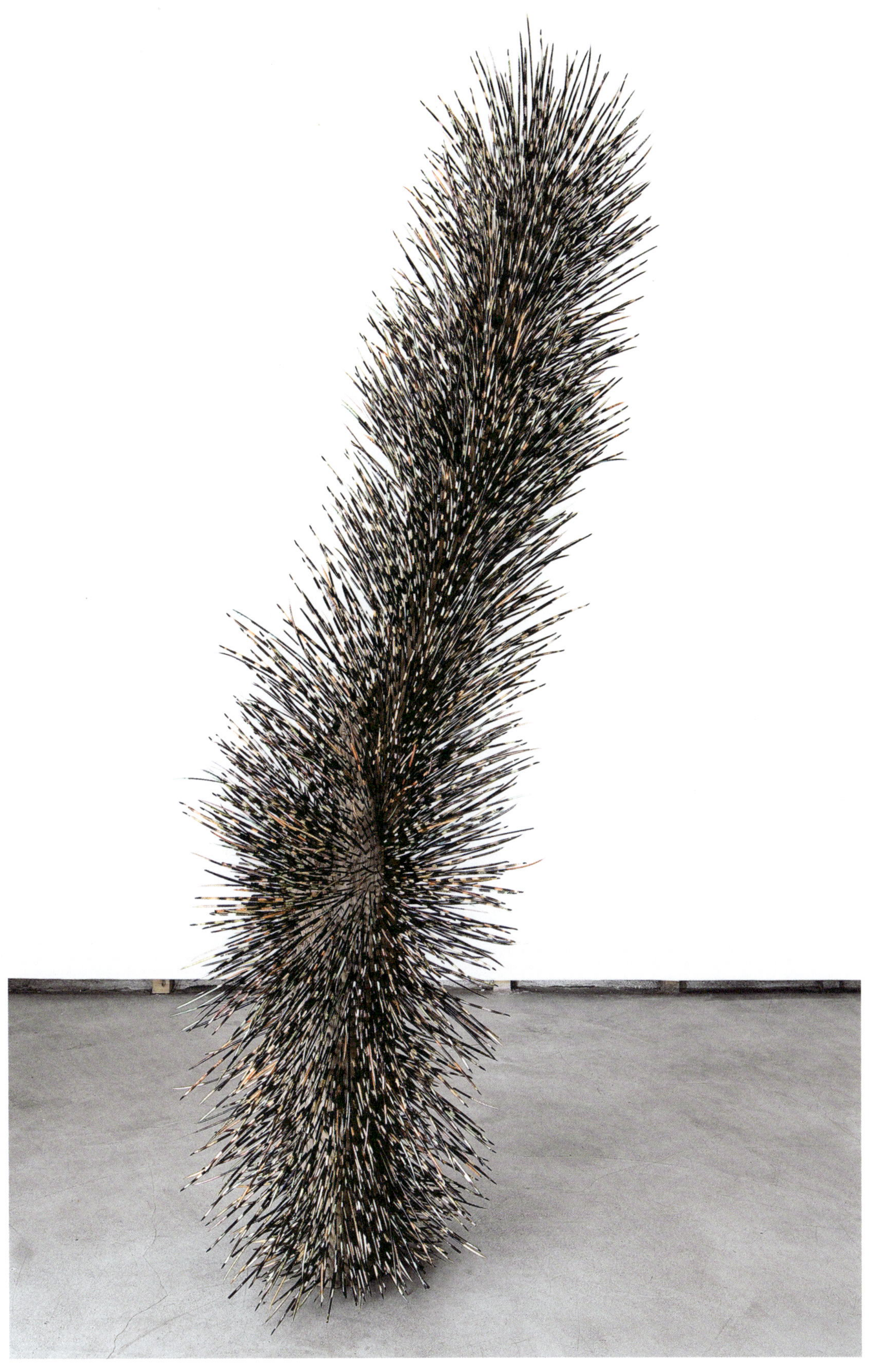

Opposite: *The Thought Before the Thief*, 2011 (detail)
Ink and marker on cotton paper, dimensions variable

Above: *Creeply*, 2011
Dyed porcupine quills, driftwood, and steel, 79 1/2 × 29 1/2 × 29 1/2 inches, 202 × 75 × 75 cm

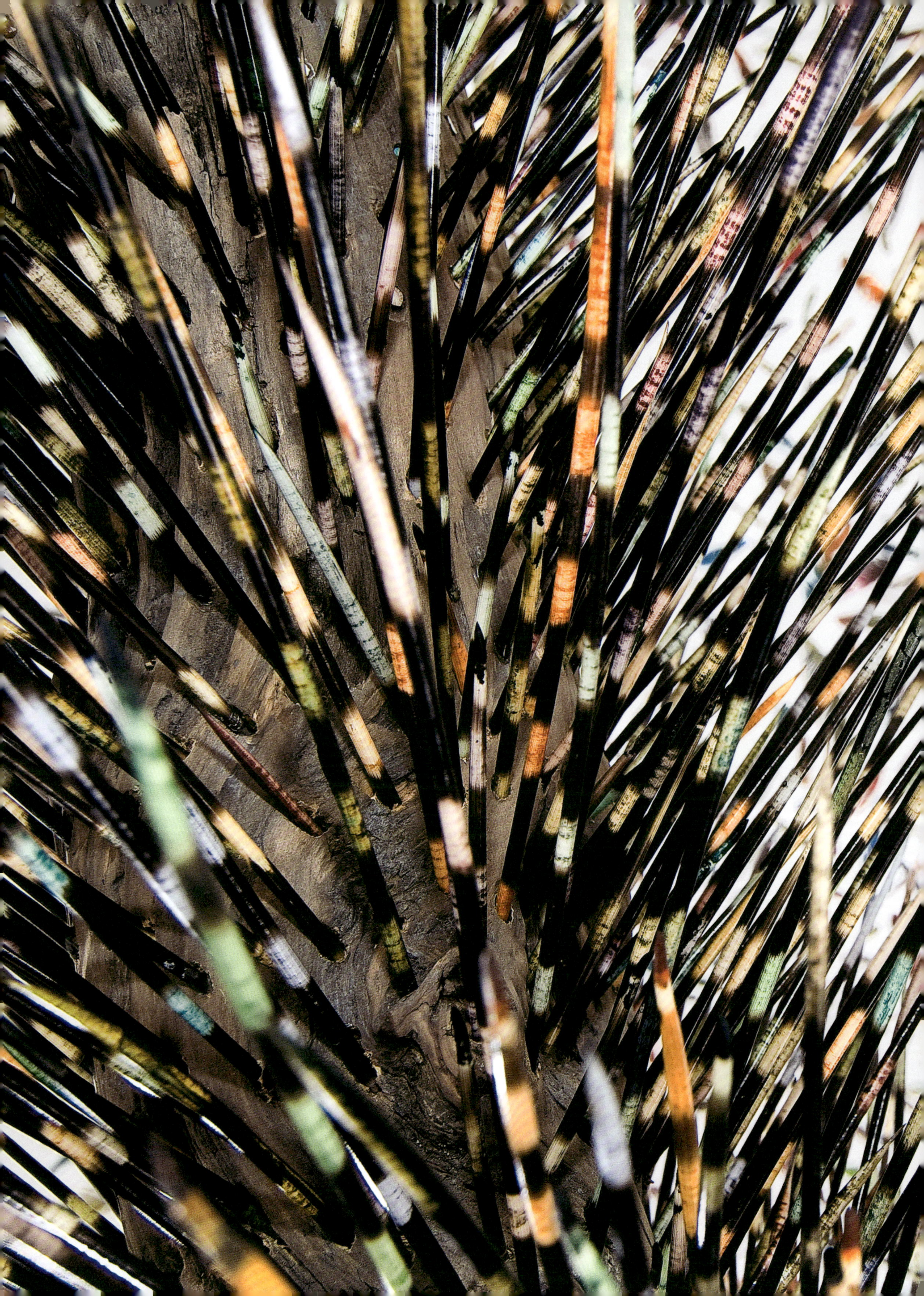

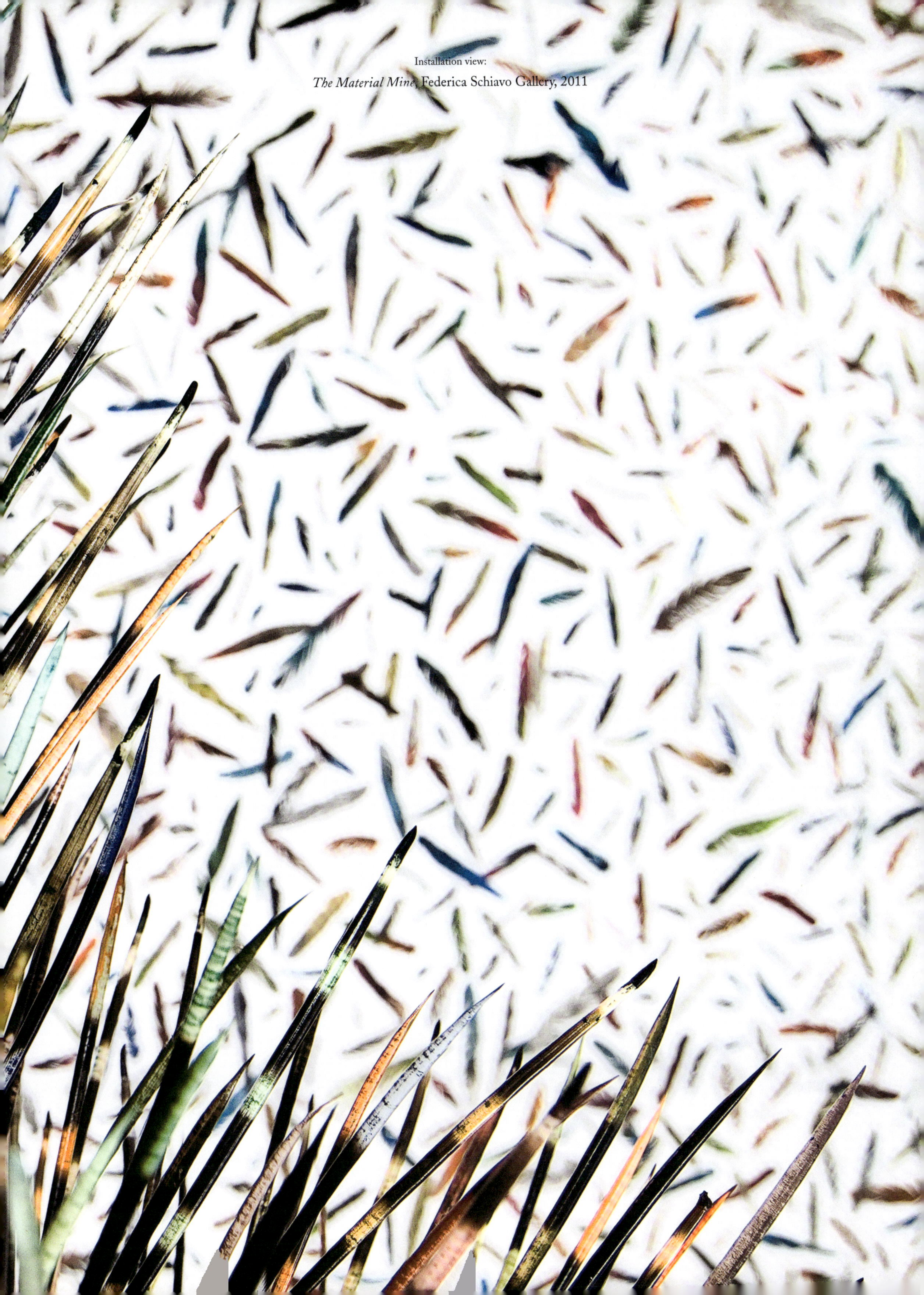

Installation view:
The Material Mine, Federica Schiavo Gallery, 2011

Jay Heikes's Deep Depravity

Sarah Lehrer-Graiwer

When somebody does something wrong, I want to feel sure it is done purposely.[1]
   —MIKE KELLEY

Are you the skunk at the family picnic? Sowing awkwardness and confusion, knocking over the popcorn, getting sand on the strawberries, leaving an unshakeable stink? Is your ability to express vulnerability and doubt (in yourself, above all) your great strength and awesome talent? Is deflation your peak performance mode? Are all your best take-downs of yourself? Are disappointment, disillusionment, disgust, and the dark comedy that makes it all barely bearable the very currency of your style and thought? Are lack, uncertainty, and feelings of emptiness, paradoxically, the wellspring of your significant aesthetic powers, trusting that what's missing will be transfixing? Do you go for marginal over mainstream? If so, you may be an artist. More than that, you may be that rare breed of vanishing American artist, like Jay Heikes, that we so badly need—that any cultural ecosystem so badly needs.

     Throughout and underneath all his objects, images, and videos, an artist like Heikes is fundamentally preoccupied with constantly reconsidering, reclaiming, and reconnecting with what the role of the artist in culture is. He worries, for instance, whether there could be such a thing as a contemporary avant-garde and, "if the avant-garde exists, is it a life-long desire or condition, in which the artist finds the tools of the present to be inadequate, giving rise to an irresistible urge to change something, even if the goal is unattainable and foolish?"[2] The nuances and emotional complexity of inadequacy have long been irresistible for him. While the materials Heikes uses and the way he combines and transforms them are consistently distinctive—including wire, wood, branches, rope, burlap, dirt, ink, tacks, leather, even porcupine quills, and lots of cast bronze, iron, steel, and copper, typically rusted or corroded in wiry, tangled, angular constructions that often roughly conjure junkyards and factory floors . . . a latter-day Arte Povera master—his works' soulful manifestation of discontent and unease emphasizes the searching psychic energy contained in an entire practice and worldview. Every body of work speaks to the aspirational if debased pursuit of embodying a subject position as an artist that stands for something apart from and beyond mere professional identification or status, something private and internal, something endangered and nearing extinction in a time of art fairs, art stars, multinational gallery chains, mega-collector ego-seums, auction house record busting, and art tourism selfies on the 'gram. Heikes's romantic conception of the artist as an uninstrumentalized misfit and intellectual outcast who both steals attention and shirks the spotlight is increasingly out of date in such a fully professionalized and spectacularized field.

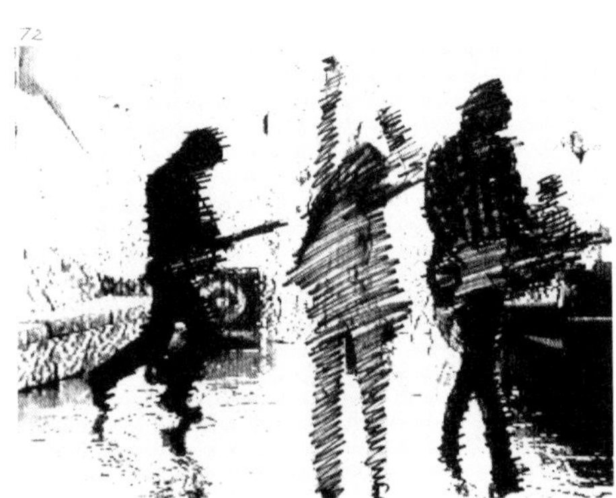

Fig. 1
White Light (Still 72), 2002
Marker on photocopy
32 × 40 inches, 81.3 × 101.6 cm

Failure, self-effacement, dissent, and marginality are among his art's foundational ideals. Since his first forays, he has drawn energy from the tension between hyperactive self-analysis and dreams of uninhibited unselfconsciousness. A self-deprecating self-awareness punctures everything: "Have you ever taken a band photo? Posed transgression is a life-changing moment," said the artist who made music before pivoting to visual art.[3] Aspirations of private transcendence and actual magic hit the wall of middle-aged exhaustion again and again, fizzling into notational shorthand and aborted gestures; it's so much mental effort just imagining what could be mind-blowing that going through every laborious step of actually attempting to actualize it is not, in the end, in the cards—like a slacker magician, waving off the ending of a trick . . . You get the idea. You are charmed.

Essentially existentialist, the claustrophobia of incessantly circling the interior of his own consciousness proves both a generative condition of selfhood and thought as well as the cause of unresolvable frustrations and mental collapse: traps, hooks, blocked paths, static fields, and closed closets, doors, and windows are recurring tropes in Heikes's work that hold the subject twitching but immobilized in a tight vice. He is torn and asks, "Do I always have to search for unexplored possibilities, or can I just present a kind of deadpan futility that acts as satire?"[4] In terms of attitude and polemics, he is cut from the same cloth as Mike Kelley, who decisively articulated artistic purpose around his attraction to rejection and negativity: "I chose to become an artist because I wanted to be a failure. When I was young, if you wanted to really ostracize yourself from society, you became an artist. . . . And I wanted to make something really, really ugly. . . . In America, artists, traditionally, are peripheral, unimportant, un-glamorous figures."[5] To be a happily disgruntled contrarian, to be willfully inappropriate and out of joint, with an anarchic sense of humor, is a deep calling and necessary cultural function, one on which much else depends.

The artist, for Heikes, is essentially a comic—or tragicomic—figure of trained, practiced irreverence and performed vulnerability, like the jester, fool, clown, and stand-up comedian. Citing the influence of Neil Hamburger's aggressive and discombobulating negativity, he helps us understand that we are all idiots. Fantasizing that art-making is "a sort of misanthropic last laugh in which the artist jester escapes being beaten up by the jock of history, a daydream where the most popular kid in school endlessly steps in dog shit," Heikes makes clear his underdog allegiances.[6] Forgoing artistry and stagecraft, the artist carries a broader mantle of pathos together with losers, bums, loners, cranks, outsiders, and other degraded proxies for social dysfunction like the unemployed, non-productive, disobedient, and unruly citizen consumer. In a large group of hand-dyed palladium prints from 2008–10 called Civilians, Heikes posed a deformed, limp dummy—plaid button-up shirt signaling basic masculinity, hornet nest as a nearly featureless head, rip-hole gash for a mouth, broken glasses for eyes—to depict and defend certain choice states of being, which serve as each picture's subtitle and stake out the more beleaguered realms of the human condition for artistic content: embarrassed, appalled, drunk, crawling, brooding, belligerent, frozen, imploding, lost, pointing, poking, relaxing, resting, screaming, shivering, surprised, unimpressed, brooding, frazzled, confrontational, gasping, hopeless, nodding off, obliterated, severed, haggard, howling, and unaware. His dramatic dummies could be goofy, like homemade Halloween decorations, but as Kelley remarked several decades ago about his own work, their "function as art actually makes it more uncomfortable."[7] Or as Heikes himself wrote, commenting on Kelley's work, images like these live for "a new dawn in which ugliness and awkwardness become a cherished raison d'etre."[8] Standing in, to one degree or another, for the artist, the Civilians suggest that to make a truly empathic member of society, we must reckon with these peeling and falling apart fools, these Paul McCarthy-esque grotesqueries. We need to wallow in this dim ditch, too. Radicality demands being in touch with everyday darkness. Heikes's civilians do not moralize or judge. They do not work. They unwork and devolve, they are spent and wasted. They are both numb and highly sensitive, feeling a lot. They wear their flaws on their sleeve. They are antiheroic, like so many of Heikes's objects. They turn inward, lost in themselves, and dysfunction magnificently—they insist that, above all, art must allow for and defend dysfunction, being that much more interesting and vital for including it. Though often the product of laborious, skilled, or time-consuming processes, Heikes's art continually argues for the disproportionate and unpredictable relationship between labor and meaning in art works, where affective power and resonance are not correlated to displays of monumental effort but rather to the most effective, poetic transmission of some intensity of gesture, thought, and emotive energy.

A decade and a half ago, Heikes seeded his practice as an exhibiting artist with an opening act that was something of a joke. In *So There's This Pirate . . .* (2005), the artist appears as a slacker stand-up delivering a weird riddle of a joke in a short looping black-and-white video, directly addressing the camera in front of a vertically striped fabric backdrop. His dark hair is combed straight down over his eyes with glasses placed on top. We can mostly see just one eye through the glasses and absurd bangs. He takes his time building the setup with a delivery that's nearly stoned, embodying an unmistakably cool, buzzed daze that hints at Mitch Hedberg's comic stylings or that lanky skater dude you crushed hard on in

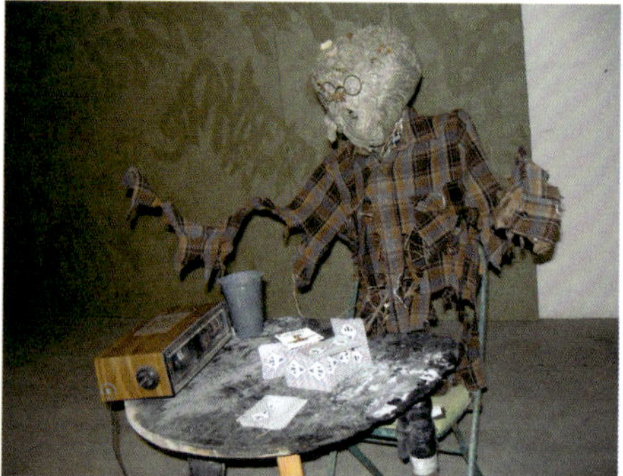
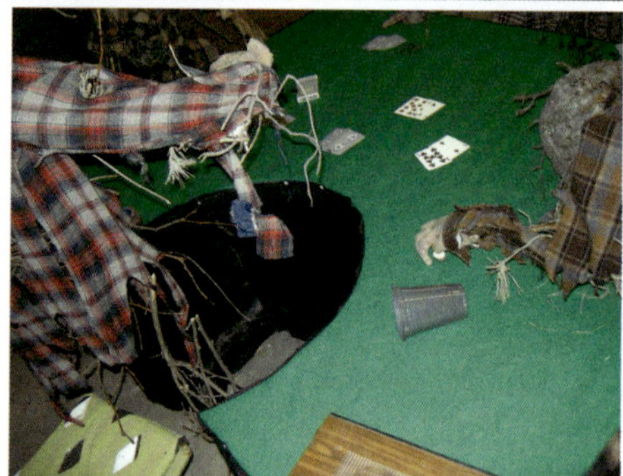
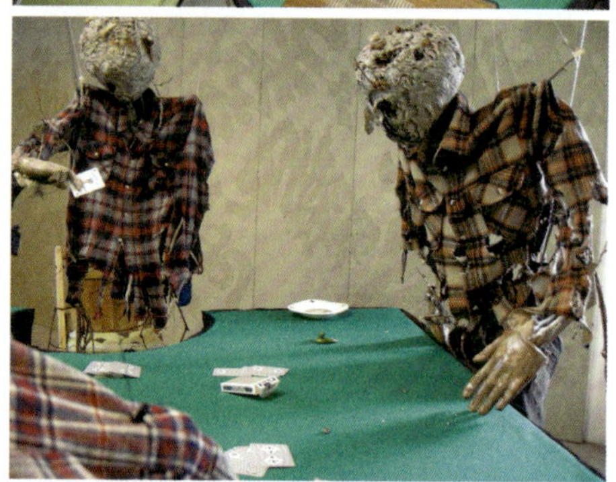
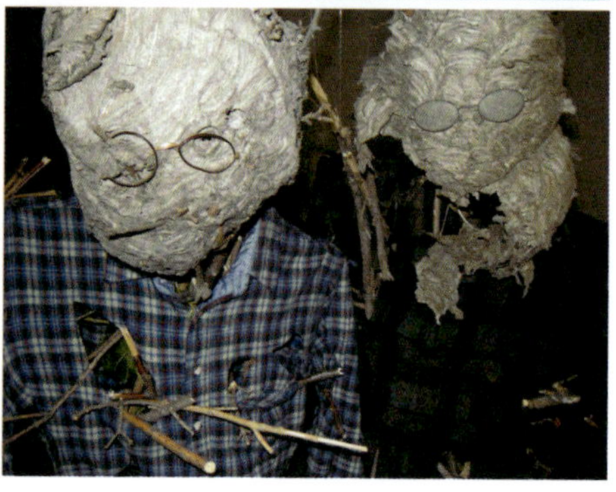

Fig. 2
Civilians in process in the artist's studio, 2008

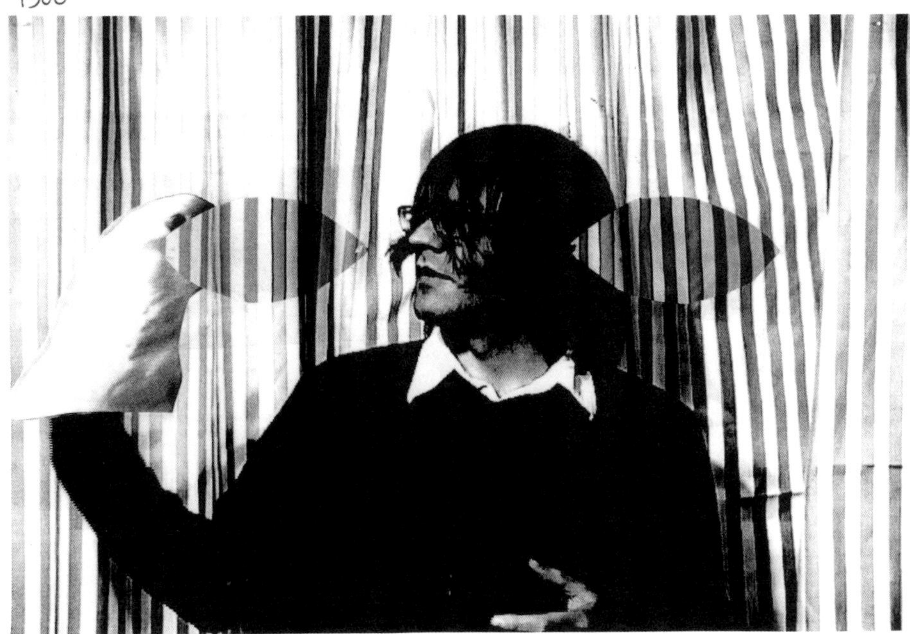

high school. The punch line is pure adolescent, no-fucks-given punk, too, in the strongest possible sense. Heikes tells the story of a lonely pirate who gets a parrot to keep himself company but quickly discovers the parrot has a serious attitude problem. When the pirate offers Polly a cracker, the parrot spits back, "FUCK YOU, ONE-EYE!" with utter disdain, taunting him. The pirate tries to punish the parrot's rudeness, first attempting unsuccessfully to teach it a lesson with the silent treatment and then, soon after, shutting the bird in the freezer. It makes no difference. Polly does not crack. The pirate's disciplinary efforts backfire and only expose his impotence, further weakening his position. The bird's insolence is total, absolute, hardwired, and uncompromising—one could say it is ideological and righteous. Even when stuck shivering in the freezer, the parrot still sneers, "FUCK YOU, ONE-EYE!" This is one badass bird. This bird's chutzpah is so rigorous you'd think it had just graduated military RTI training, resisting torture instead of rebuffing treats. So, anyway, the irate pirate has had enough and leaves his surly pet in the freezer all night, thereby killing it. But, even in death, the feathered rebel maintains and even escalates its defiance, dying in frozen rigor mortis flipping the bird with one wing and covering an eye with the other—rude to the bone, rude to the grave. The animal is that wild and that mad that its anger converts into performance and the transformation of self into sculpture, life into aesthetic gesture. At bottom, this is a parable of expression claiming the ultimate stakes. The bird's outrageous offensiveness is stunning and transcendent, moving in its courage and fearlessness. Even the pirate, so antagonized, cannot help but admire the beauty of the parrot's act and, as the artist says in narration, stands "in awe of his rudeness." In fact, to be in awe (of rudeness, of radicality, of extremity) is perhaps the key here, not only to the joke but to Heikes's project and passion. Rudeness and being difficult are reframed as great strengths, signs of intelligence, independence, and critical thinking that are essential antidotes to herd mentality, mainstream culture, and nascent forms of authoritarianism.

It's not just one early video that's based around this story, but several early exhibitions and related bodies of work spun off of and referred to it as source material that then got reframed and attenuated. In *Like a Broken Record*, a group of sculptures from 2007 shown at Marianne Boesky Gallery, the pirate joke is the distant pretext for repetitions issued past the point of legibility or comprehension, where the decay of information resulting from reiteration and recombination steers the original story further toward themes of fatalism, interminability, exhaustion, interference, static, and breakdown. The story itself barely even works as a joke; its humor is dark, bleak, anarchic, nihilistic, suicidal. The absurdity of the parrot's extreme, self-destructive behavior is so complete and irrepressibly forceful that it becomes a work of art. It's really a paean to hardcoreness and total die-hard commitment, follow-through, charging off a cliff, full body-and-soul resistance, and persistent difficulty as a way to be. And isn't "parrot" rather close to "pirate," in fact just a slip of the tongue or tonal shift away? They are basically homonyms, and the two are basically the same figure, split sides of the same character, both played by the artist with the mounting tension between the two representing him as a self-avowed, if failed, antiestablishment figure in society who risks impropriety, madness, and unpleasantness—sometimes, but not necessarily, in service to that culture's health. Again, much like the court jester, doofus, buffoon, or fool, from Shakespeare's stage to Chaplin's screen. Warhol's deadpan dumbness not only concealed a baroque genius but amplified it. One thing we know for sure, an artist can't be afraid to play the fool. Stupidity and absurdity are so often the near shore of a very vast intelligence.

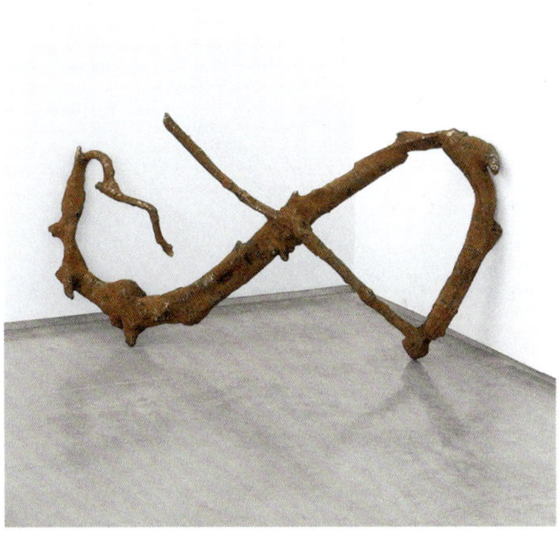

Fig. 4
Generational Anxiety, 2008
Cast bronze, iron, and rust
24 × 48 × 7 inches, 61 × 122 × 17.8 cm

Failure is funny. Traps are funny. Ugliness, fear, and falling down are funny. Cracked, smashed glasses are funny. Feeling moved and just feelings in general are funny. Self-awareness is funny. People—overgrown children all of us—are funny in their psychological insecurity and physical frailty. Death is funny. Beckett cuts the shit, having Nell spell it out plainly in *Endgame*: "Nothing is funnier than unhappiness, I grant you that." The right distance and vantage on anything makes it funny. Indeed, comedy is the direct and inevitable consequence of consciousness, self-distanciation, and metacognition, seeing oneself from outside oneself. Humor goes even further than release, relief, and coping mechanism. It's the expression of one's worldview and way of processing limitation, futility, irrationality, inequity, mortality, and all that is unknown. It can be an organizing principle of thought that folds back on itself in a heady loop, spinning off jokes about jokes so that the funniest joke may be the worst, flagrantly bad, failed, ironic, dumb ones. One person's bomb is another's smash hit. Bombing and flopping promise their own intense rush for those ready to receive it. For the masochist in each thinking person who considers authorship and wrestles with ego, playing with rejection can yield powerful, perverse highs. And if you're the kind of artist who feeds off strong feeling, lows are their own highs. Titles of many jagged, disjointed, frail, sharp, and frankly dangerous-looking sculptures, from *Dead Air*, *Nervous Laughter*, and *Awkward Pause* to *Generational Anxiety*, *Uncomfortable Silence*, and *Career Ender* (all 2008, except the last, 2009) speak to that adrenal feeling of free fall where comedy mingles with a vast internal reservoir of darkness, suspended over one's own private abyss. Death, dismemberment, mummification, paralysis, horror, foreboding, and fear surface and resurface as recurrent presences that shadow Heikes's sense of humor. The point, if there is any, is not merely to laugh at a joke but to laugh at the entire situation in which joking can and must occur, as a matter of survival or abandon—the scene, the communication, the delivery, the reception, the performance, the coming down, the people involved, yourself. It's a way to connect with an audience (other people, other artists, other loners) and form community, opening channels of collaboration and conversation, preferably through degrees of aversion. It's like Heikes mused years ago—wistfully, perversely, ecstatically—"In my dreams, I want to tell the worst jokes to the biggest crowds."[8] Or, perhaps even more to the existential point, in reverie, "I can only dream of the day when my work gives people hives."[10]

1. Mike Kelley, "On Folk Art," in *Minor Histories*, ed. John C. Welchman (Cambridge, MA: MIT Press, 2004), 146.

2. Jay Heikes, "Manifesto," *Art in America* 101, no. 2 (February 2013), 40–41.

3. Jay Heikes, quoted in Claire Barliant, "Emerging Artists: Jay Heikes," *Modern Painters* (October 2006), 58–60.

4. Jay Heikes quoted in Bartholomew Ryan, "A Table of Curious Elements: Jay Heikes on *Filthy Minds*," Walker Art Center, July 3, 2013, https://walkerart.org/magazine/a-table-of-curious-elements-jay-heikes-on-filthy-minds.

5. Mike Kelley quoted in Glenn O'Brien, "Mike Kelley," *Interview* (November 24, 2008), https://www.interviewmagazine.com/art/mike-kelley.

6. Jay Heikes, "Grade and Point to Average," in *Mike Kelley: Timeless Painting*, ed. Jenelle Porter (New York: Hauser & Wirth, 2019).

7. Mike Kelley quoted in "Mike Kelley by John Miller," *BOMB* 38 (winter 1992), https://bombmagazine.org/articles/mike-kelley/.

8. Heikes, "Grade and Point to Average."

9. Heikes, quoted in Barliant, "Emerging Artists: Jay Heikes."

9. Heikes, quoted in Ryan, "A Table of Curious Elements."

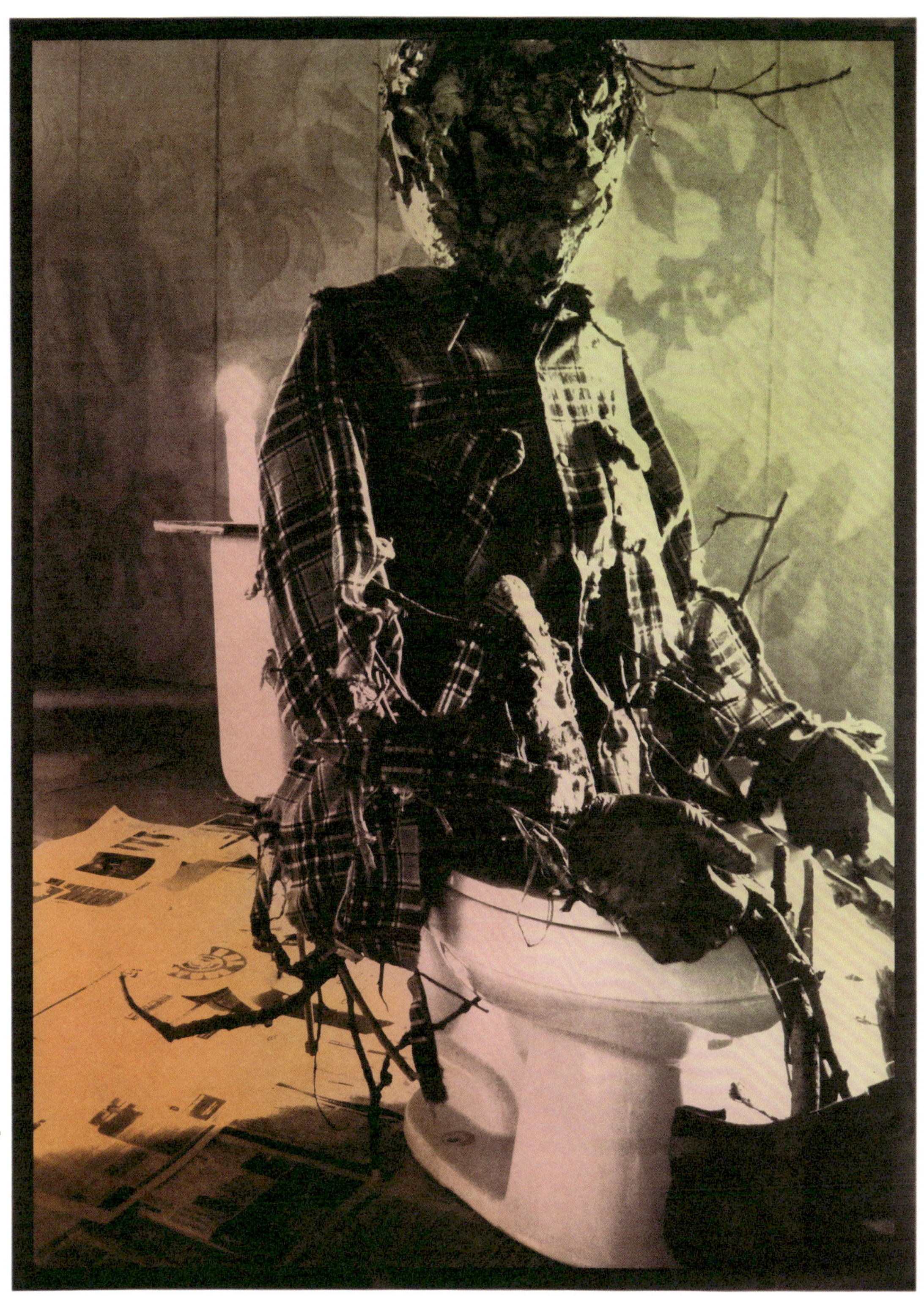

Civilian (hopeless), 2009
Hand-dyed palladium print, 56 ¼ × 41 inches, 142.9 × 104.1 cm

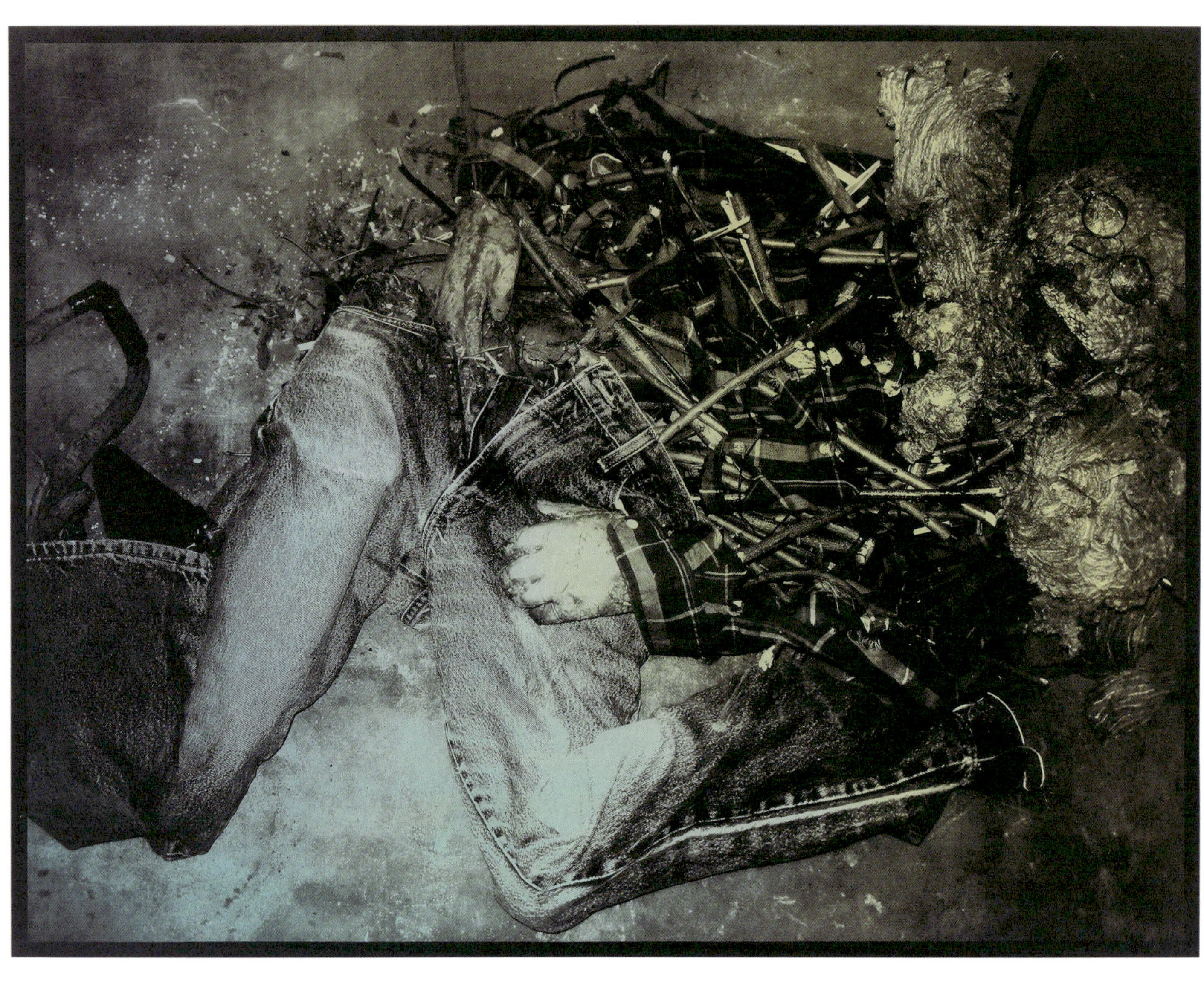

Civilian (resting), 2008
Hand-dyed palladium print, 41¼ × 54⅝ inches, 104.8 × 138.7 cm

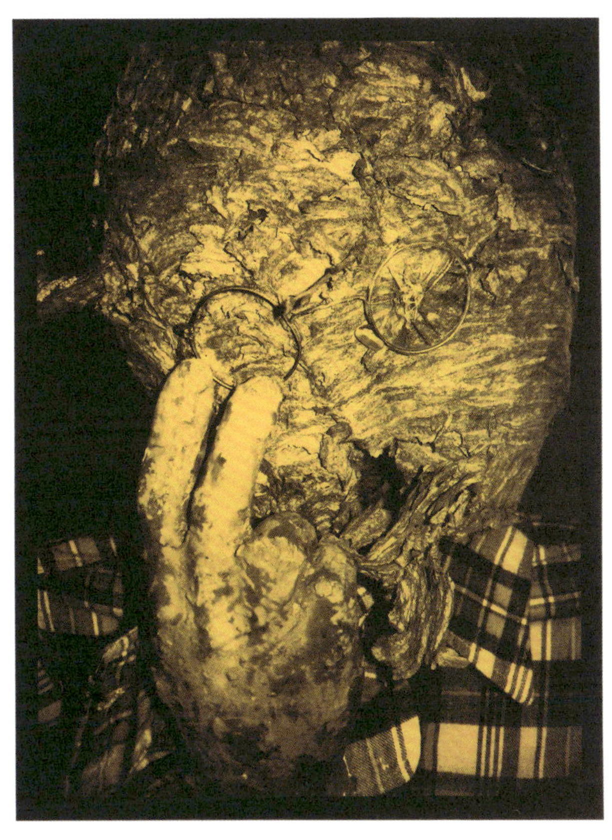

Civilian (poking), 2008
Hand-dyed palladium print, 18 × 13 ¾ inches, 45.7 × 34.9 cm

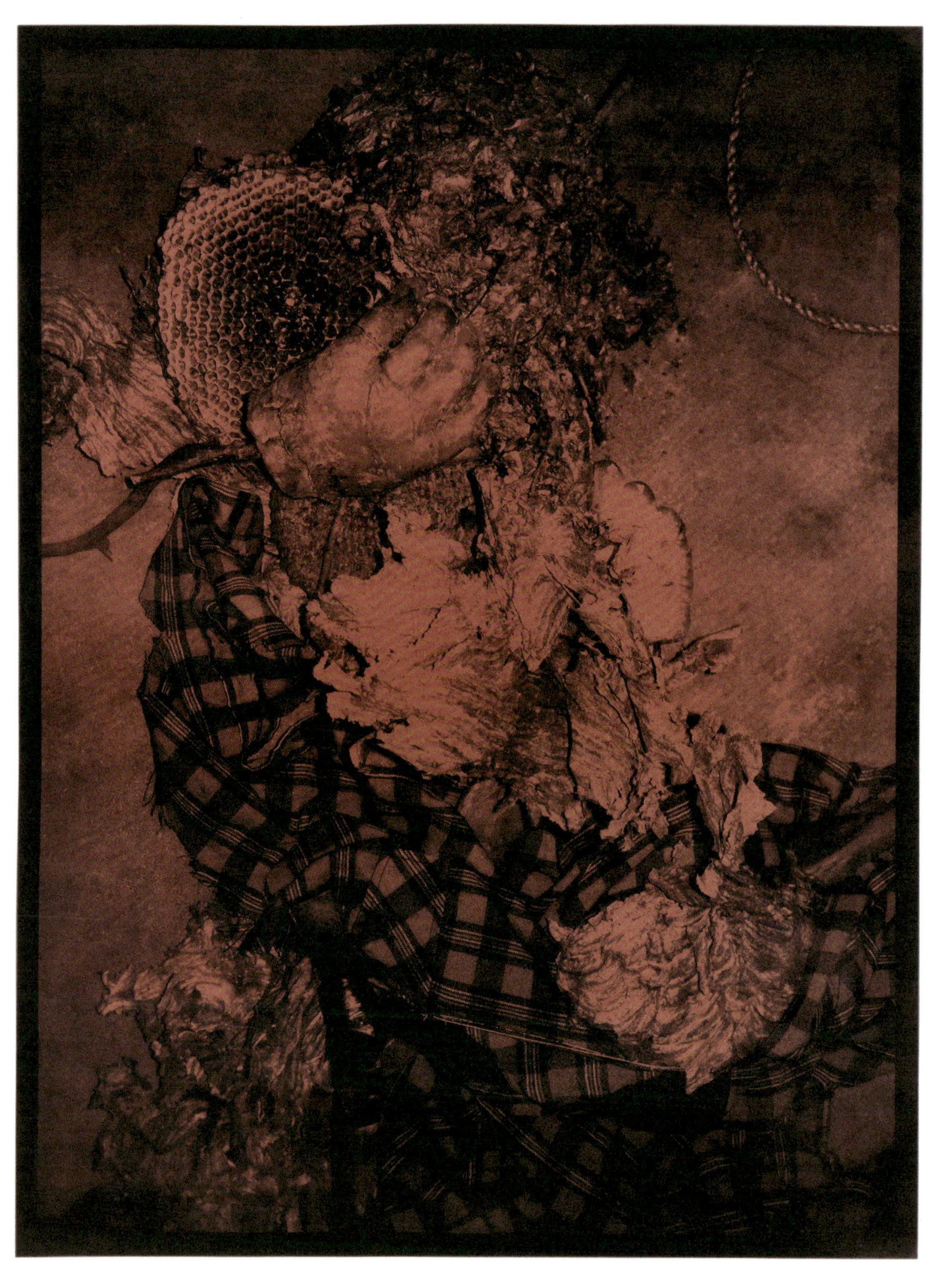

Inanimate Life, 2009
Hand-dyed palladium print, 38 ¾ × 29 ⅜ inches, 98.4 × 74.6 cm

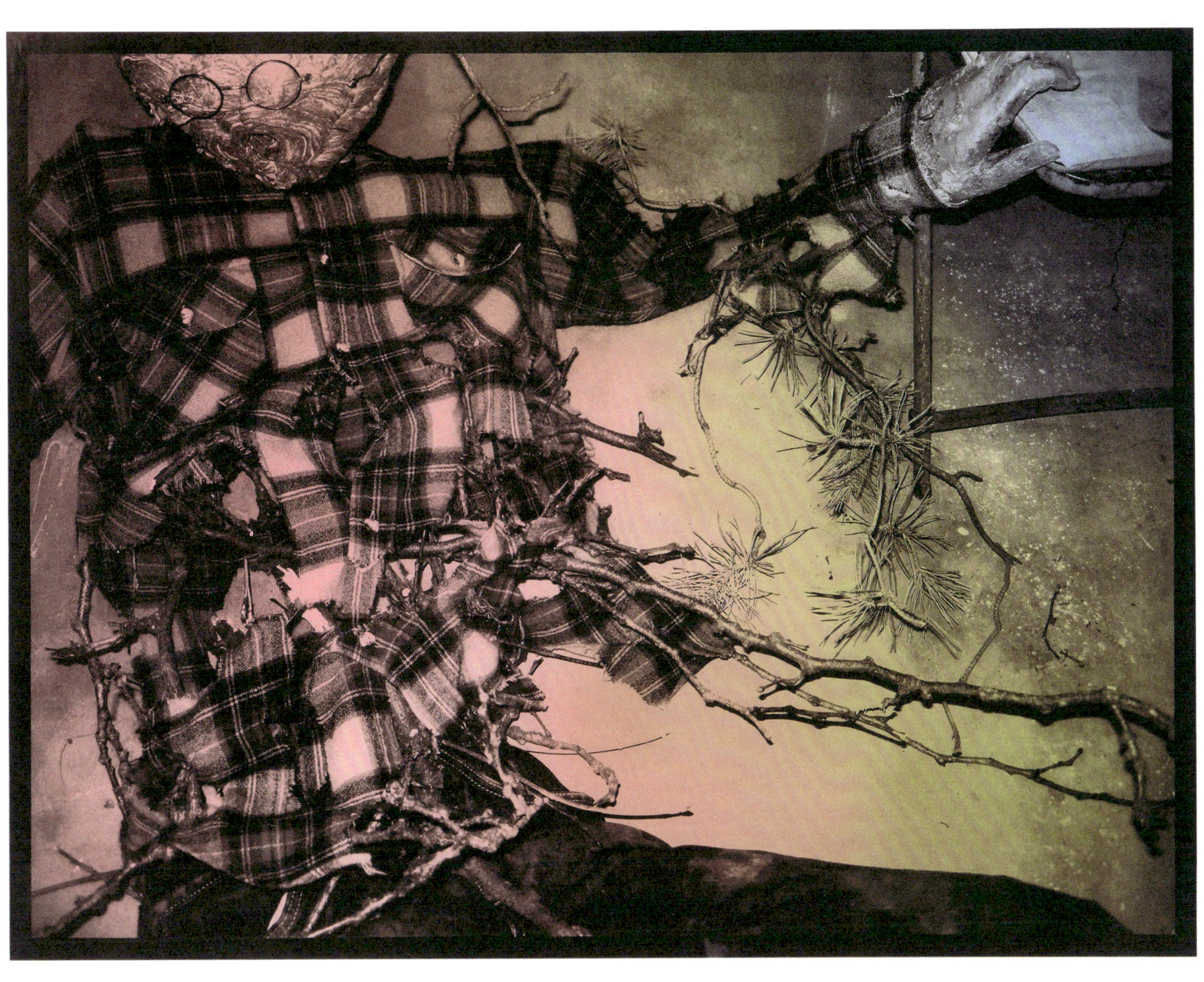

Civilian (drunk), 2008
Hand-dyed palladium print, 31 ⅜ × 41 ½ inches, 79.7 × 105.4 cm

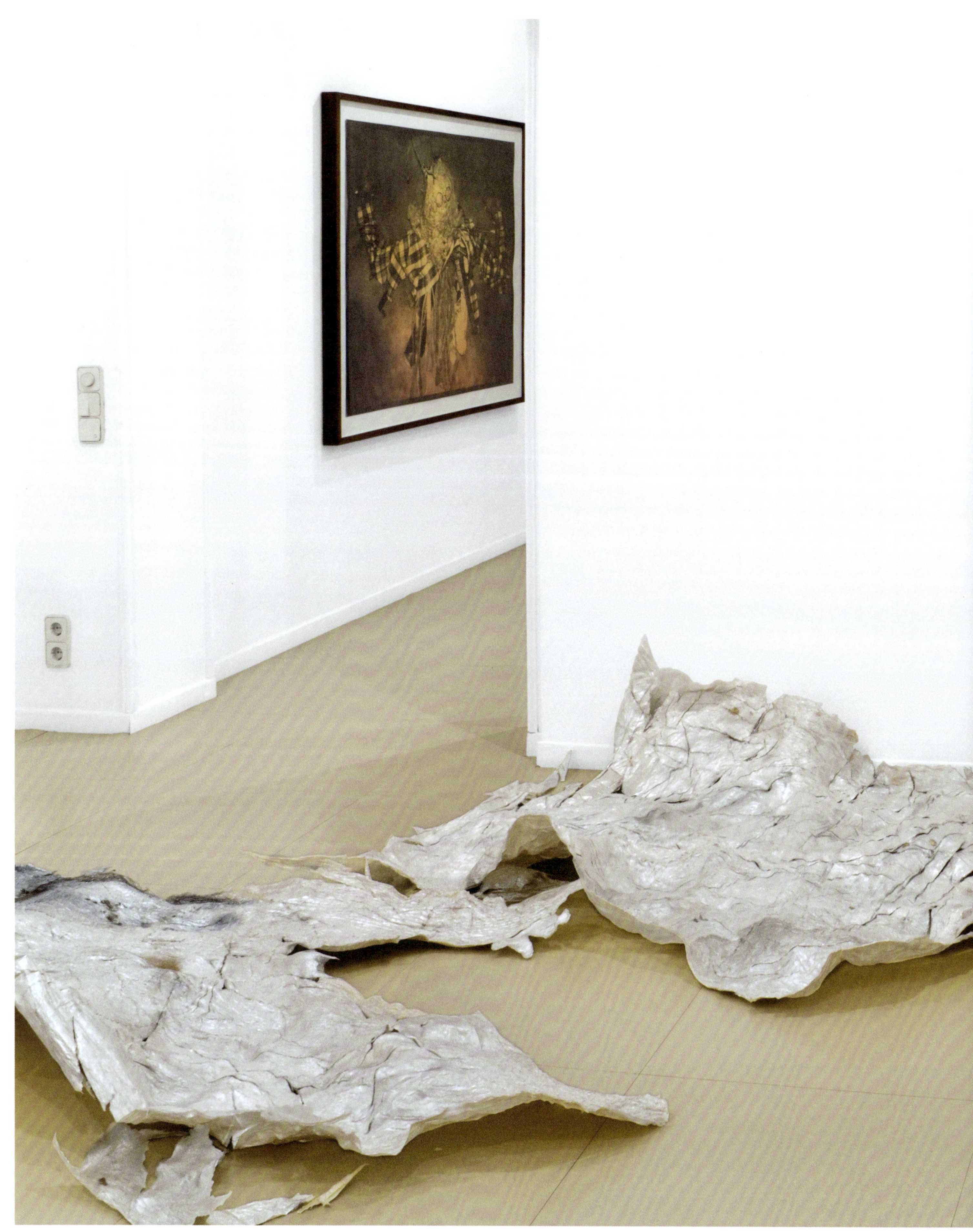

Installation view:
Jay Heikes, Galleria Marta Cervera, Madrid, 2010

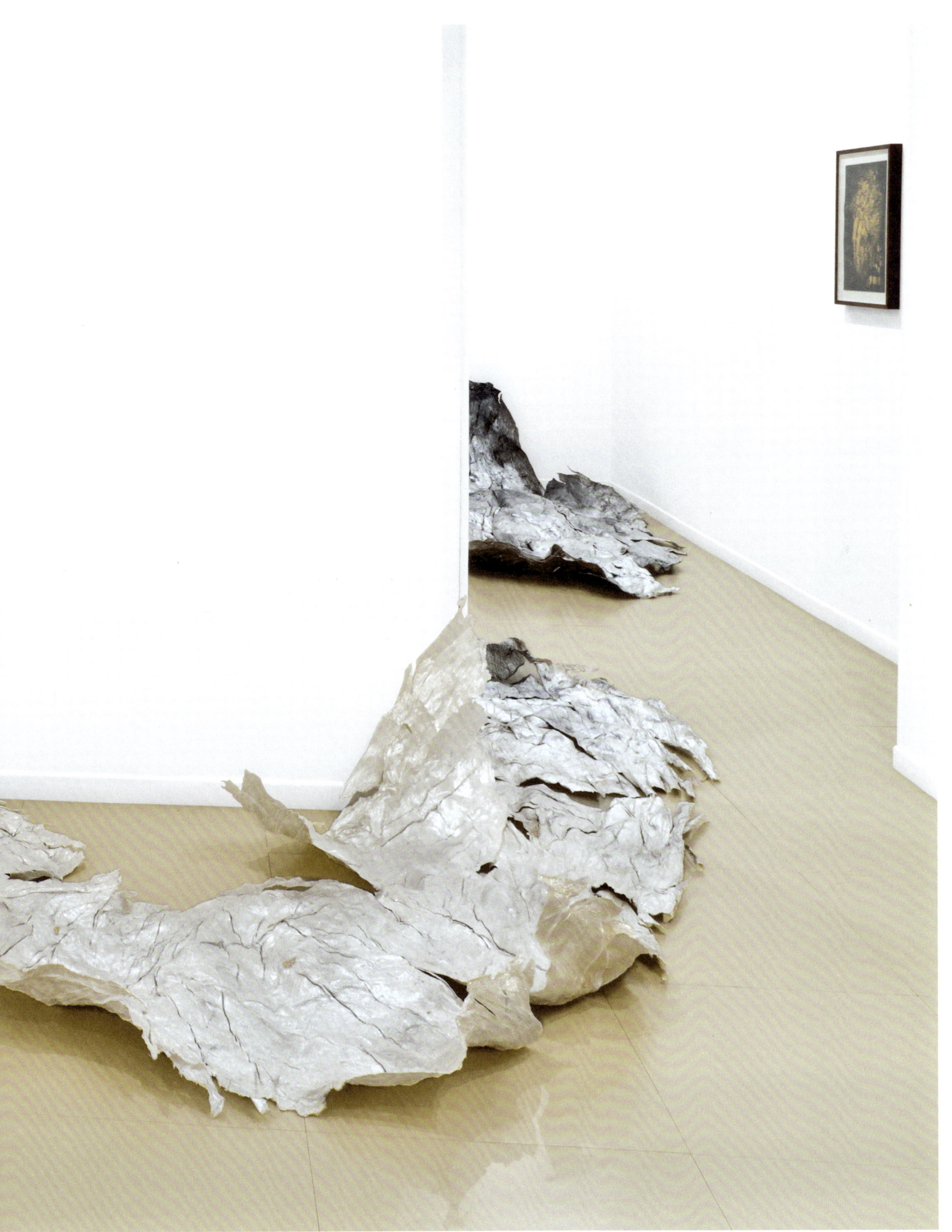

Left to right:
Civilian (severed), 2009; Molting, 2010; Civilian (poking), 2008

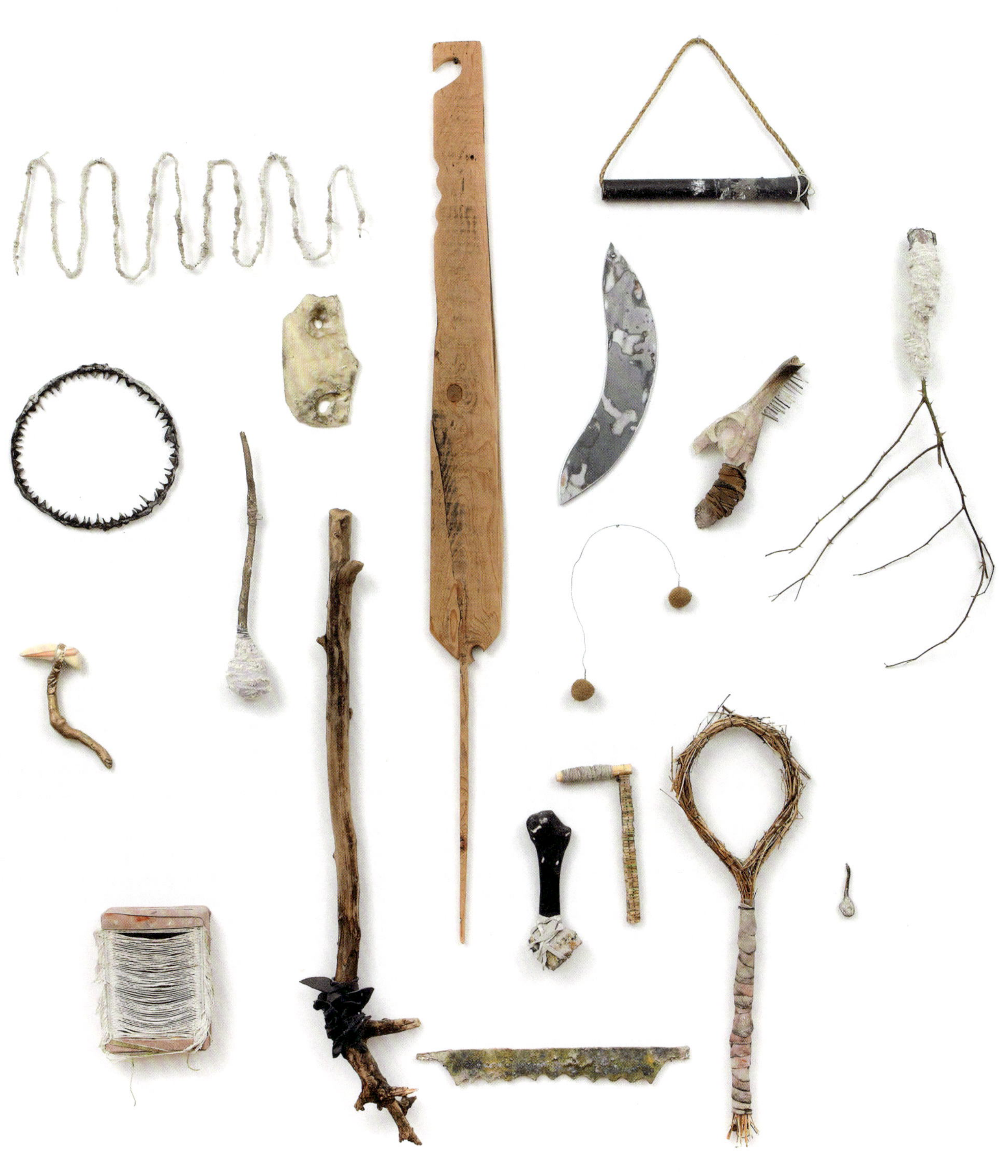

No Age, 2012

Cotton, steel, wood, rope, leather, bone, sea balls, hardened corn syrup, cast bronze, cast bismuth, shark teeth, string, and canvas,

overall: 74 × 70 × 5 inches, 188 × 177.8 × 12.7 cm

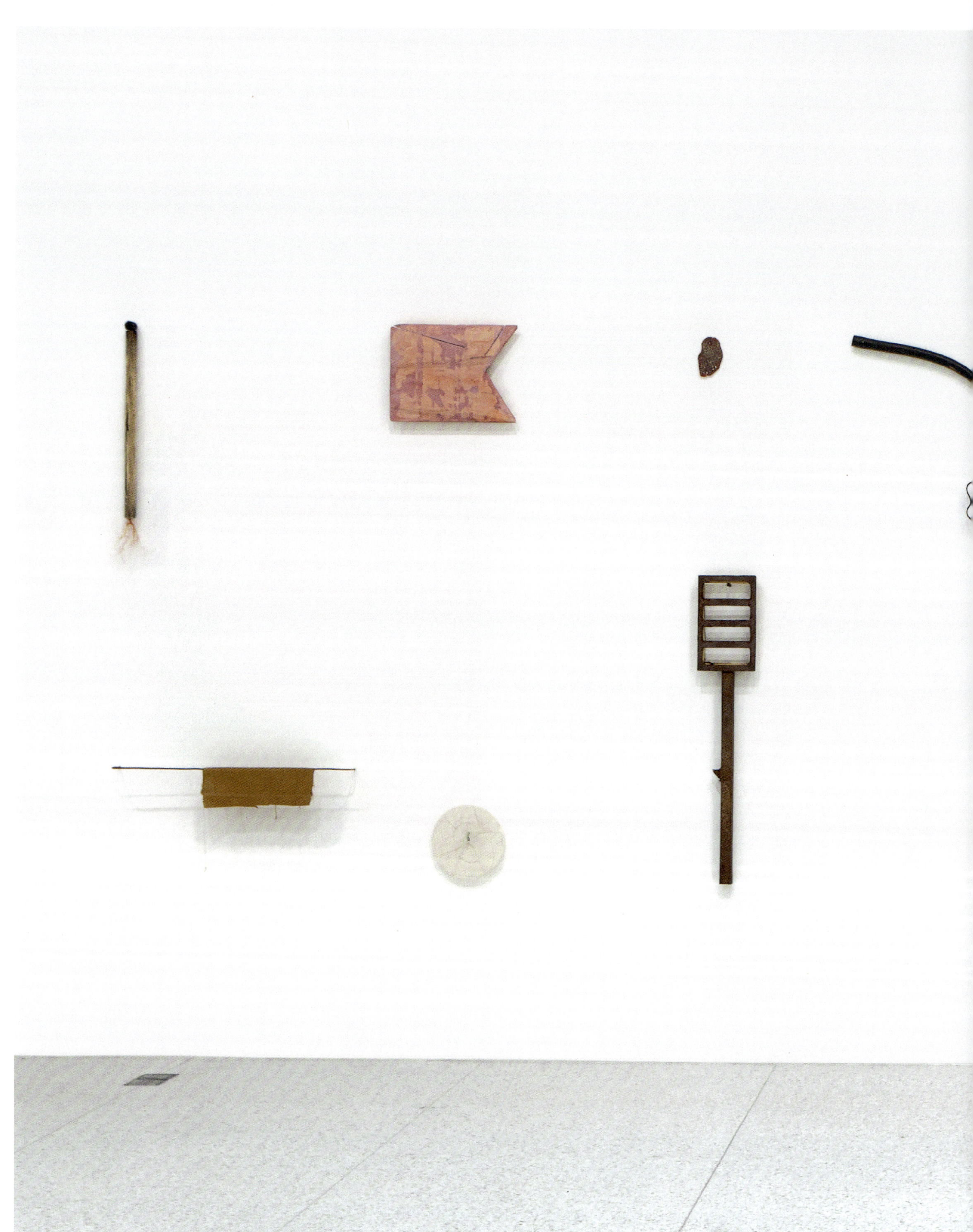

Installation view:
Painter Painter, Walker Art Center, Minneapolis, 2013

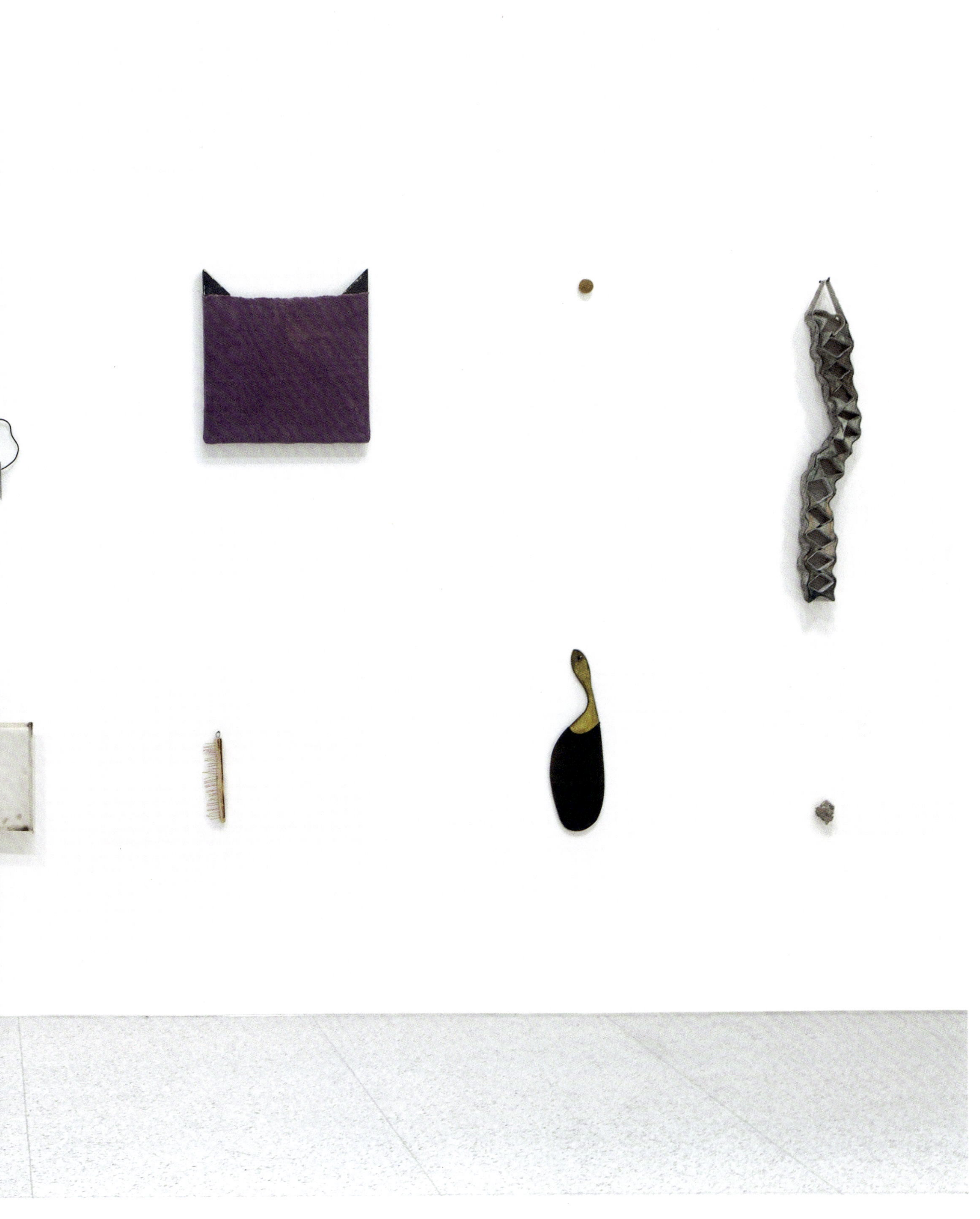

We lead healthy lives to keep filthy minds, 2013
Wood, latex paint, copper wire, stained canvas, fired clay, steel, wax, dirt, iron, rust, plastic, cheesecloth, nylon, concrete, leather, and sea ball,
overall: 70 × 216 × 6 inches, 177.8 × 548.6 × 15.2 cm

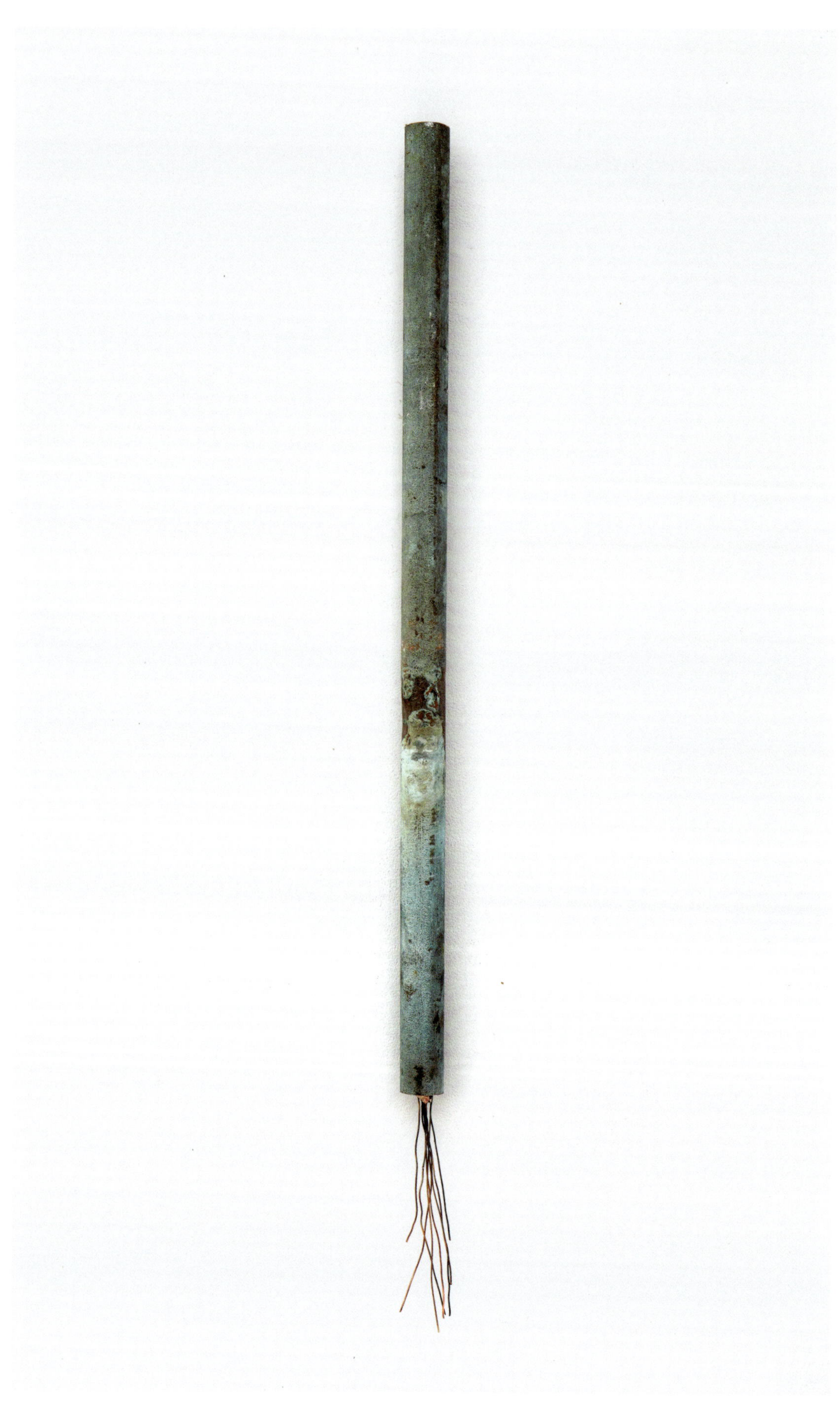

Charisma, 2013
Copper and bronze, 45 × 4 × 2 inches, 114.3 × 10.1 × 5.1 cm

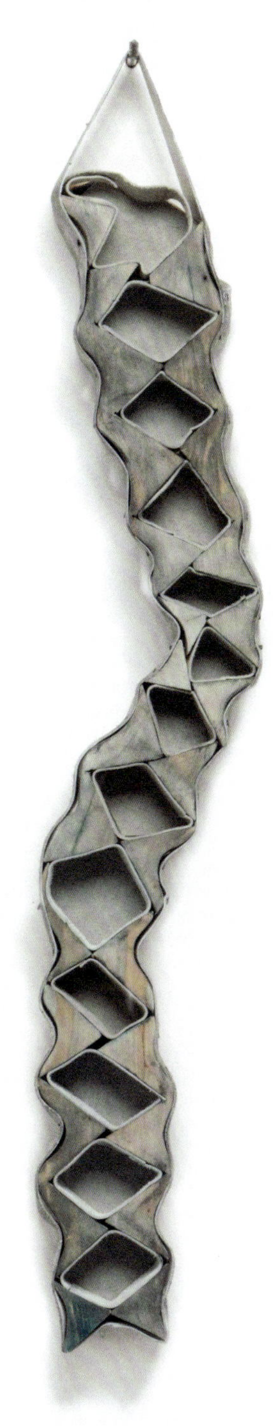

We lead healthy lives to keep filthy minds, 2013 (detail)
Stained wood, leather, and upholstery tacks, 40 × 7 × 3 inches, 101.6 × 17.8 × 7.6 cm

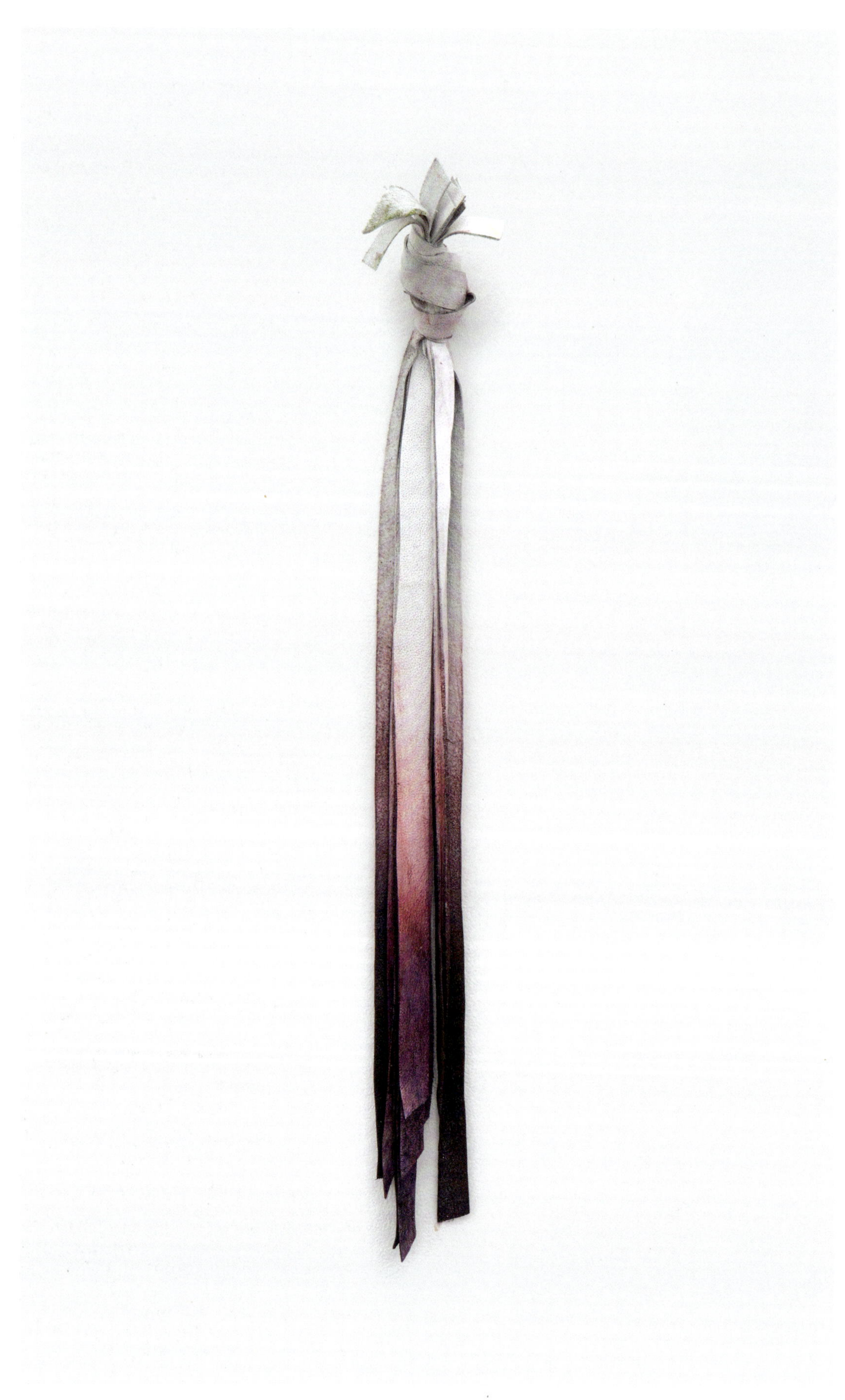

Painting Whip, 2013
Ink on leather, 31 × 3 × 3 inches, 78.7 × 7.6 × 7.6 cm

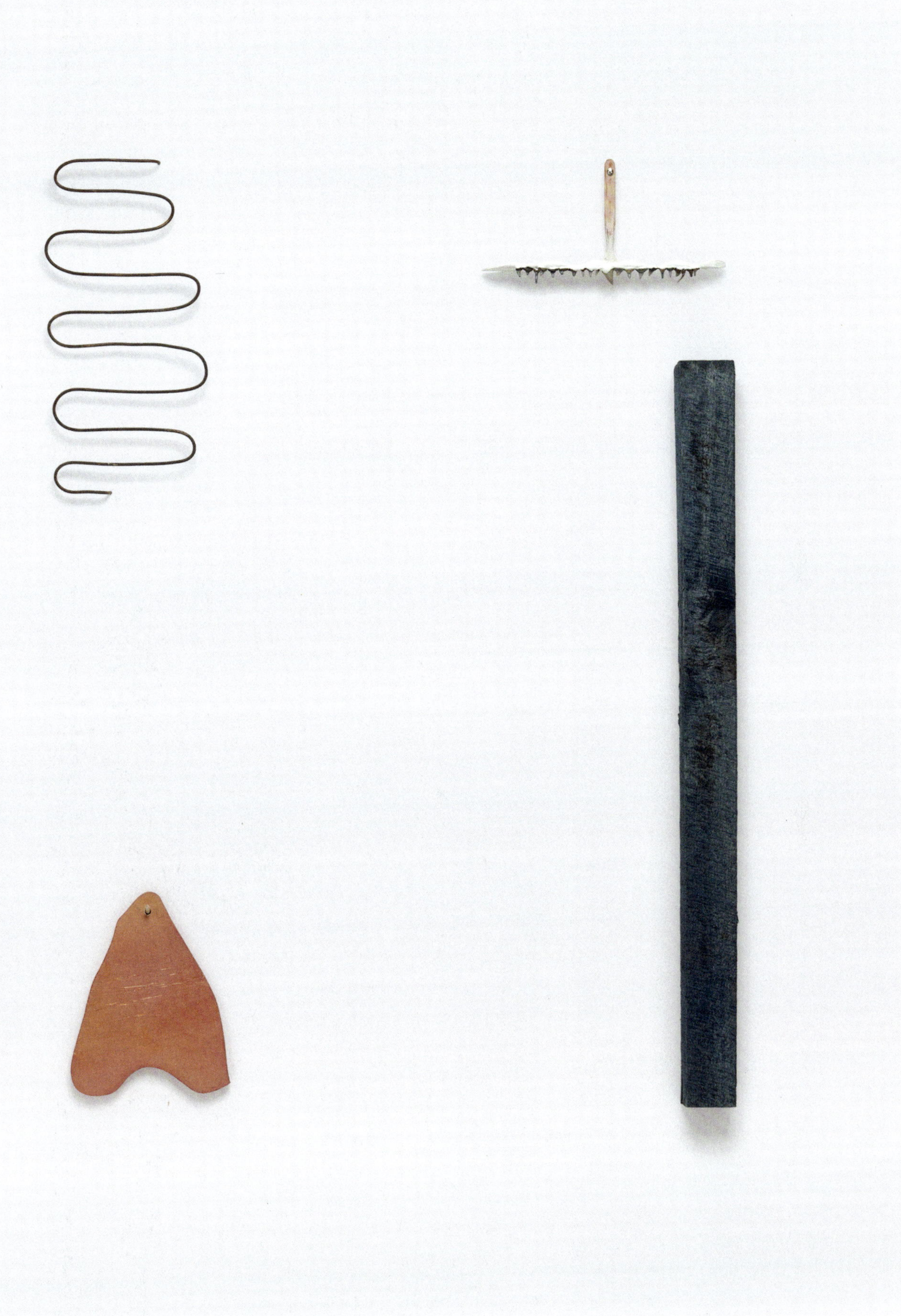

We will destroy this museum, 2012
Copper, stained wood, dye, shark teeth, and mortar, overall: 62 × 50 × 4 inches, 157.5 × 127 × 10.2 cm
Walker Art Center, Minneapolis, Gift of Gayle and Mike Ahearn, 2014

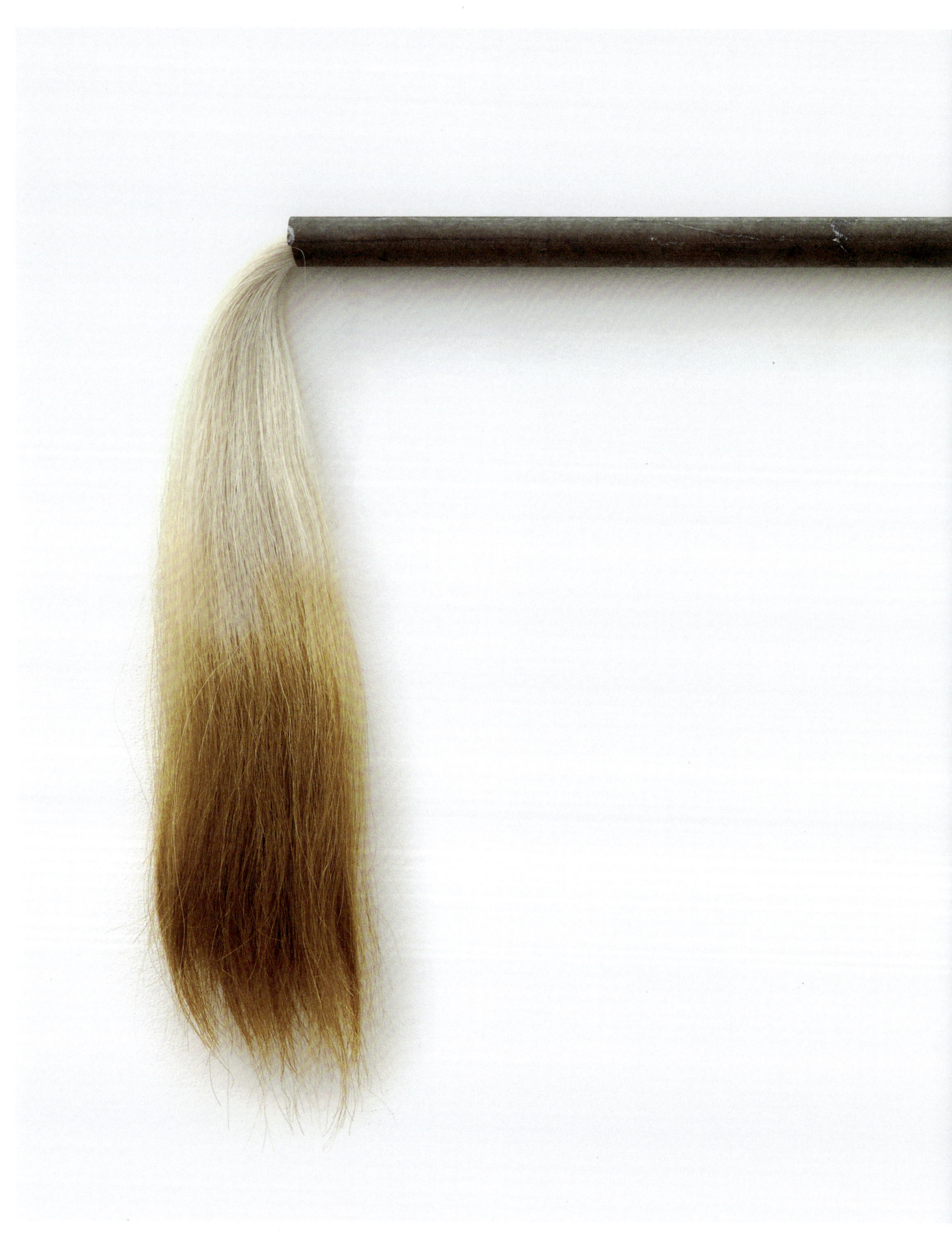

County Line, 2013
Dyed horsehair and steel, 23 × 46 × 2 ½ inches, 58.4 × 116.8 × 6.4 cm

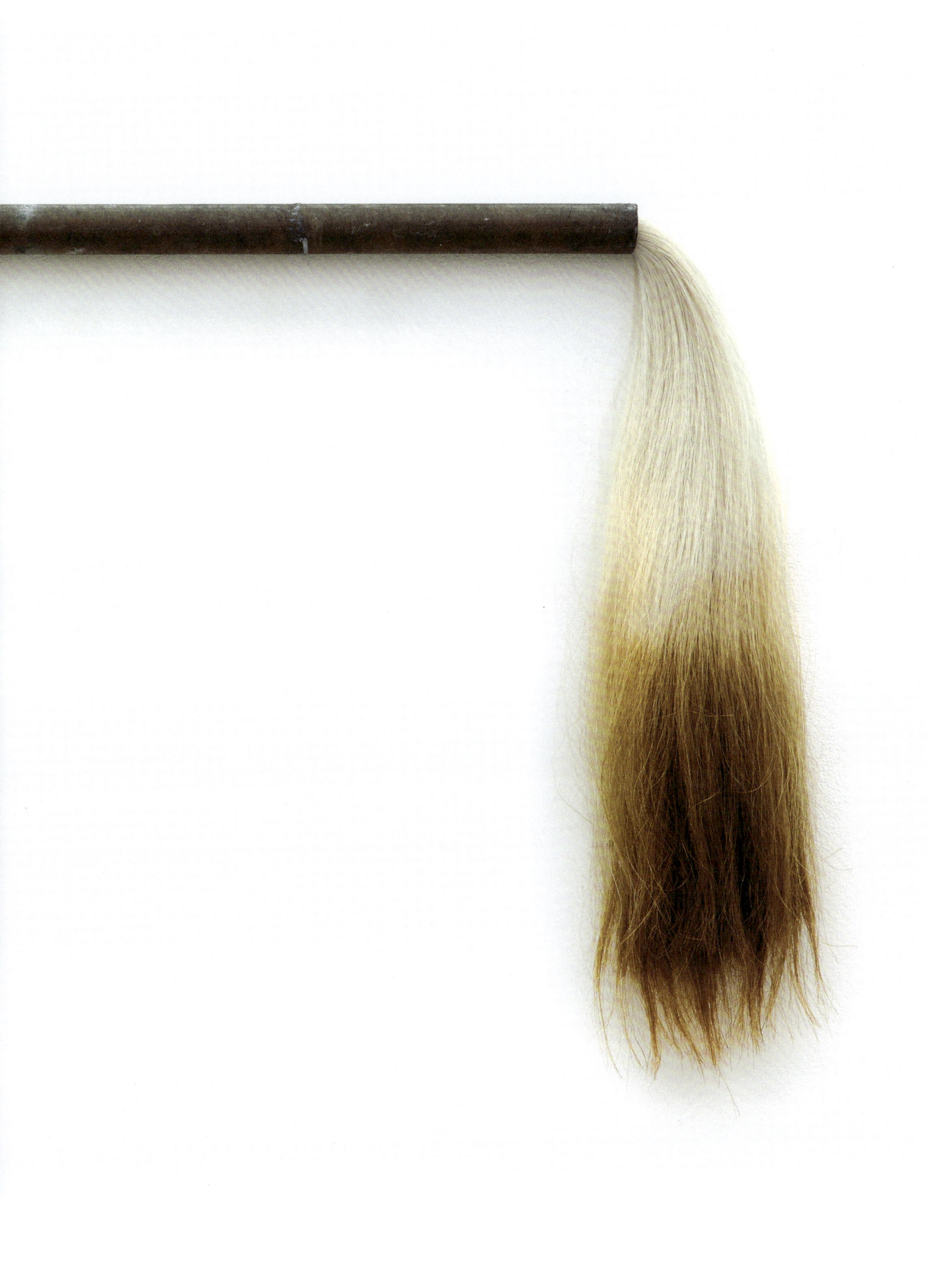

<u>Manifesto for the anti social</u>

We lead healthy lives to keep filthy minds.

Manifesto for the anti social, 2012
Typewriter toner on paper, 12 × 9 inches, 30.5 × 22.9 cm

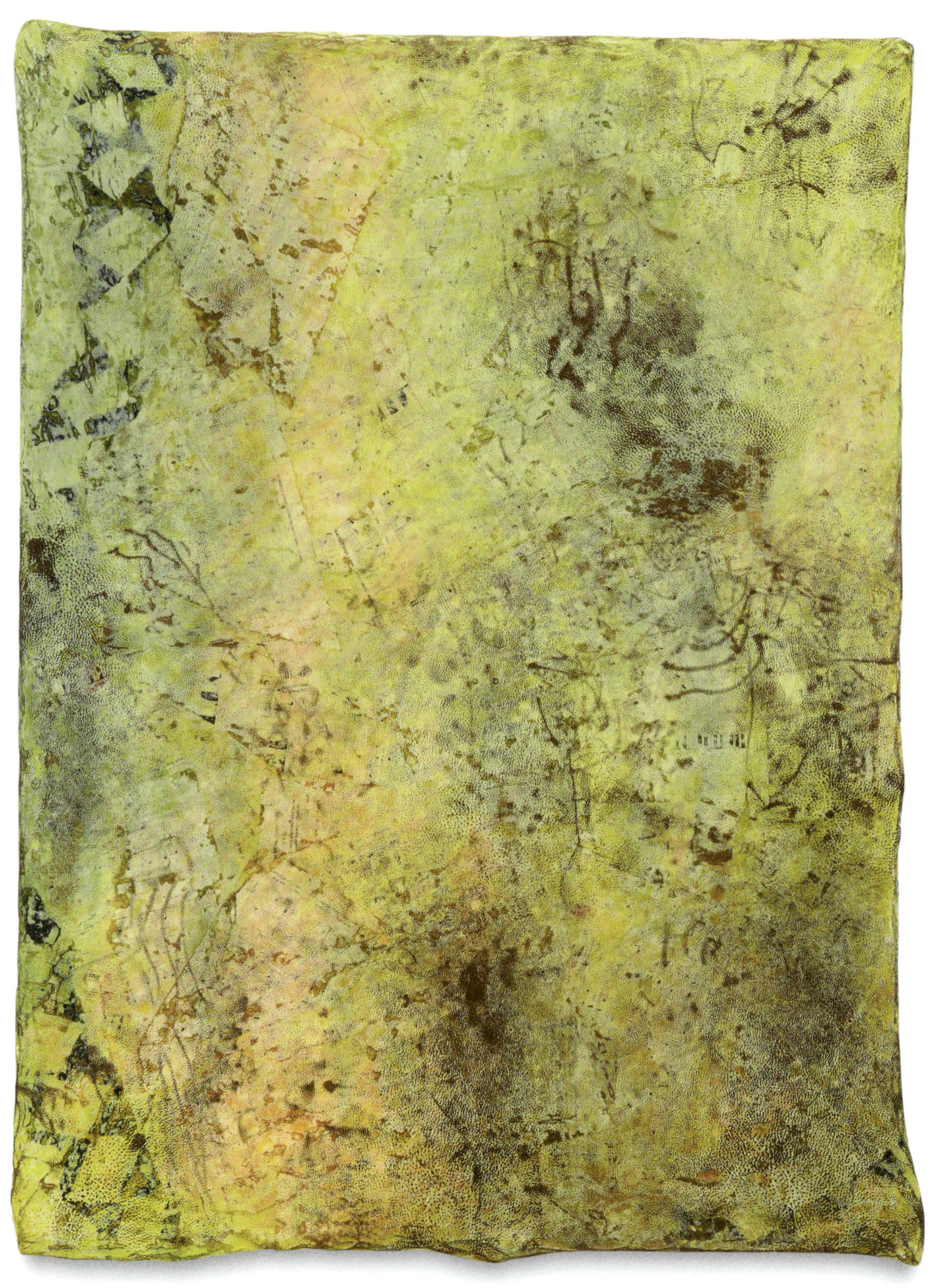

Paper, oil-based ink, gesso, wood glue, and expanded aluminum on wood stretcher, 48 × 36 inches, 121.9 × 91.4 cm

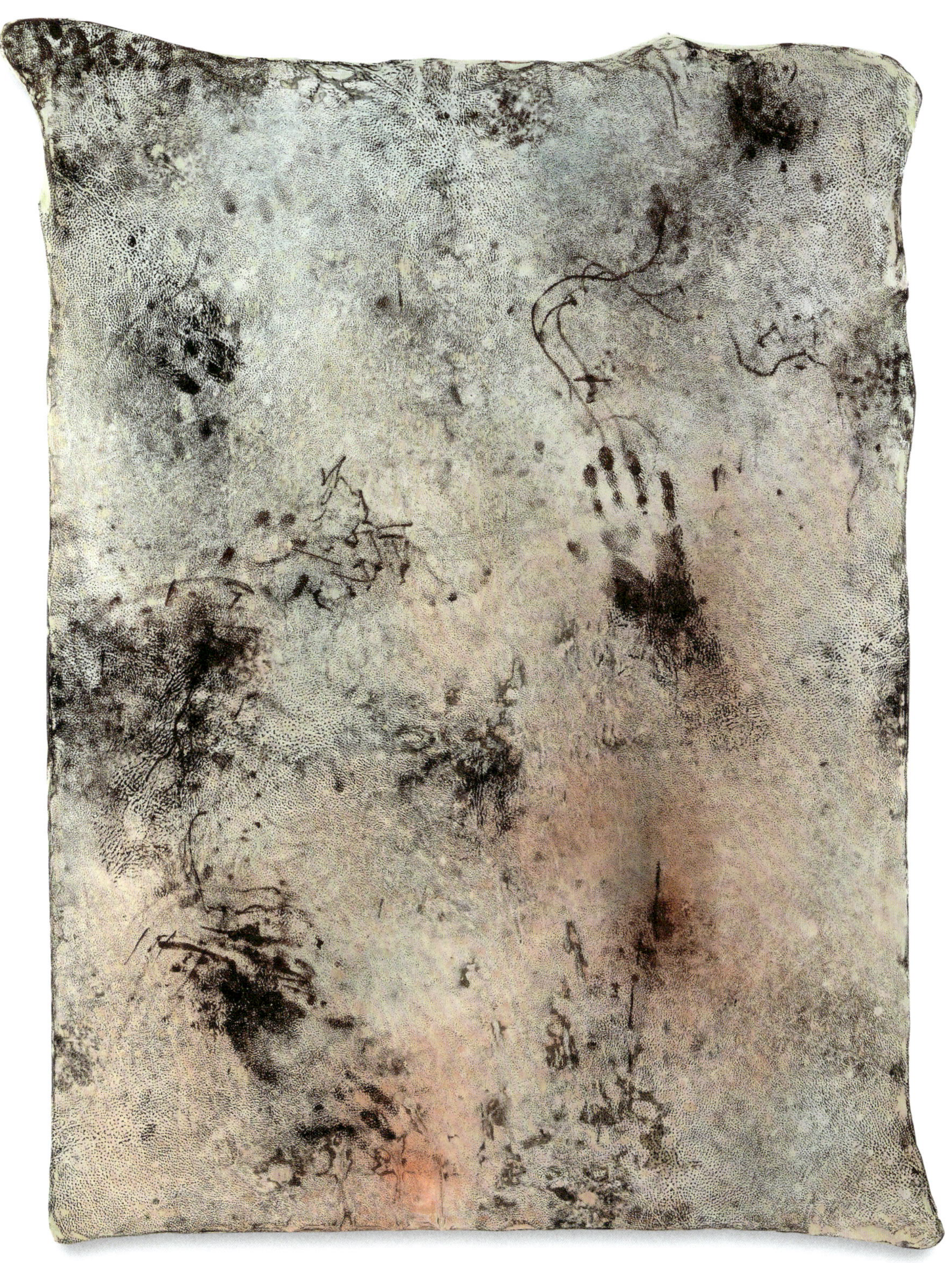

Bell Witch, 2012
Paper, oil-based ink, gesso, wood glue, and expanded aluminum on wood stretcher, 50 × 39 inches, 127 × 99.1 cm

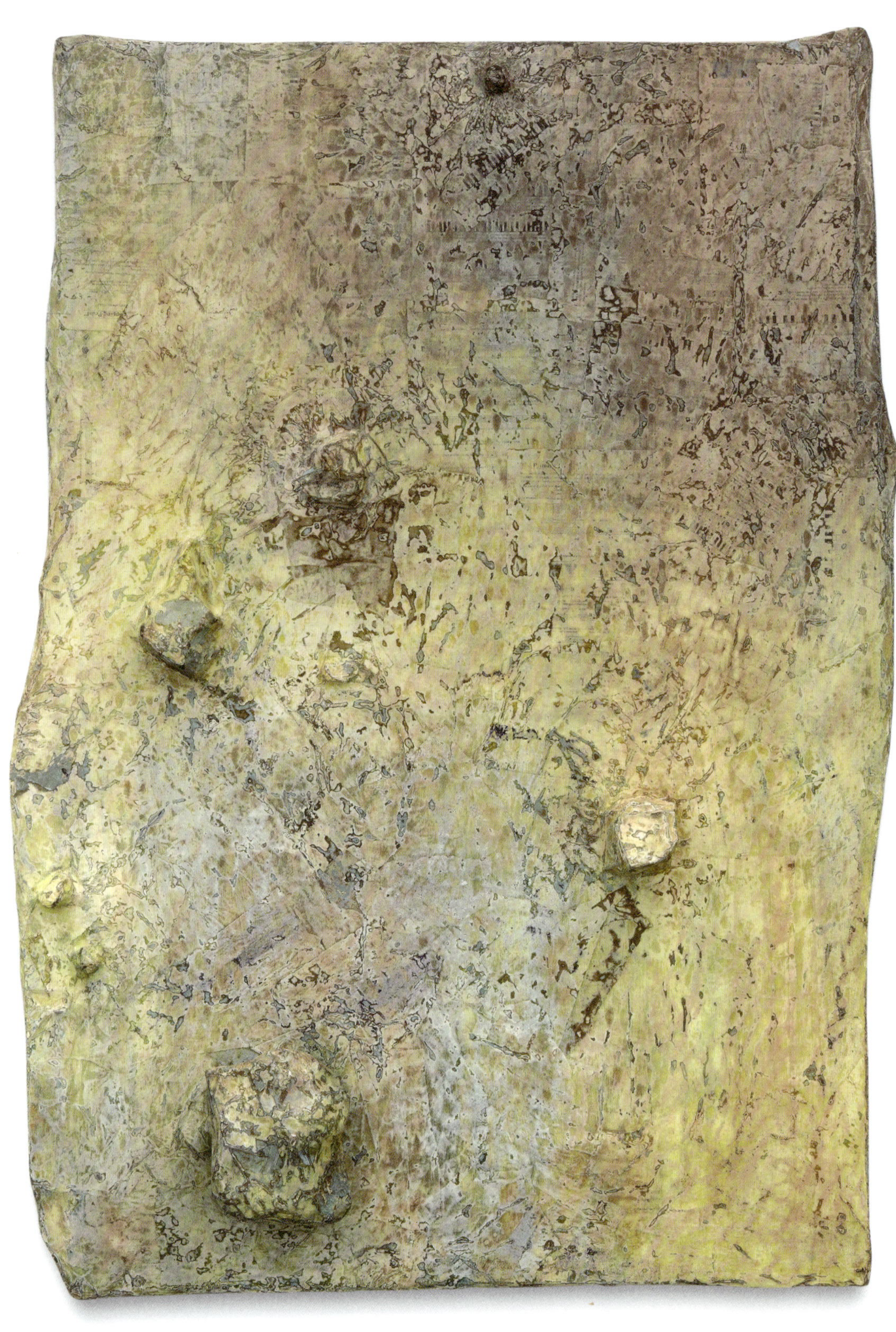

Fur Elise, 2012
Paper, oil-based ink, gesso, wood glue, copper ore, petrified wood, wire, and expanded aluminum on wood stretcher,
72 × 48 × 8 inches, 182.9 × 121.9 × 20.3 cm

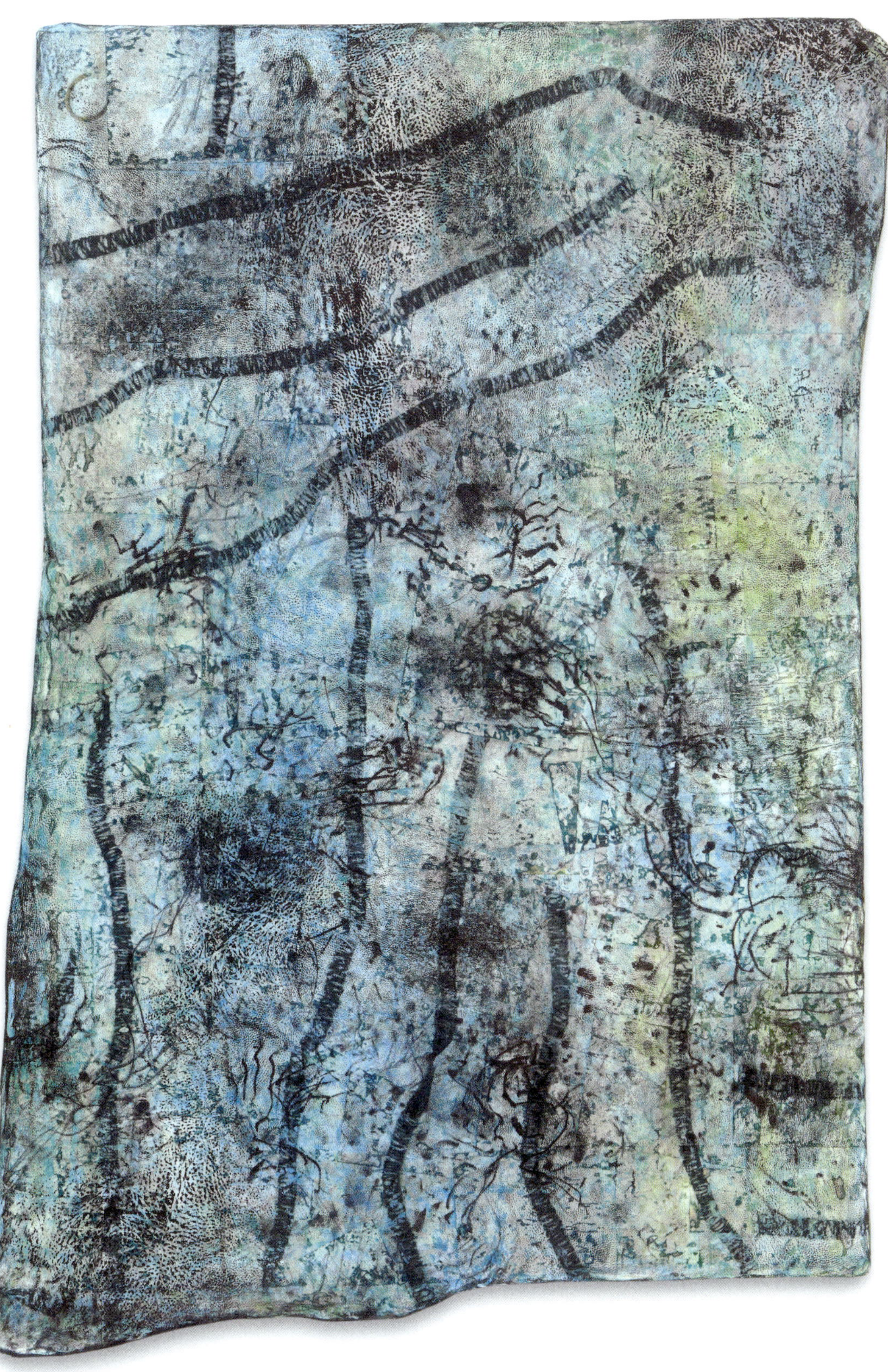

Repeater, 2012
Paper, oil-based ink, gesso, wood glue, and expanded aluminum on wood stretcher, 75 ¼ × 55 ¼ inches, 191.1 × 140.3 cm

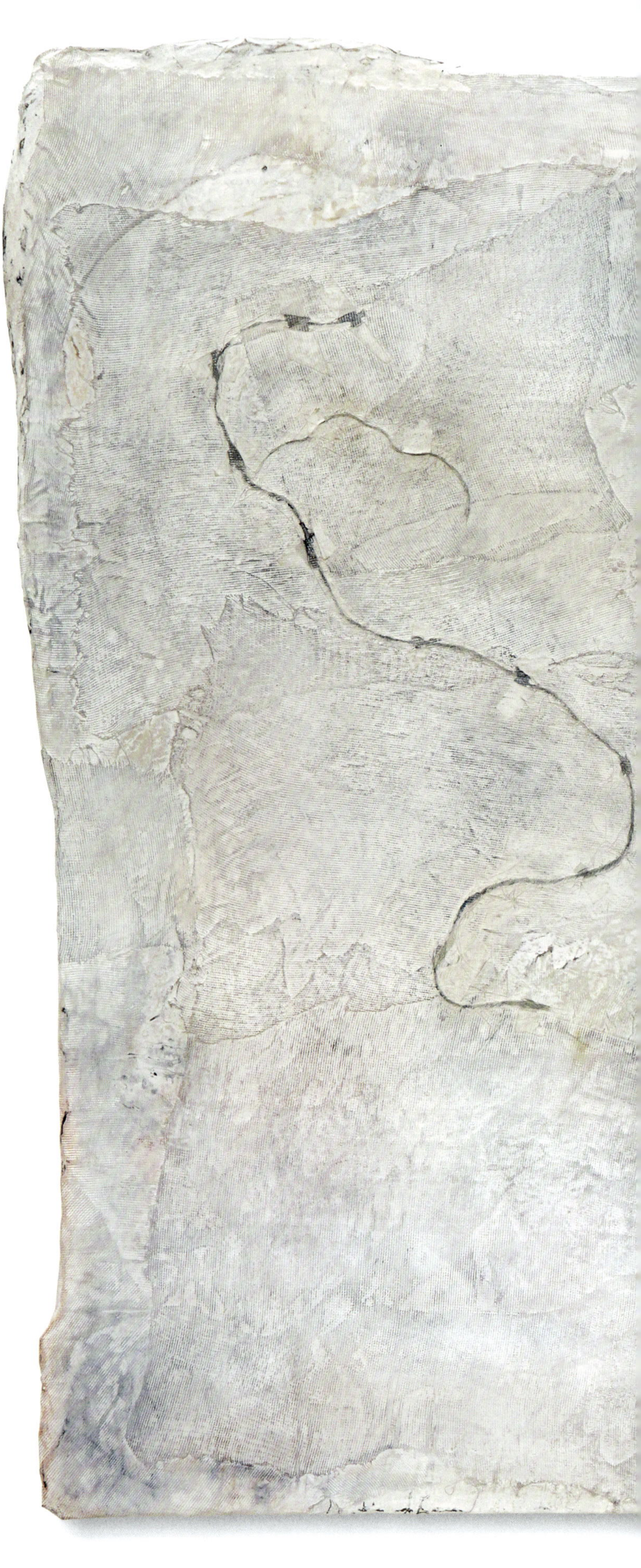

Nature Morte, 2013
Cotton scrim, gesso, twine, wood glue, paper, oil-based ink, and expanded aluminum on wood stretcher,
79 × 102 × 2 inches, 200.7 × 259.1 × 5.1 cm. Baltimore Museum of Art, Maryland

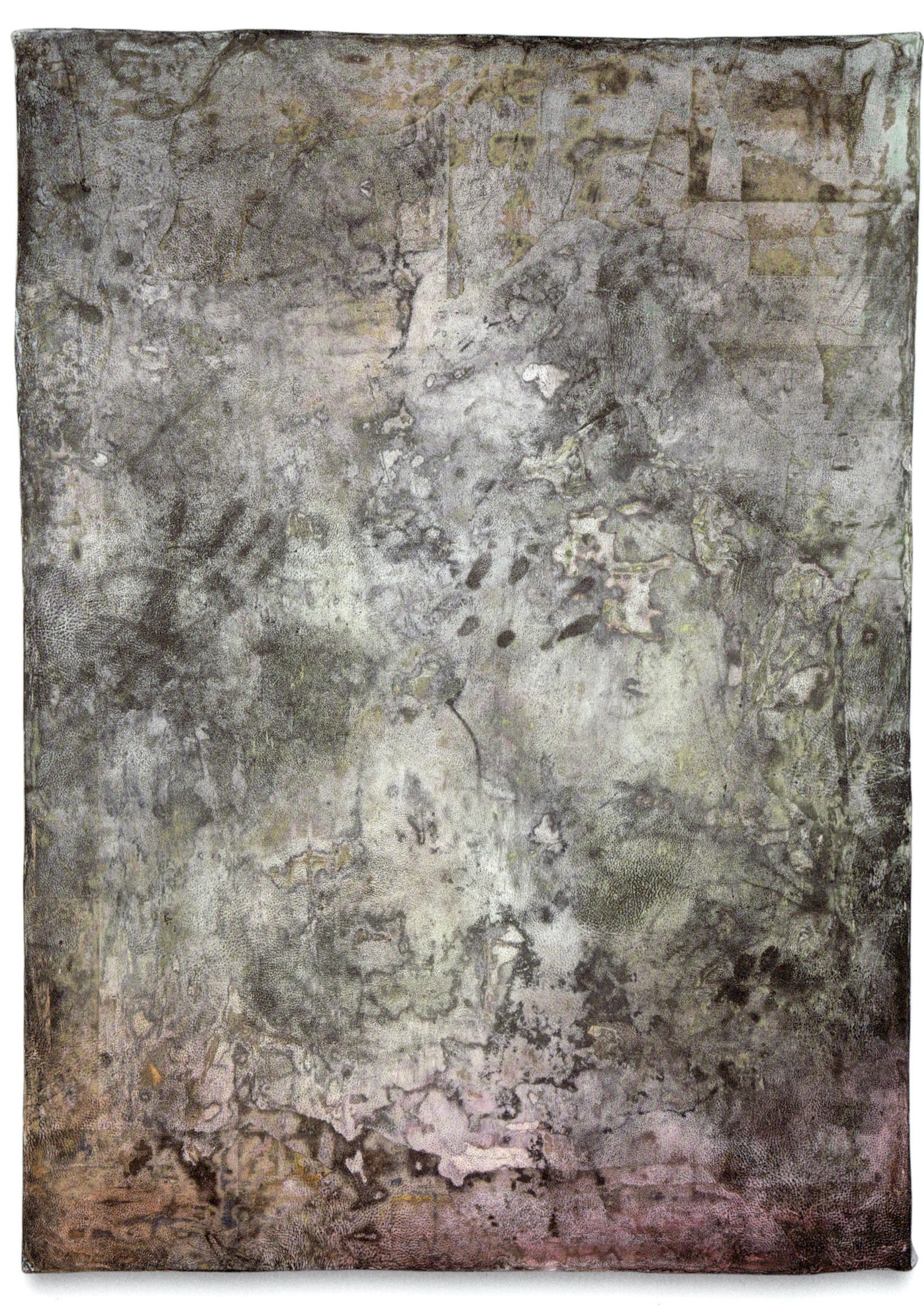

Ear of Dionysius, 2011
Water-based ink, dry pigment, gesso, wood glue, paper, and expanded aluminum on wood stretcher,
50 × 38 inches, 127 × 96.5 cm. Walker Art Center, Minneapolis, Butler Family Fund, 2012

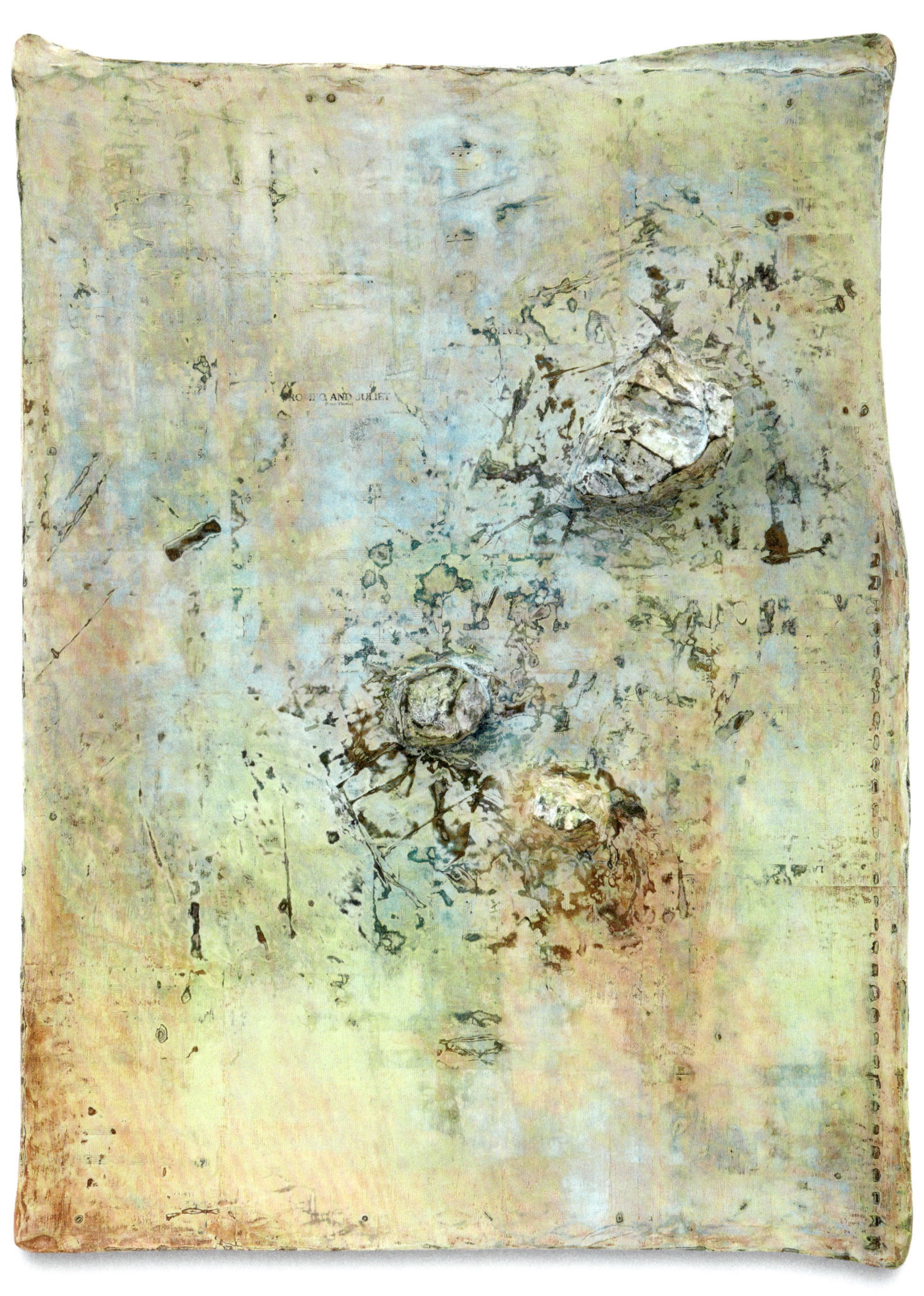

Romeo & Juliet (Love Theme), 2012

Paper, oil-based ink, gesso, wood glue, copper ore, petrified wood, stone, and expanded aluminum on wood stretcher,
50 × 38 × 5 inches, 127 × 96.5 × 12.7 cm. Joslyn Art Museum, Omaha, Gift of Adrian M. Turner, New York, 2017

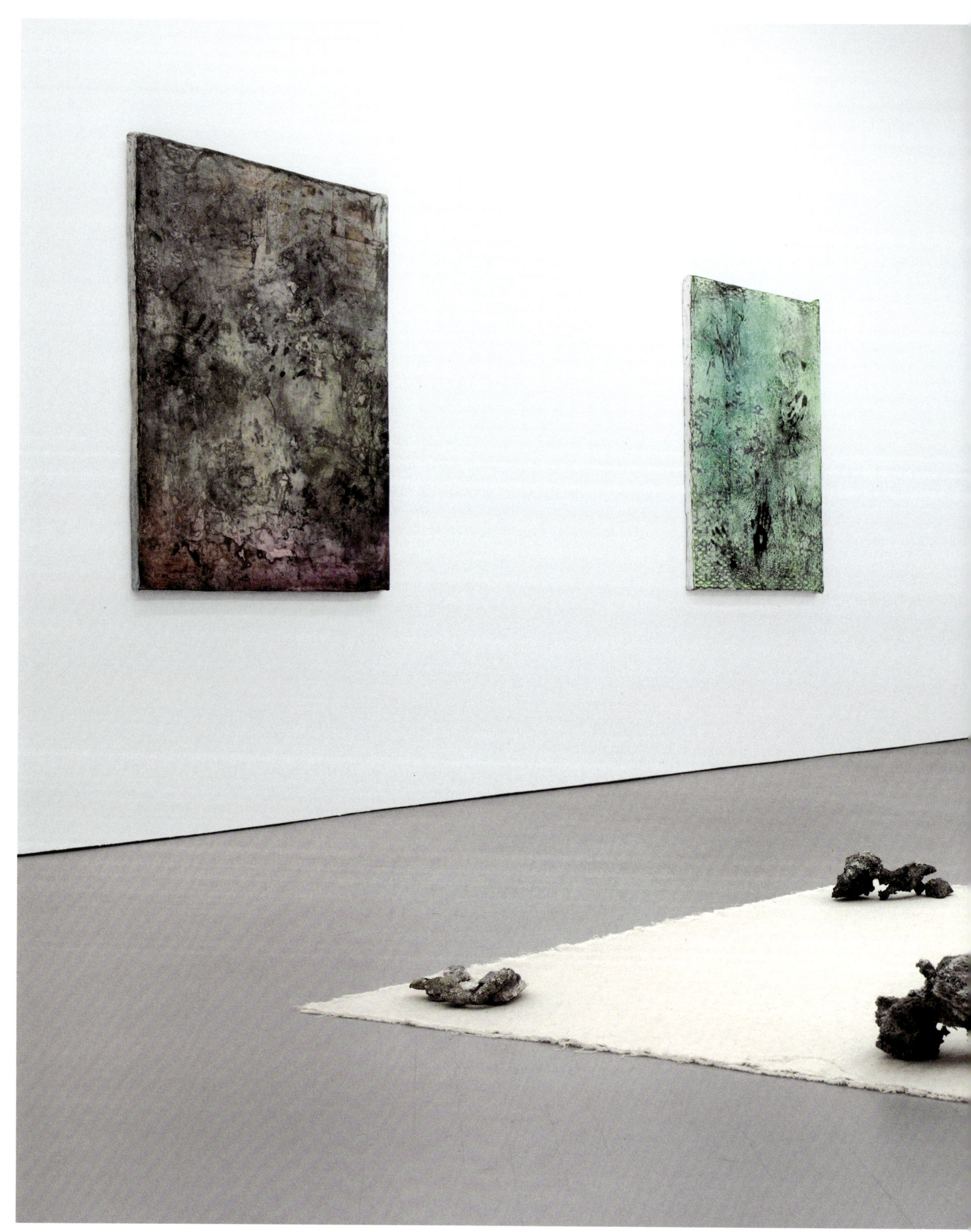

Installation view:
Subterranean Isle, Shane Campbell Gallery, Chicago, 2011

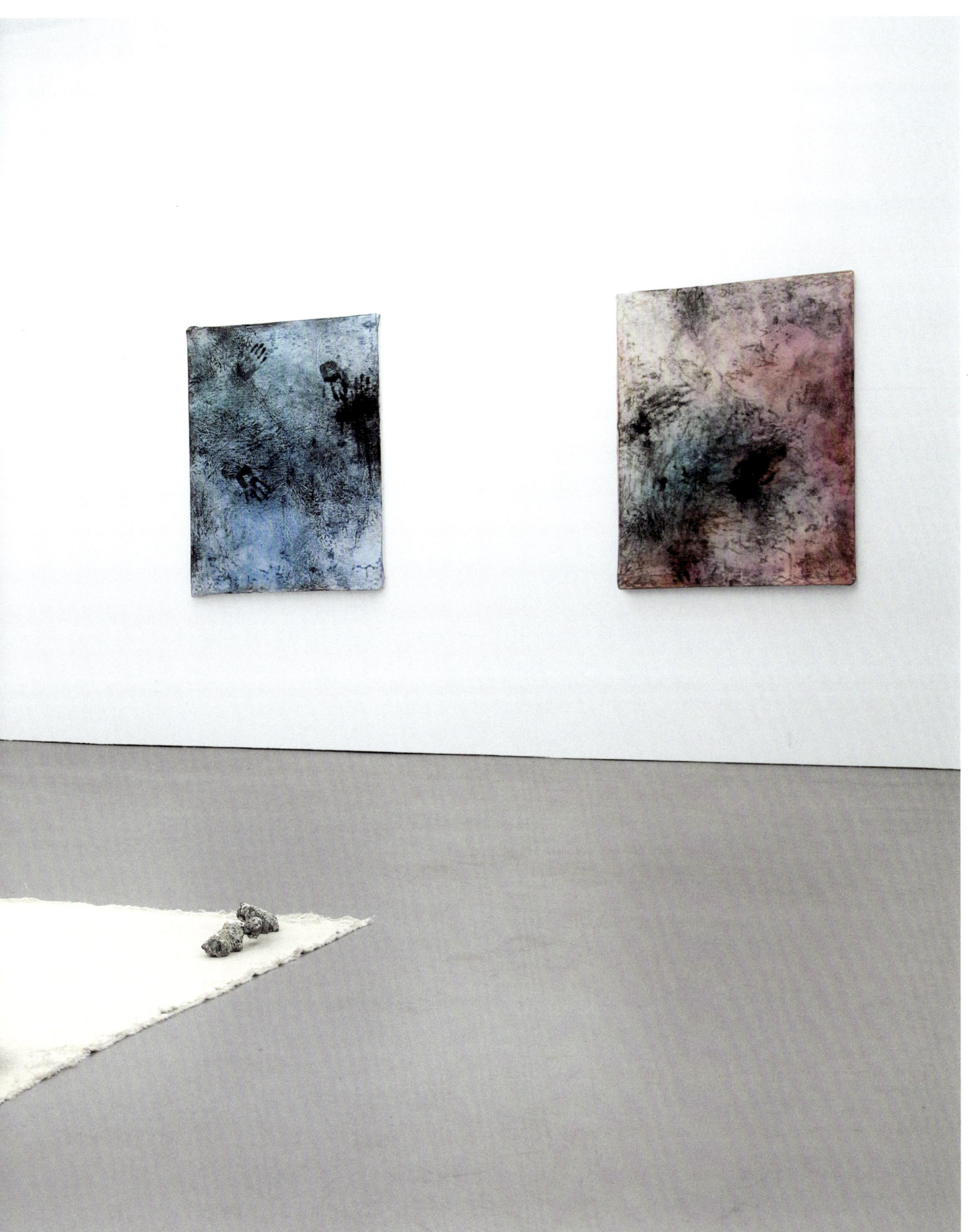

Left to right:

Ear of Dionysius, 2011; *Mermaid's Hole*, 2011; *Moonshine*, 2011; *Margin Walker*, 2011; on floor: *Methcathinone Blues*, 2011

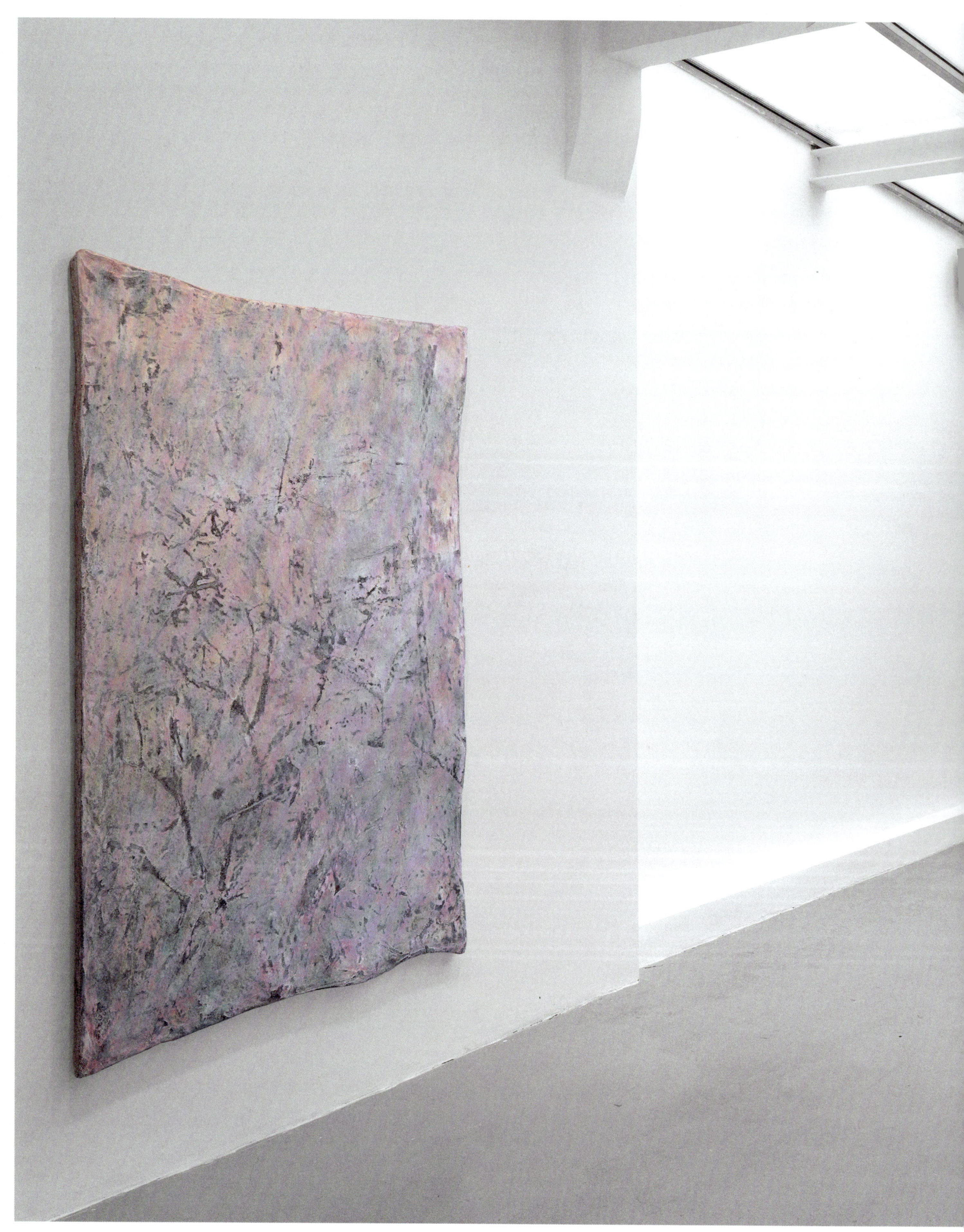

Installation view:
Trieste, Grimm Gallery, Amsterdam, 2014

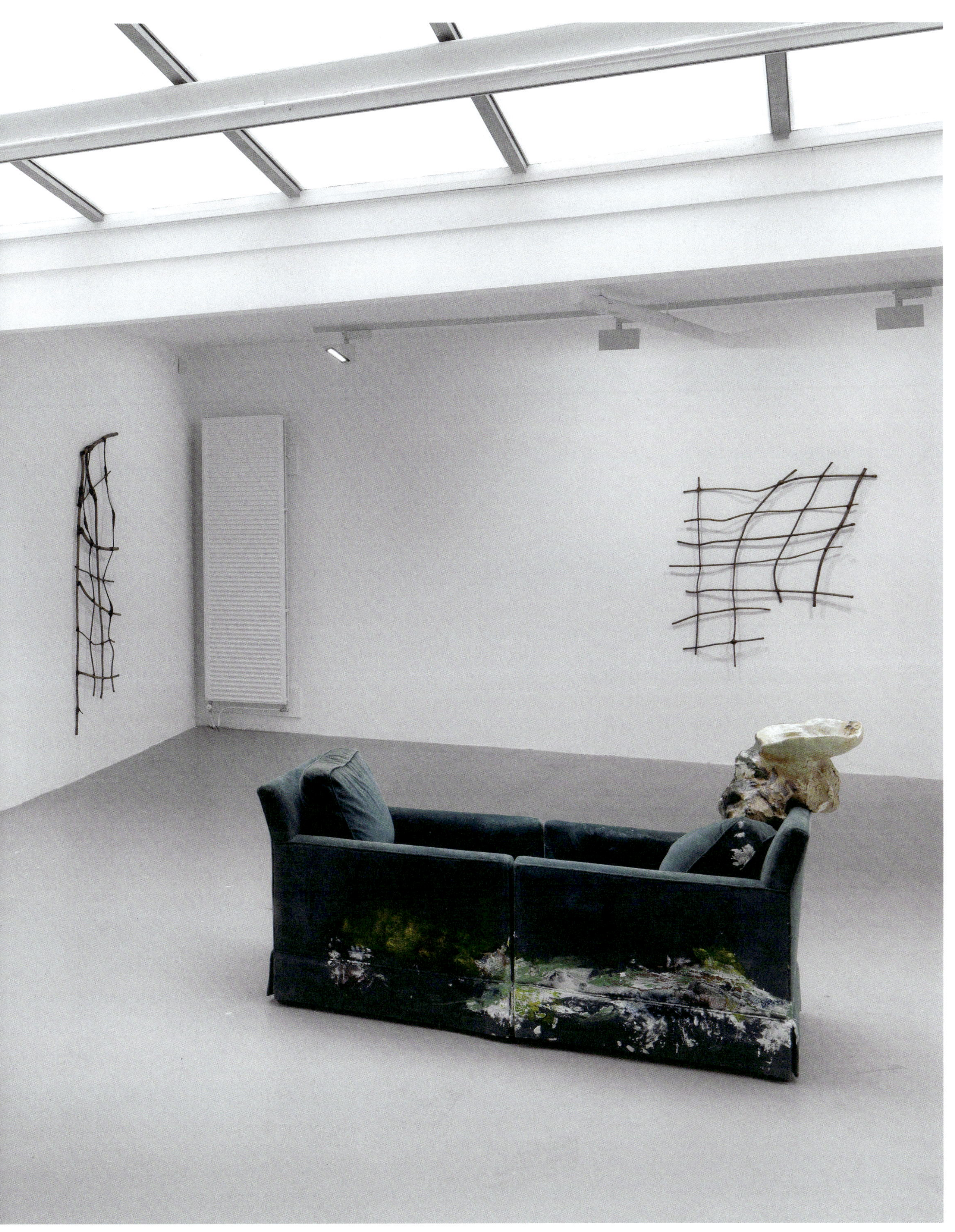

Clowning, 2013; *fragment from the Theory of Everything*, 2013; *fragment from the Theory of Everything*, 2013;
on floor: Jessica Jackson Hutchins, *Wedding Present*, 2013

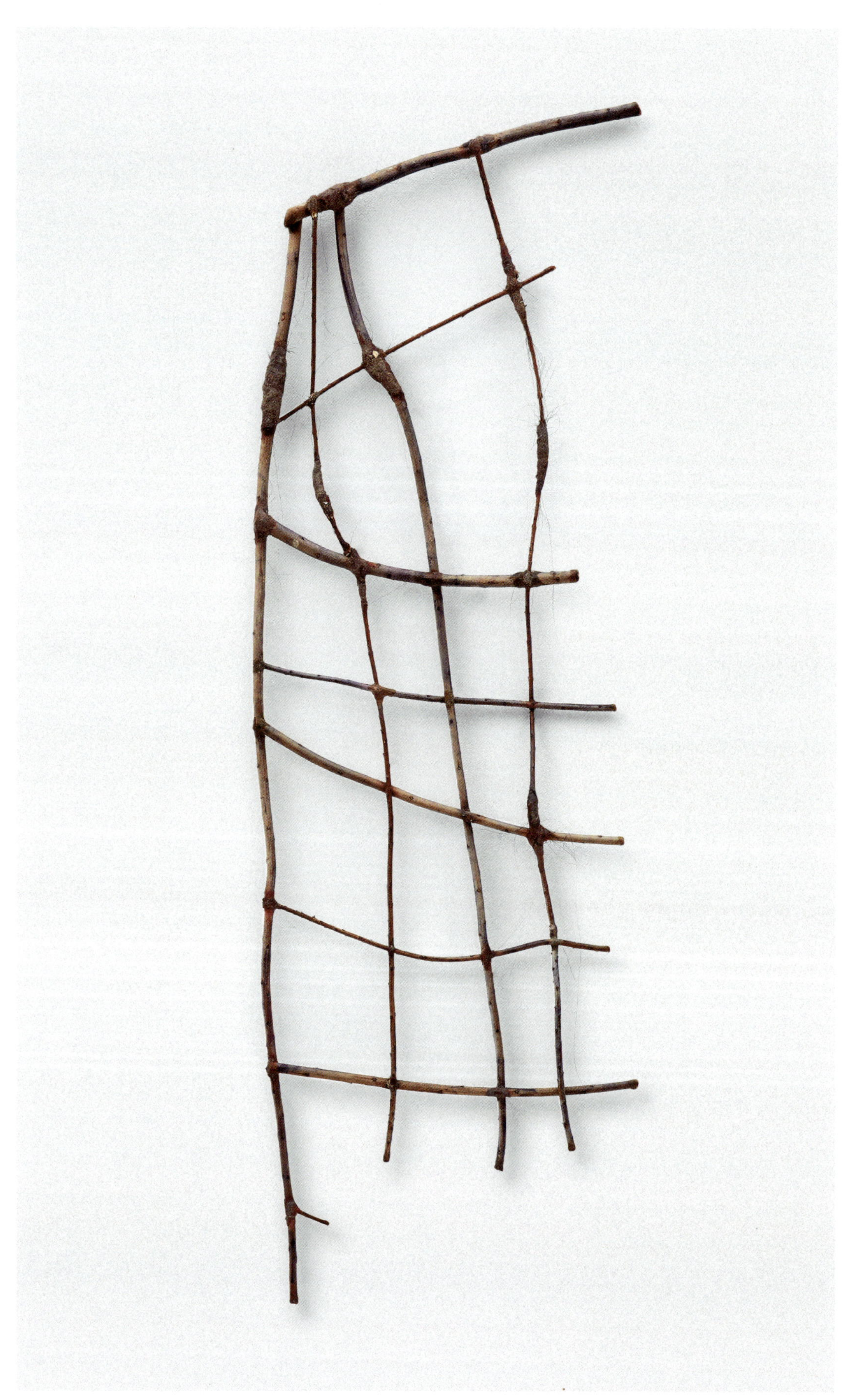

fragment from the Theory of Everything, 2013
Wax, wood, horsehair, ink, and steel wire, 73 ⅝ × 29 ⅛ × 4 ¾ inches, 187 × 74 × 12 cm

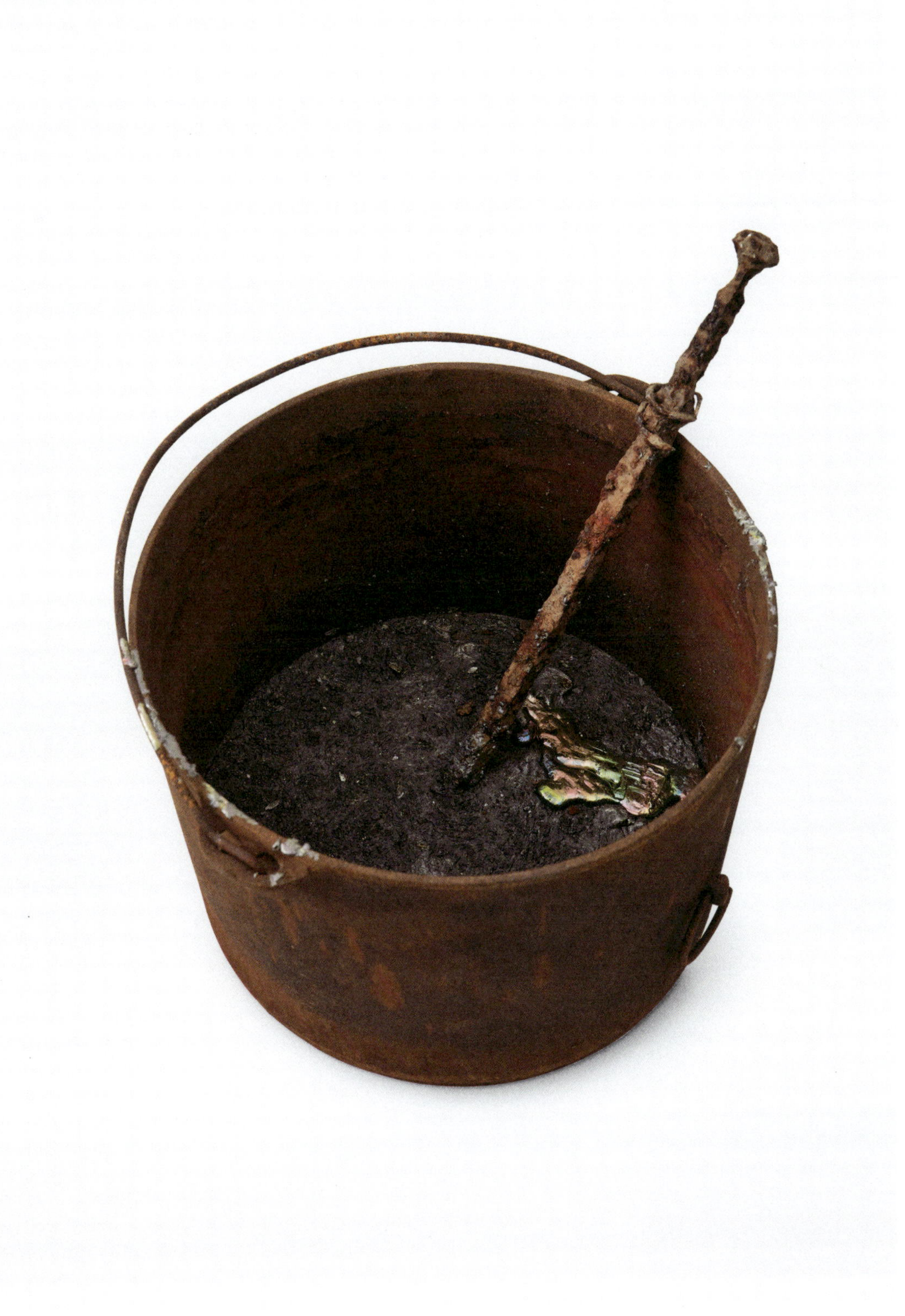

This is Magic, 2013
Iron cauldron, iron stake, and poured bismuth, 12 ¾ × 9 ¾ × 10 inches, 32.4 × 24.8 × 25.4 cm

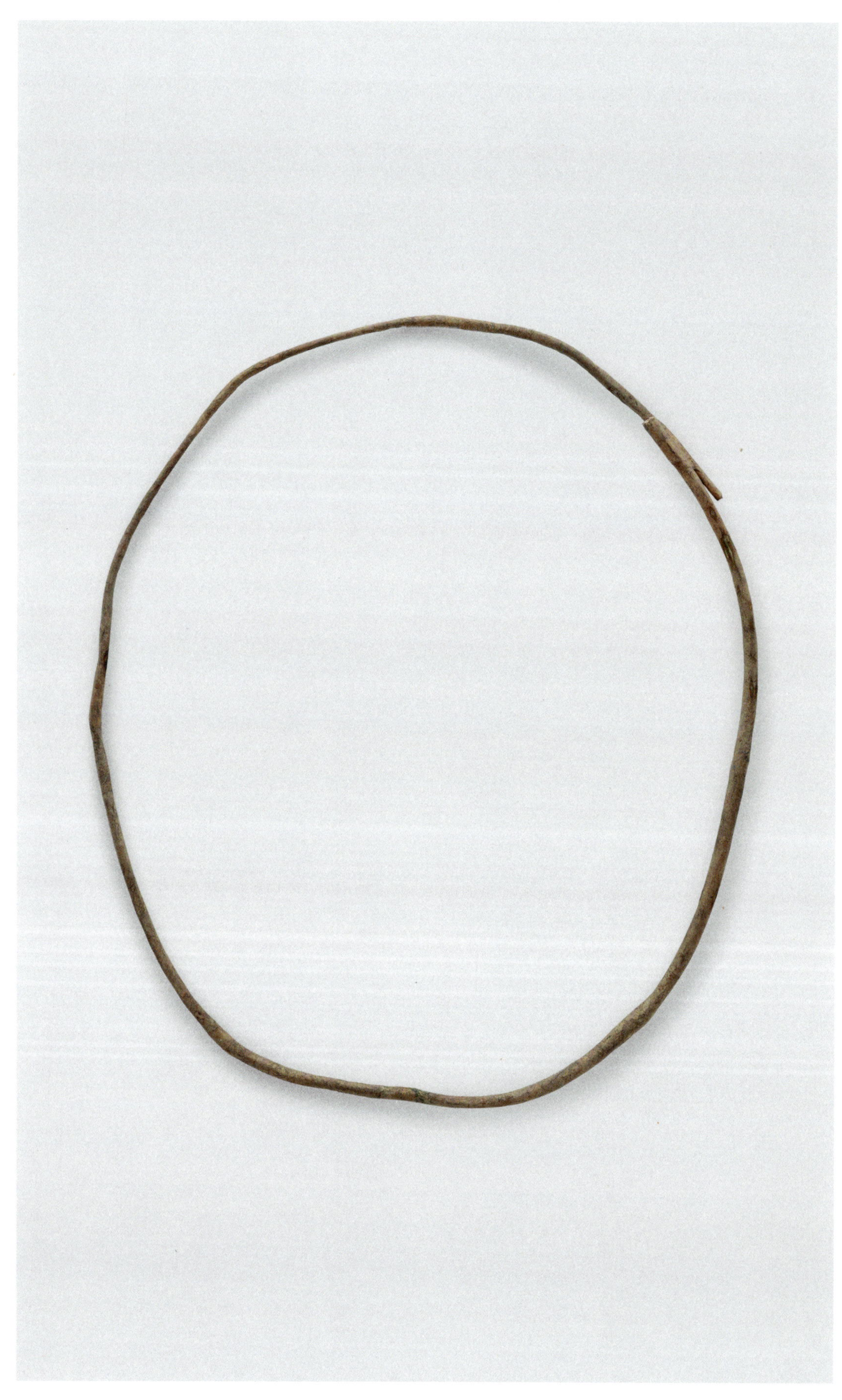

Naive Melody, 2013
Wood, paper, ink, and graphite, 49 ¾ × 43 ¼ × 3 inches, 126.4 × 109.9 × 7.6 cm

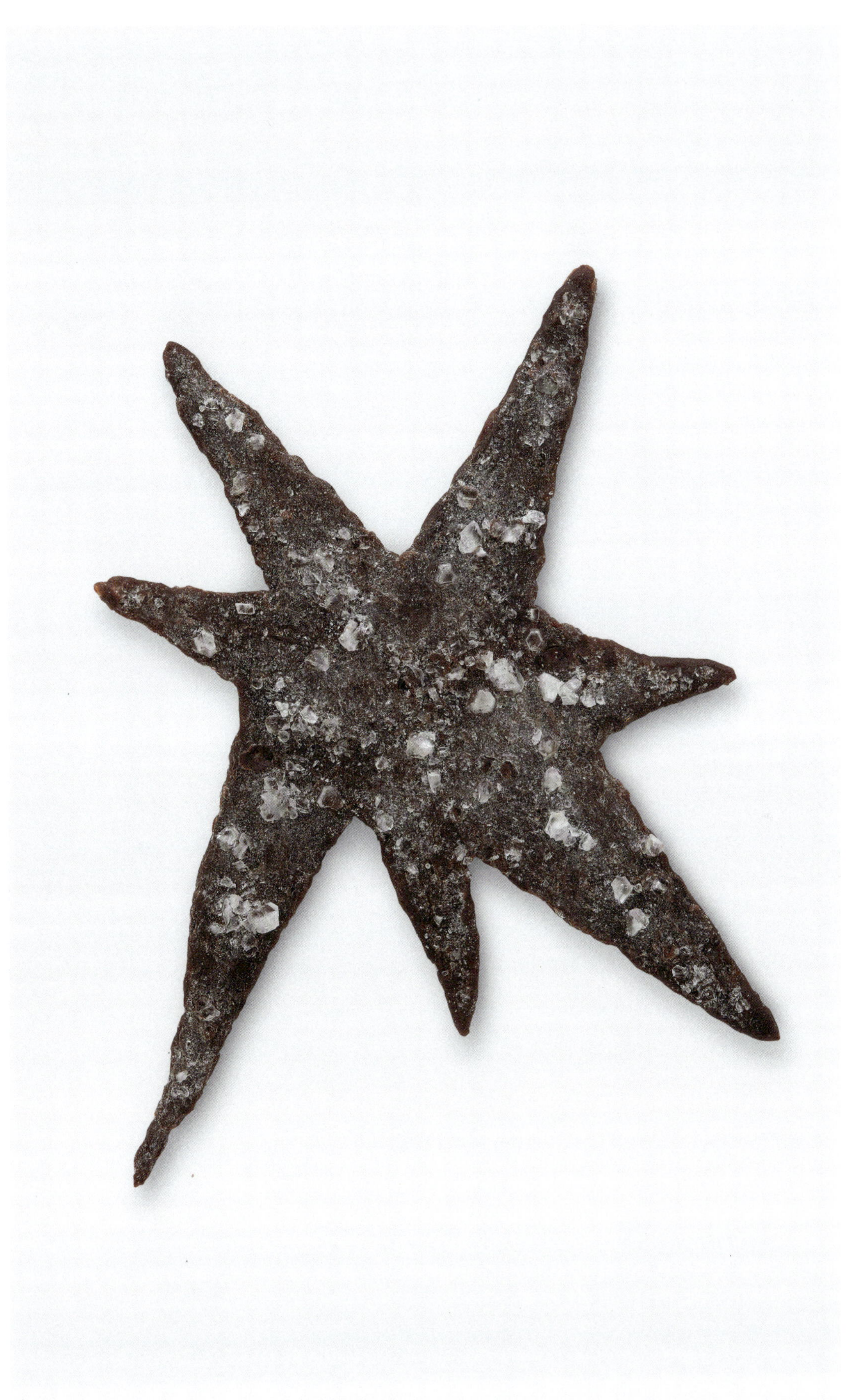

Quintessence, 2013

Wax, aluminum sulphate crystals, and expanded steel, 22 × 16 ¾ × ½ inches, 55.9 × 42.5 × 1.3 cm

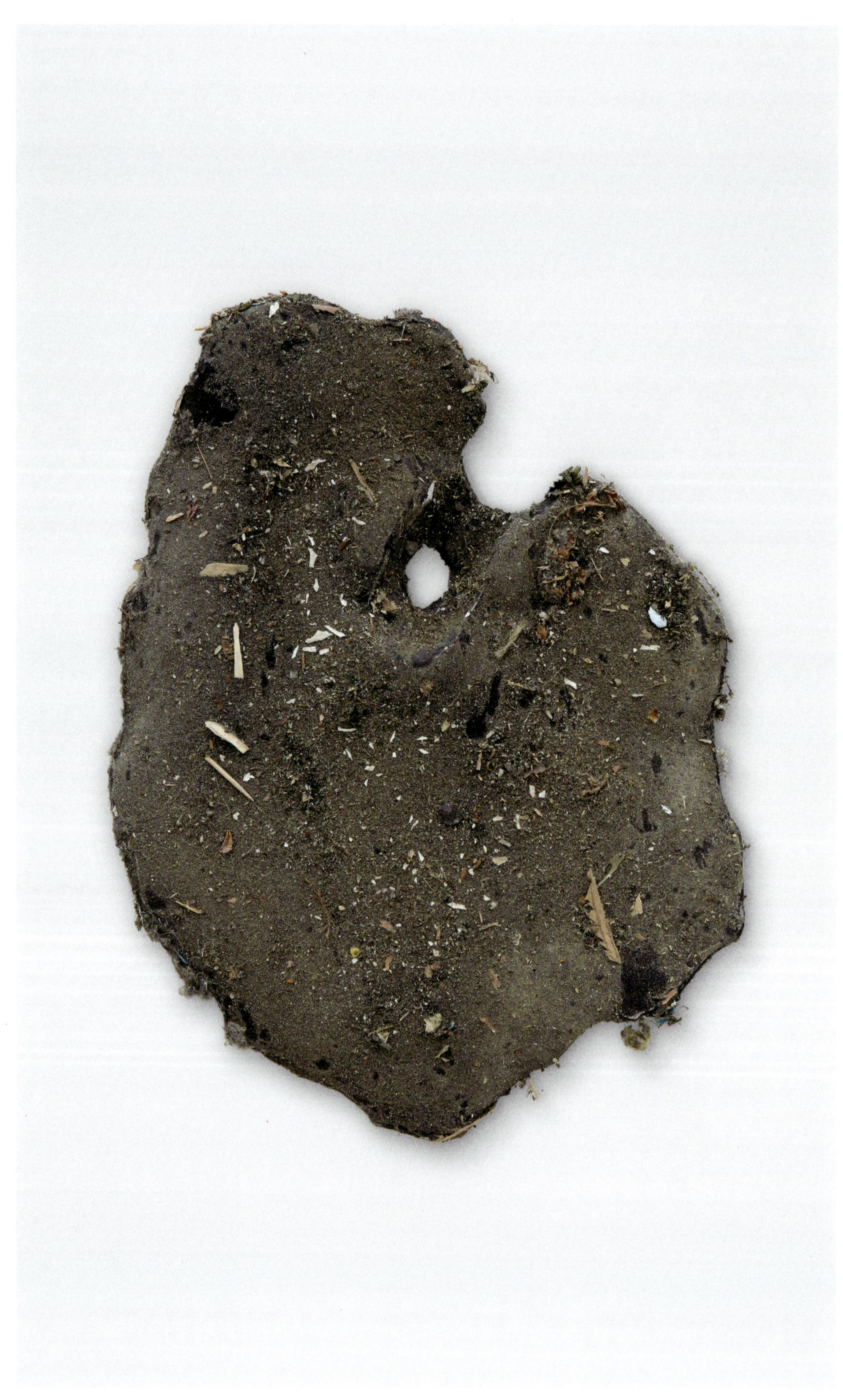

The Wrong Way, 2013
Plastic, paper, latex, and studio dust, 16 ¼ × 12 ½ × 1 ¼ inches, 41.3 × 31.8 × 3.2 cm

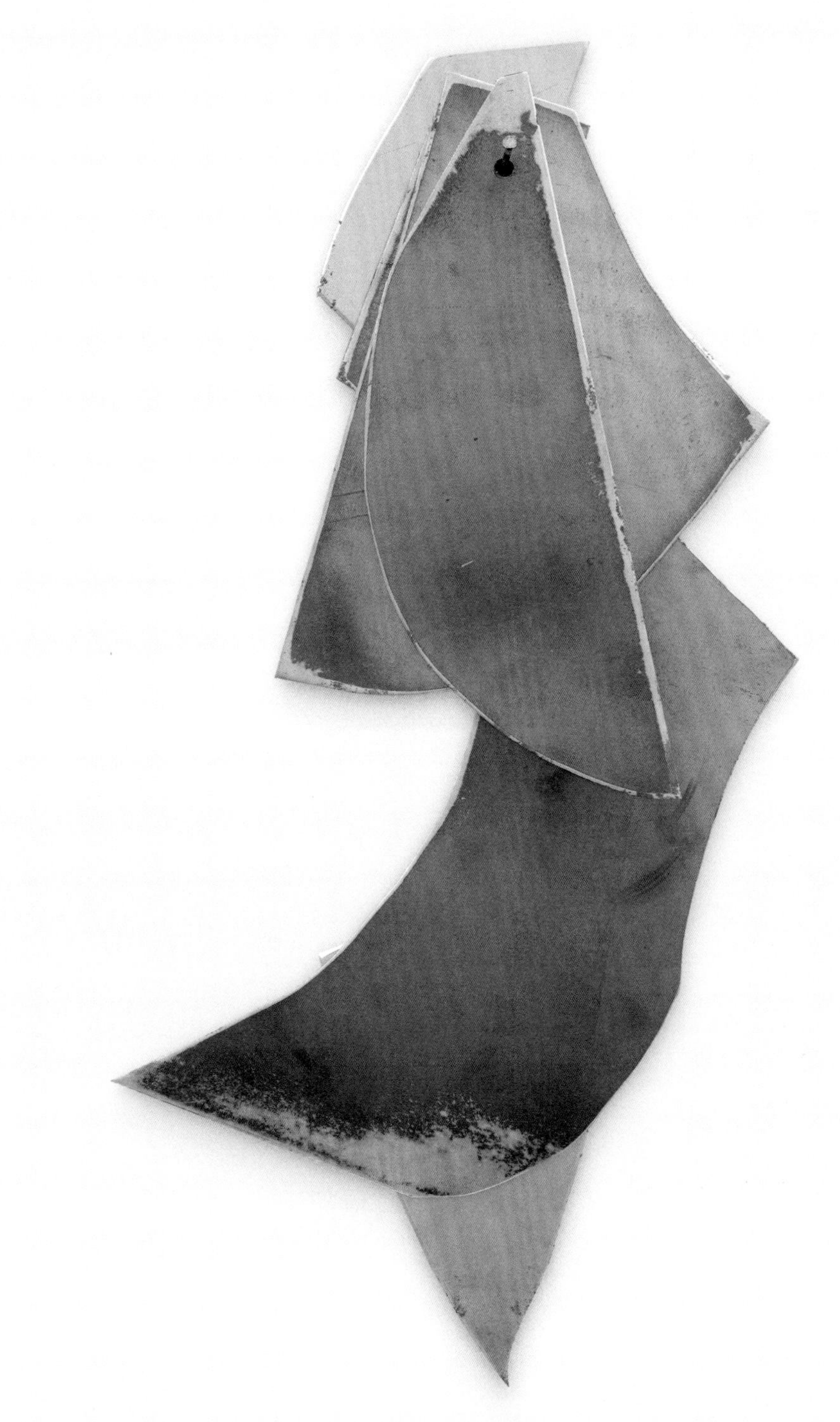

Intermission, 2013
Steel, 26 × 18 × 1 inches, 66 × 45.7 × 2.5 cm

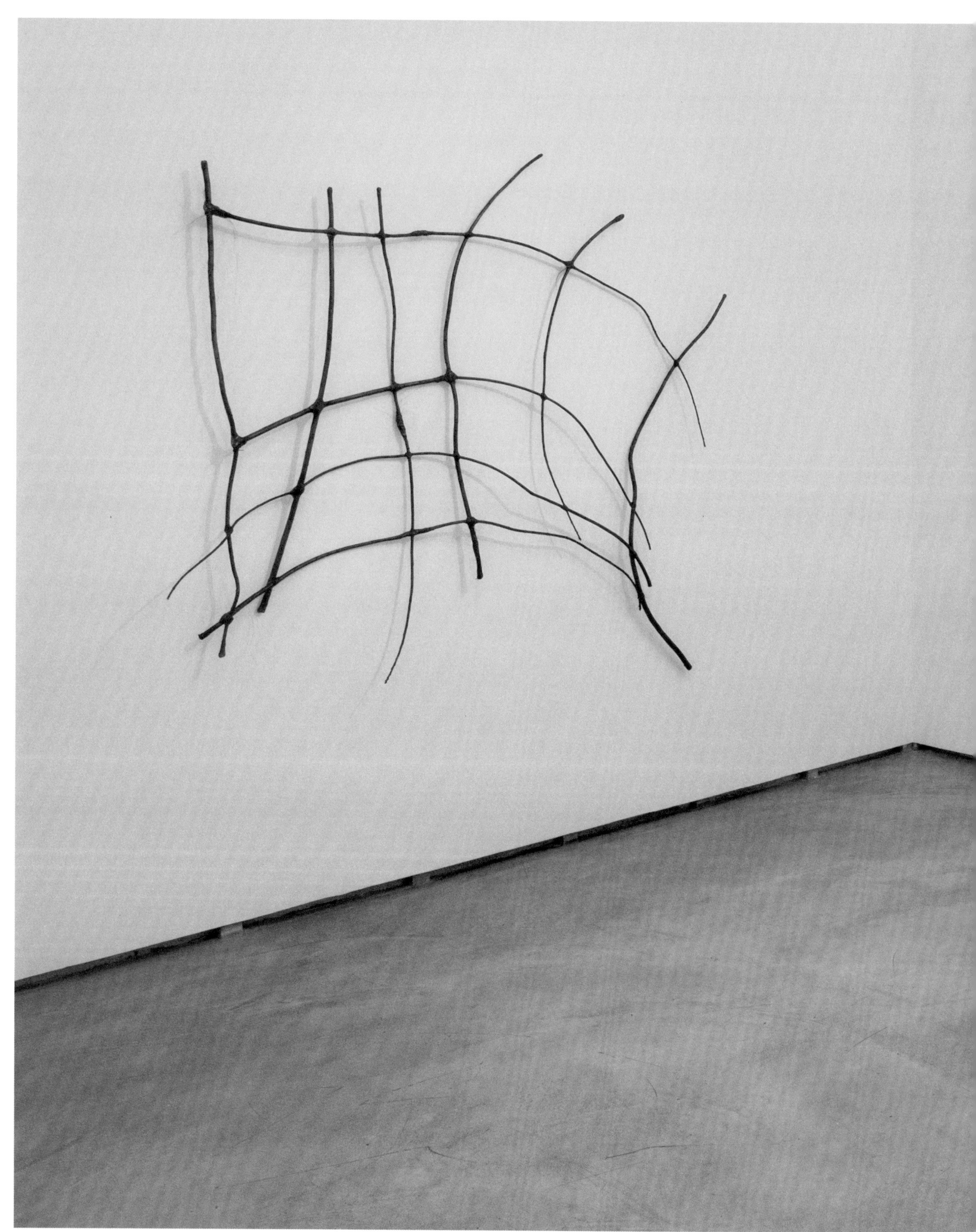

Installation view:

Ra, Federica Schiavo Gallery, Rome, 2014

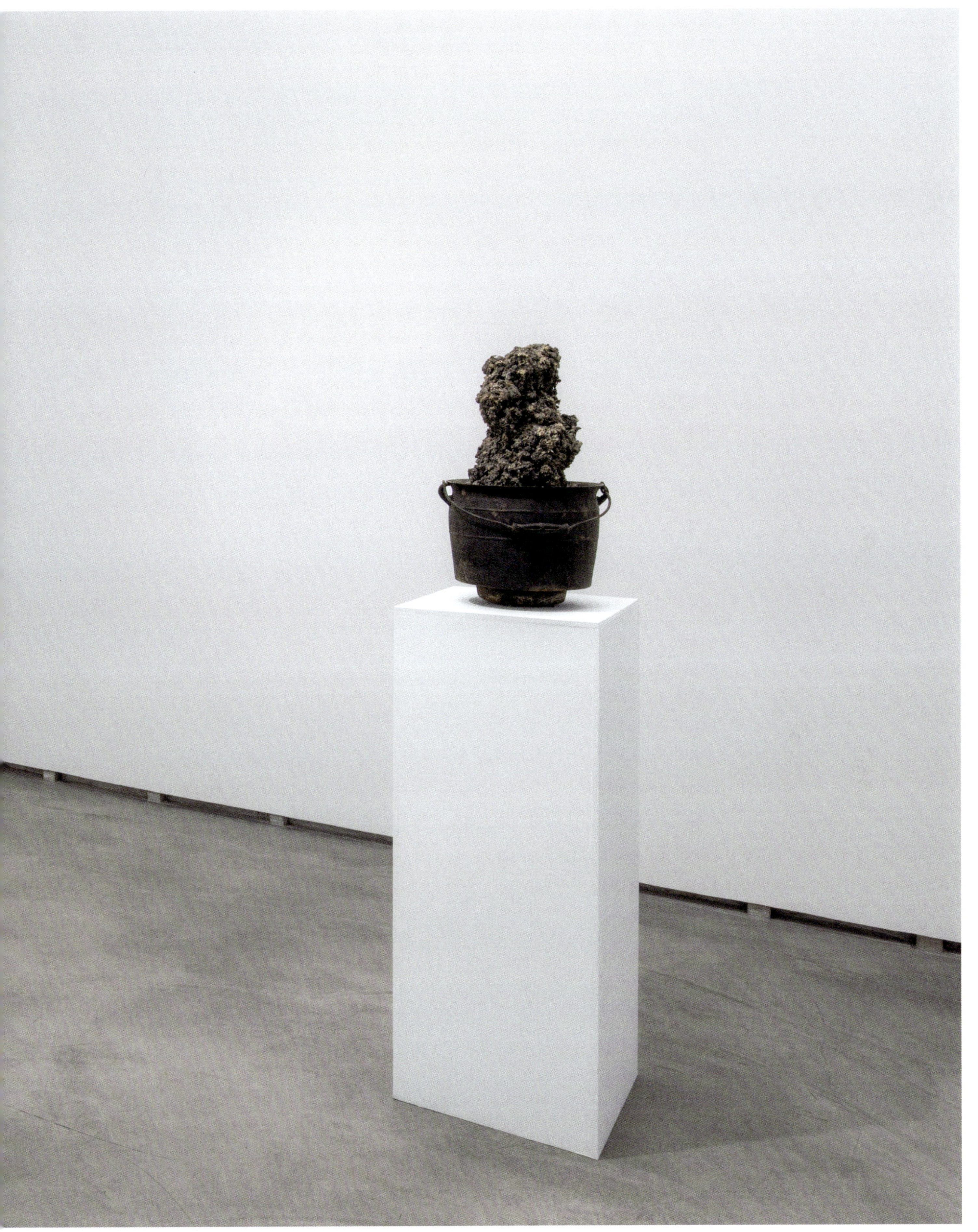

Left to right:

fragment from the Theory of Everything, 2014; *Desire*, 2014

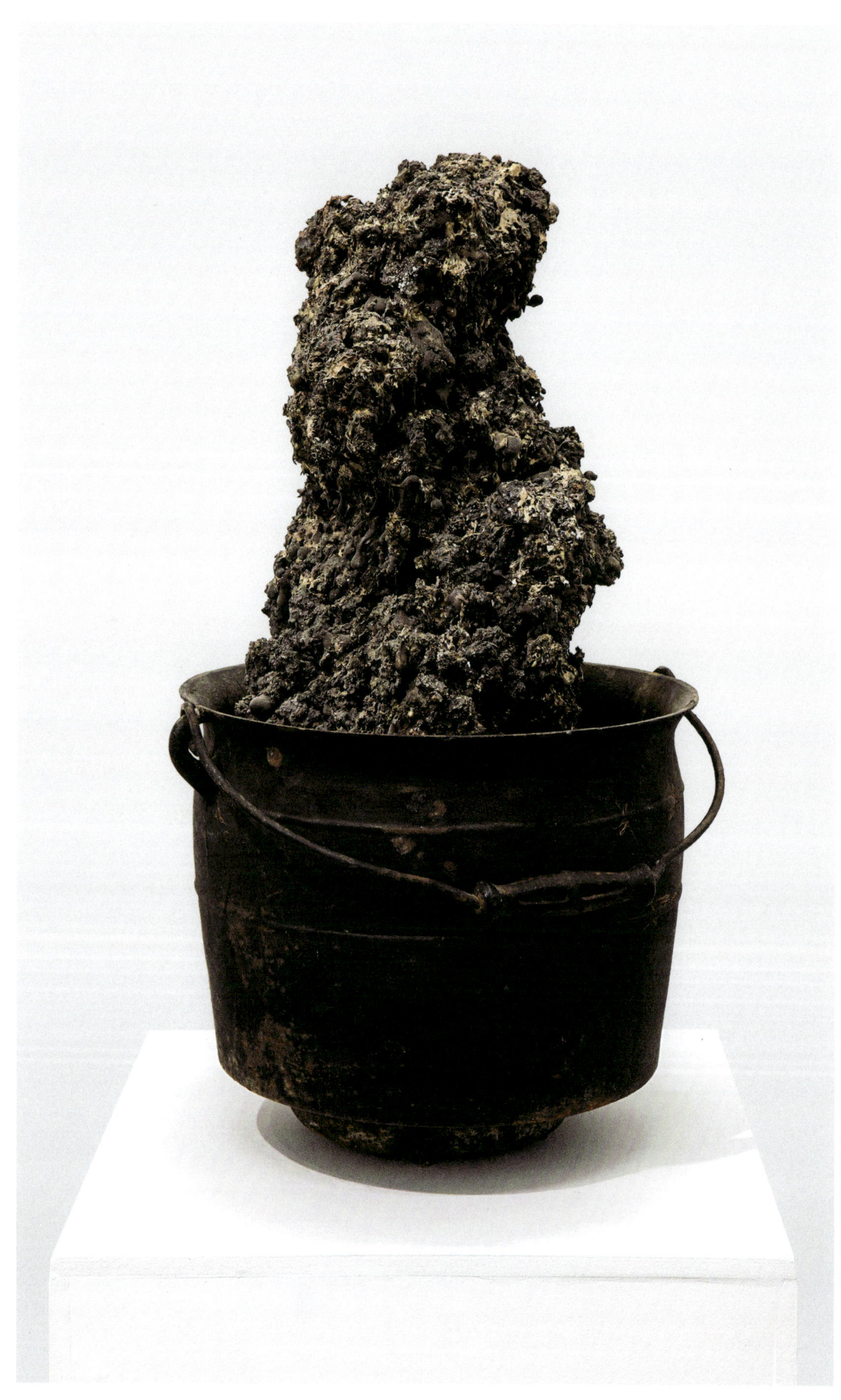

Desire, 2014
Iron cauldron, bronze slag, and cement, 22 × 12 inches diameter, 56 × 30.5 cm diameter

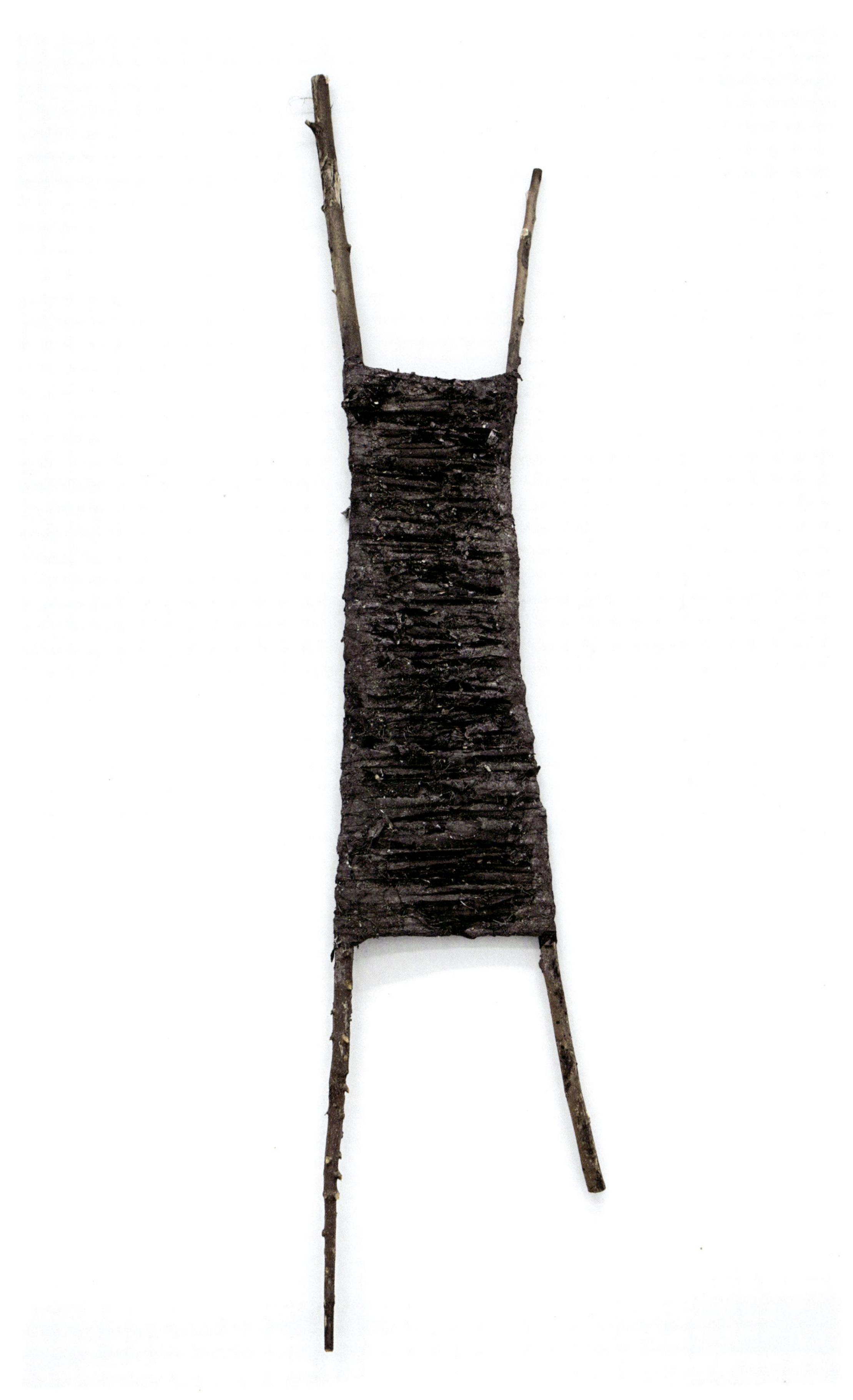

Self Portrait in Ultra Violet Light, 2014

Wood, leather, paper, pine needles, studio dust, and phosphorescent pigment, 94 1/8 × 22 × 3 inches, 239 × 56 × 7.6 cm

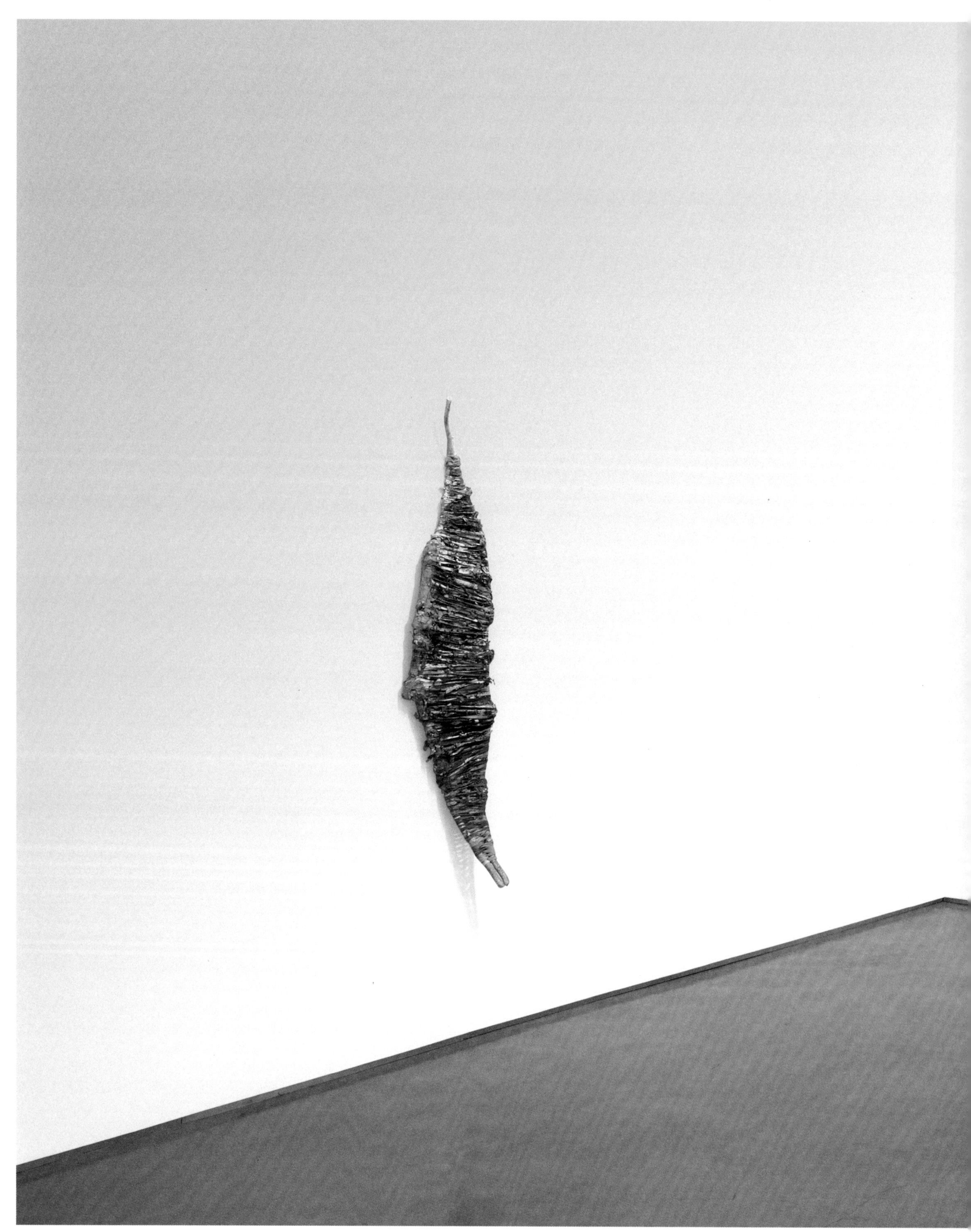

Installation view:
Walkabout, Marianne Boesky Gallery, New York, 2013

Left to right:
Self Portrait with Frostbite, 2013; *Storytelling*, 2013

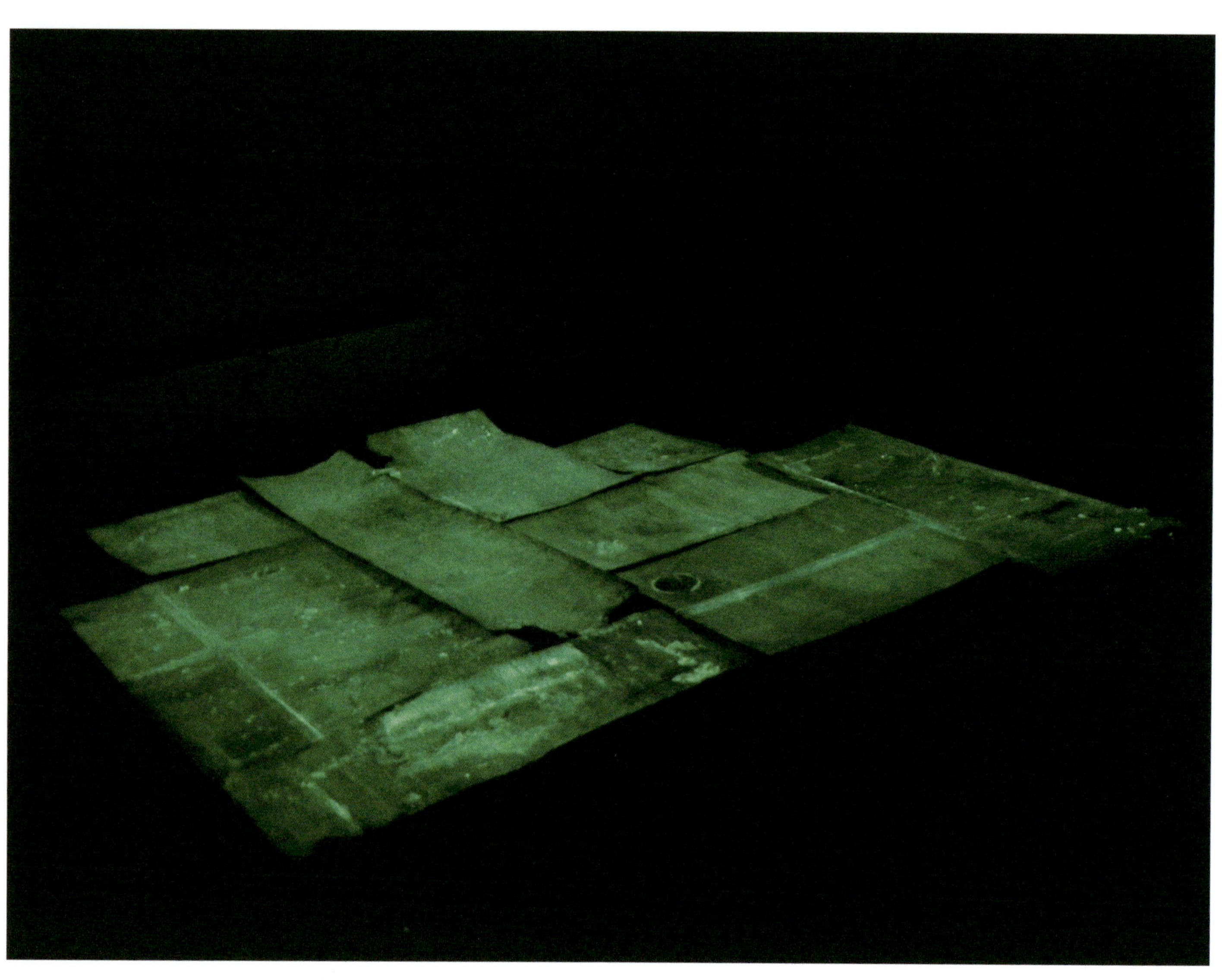

Studio Ra, 2014
Phosphorescent pigment and acrylic on cardboard, dimensions variable

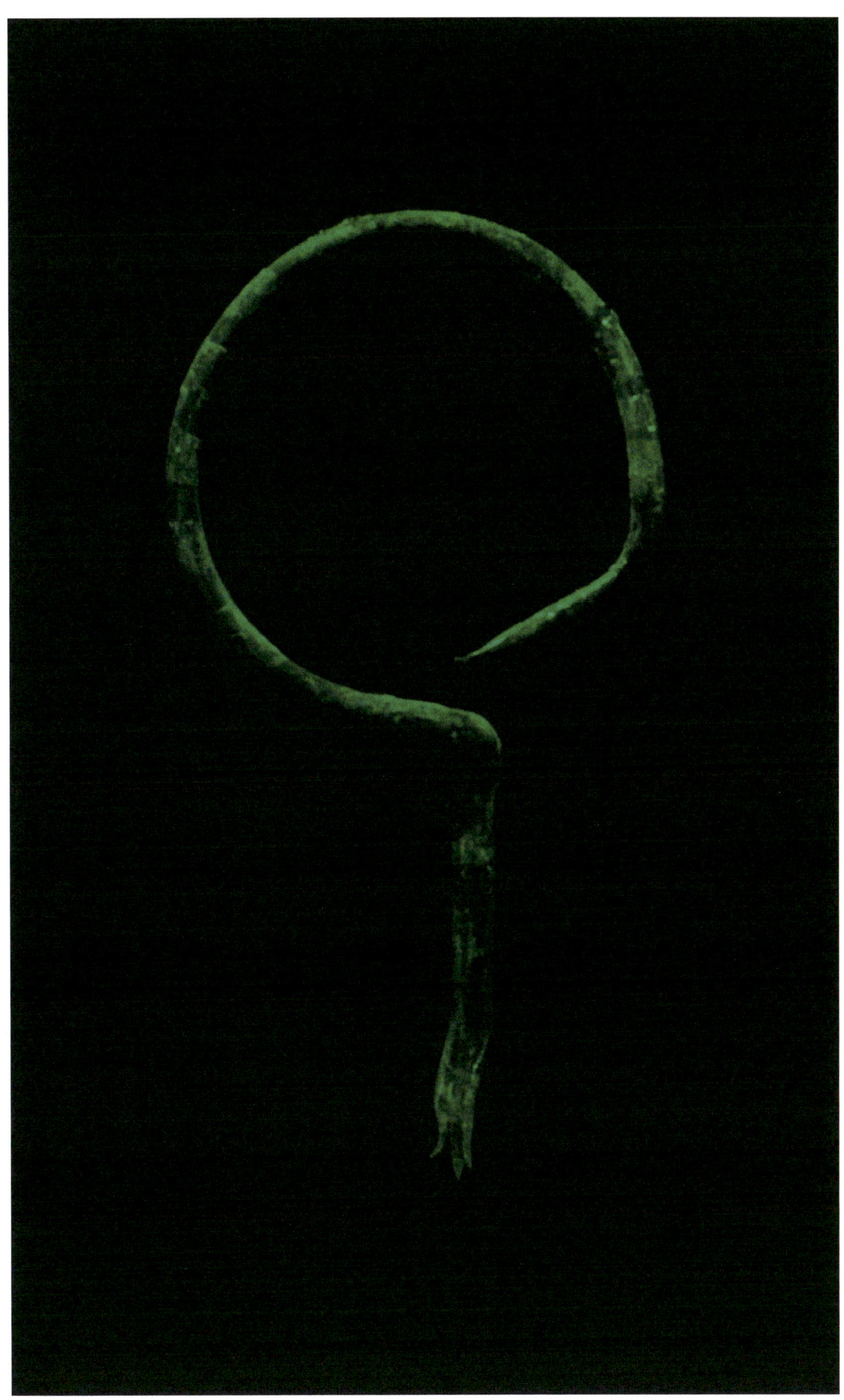

Year of Ra, 2014
Wood, ink, paper, rubber, acrylic, and phosphorescent pigment, 33⅛ × 18⅛ × 4⅜ inches, 84 × 46 × 11 cm

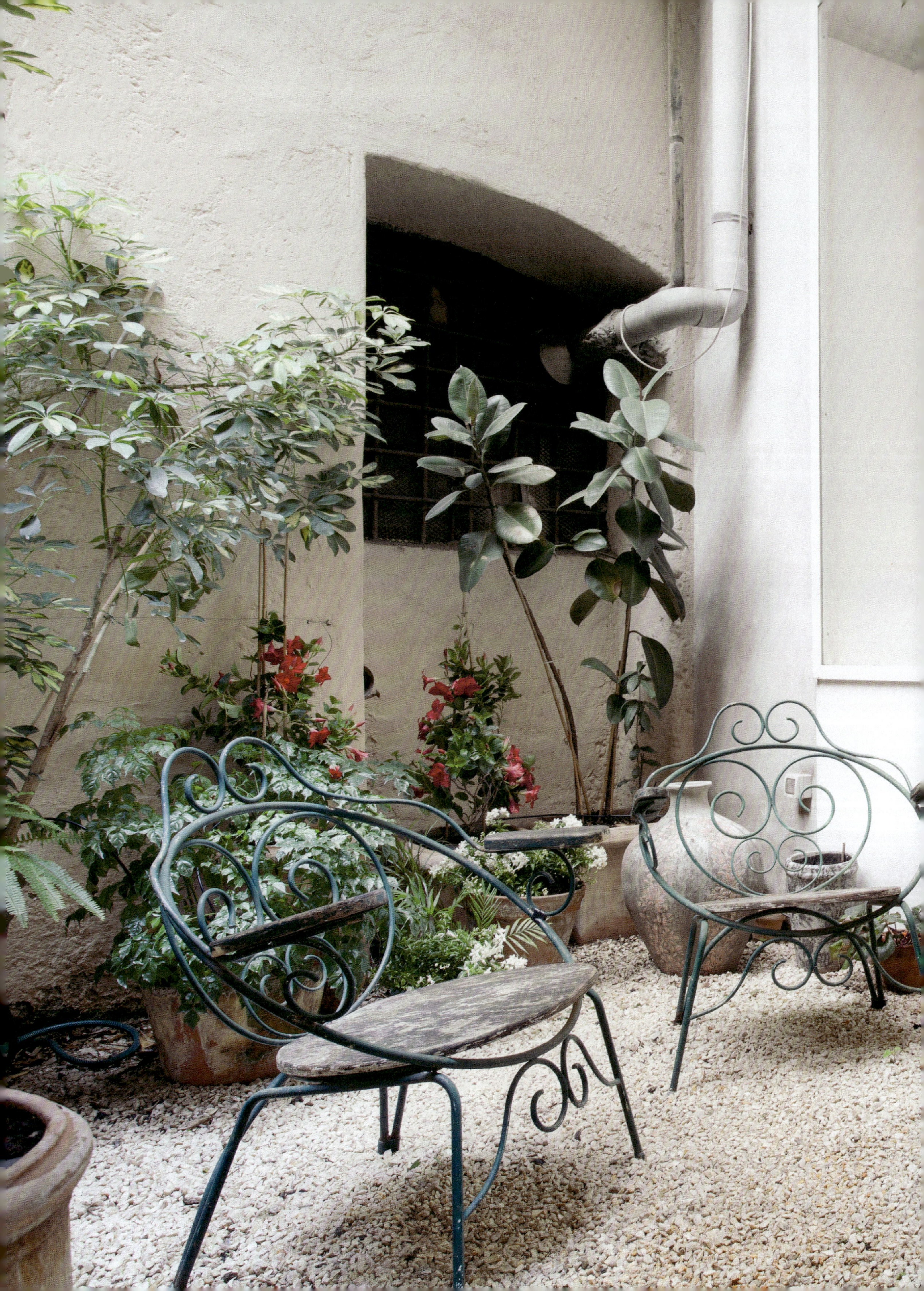

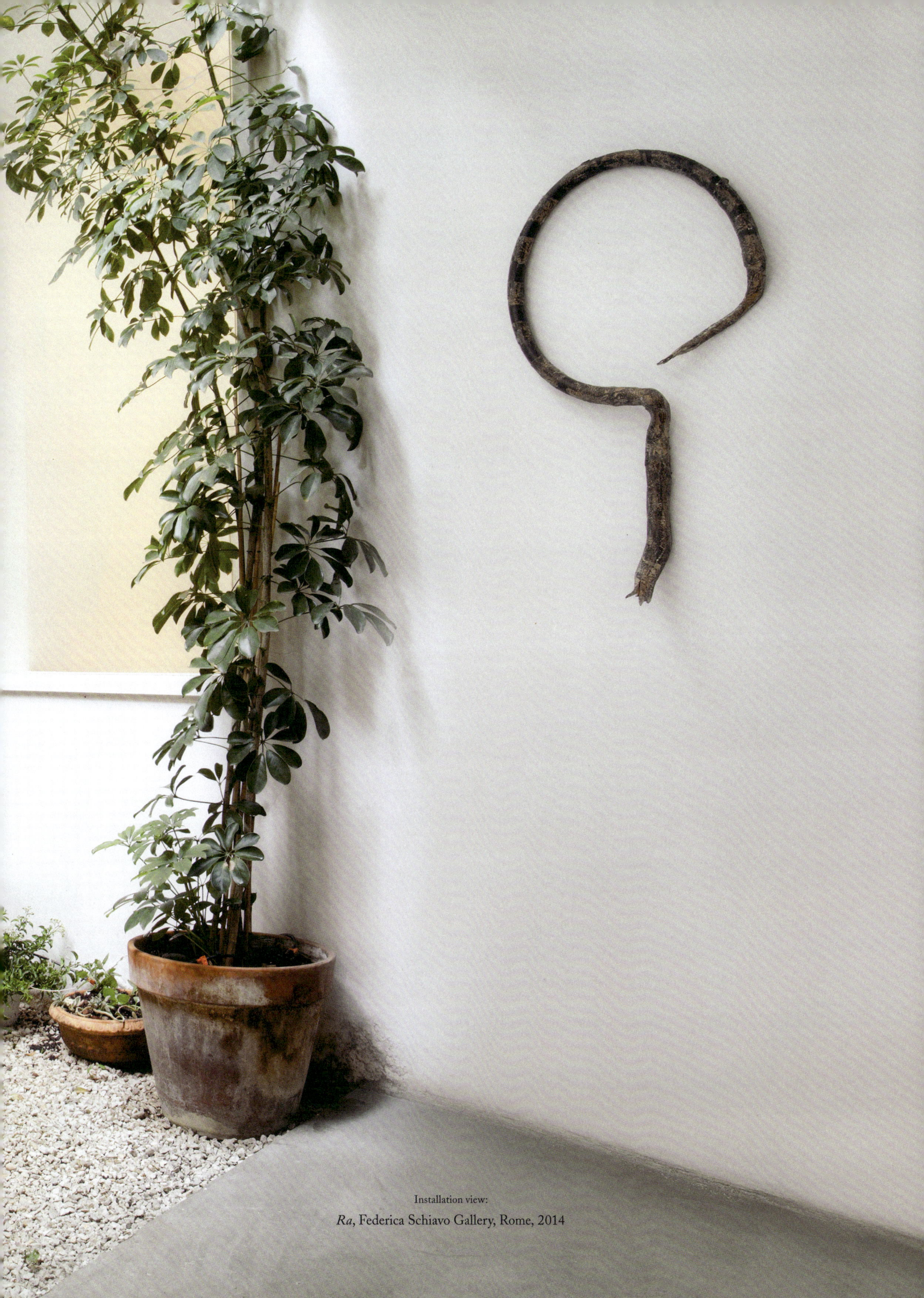

Installation view:
Ra, Federica Schiavo Gallery, Rome, 2014

The Great Aesthetizator and the Gaucher Boiteux

Philippe Vergne

Language. Jay Heikes's work has been, from its very early stages, about an exploration of existing languages and the processes of elaboration; that is the logic, at times deceptive, of visual linguistics and semantics. Over the last twenty years, he has built a versatile practice that demonstrates his ability to resist the limitations of aesthetic tropes, the traps of style. What can be superficially perceived as a heteroclite body of work is the result of rigorous development and growth cycles; one aesthetic move after another, one decision after another, one critical approach to art making after another. But at its core is an interest in the transformative, and transformational, potential of an art object to trace the boundaries of languages and their sources in music, literature, science, alchemy, storytelling, or natural phenomena.

Heikes's interest in language is not limited to his practice as a maker of objects and images. He writes and wrestles with words in a programmatic way, laying down and articulating a discursive equivalent of his visual work. His *Manifesto*, published in *Art in America* in January 2013, cites well-known predecessors—from the 1909 *Manifesto del futurismo*, which proposed the diversion of canals to flood museums, to Valerie Solanas's feminist *Scum Manifesto* and the *Dogme 95 Manifesto* of filmmakers Lars von Trier and Thomas Vinterberg—to reflect on the legacy of radical aesthetic languages. With an elliptical twist, Heikes bases his own manifesto on his anthropophagic digestion of these illustrious forerunners and his urge to kill idols. Extracting from an already formed language, Heikes points to a paradoxical need to reset the basis of language and to invent the possibility of a pre-language from which a new form of representation might emerge.

Heikes's desire to shed old language is manifest in artworks such as *Molting* (2010), with its larger-than-life silvery flakes resting, structureless, on the floor. But because they look slightly familiar, possibly mined from the taxonomy of sculptural formlessness born from the 1960s aesthetic and political call to undo dominant models, they are the emperor's new clothes: no attempt is made to hide the masquerade; it's all left on the floor to rot, decompose, and nurture the shape of things to come like so much aesthetic dandruff. But Heikes's efforts, though genuinely iconoclastic, are not in pursuit of a tabula rasa but rather a systematic and programmatic evolution through an analysis of language. His works from the early 2000s directly played with language and with formlessness. These works—swarms of language elements made of cut-out felt letters that are dumped on the floor, arrayed on pedestals, or hung on the wall, such as *Untitled* and *Kingdom* (both 2001)—pushed the text toward the indecipherable without losing the specificity of their sources. The letters, if

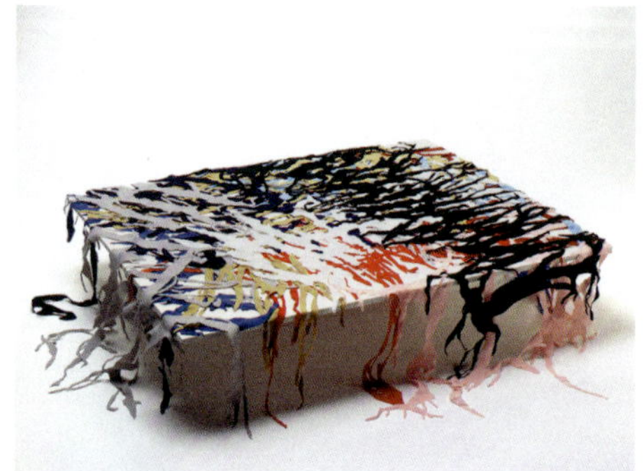

Fig. 1
Untitled, 2001
Felt
15 × 48 × 66 inches, 38.1 × 121.9 × 167.6 cm variable
Walker Art Center, Minneapolis, T. B. Walker Acquisition
Fund, 2002

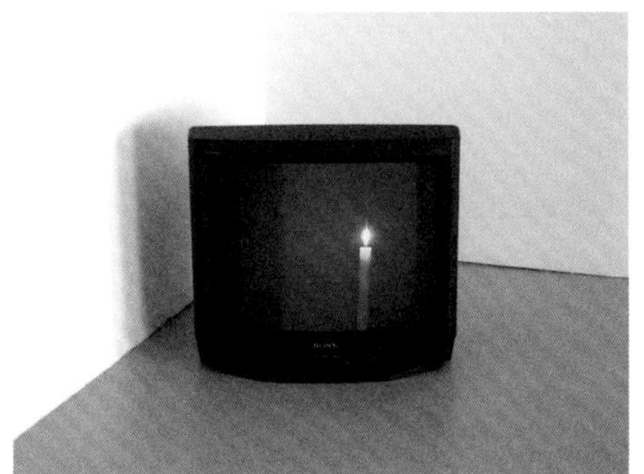

Fig. 2
Daydream Nation, 2000
Video transferred to DVD, color, silent
40:00 minutes

"properly" sequenced, would spell out song lyrics, band names or logos, random words, all unreadable but still projecting the ethos of the popular culture they honor and quote. They pause as dead skins and limbs, the remains of the late 1950s and 1960s passage between high and low culture and art. From pop art to the "Pictures Generation," driven by the logic of straightforward appropriation of images and icons, this period produced some of the most radical and now iconic artworks of the last fifty years. But Heikes's work suggests that it is time to move on, before the radical gesture becomes its own travesty, just another academic style. Without denying its importance, without ignoring his own interest in this aesthetic or in music (Heikes is a musician and former band member), he quietly advocates for a tectonic shift.

Daydream Nation (2000), a single-channel video showing a burning candle on a greenish background, is a bit of a swan song in this regard. First, the title is a direct appropriation of one of the most iconic albums of the post-punk band Sonic Youth, itself an icon of radical rock that was fully immersed in the radical art community. Their albums featured artwork by Mike Kelley, Raymond Pettibon, and in the case of *Daydream Nation*, Gerhard Richter—his 1982 painting *Kerz (Candle)*, a moody memento mori. Heikes's video of the burning candle is a live restaging of the painting in its guise of album cover. It is almost too perfect, a constellation of references that turns the notion of *mise en abyme*—the traditional painting technique in which a copy of an image is inserted within itself—into an abyssal exercise with no end in sight. In Heikes's case, this tongue-in-cheek work, respectful but not deferential, signified a turning point, a point of departure from which, step by step, a language—a singular language, a sui generis language—would autonomously follow. Subsequent bodies of work deepened this rupture, at times signifying the difficulties, the hesitation, in retiring an aesthetic model. This wrestling in the studio, with no romanticism and only the drive to produce a new language, is a courageous and risky path. First, it shows work "at work" without indulging in the often-abused notion of exhibiting process. Second, it might feel like learning to walk or to talk again.

So There's This Pirate . . . and *New Heaven Hook* (both 2005), are two works that produce this rupture and, porously, push and pull through it. *So There's This Pirate . . .* is a series of twenty-four images, some abstracting a stage curtain, some showing a photographic portrait of the artist holding a parrot, and a final image of the artist's hand flipping us the bird. Heikes tells a stereotypical joke, but the punch line is never revealed and the only thing we get is the artist's finger. The joke is therefore on us and we are left to decide for ourselves what the joke was and why it ends with a seemingly hostile gesture. Artists are always on call to perform, to play the game, to be on stage, to deliver, to entertain us … until they turn their backs to preserve the space and time necessary for their work. *So There's This Pirate…* might be intended to ensure that ultimately the joke is not on the art or the artists. It is about the urgency of *le pas de côté*, the side-step that positions the mind to embrace the oblique or the diagonal in order to privilege clear thinking and invention. This approach is close to what French philosopher Michel Serres articulates in *Le gaucher boiteux*, in which he advocates for "limping thoughts" that defy established and rigid systems of truths and well-balanced certitudes.[1] Serres argues for a "gai savoir," where minor stories, tales, and clumsy know-how gain more relevance than the dominant narratives and show themselves as the authentic engine behind true innovation. Thus Heikes's need for *New Heaven Hook*, a cast aluminum sculpture shaped like a vaudeville "hook" designed to open theater curtains and repurposed to pull mediocre or bad performers offstage by the neck. Heikes might have used it to pull himself transversally off the stage, the "scene," so he could get back to the concentrated, focused space of the studio.[2] The hook also signals that his methodology was evolving away from that of the "idols" and icons, whom he was now pulling offstage, and simultaneously toward a body of work centered on the notion and apparatus of stage presence, specifically the contemporary myth of the romantic artist as akin to the fetishized caricature of a punk martyr.

Heikes's 2005–6 series Roadgear is his version of Michelangelo Pistoletto's Minus Objects of 1965–66. With the Minus Objects, Pistoletto intended to disrupt the dogma of the uniformity of individual artistic style that was increasingly applied to his critically and commercially successful mirror paintings. The Minus Objects acted as aesthetic liberators and as the taxonomic foundation of the shapes and forms that would inform Pistoletto's work for years to come. Heikes's Roadgear works operate as a disruption not only of his own work but also, as with *New Heaven Hook*, of the cliché of the artist as rock star.

The Roadgear installations are composed of objects that mimic the apparatus of a rock concert: a collection of what you might see listed on any backstage rider for sound equipment. It is the ultimate checklist for "roadies" (concert technicians): speakers, amps, racks, PA systems, stands, and drum risers — all painted in matte black. But the elements are stripped of their electronic guts and therefore deprived of their function. They are empty vessels, placebo equipment relegated to décor; the core is gone, pulled offstage long ago by the vaudeville hook of cool consumerism in both retail and art. They are to rock, to music, what Urban Outfitters is to street cred: pure style, removed from the urgency of "teenage riot," to borrow another Sonic Youth title. What is left is the

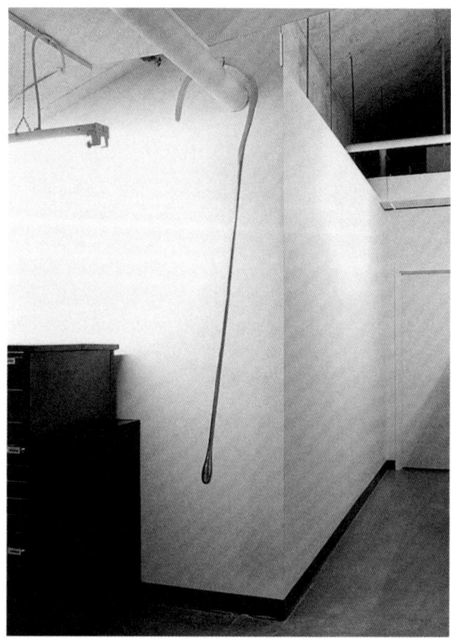

Fig. 3
New Heaven Hook, 2005
Cast aluminum
83 × 17 1/2 × 2 inches, 210.8 × 44.5 × 5.1 cm
Walker Art Center, Minneapolis, Butler Family Fund, 2006
Installation at Walker Art Center

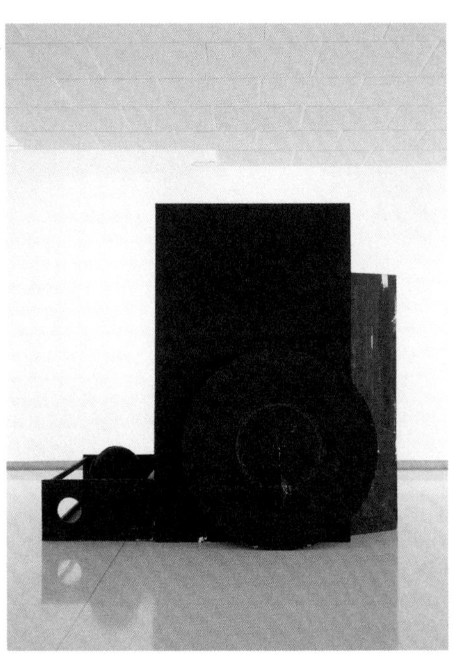

Fig. 4
Roadgear (Staircase, Severing Box, Beach Ball, Milk Crate,
Extension Cord, Frying Pan and Light Bulb, Bocce Ball, Clock,
Giant Toblerone, Rain Stick, Duffle Bag Box), 2006
Wood, paper, staples, flat black latex, plastic milk crate, cotton,
painted extension cord, painted coconuts, string, painted bocce
ball, painted rain stick, painted light bulb and cast iron frying pan
Overall: 80 × 84 × 92 ½ inches, 203.2 × 213.4 × 235 cm

stereotypically muscular, if slightly macho, silhouette. The forms are not deprived of aesthetic virtues, though, and possess a minimalist theatricality in the way they occupy and structure space without sharing the monumental gestalt of minimal art. Quite the opposite. They are vulnerable, closer to Fluxus and Robert Filliou's equivalent principle "*bien fait, mal fait, pas fait*" than to Robert Morris's primary structures. They are more sarcastic than ironic, and the sound they project is not that of music but of silence. The party is over. And from this moment it seems that Heikes commits himself to reinvent, step by step, his own language, not unlike a "gauche" alchemist.

In Heikes's *This Is Magic* (2013) an iron bucket with a stir stick resting in a drop of bismuth at its bottom is the trace of investigations that involve the transmutation of matter. Anachronistic as it may look, it comes from a quasi-archaeological past. But it contains the transformative magic that Heikes is looking for. The bucket, the stick, and the puddle of leftover matter are traces of an activity. Someone was experimenting with something, something small-scale and humble. But the endgame is open-ended; no success, no failure—or both at once. *Bien fait, mal fait, pas fait*. What matters is the process, the transmutation, the minor trials, accidents, and errors.

A subsequent body of works expands on this transformative ethos, within the sculptures and beyond them into real space. In 2008–9, Heikes produced a series of exquisite corpses, hybrid objects that at first sight superficially evoke tree branches. They lie on the floor, creep along the wall, convulse in torqued angles. Their presence in a space alters how one experiences and perceives it. A closer look reveals that they are made of bronze and iron, the combination of which causes corrosion. They present their "wounds," that is, they're cast from pieces of wood attached with tape. They are "*boiteux*," as Michel Serres would write, meaning they limp and are slightly unstable. They are definitively and defiantly against nature, and their titles reveal Heikes's process and strategically limping attempts to elaborate a transformed and transformative language through matter: *Wave of Mutilation* (2008), *Awkward Pause* (2008), *Technical Difficulties* (2009). One of them is very tongue-in-cheek and self-deprecating: *Career Ender* (2009). It's shaped like *New Heaven Hook*, but it is less perfect, roughed up with asperities. The title suggests that Heikes might see his investigation and exploration of matter manipulations as a risky career move, a point emphasized by the ultimate symbol of traditional, monumental, conservative sculpture: bronze. *Career Ender* is his own vaudeville hook, casting doubts, aspersions on the direction of the work. These sculptures are contradictions, only superficially "definitive." The chemical reaction of bronze and iron makes them living organisms at the edge of being toxic.

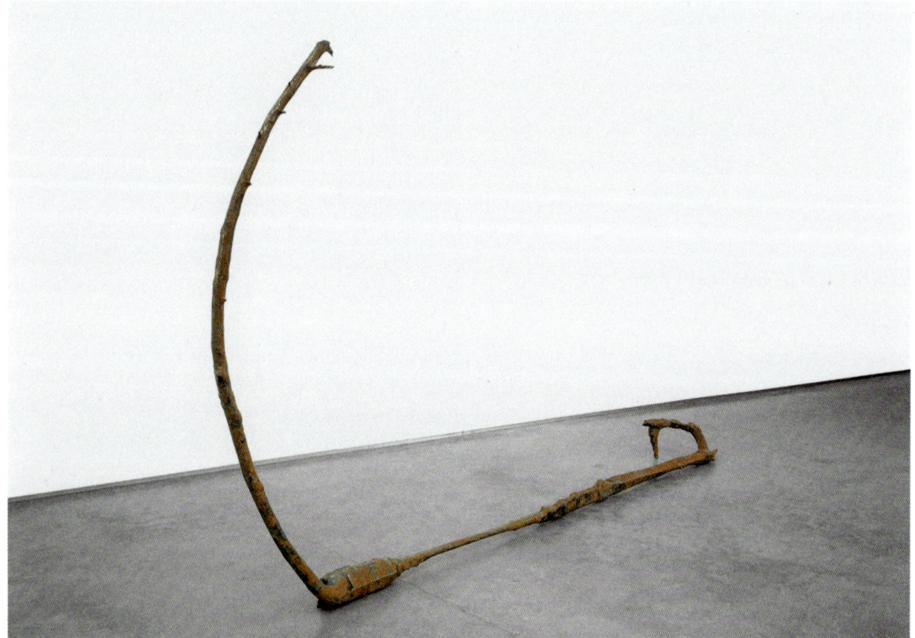

The gestures that constitute these sculptures—joining, taping, and mending—are motions of tender care, like those afforded broken tools or limbs. Their jointed oddities result from Heikes's ability to trigger the transformation of ordinary materials and matter through the performance of elementary gestures. The same gestures sustain the emergence of two other series, in 2012 and 2013, that distinguish themselves by their modesty, their vulnerability, and their transformative (or seemingly transformative) qualities. The first series is composed of small tools handmade from natural and found materials that suggest rural needs and utility: they appear to be devices for gathering, tracing, cutting, or trapping (*No Age*, 2012). Though their ultimate function remains elusive (*We will destroy this museum* or *Drawn & Quartered* [both 2012]), they evoke humanity's perennially primary activities: predation and survival. They are bricolage about bricolage.

Hung on the wall as precisely organized pictorial compositions, these tools become about painting in a convoluted way, one that critically invokes the possible tools for a painting that has not yet been painted and might never be. What comes to mind is the 1970s French movement Supports/Surfaces, and more specifically the artist Daniel Dezeuze, who in the early 1990s produced a group of objects he named *objets de cueillette* that mimic harvesting tools. But true to the early mandate of the Supports/Surfaces ideology—to deconstruct painting in order to reexamine its nature, its history, its status, and eventually its

134

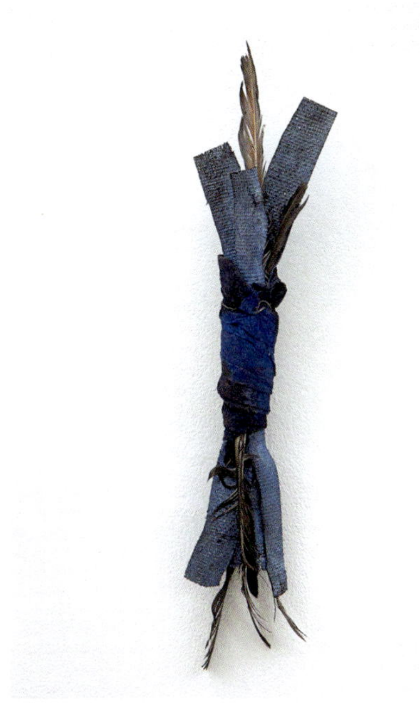

potential—these objects carry a subtle pictorial quality that takes precedence over their function. The fictional archaism of Heikes's "tools" might be a reminder of how archaic painting is and has been for a long time. Thus the body of paintings that Heikes contemporaneously realized, Cave paintings, appears to be excavated from the ground in an archaeological dig. *Moonshine* (2011), *Coba* (2011), and *Cutter's Folly* (2012), exhibit an alchemy of time, material attrition, and mineral sedimentation adorned, on occasion, with Lascaux-like handprints and human stains. Heikes could well be engaged in an authentic and critical endeavor to advance the transformative potential of painting.

The second group of transformative objects shares the haptic quality and modest, anti-monumental scale of the "tools." They are not tools, however, but conduits. Composed of detritus, pieces of fabric, and wood, the description of these sculptures matches that of medicine bundles or folk fetishes. If anything, they recall the dense little sculptures of the legendary and still anonymous folk legend Philadelphia Wireman. Heikes's *Anti Magic, Charm, Dreggs*, and *Self Portrait with Frostbite* (all 2013), have the appearance of sacred ceremonial or medicinal items, arbiters of protective powers and condensed shamanistic energy. These objects suggest the cathartic, if not magical, power to cure and the occult faculty to heal.

The question, in consideration of Heikes's still-developing practice, is to assess the finality of this healing process, and whether or not Heikes is a charlatan, a showman, or a genuine shaman. None of these categories would actually shield him from the status of artist. In fact, he would join a family of artists, including Alighiero e Boetti, Joseph Beuys, and Andy Warhol, for whom being a shaman and a showman was integral to their aesthetic programs. With *So There's This Pirate . . .* , *New Heaven Hook*, and Roadgear, Heikes removed the showman from the equation. As constructed as it might be, the arc of his work toward transformative objects aims, ambitiously and genuinely, at the transformative power of art, the ability of art to change itself, and the expectation of art to be an agent of change. A simple belief and a tall order, often ridiculed as romantic and naive.

Between 2008 and 2010, Heikes produced a group of uncanny photographs, Civilians, that pictured in saturated, overexposed colors the figures of disheveled scarecrow characters, each made of tree branches, a hornet-nest head, a plaid shirt, and jeans. The images, moody and dark, document the "civilian" expressing human emotions or conditions: flirting, crawling, howling, screaming, haggard, severed. The Civilian series is about humanity, or the loss of humanity, about violence and war.[3] The hornet's nest, a model of social organization as well as a colloquial phrase describing the anger stirred up by a troublesome situation, suggests civic unrest or despair. A discrete group of images, the Civilians crystallize Heikes's aesthetic program and his motivation for attempting to create a singular visual language that restores humanity to art, far from postmodern irony. In his most recent book, *What Comes After Farce*, art critic and historian Hal Foster contemplates arts, culture, and media from the post-9/11 era to the present Trump era. In the chapter "Machine Images," he considers "a culture in which the vast majority of images are produced by machines for other machines, with humans left out of the loop."[4] These images, rendered from a conjunction of surveillance technology and algorithmic inscriptions, are no longer a spectacle projected at us, a representation. Rather, they intervene on us, impose order upon us, the civilians, through the tragic manipulation of visual language.

Foster's words strangely echo one of Heikes's favorite short stories, Roald Dahl's "The Great Automatic Grammatizator," in which the author narrates the invention of a machine, pre-algorithms, that has the capacity to produce literary masterpieces by rationalizing and systemizing grammar, syntax, style, and literary genre through mathematical and mechanical principles.[5] The ultimate consequence of this commercially motivated endeavor is the sad removal of humanity from any creative and transformational process. Heikes goes the other way. His own aesthetic revolution and machinery, his embrace of language, his endless desire to experiment, to bring back the hand, all rage against the machine. He is "the great aesthetizator" and "gaucher boiteux," who still believes that art can, if not change the world, at least bring music to our minor planet one civilian at a time.

1. Michel Serres, *Le gaucher boiteux: Puissance de la pensée* (Paris: Éditions Le Pommier, 2015).
2. After graduating from the Yale School of Art in 2005, Heikes relocated to Minneapolis, having decided to work away from art world centers.
3. Heikes notes that the Civilian series was made in consideration of all the civilian victims of the Iraq war. Conversation with the author, July 30, 2020.
4. Hal Foster, *What Comes After Farce: Art and Criticism at a Time of Debacle* (London: Verso, 2020).
5. Roald Dahl, *The Great Automatic Grammatizator and Other Stories* (London: Puffin Books, 2001).

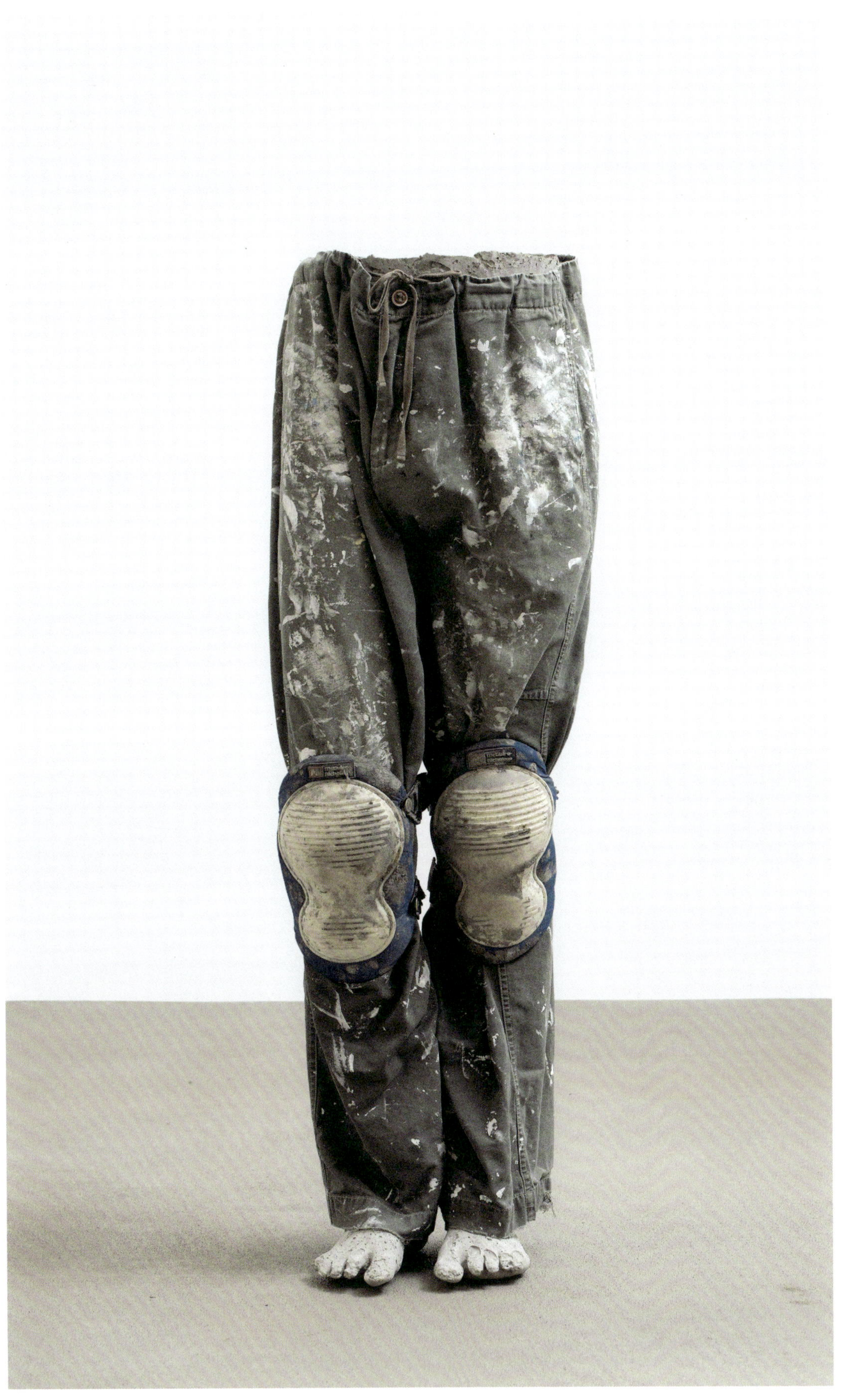

Our Frankenstein, 2015 (bottom)
Concrete, steel, plastic, fiberglass, cotton, and oil paint, 43 ¼ × 13 × 9 ½ inches, 110 × 33 × 24 cm

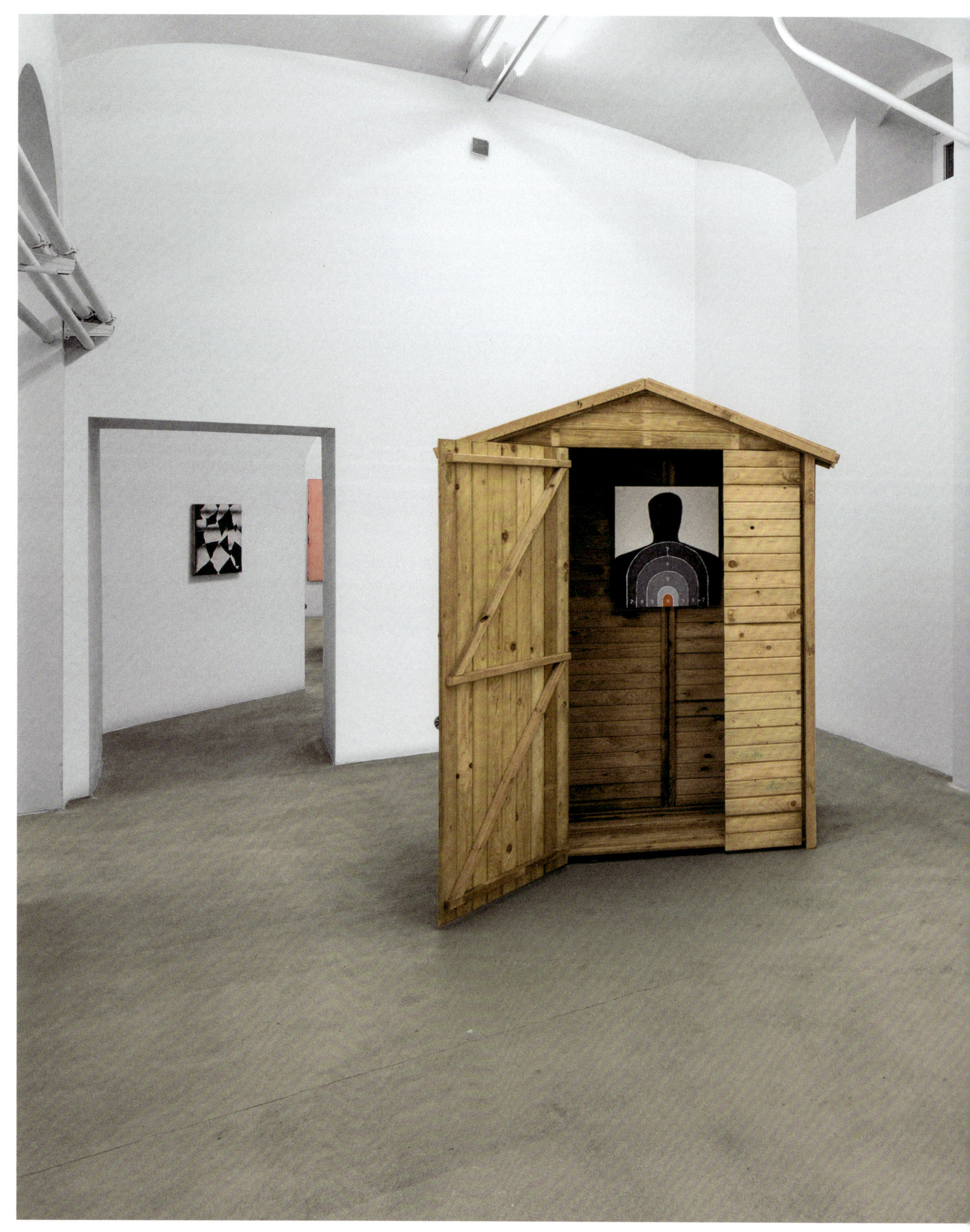

Installation view:
Consequences, Fondazione Giuliani, Rome, 2015

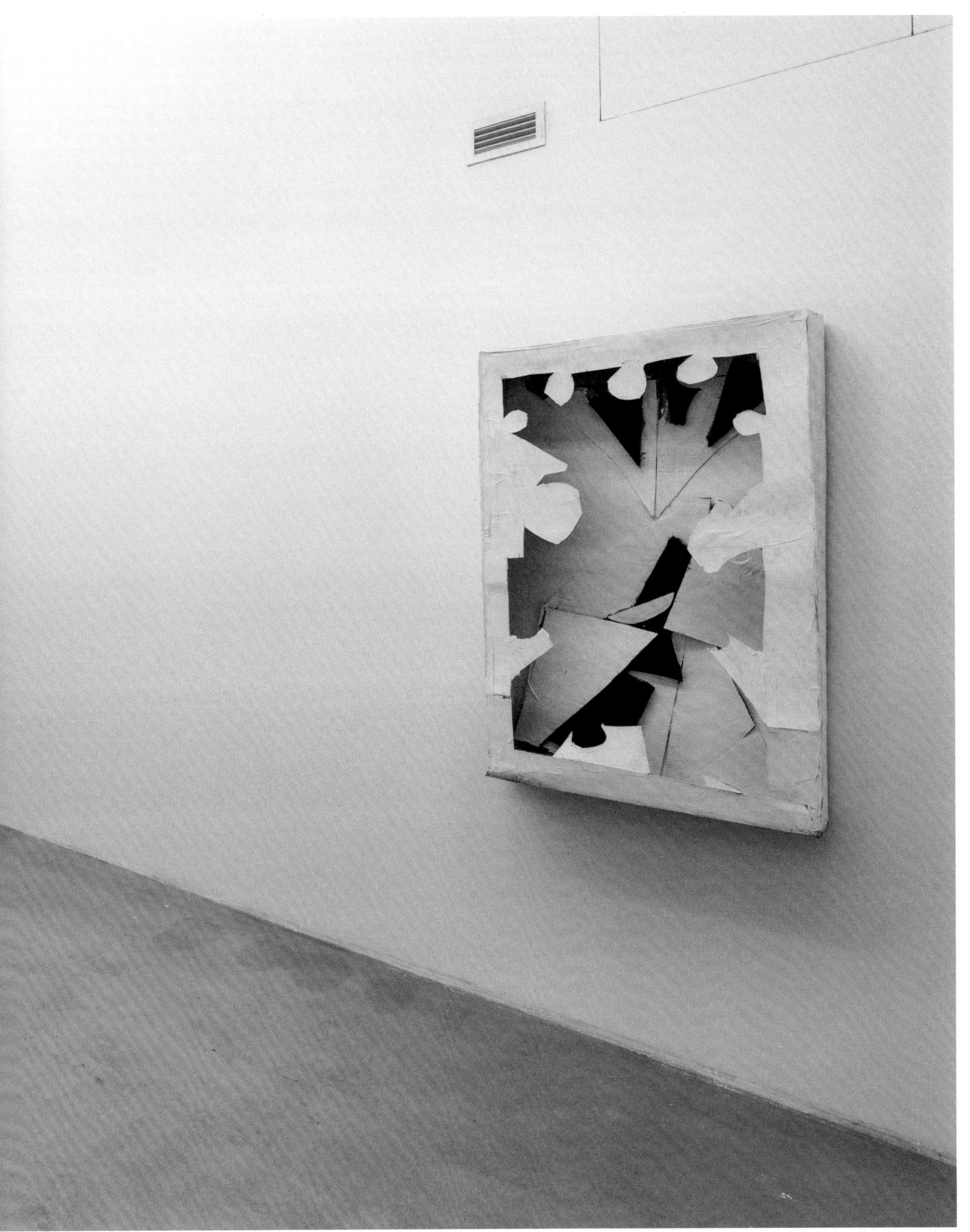

Left to right:
Conny Purtill, *The Ground: Carl the Eagle*, 2009; Jay Heikes, Todd Norsten, and Conny Purtill, *Ufficio*, 2015
(with painting by Todd Norsten, *1962*, 2015); Gedi Sibony, *Fountain Feet*, 2015

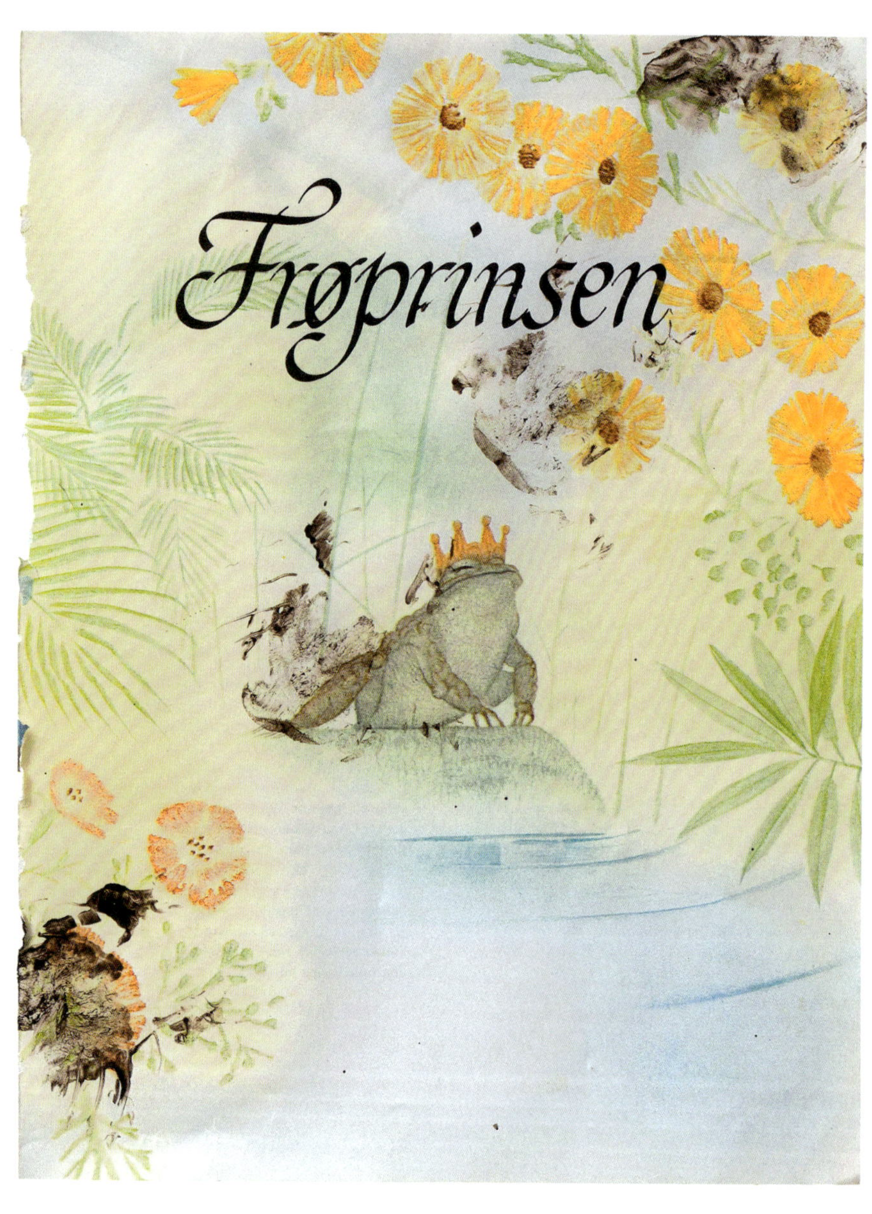

Jay Heikes and Michael Stickrod, *Frog Prints*, 2008
Water-based ink on children's book page, 15 ¾ × 12 ⅝ inches, 40 × 32 cm

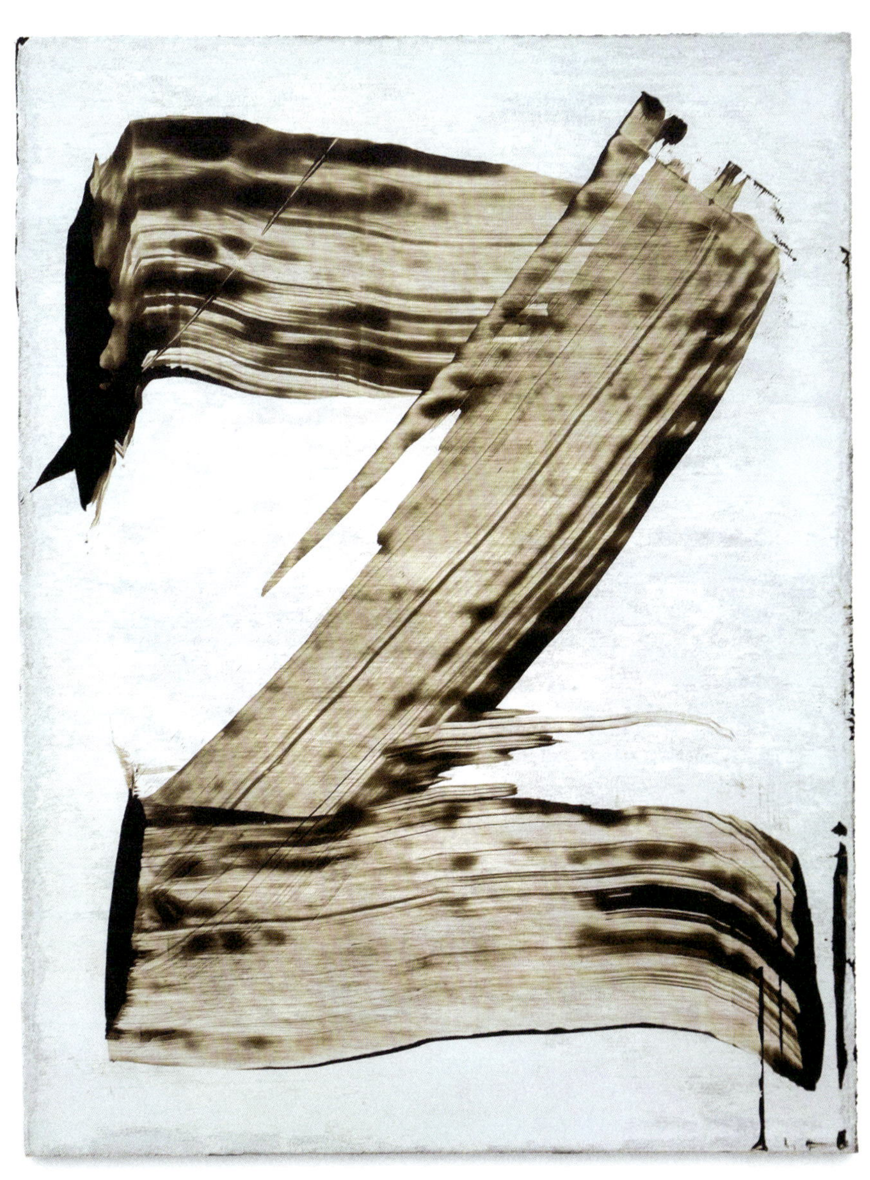

Jay Heikes and Conny Purtill, *Z*, 2015
Asphaltum, gesso, india ink, and pencil on canvas, 22 × 16 ⅞ inches, 56 × 43 cm

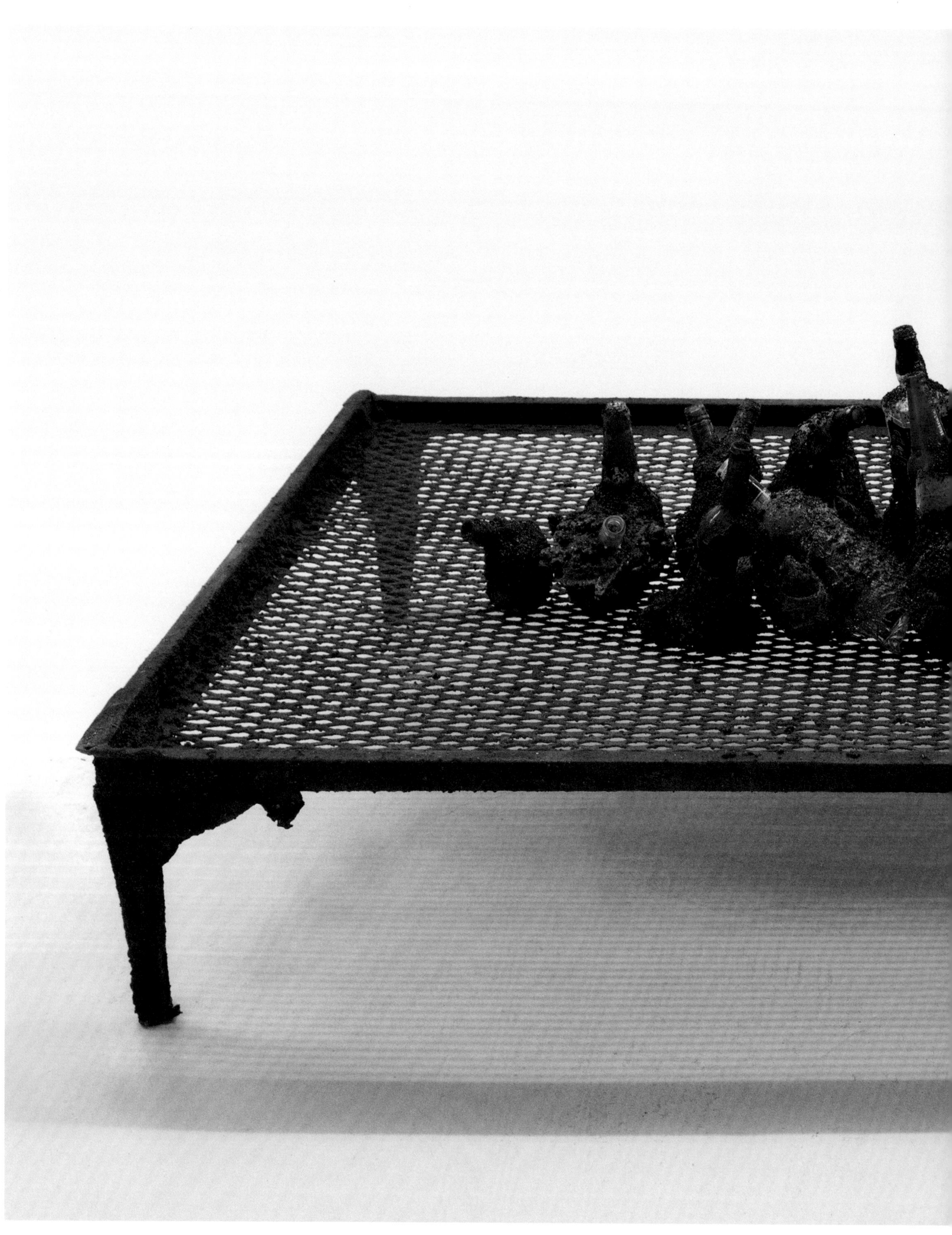

Artist's Artist, 2015
Wood, glass beer and liquor bottles, steel slag, sand, paper, burlap, and expanded aluminum, 14 × 78 × 44 inches, 35.6 × 198 × 111.8 cm

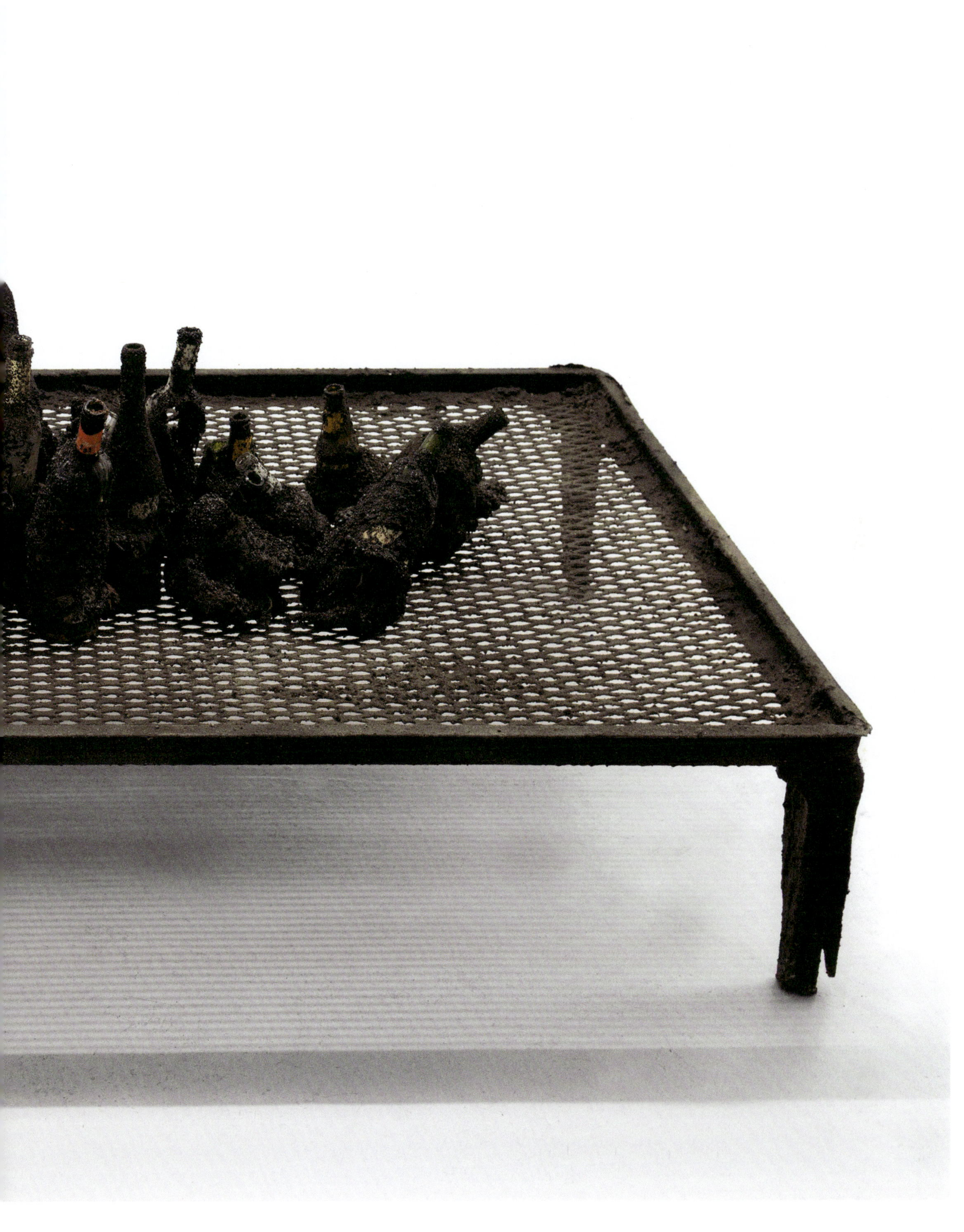

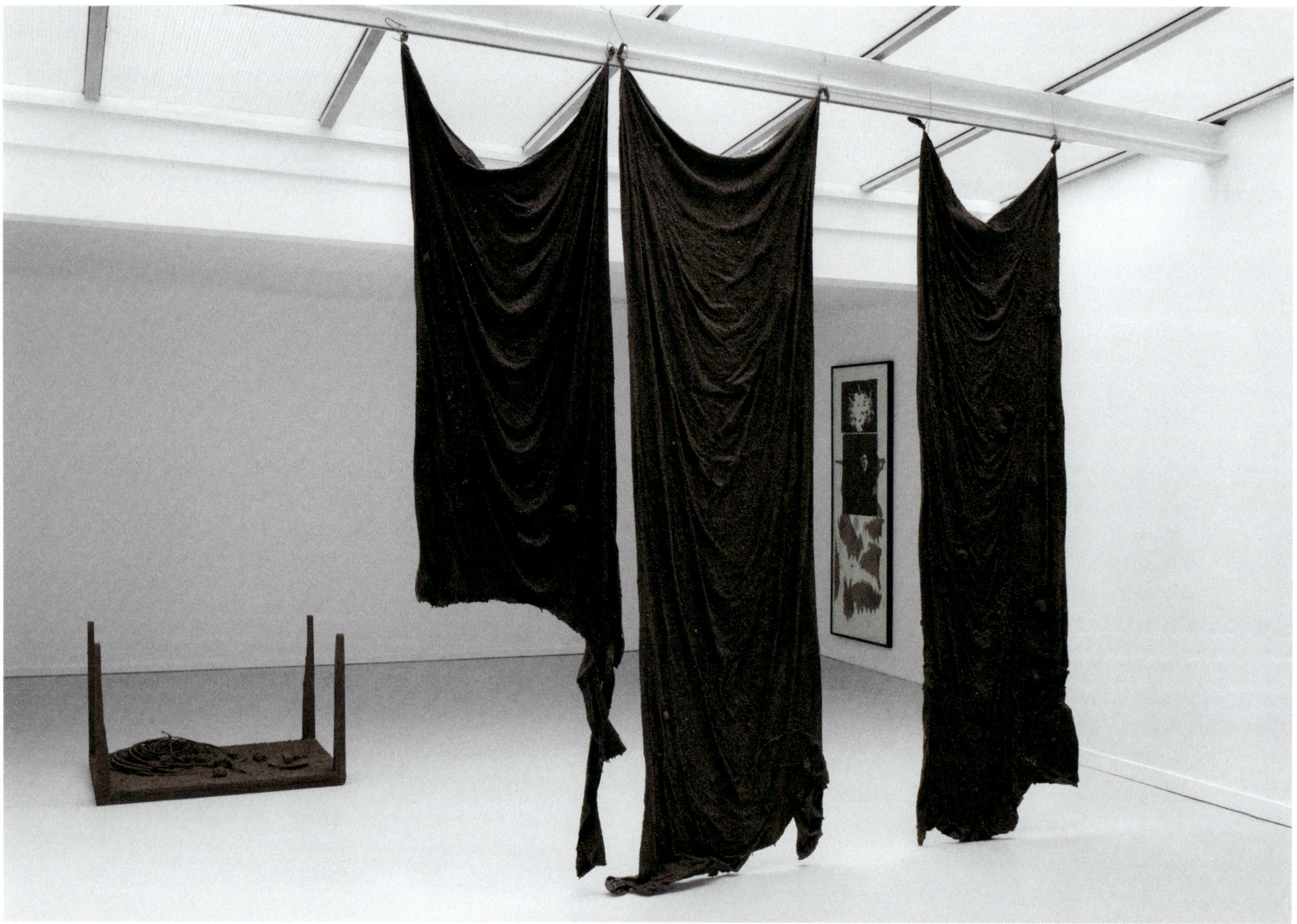

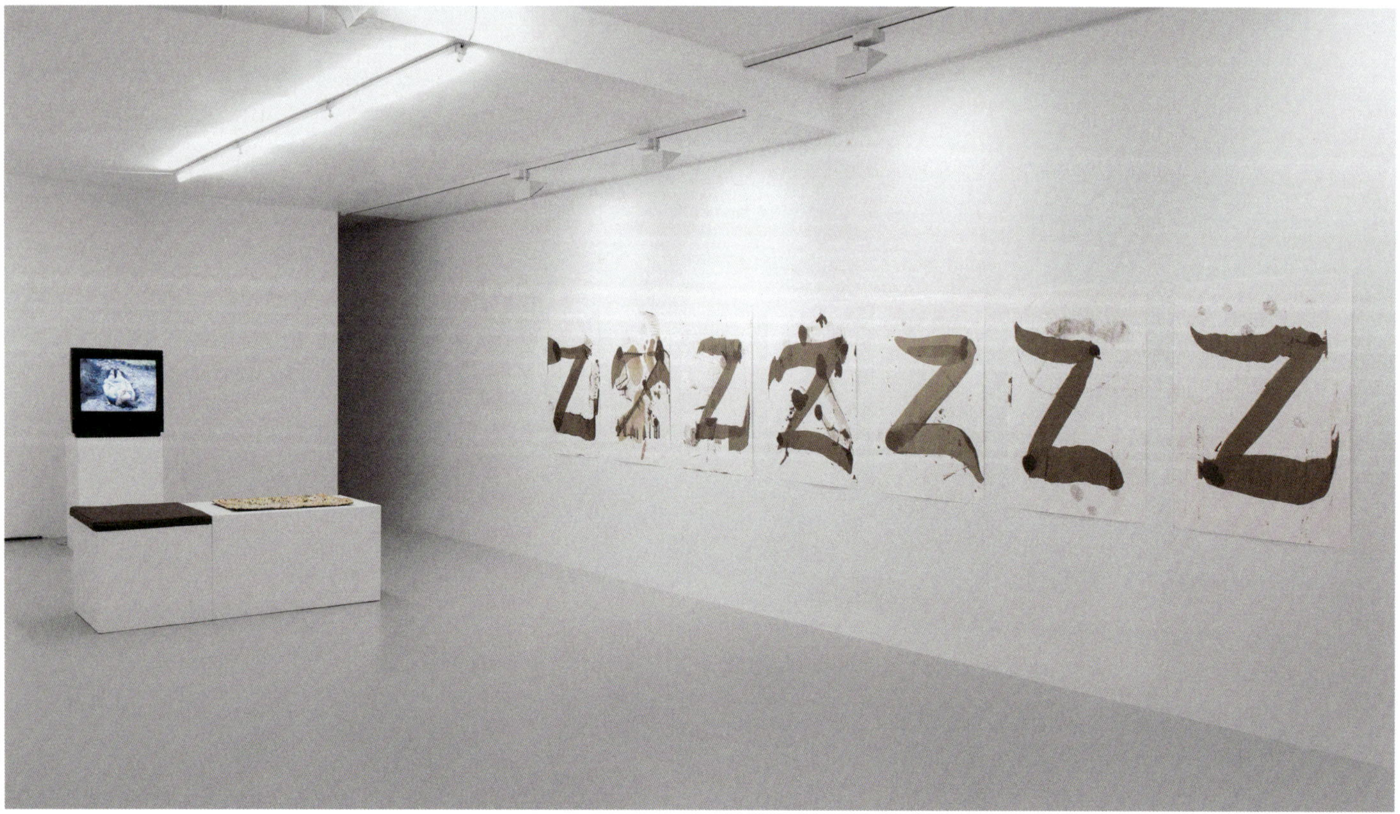

Installation views:

Necrophiliac, Grimm Gallery, Amsterdam, 2016

Top, left to right: *Appetite for Destruction*, 2015; *Nostalgia*, 2015; *Niet voor Kinderen*, 2015

Bottom, left to right: *Daily Rituals (Newday)*, 2015; *Welkom*, 2015; *Zs*, 2015

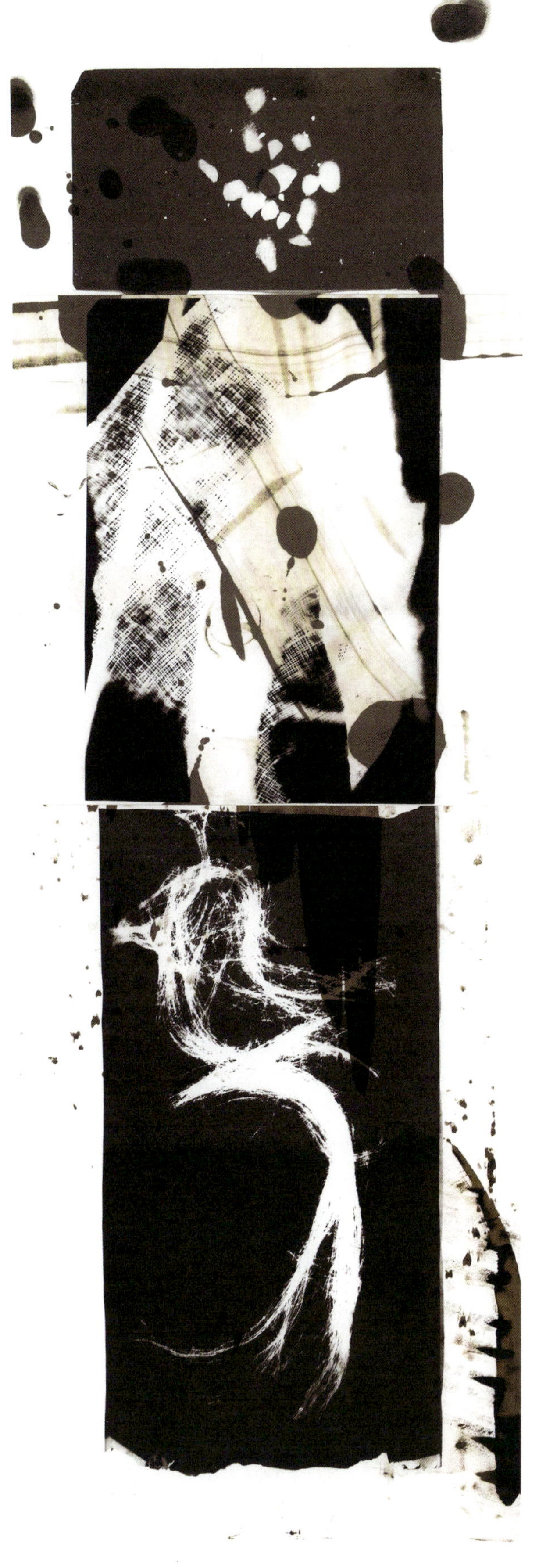

Niet voor Kinderen, 2015
Asphaltum on paper, 86 ⅜ × 27 inches, 219.4 × 68.6 cm

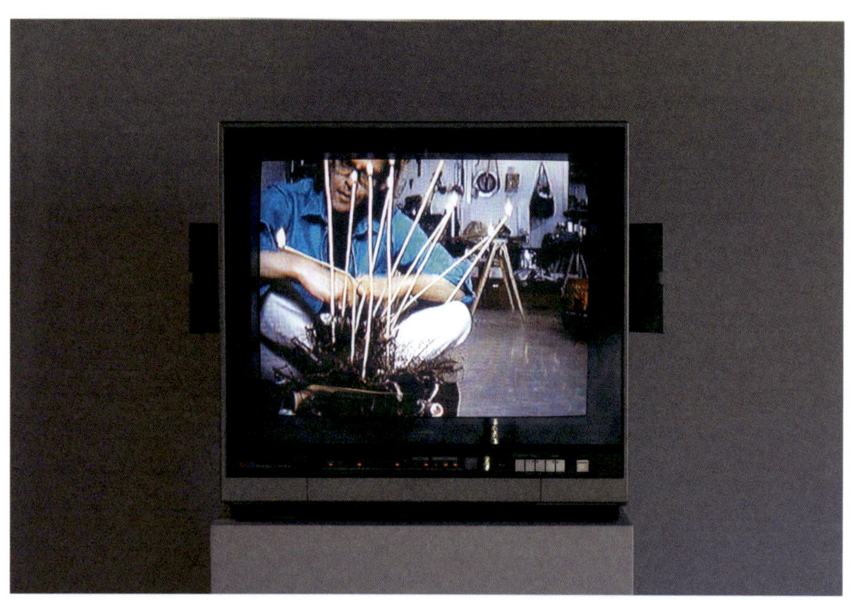

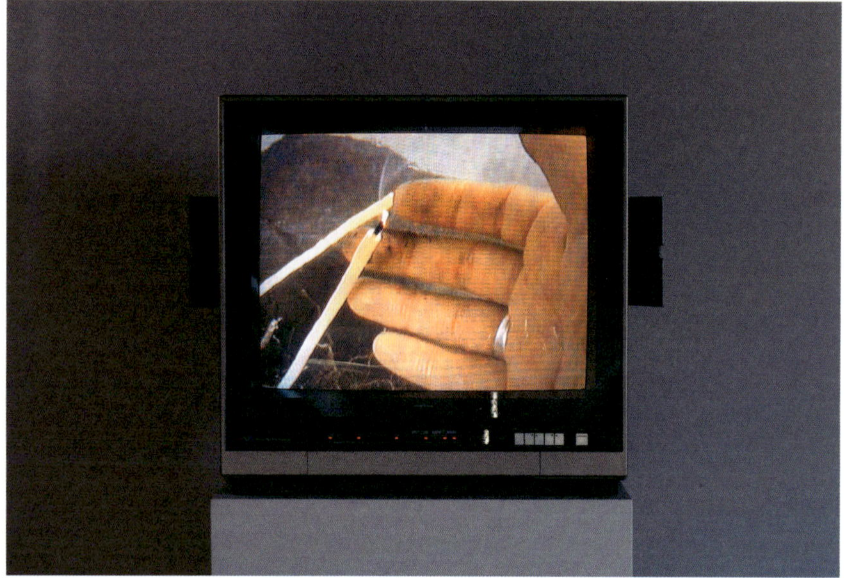

Top and bottom:

Daily Rituals (Tuesday), 2014

Digital video transferred to DVD, color, sound, 39:41 minutes

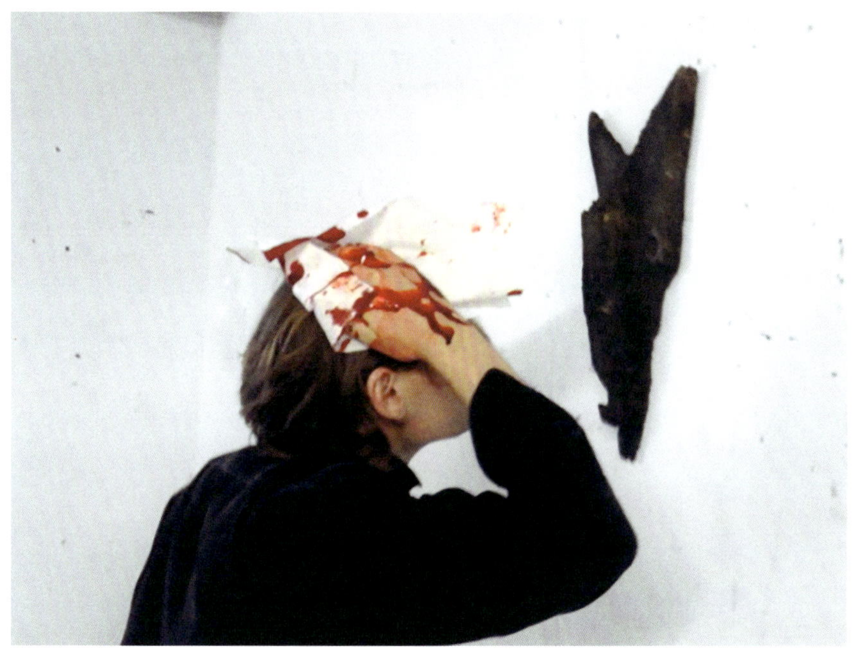

Daily Rituals (Friday), 2014 (still)
Digital video transferred to DVD, color, sound, 36:12 minutes

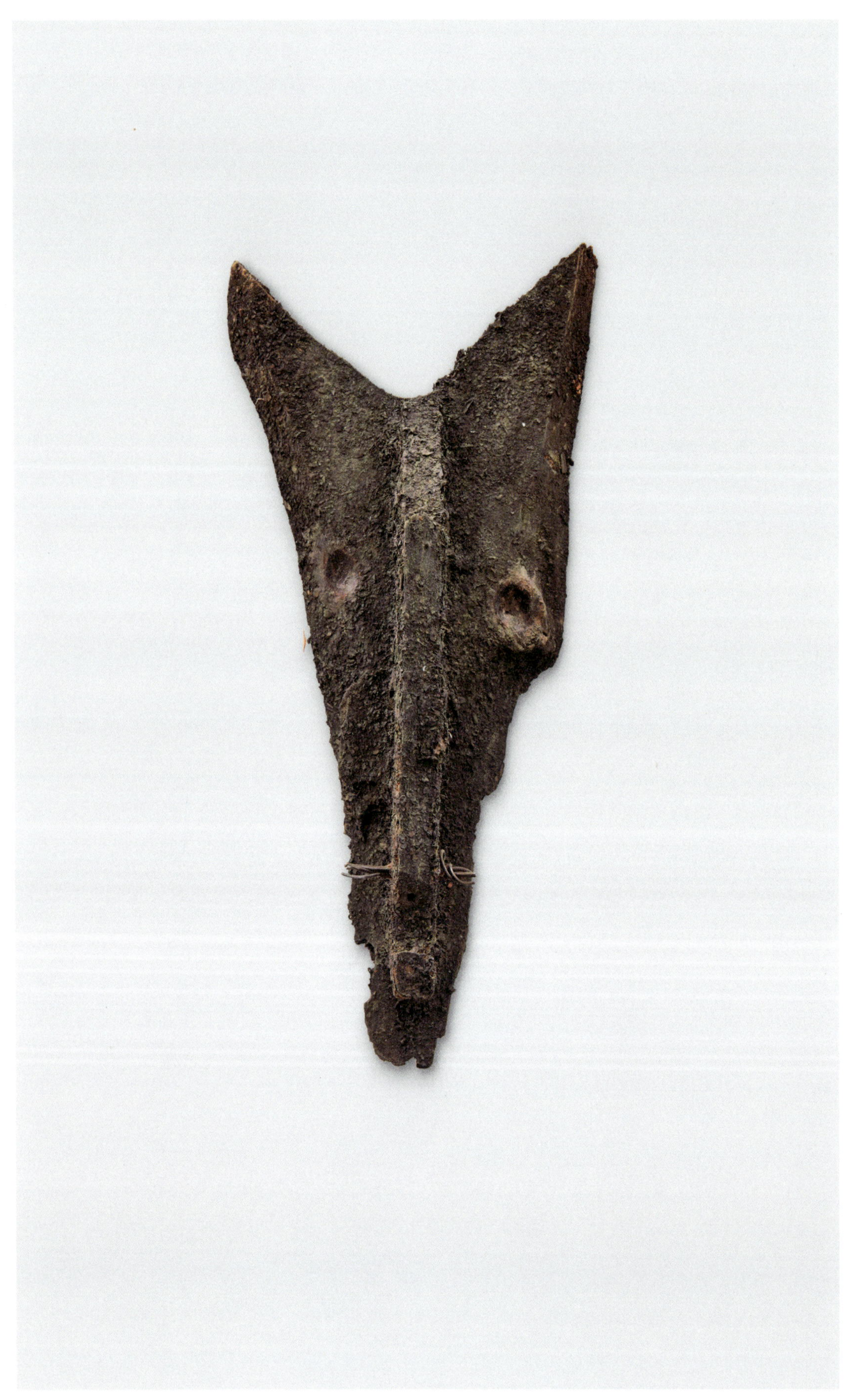

Dog, 2016

148   Wood, wax, iron wire, wood chips, sand, wood glue, studio dust, and pigment, 19½ × 9 × 4 inches, 49.5 × 22.9 × 10.2 cm

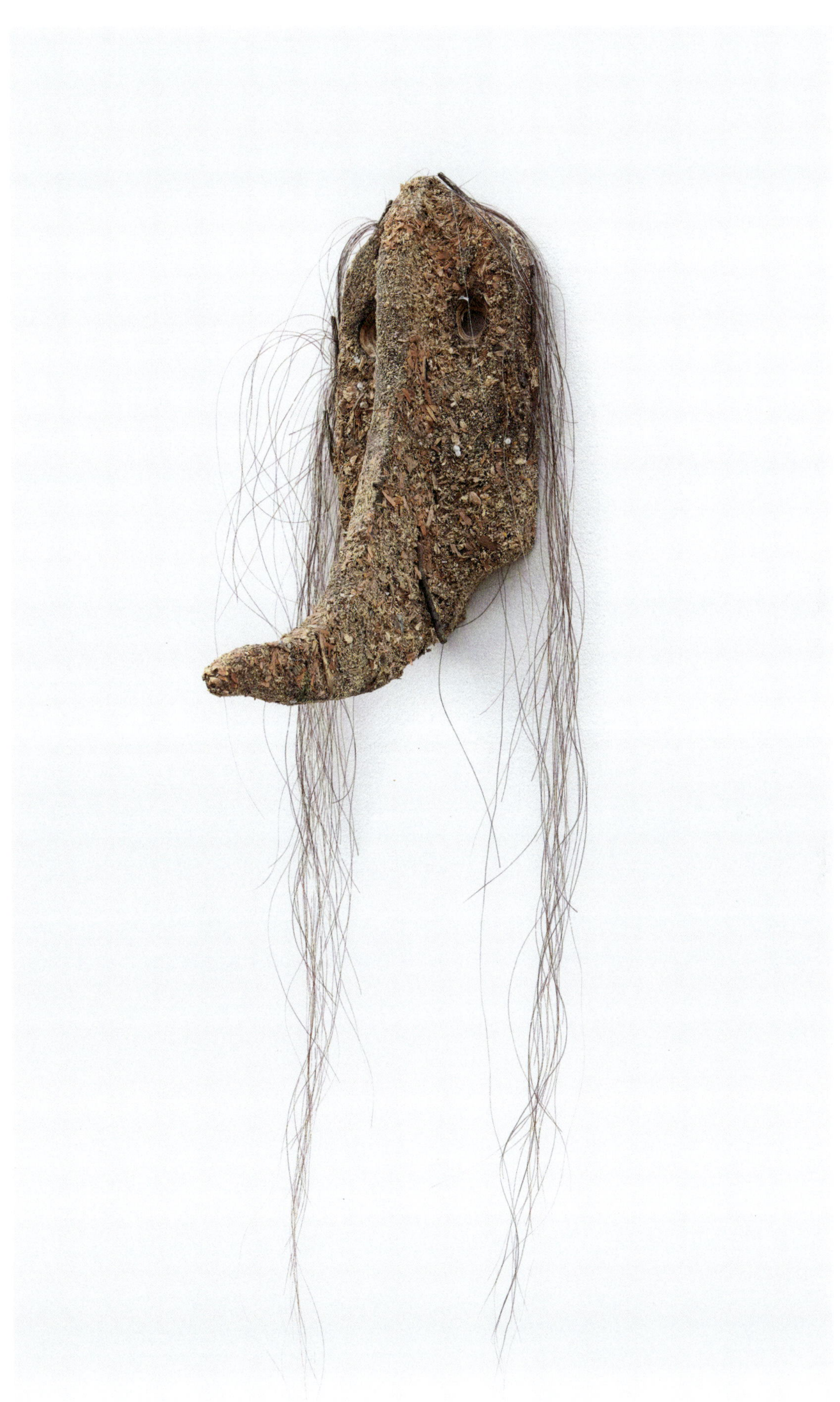

Elephant, 2016
Wood, horsehair, wood glue, iron, studio dust, and steel, 36 × 10 × 12 inches, 91.4 × 25.4 × 30.5 cm

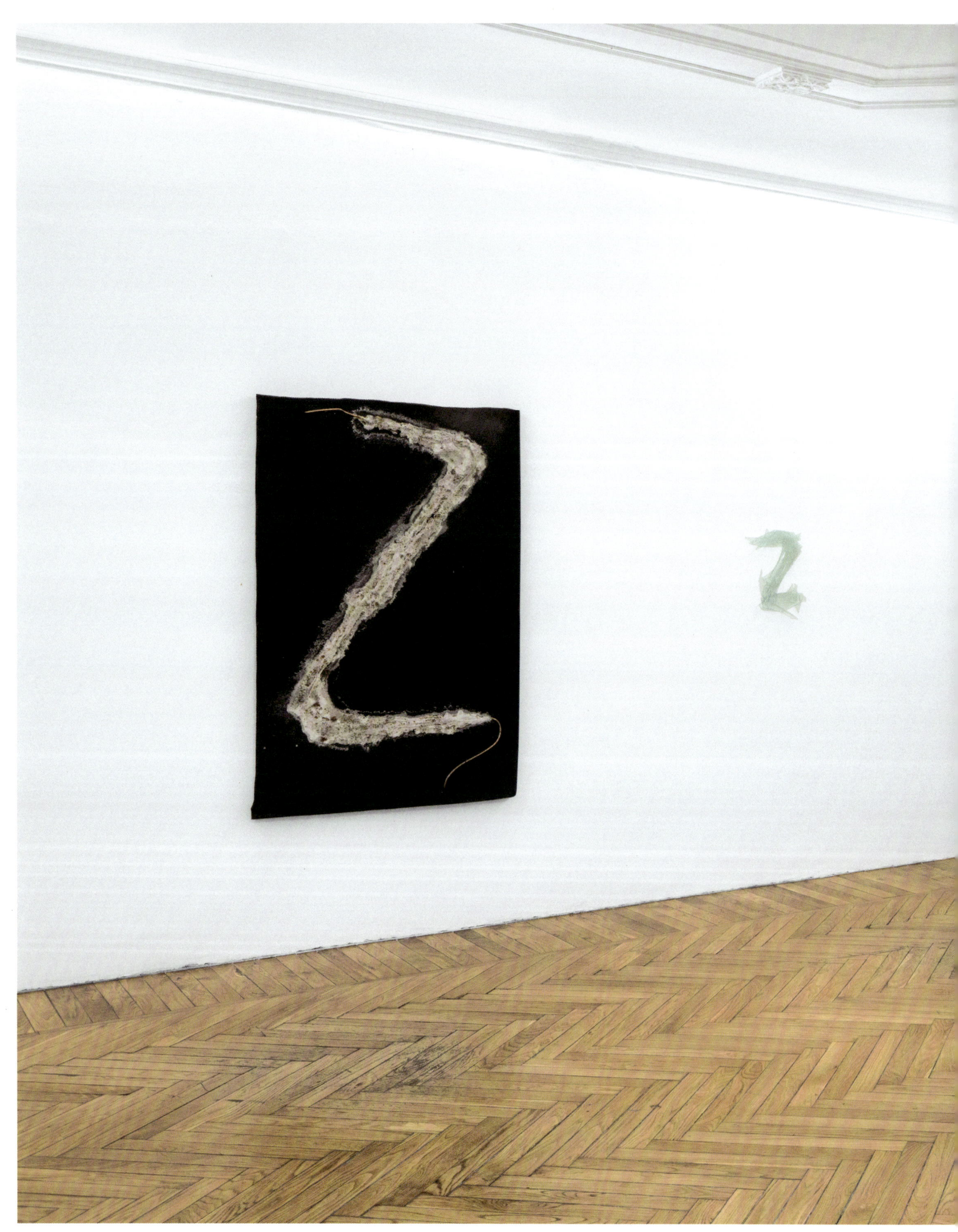

No future ism, Federica Schiavo Gallery, Milan, 2016

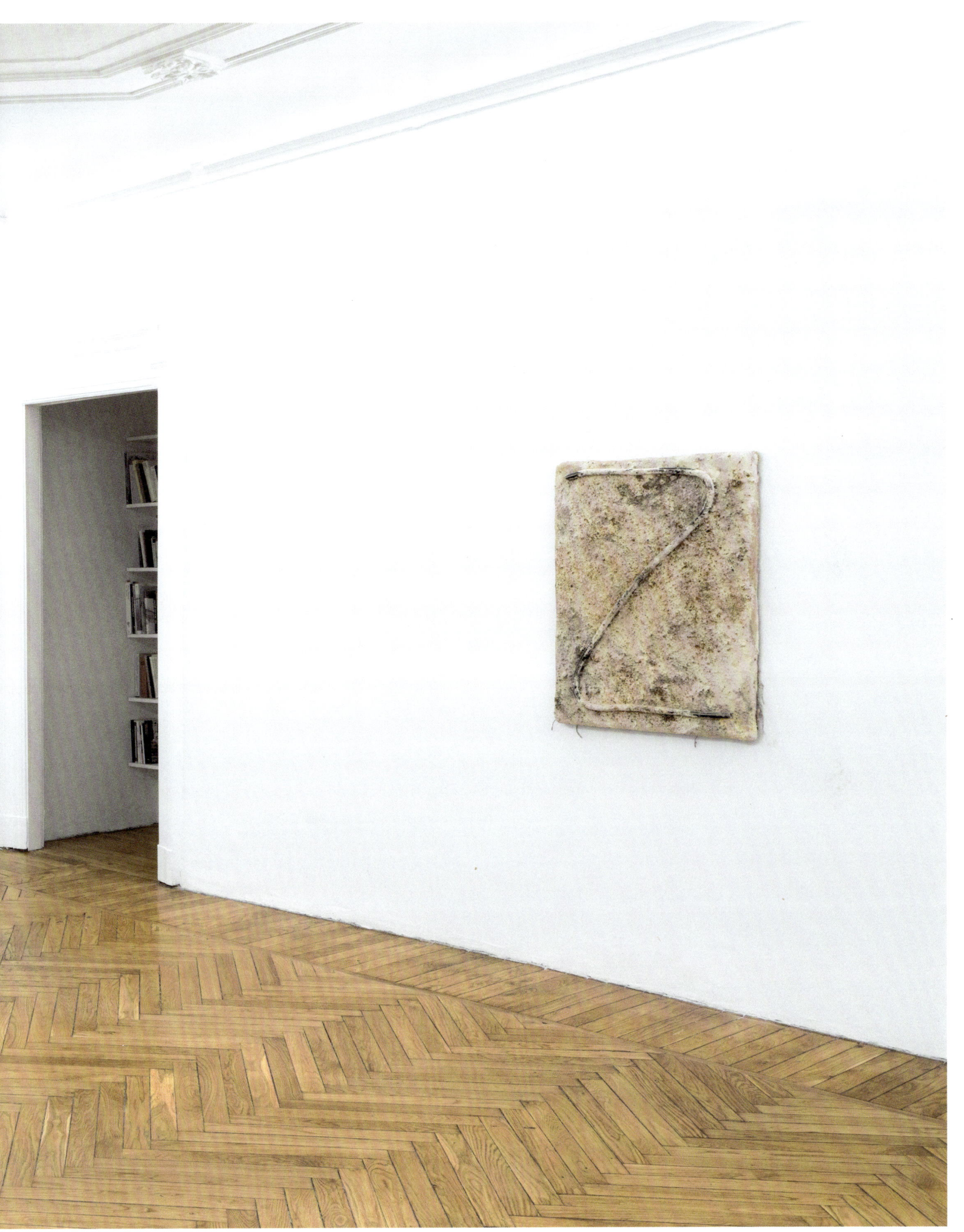

Left to right:
Zs, 2016; Zs, 2016; Beyond Zebra, 2016

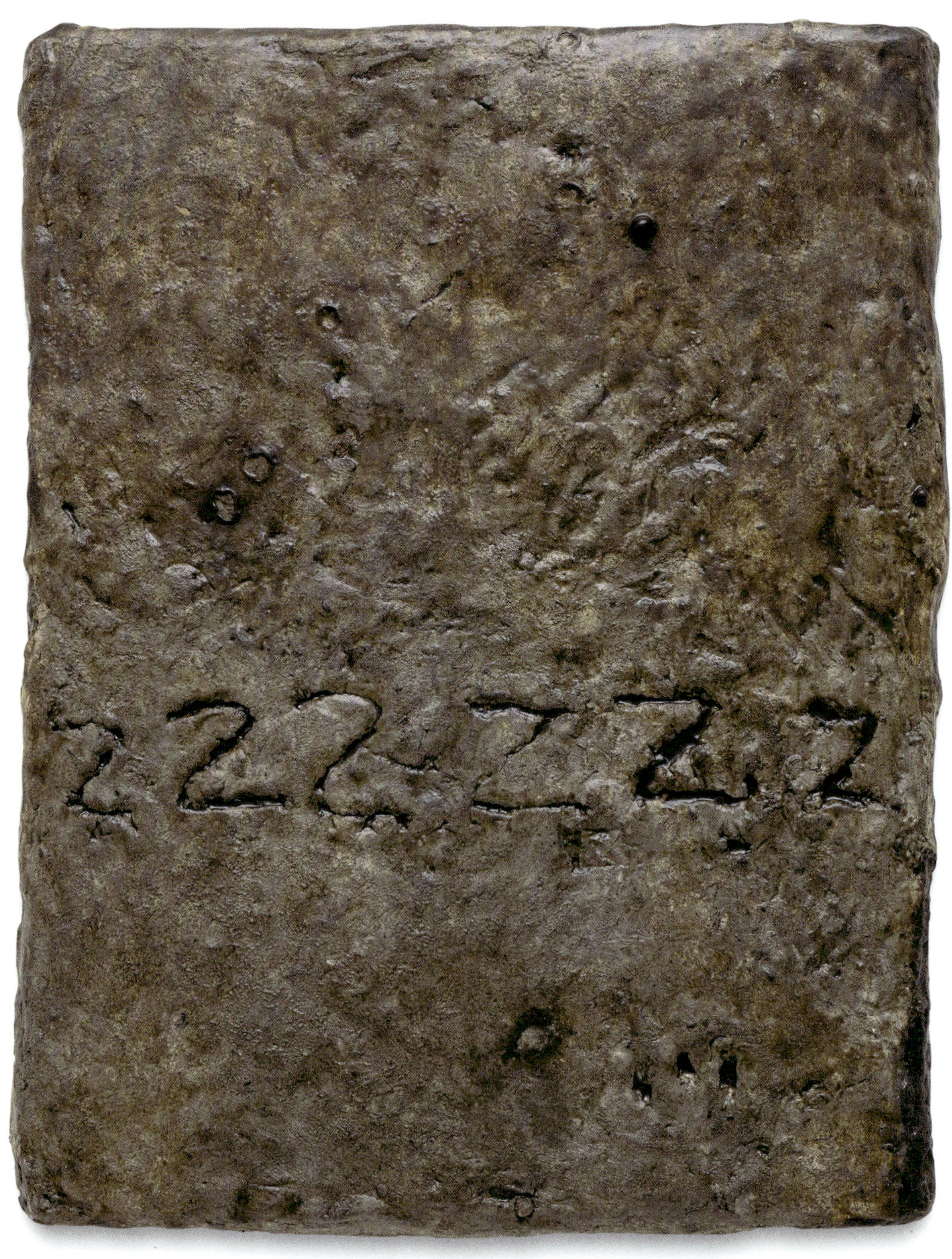

Zs, 2016

Concrete, mortar, wax, and expanded steel on wood stretcher, 36 ⅝ × 28 ¾ × 1 ⅝ inches, 93 × 73 × 4 cm

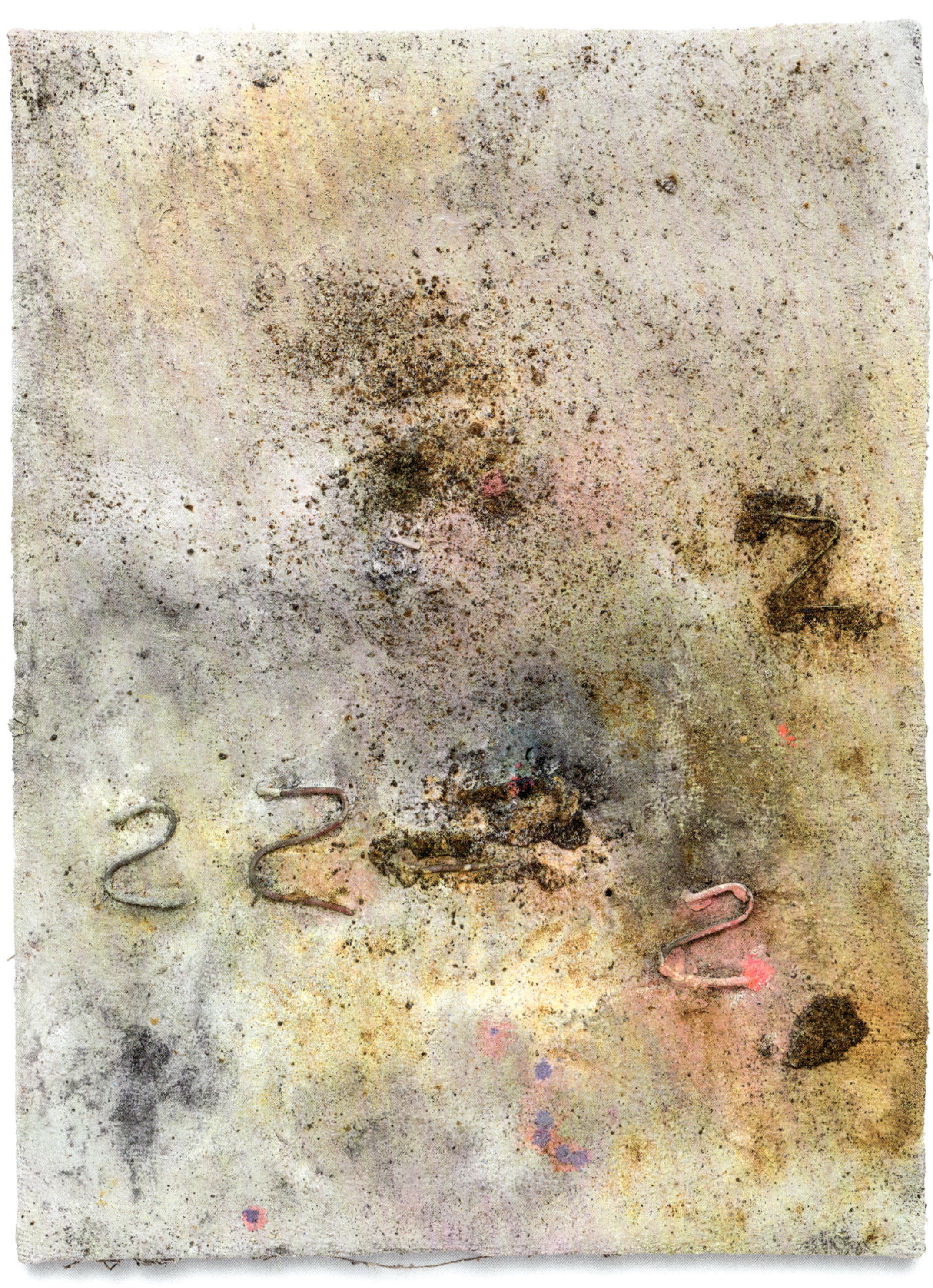

Zs, 2016
Pigmented mortar, dyed burlap, salt, steel slag, wood glue, copper wire, enamel, and expanded steel on wood stretcher,
40 ⅛ × 30 ¾ × 2 inches, 102 × 78 × 5 cm

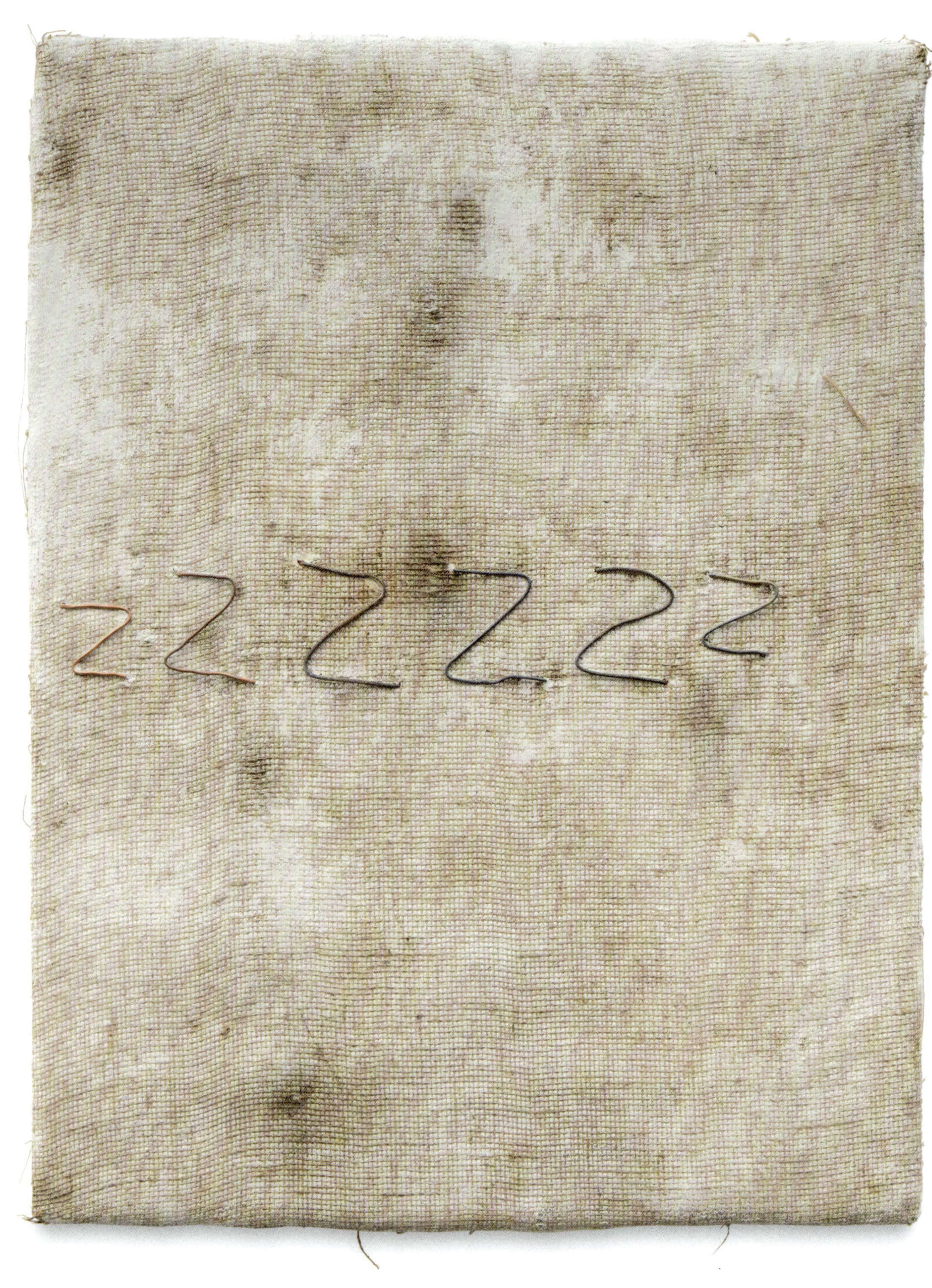

Zs, 2016

154   Burned burlap, mortar, copper wire, steel wire, and expanded aluminum on wood stretcher, 36 × 28 × 2 inches, 91.4 × 71.1 × 5.1 cm

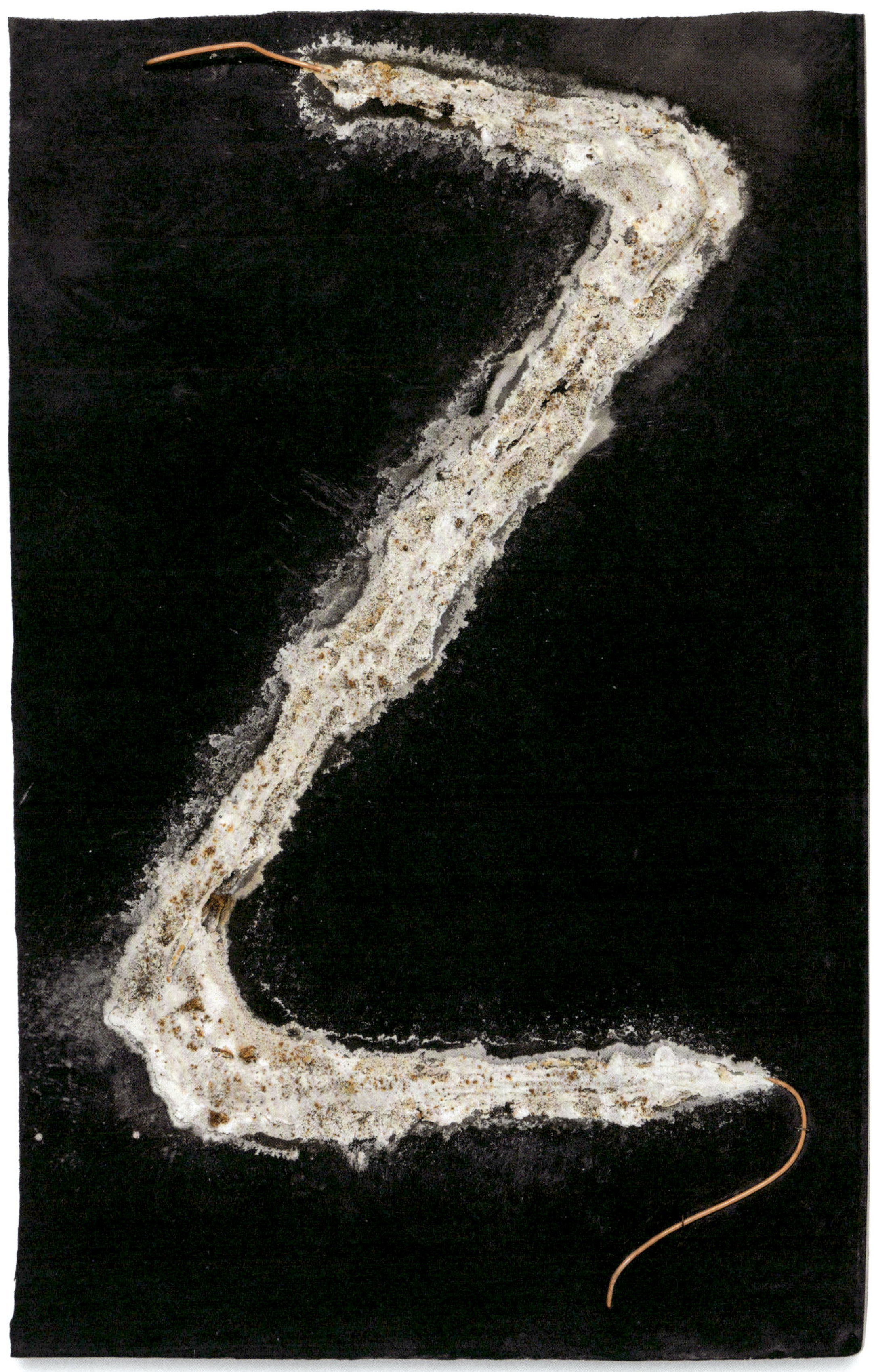

Zs, 2016

Neoprene, salt, steel slag, copper wire, and wood glue on wood stretcher, 62 ⅝ × 41 × 2 ⅜ inches, 159 × 104 × 6 cm

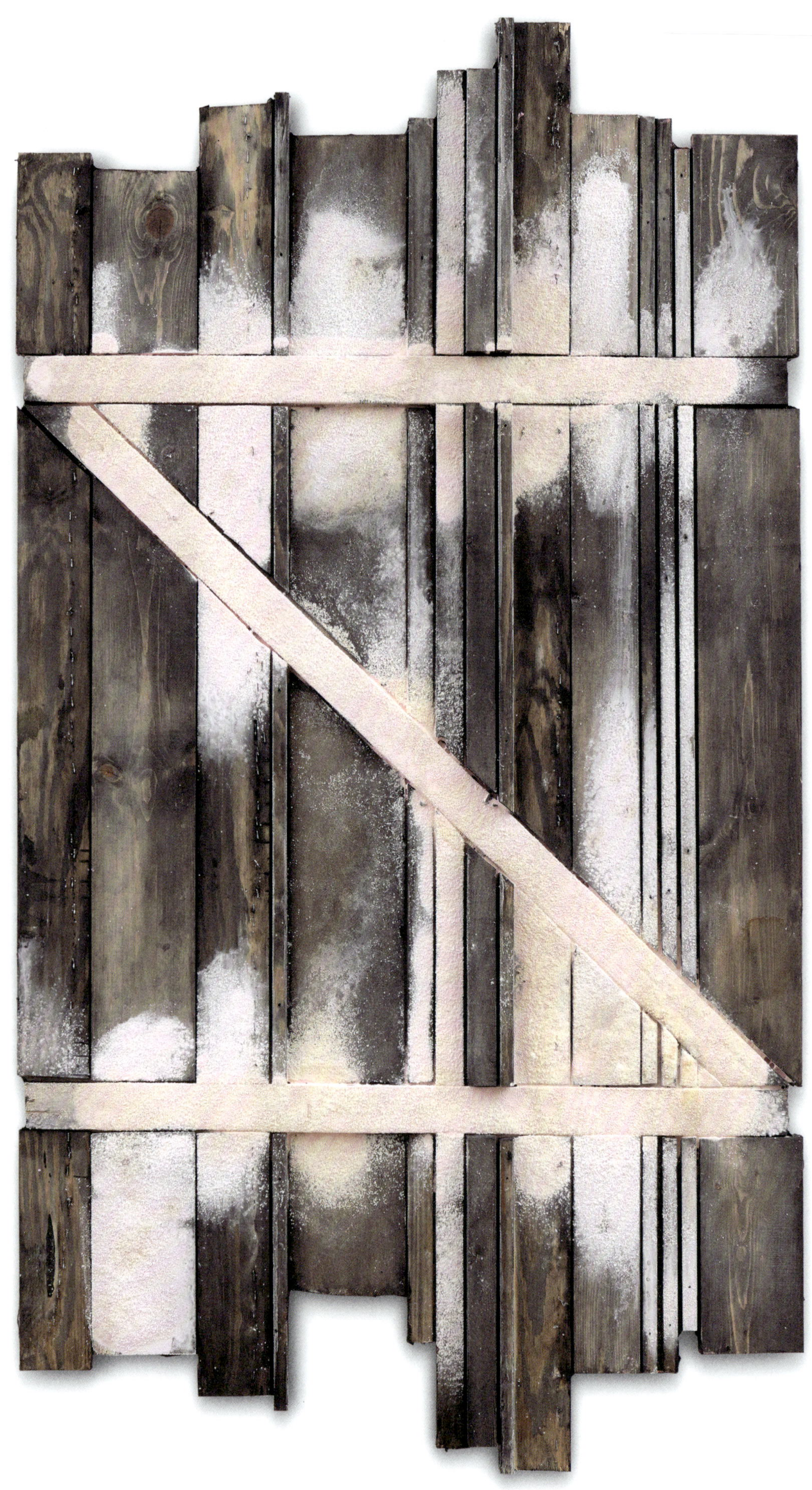

Zs, 2017

 Wood, paper, wood glue, salt, ink, coffee, acrylic paint, and staples, 70 × 44 × 3 inches, 177.8 × 111.8 × 7.6 cm

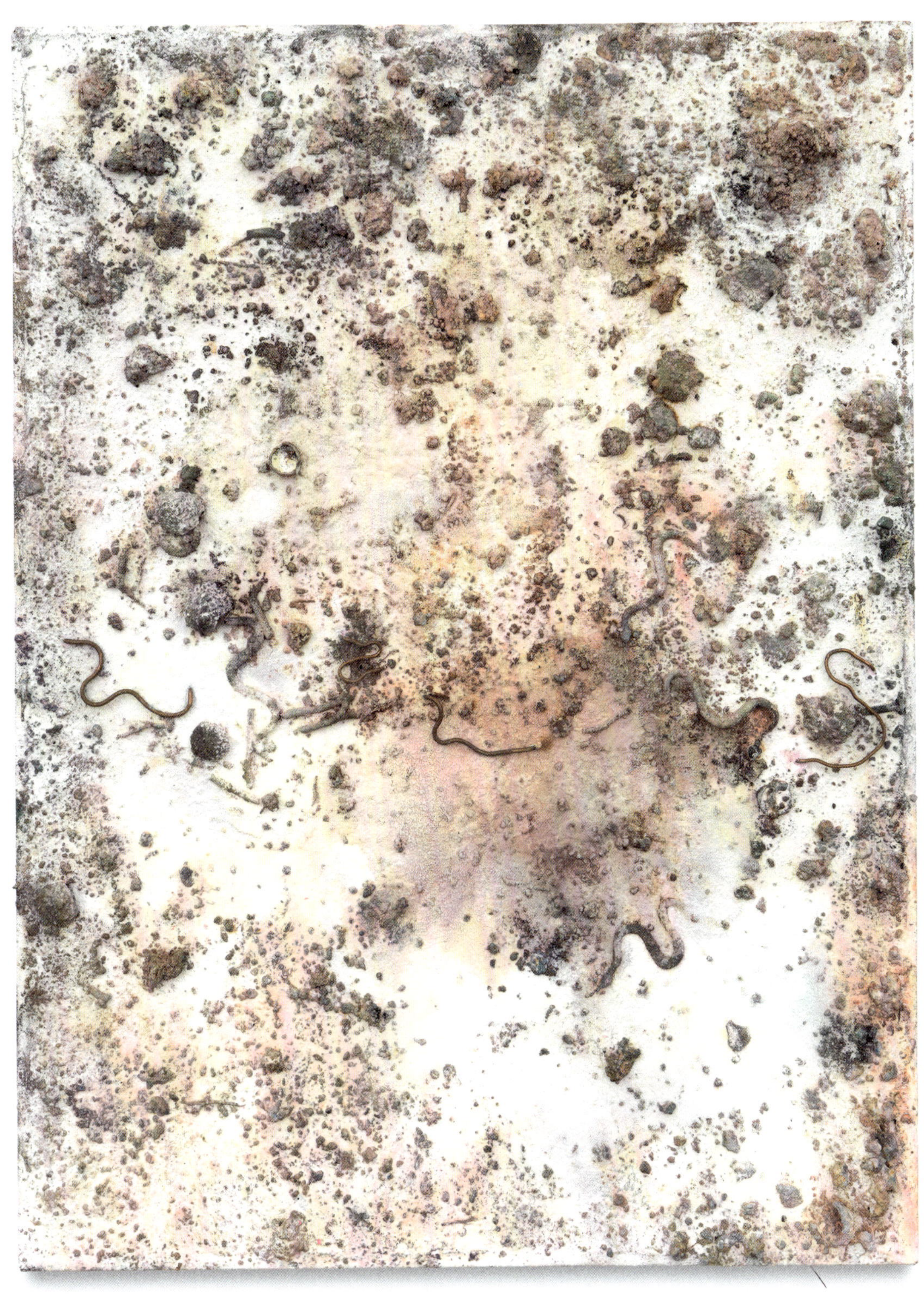

Zs, 2017

Steel slag, salt, glue, pigment, ink, fiberglass, rubber snakes, copper wire, acorn husks, rocks, and dirt on wood stretcher,
51 × 38 × 4 inches, 129.5 × 96.5 × 10.2 cm

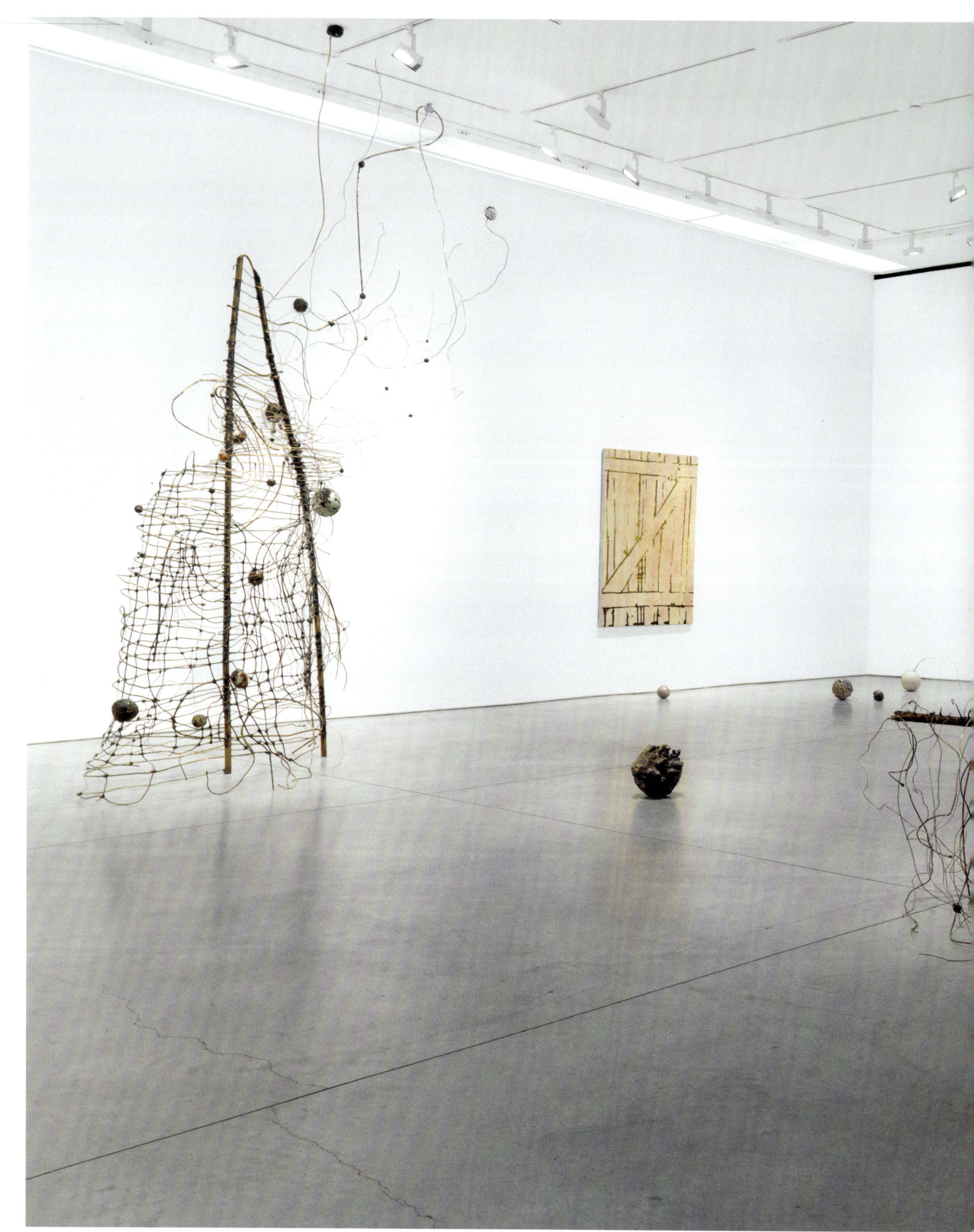

Installation view:
Keep Out, Marianne Boesky Gallery, New York, 2017

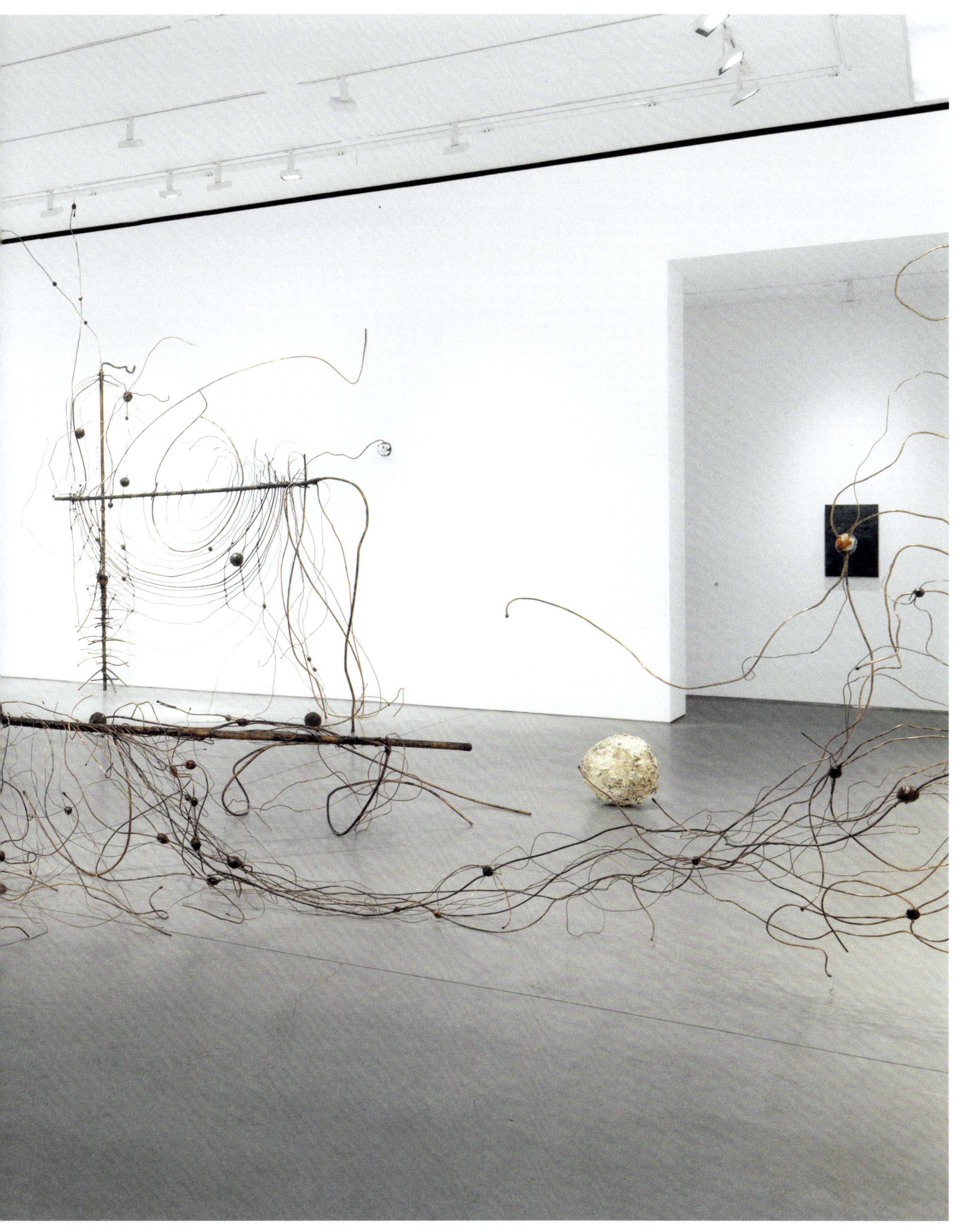

Left to right:

Death Spiral, 2017; on wall: *Zs*, 2017; *Couper l'oeil*, 2017; *Minor Planets*, 2017; *Winter is Coming*, 2017; on wall, rear: *Zs*, 2016

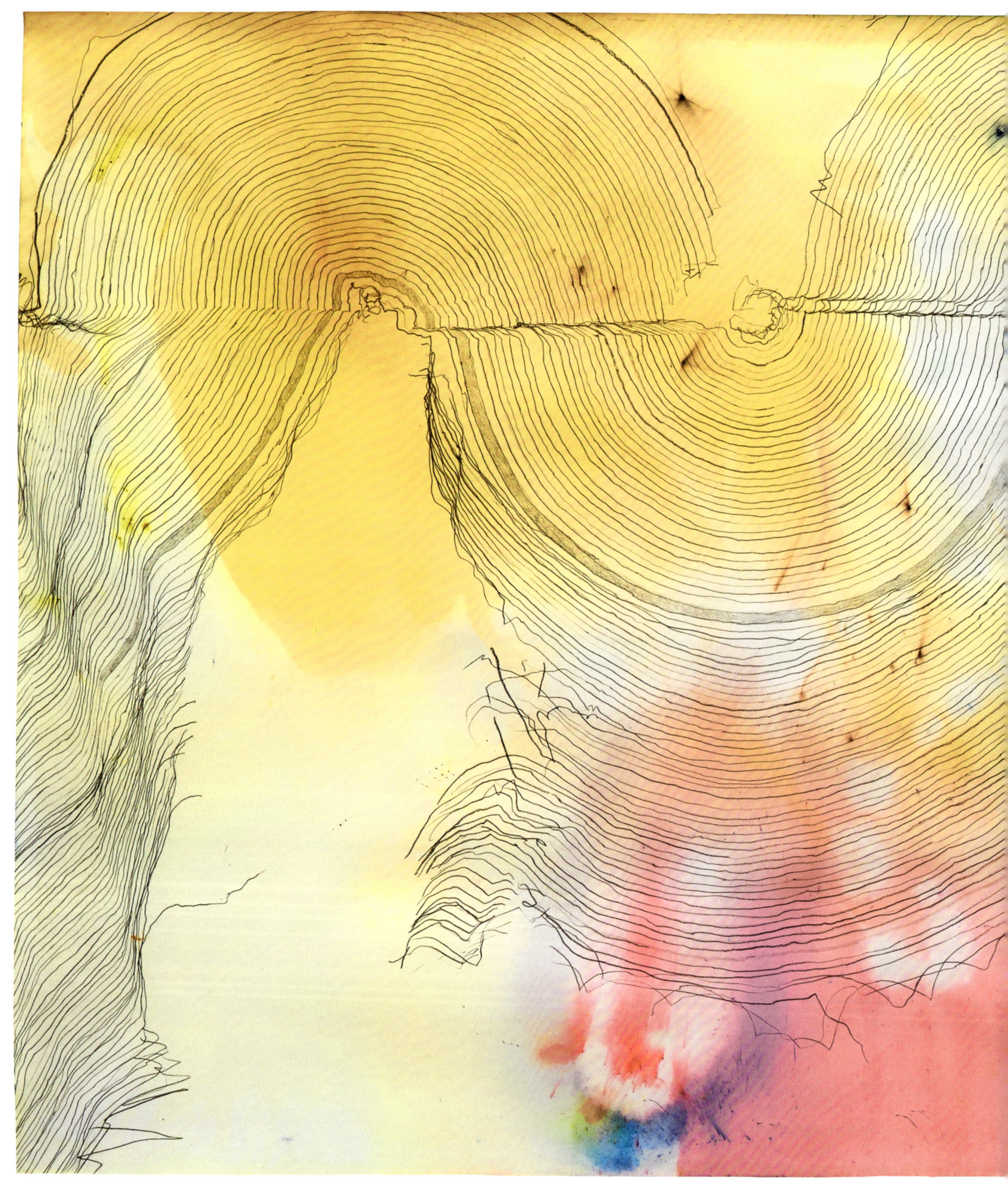

Music for Minor Planets (Oz), 2015
Graphite, coffee, and pigment on dyed and bleached paper, 50 ⅛ × 86 inches, 127.3 × 218.4 cm

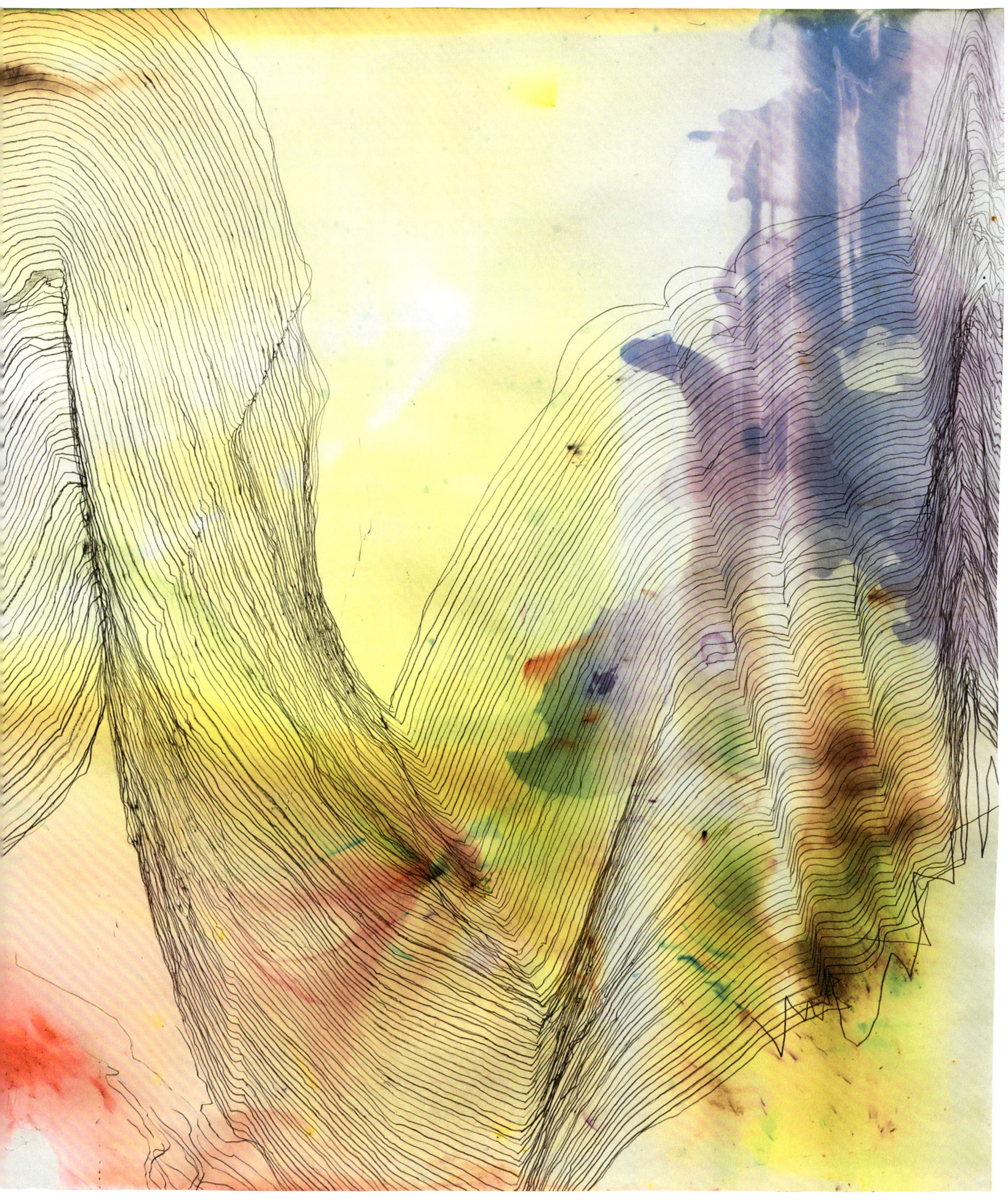

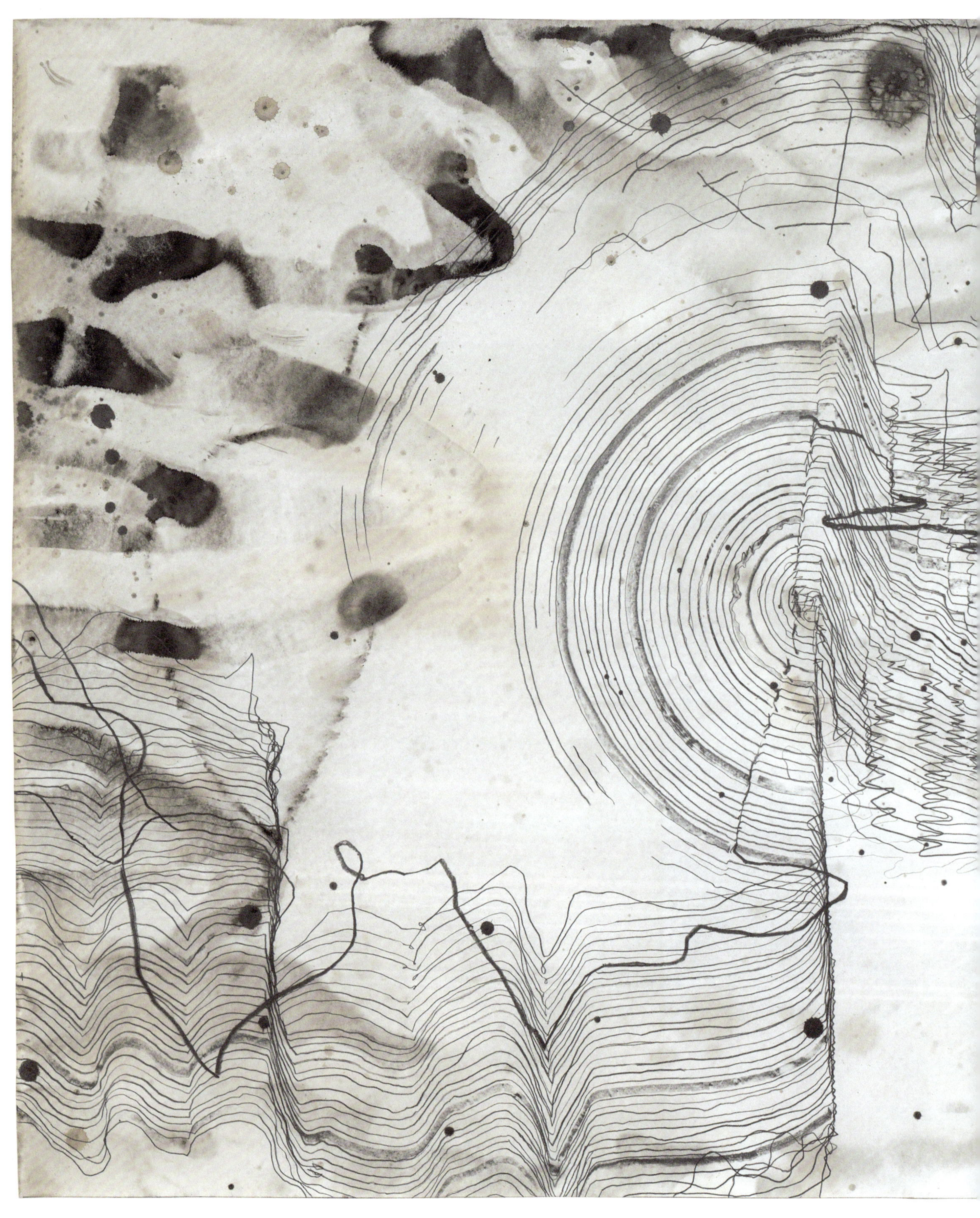

The Devil Has Left My Building, 2015
Pencil and ink on paper, 51 1/8 × 85 inches, 129.9 × 215.9 cm

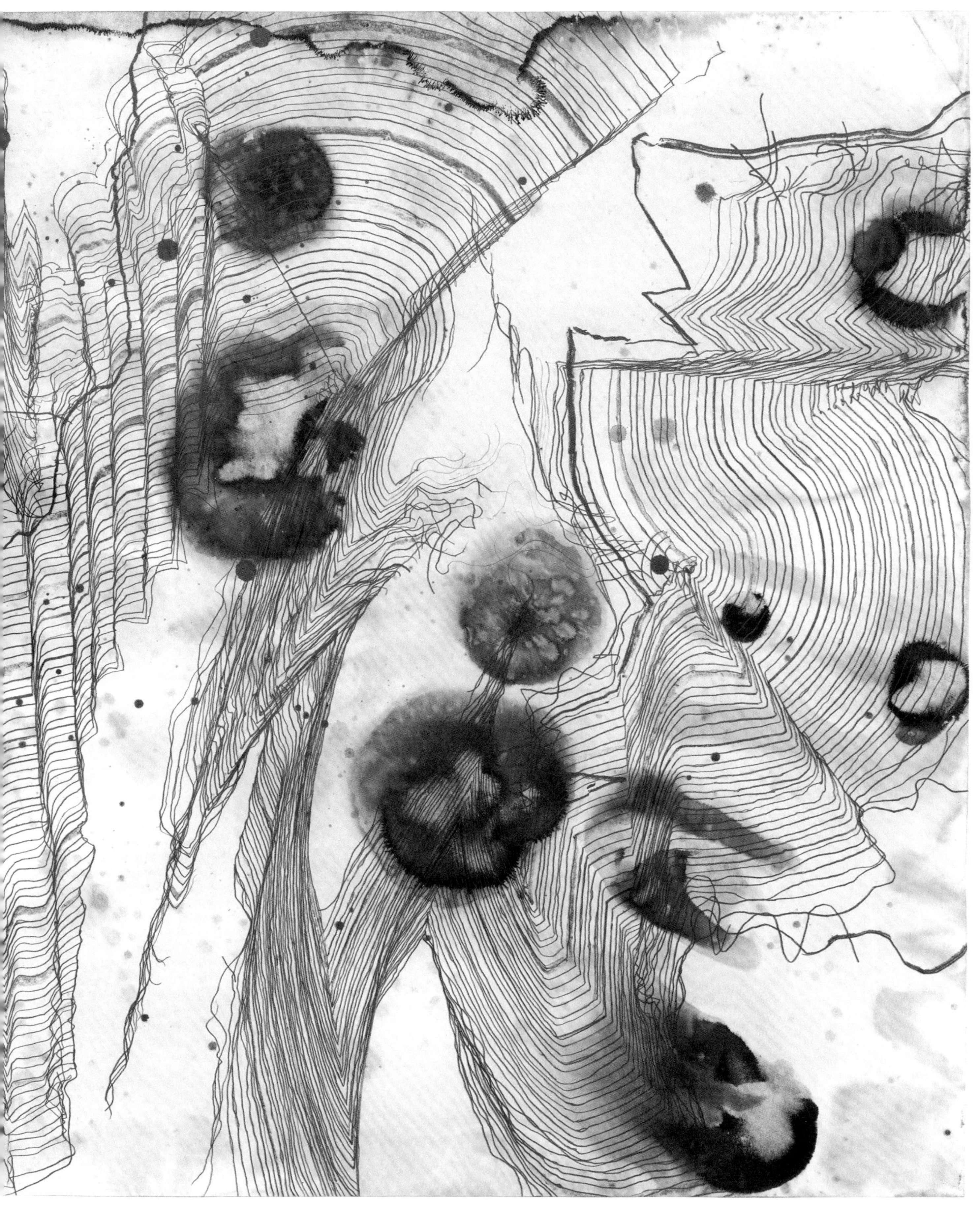

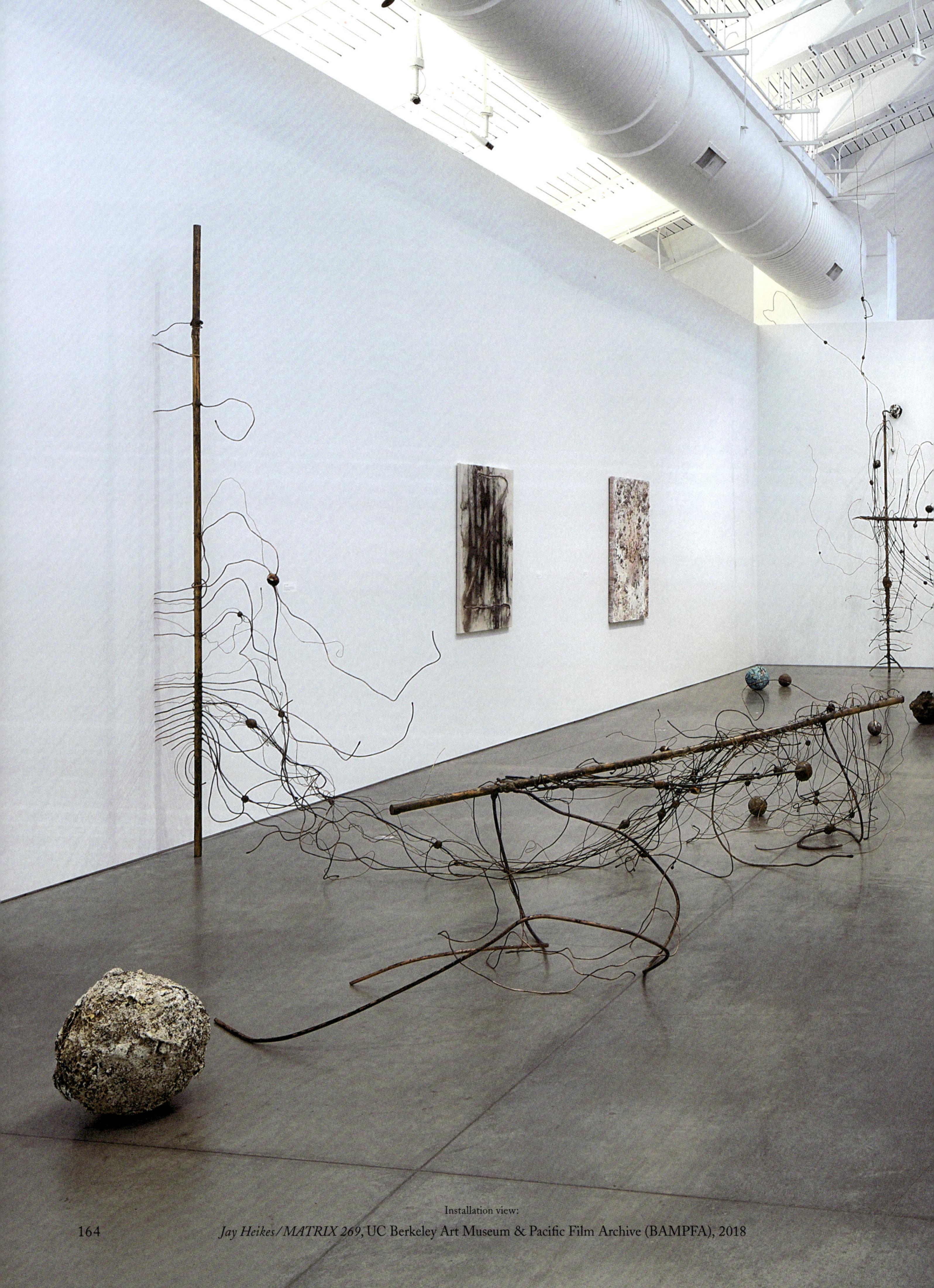

Installation view:
Jay Heikes/MATRIX 269, UC Berkeley Art Museum & Pacific Film Archive (BAMPFA), 2018

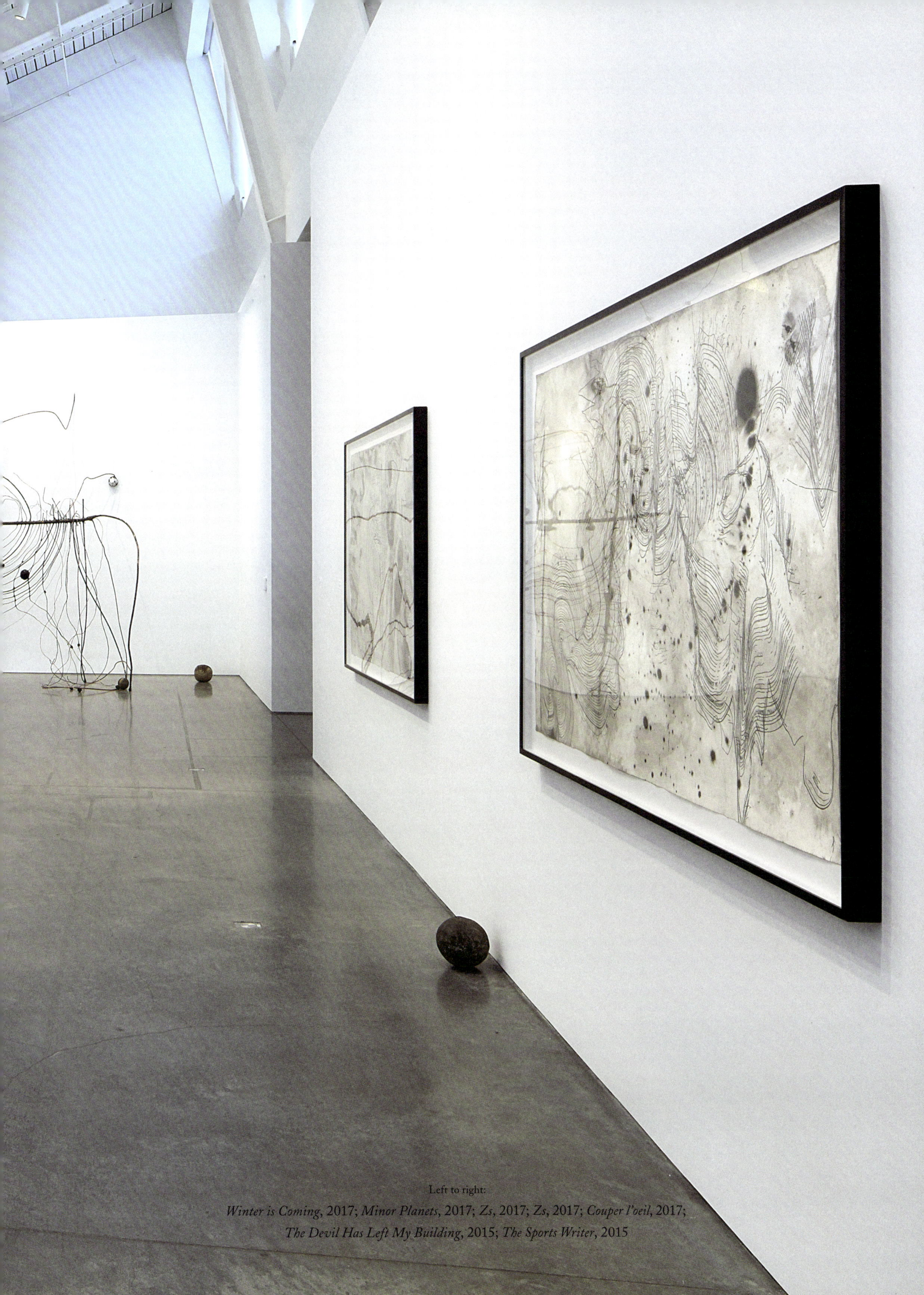

Left to right:
Winter is Coming, 2017; Minor Planets, 2017; Zs, 2017; Zs, 2017; Couper l'œil, 2017;
The Devil Has Left My Building, 2015; The Sports Writer, 2015

Field Recordings for the Faint of Heart

Hamza Walker and Jay Heikes

[HAMZA SIPS HIS MINT TEA AND SETS HIS MUG DOWN]

HW: So tell me about this score you created.

JH: I did a show two years ago in the Matrix space at the Berkeley Art Museum and the curator I worked with on the exhibition, Apsara DiQuinzio, invited Zeena Parkins and William Winant to perform my score, *Music for Minor Planets.*

HW: I went through the whole score and I didn't realize how deep in you were. At first I was like, Oh wow, look at this graphic score!

JH: I started doing these kinds of drawings around 2012, and then they turned into the score and I thought, Wouldn't it be amazing to have someone interpret it? But I have to admit it was all Apsara getting those people to do it.

HW: Well, she got top-shelf players.

JH: Yeah, top-shelf. When I watched them perform the score I thought so much about what it means to "read" music, which was truly the most fascinating part of the experience. For instance, if there was a circle on the page, Willie would be rubbing the wall with a mallet in the form of a large circle to make a sound, and to mimic the lines I'd drawn, Zeena was weaving felt into the strings of the harp. But in some ways I thought it was peculiar that they would even approach reading the score instead of using it as simply a starting point.

[STRANGE, HIGH-PITCHED-HORN SOUND EMANATES FROM OUTSIDE, BUS WHIZZES BY FOLLOWED BY GARBAGE TRUCK BEEPING WHILE BACKING UP]

HW: Oh yeah, yeah, yeah, there's all kinds of ways you have to deal with that. How do you structure things — is it improvisation, is there a way to notate, to still maintain the integrity to structure, or should improvisation be structured, and in what sense?

[BEEPING CONTINUES . . .]

JH: Yeah, these are people interpreting the graphic score, not machines. I've thought a lot about precedents with regard to the interpretation of graphic scores over the years. Do you know Daphne Oram and Oramics? You know the BBC Radiophonic, that whole early British radio show of soundscapes and sound experiments?

HW: I know the BBC Radiophonic, but I'm not familiar with Oram.

JH: Musique còncrete was a huge influence on them, obviously, but the BBC Radiophonic group is most interesting to me because of Oram. She's a truly revolutionary figure because she invented a machine that was called the Oramics machine. She would paint shapes on 35mm film, obsessively studying the way sound produced wave forms and trying to figure out whether the process could reverse: whether a machine could read the wave forms to produce sounds. Even during her early years of music education she inquired about these possibilities, but her professors all agreed, that "no, that definitely can't happen." So Oram took that as a challenge and invented this machine that could make sounds based on her graphic scores. And when you hear the sounds that it made, you realize she barely tapped into the possibilities of this machine that she worked so hard to bring to life, but her contribution was a phenomenal breakthrough in the early days of electronic hybrids of sound and form. I thought about her contribution in relation to my score, specifically the fact that a machine was interpreting her marks—not a musician—so I realized a divergence of interpretation was necessary; a human presence became vital for me when I considered its possible performance.

[CLANGING SOUND ON DESK, JAY CLEARS HIS THROAT]

HW: *Mhm . . .*

[CAR HORN HONKS]

JH: So during the Berkeley performance, when I was watching Zeena and Willie kind of flailing at points, weaving felt into the harp, blowing up balloons, etcetera, I was so pleased by the unpredictable behavior and variety of instruments being played. At one point Willie was using this Australian, um, what is it called, it's called a . . .

[TAPPING SOUND DISTORTING PHONE MIC AS JAY GOOGLES "AUSTRALIAN INSTRUMENT ON A STRING"]

. . . a bullroarer. Do you know this?

HW: *No.*

JH: It's basically a string attached to a thin piece of wood that makes a subtle, whirring sound. Maybe Zeena and Willie looked at the score and thought, What bag of tricks can we bring to make different sounds that would relate to the graphic nature of the lines and dots and feeling of disintegrating and rematerializing forms? The inclusion of the bullroarer, and other unexpected instruments, created a bridge to a more sculptural and material-based language. But while I was sitting through the performance, which was about an hour long, I thought about the limitations of legibility from a particular avant-garde perspective and how the score could evolve, or be reinterpreted the next time around by a different set of musicians. Soon after Berkeley, I made an exhibition for the Joslyn Museum in Omaha, and these young guys who were students (playing as a collective under the name TAPEnsemble) at the University of Nebraska, Omaha, got wind of the previous performance and approached me about wanting to interpret the score. They performed it at the opening reception. Thinking back on it now, they were jammin' on their keyboards and horns and bringing out the sounds in their heads, and it was all so airy. Afterwards I asked them, "Did you *read* the score?" And they said, "Oh yeah!" I immediately laughed and realized there was once again a disconnect with the way I think a musician reads music.

[ADJOINING OFFICE PHONE RINGS]

HW: *Sure, that's what they're trained to do.*

JH: I've always played music but I have never been able to read music. After that first performance, Zeena and Willie said to me, "Oh, well the score is so musical!" [*laughing*] Which is funny, because that's what I was hoping but, at the same time,

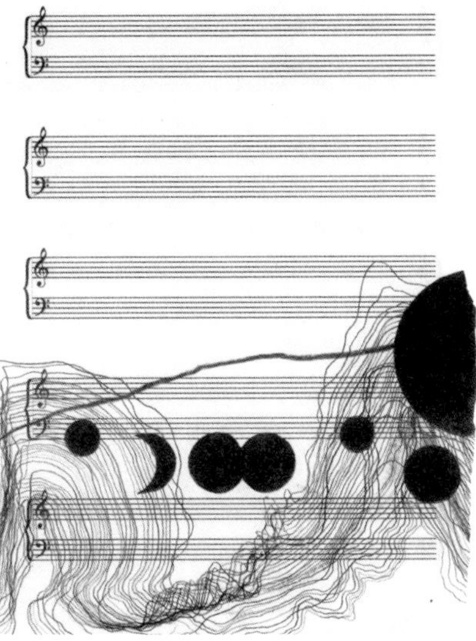

Fig. 1
Page 11 from *Music for Minor Planets*, 2018
Graphite on sheet music
10 × 8 inches, 25.4 × 20.3 cm

I wonder if there will be a musician who will think it's illegible, or overly decorative, and just look at me like, Stop wasting my time!

HW: Zeena and Willie are both seasoned musicians of a particular caliber, and you know, in terms of questions of music qua *music, as opposed to someone outside the discipline, they might be more trenchant in how they address fundamental aspects of abstract music and take them for granted.*

[SWALLOWING SOUND]

JH: Mhm . . .

HW: For instance, Yves Klein's Monotone–Silence Symphony*—twenty minutes of a single note, twenty minutes of silence. To think he started working on that in 1940, in advance of John Cage's silence, and how revolutionary it was then to work with those concepts. Marcel Duchamp also wrote music, and I wonder how his scores were interpreted. The way that visual artists have engaged with music has been welcomed by musicians and composers consistently, but also bear in mind that, you know, there are European composers who DON'T LIKE JOHN CAGE.*

JH: And why do you think they don't like his works? Because they are too abstract or too ephemeral or too something?

HW: Or is it the extent to which it could even be considered music? Cage has written things that fall into the category of music, but it's more of a kind of ontological investigation into the nature of music, its very being, and what constitutes composition, to strip it down, and to say this is about organizing or structuring time. But what to do with notes or soundness, what's the relationship with sound and noise, etcetera?

[CAR HORN BLARES]

So to what extent does asking those kinds of questions fall under the purview of music? Or does that represent a threshold in music? I'm thinking about the way that visual art has deconstructed, even wholeheartedly welcomed, the dismantling of itself. Are other fields as self-reflexive or critical as the visual arts, to the extent that we could consider visual arts to be, at times, anti-retinal*?! It's still called "visual art," but it often questions the very premise of what constitutes the visual, and to sustain that through the legacy of an avant-garde, that kind of rigorous investigation and willingness to deconstruct and dismantle the very tenets upon which the field is built, could it then be used as a framework that would then be applied to other disciplines?*

[TRUCK SCREAMS]

JH: And for me, sitting through Zeena and Willie's performance, I realized it was an avant-garde presentation that had a historical reference. I was familiar with the look and sound of the harp. I could recognize the drums, the gong, these things that lead me to go, Okay, this as an avant-garde interpretation through idiosyncratic tools, but I'm familiar with them and their vocabulary, which then led me to think about other musicians who invented their own instruments, like Theremin, or Moondog, or Maurice Martenot and his Ondes Martenot. Do you know this instrument where you put a ring on your pointer finger?

HW: Uh-uh.

JH: You slide it up and down the edge of the keyboard. It changes the pitch. It was invented in the late 1920s and most recently brought into popular music by Jonny Greenwood through the soundtracks he did for films like *There Will Be Blood* and *The Master*. It was also used by Olivier Messiaen in his *Quatour pour la fin du temps (Quartet for the End of Time)*. Do you know him?

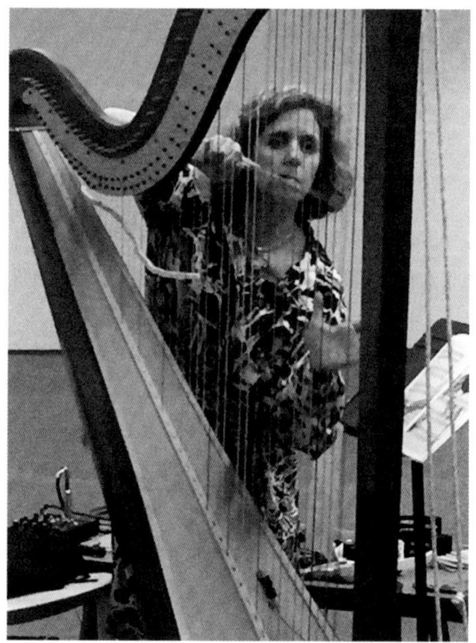

Fig. 2
Zeena Parkins performing *Music for Minor Planets* (with William Winant), April 28, 2018, UC Berkeley Art Museum & Pacific Film Archive (BAMPFA)

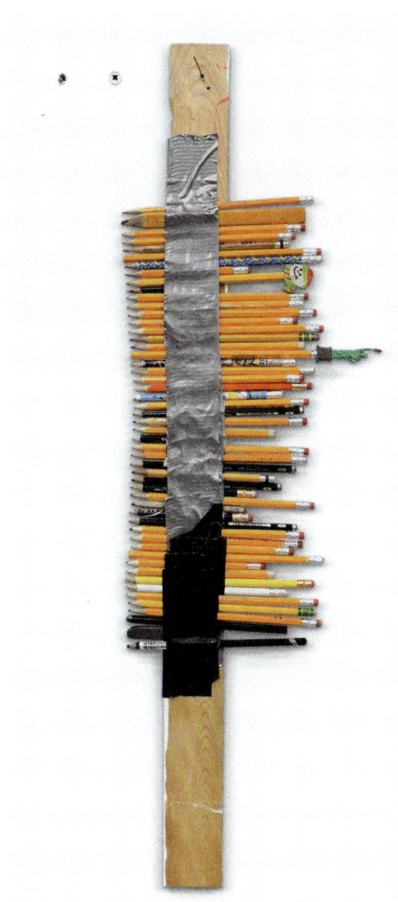

Fig. 3
Pencil rake hanging on artist's studio wall

HW: *Yeah, Messiaen, one of the greats.*

JH: Undoubtedly. And the Ondes Martenot was based on military radio transmissions when soldiers were trying to find frequencies to send messages.

[JAY IMITATES A RADIO TUNER SQUEALING TO FIND A CLEAR CHANNEL]

He wanted to mimic the sound. The Theremin is similar because you have two antennas creating the possibility for interference. So I kept thinking about, with Oram and Theremin, Moondog and Martenot, this reinvention of the instrument they are playing.

HW: *Yeah, you change the tools . . .*

JH: Change the tools, right, which is what I was trying to do with those drawings, from the beginning, by making a new tool I called the pencil rake. It's a piece of wood with various pencils taped to it so it can mark grooves, much like the emotional lines of a polygraph or recorded vibrations of a seismograph. When I was making the drawings I kept thinking about what kind of instrument could interpret this score. I loved having Zeena and Willie interpreting this, but I was also wondering, What if I gave them different instruments? Is it about the tool? No, obviously it's about the person *and* the tool. There's a specific form in the score that looks like a pie-shaped fan, or like a cross section of granite that's been cut in a wedge, and I kept waiting to *hear* that fan.

When I first conceived the score back in 2018 I had this idea to buy one of those industrial belt sanders because they almost look like pianos. It's just a huge hunk of metal with a big red button and a bed that comes out with a giant piece of sandpaper on a belt. I wanted to replace the sandpaper with guitar strings or some kind of metal strings. And then, in my imagined perfect world of alternative instruments, if you hit the big red button the stringed belt would start going around and around, and it would look like glimmering lines of metal that then could be played by moving something in a fan motion across the strings. What would that sound be like? So I'm saying that when I made the original drawings I had this sound in my head, and when I didn't hear it during the performance, I thought, Oh, they didn't play the sound of the fan. But how would they know that if I hadn't pointed it out? I guess I had hoped they would see what I saw and hear what I heard without me having to point it out. My point is that when I didn't hear it, I thought the only way to hear that sound would be to make the instrument myself, and play it, and I wondered if that impulse was what led so many of these people I've mentioned to invent their instruments.

HW: *Yeah, yeah, yeah, you know, the great saying is "You build the bars of your own cage," right, so if I give you something that represents an opportunity to play, how free can you be? And do you understand the nature of the exercise? And if you are given a space to do what you like, does it end up sounding like a jam session as opposed to . . . ? What's being asked of you might by its very nature involve a more critical approach, as opposed to the idea of "We're just gonna play." You're supposed to question all of your default moves, and the idea of the nature of music. And so it's not just the tool but also their training.*

JH: And how much they want to reject that training.

HW: *Mhm.*

JH: Zeena's mastery of and love for the harp—I could just watch that for hours. I don't really need a new tool to create that feeling, but then I thought about the experience I had with eYe from Boredoms and that crazy eight- or seven-necked guitar thing he totes around. Do you know this instrument he has? It looks like a big cross with guitar necks that he plays with long rods, and when he hits the guitars it sounds like he's ripping open the venue. It's just such a complete and total crescendo. As a full band they set up on the floor instead of the stage so even the way you receive sound is different. It's more like a drum circle. There's a gaggle of people playing drums and then he's bashing this homemade thing and it all feels ceremonial and new. And when I think about the graphic nature of my score, the legibility, the instruments, the training of the musicians and these people who have developed new ways of interpreting the music, I find myself now suddenly thinking more about the "conditions" that surround it; conditions that are determined by something outside of our intentions and capabilities as humans. And maybe it has something to do with the earth caving in on itself, but what would this unstable stage produce, and could you make a concert for a hurricane, or is there a specific reference for that? Because we're just so used to an architecture that has provided a stage for us to focus, but what if we can't focus at some point? What emerges? Is it a natural sound, an earth sound? One that overtakes us? Or are we competing with the hurricane?

HW: *There are plenty of examples. One is Mazen Kerbaj, the trumpet player.* Starry Night *is the name of a composition he made in 2006, on a night Israel bombed Beirut. Kerbaj went up to the roof of his apartment building and recorded himself playing this self-made instrument that's a trumpet with a long piece of plastic tubing between the instrument and the mouthpiece. He played this instrument while the bombs were going off in the background, so you hear these explosions from a distance. He considered the bombs as fellow musicians to improvise with. So just an example of that kind of music, if we can call it that still, in that infinitely expanded field. I still think of these things as remnants, vestiges, of thinking and not just experimentation from the mid-twentieth century. And to what extent is a debt still owed to, methodologically, John Cage, in terms of how he may have been thinking about some of these relationships? What constitutes composition and noise and sound? Then there's the very question of improvisation, whether it came through the field of free jazz or whether it was the provenance of late twentieth-century* Neue Musik.

[TRAFFIC HUMMING ON THE OTHER SIDE OF THE OFFICE WALL]

JH: There's something that Daphne Oram wrote in her manifesto, *An Individual Note of Music, Sound and Electronics*, in which she describes the ability of the human spirit and music to coalesce through sound. Maybe that's what the people trying to interpret these squiggles are after: how to manifest something unreadable through a personal articulation. Within the things we've talked about in the past, like improvisation in free jazz and Albert Ayler and this moment where you don't need the score and you don't need the song any longer, my question is, When we build the song back up, do you think it's all reactionary?

HW: *No, hardly, hardly. It's the questions about song. Wait, I just saw a mosquito. Hold on.*

JH: It's gonna land in my soup.

HW: *Disappeared.*

If you were to hear free jazz, say a 1960s record from Ornette Coleman, he has a double quartet playing, and even though he draws a parallel between Jackson Pollock and allover painting and what he was after, the rhythm section is still playing a standard "dun dun dun dun da da da dun dun dun dun da da da." You can still follow it, and there's still a few more stages to go before a real revolution is achieved and it's like, liberate the rhythm section! And they thought, Oh, if we get rid of the piano, because the piano does the chord changes . . . But there's still a few more steps before I would say you arrive at what can be seen as a more free music. With respect to compositions, things like standards, musicians all know these songs, but it isn't that abandoning the song neces- sarily meant being free. Albert Ayler was free but he still likes songs.

JH: Oh for sure.

HW: He wants nursery rhymes and anthems and marches, and even his own compositions were a better vehicle for how he wanted to express himself.

JH: It's personal and that's what it all comes back to. In the breaking of that structure certain things remain.

HW: Right, exactly. Different figures negotiate with freedom in different ways. Is this an attack? Are they building a new structure or are they smashing to bits and pieces an older one? But freedom is not necessarily synonymous with the abandoning of structure, so you could also argue, say with some of Miles Davis's stuff, the Second Great Quintet, like Miles Smiles, *here is some of the freest music ever written. What if you could have the band float? Gravity is an issue, and I'm gonna separate whether there is or isn't gravity from the issue of velocity. What if everything in this room just suddenly floated? If I push it, it will go smashing into the wall. But what then is the relationship of one thing to another thing in the absence of gravity? We're all just floating here, so it's much more like a Calder mobile, in a certain sense, with the musicians still being connected and tethered. But I get a sense that Miles Davis lowers the gravity considerably to see if he can keep the quartet intact, but no, they're just gonna play as though they are playing in zero G.*

JH: We're so limited by our perceptive prism that I wonder if it's just about opening up that perceptive prism to allow it to float? Or do we need it to actually happen, that the musicians are actually floating? When the world intervenes and you're not able to hear something because your perception distorts, are we then witnessing a competition in sound? Or say a trumpet player is playing next to an active volcano and the earth somehow has its say in volume? Or a destabilizing force that keeps you from playing an instrument the way that you have been trained to? What then?

HW: To go back to something like Fluxus performance—which represented an assault on music, which of course is understood as a set of conventions that surround the production and reception of music and what constitutes music—I think about comparing a geo- logical event and the sound it produces relative to a musical instrument, or the pairing of the two things together. On the one hand, you could be asking me to listen to this at a formal level as though it were music, and the extent to which I'm actually understand- ing it as music might reside with somebody being there playing trumpet. I can close my eyes and listen to the relationship between these two sound events and sound sources despite their incommensurability. Or, is the revelation the question of what role music plays in a modern soundscape that is hopelessly perforated? The conditions under which we receive music, like going to the philharmonic where it's sort of removed from our daily lives, begs the question, Is music a question of how *we listen rather than* what *we listen to? Which is totally different than me listening to it as though it were music for formal relationships between the sounds.*

[HIGH-PITCHED BUS BRAKES SCREECH TO A GRINDING HALT]

JH: And could a philharmonic perform in an area where there is so much noise pollution that it is not only influenced by it but has to mutate to conceal or con- form to the noise? When so few spaces have silence in the world now, and noise pollution is increasing every year, and how we listen is changing, the question for me is, How do we intertwine? And is it based in comedy like those early Fluxus performances? If you say, We're having a concert tonight and because of nearby construction there's gonna be a jackhammer running for the first hour, what moment in this post-contemporary, dystopian jambalaya does it start to affect itself in a way that's not an illustration of what Fluxus was talking about but is actually a harsh reality that we have to accept? What if there is no space for integrity anymore? I don't think it's a question in our lifetime, but there is this non-space for integrity that our senses have become so accepting of that we can't even see or hear the distractions any longer. Maybe we would never notice it?

[EXPIRING BATTERY IN WHAT SOUNDS LIKE A SMOKE OR CARBON MONOXIDE DETECTOR BEGINS TO CHIRP]

HW: *Right. The cacophony is a model of subjectivity where a perpetual state of distraction is being. But are there things that require our undivided attention? It's interesting that you're proposing that, at a formal level, I would still be able to perceive or understand something even in a state of complete distraction. But what I think would happen before that is that distraction doesn't become the issue, it's much more a hierarchy of sounds. Beethoven or the Rolling Stones playing on the radio, it doesn't matter. You go ahead and play your thing while the jackhammer is playing outside, and then I will be able to reconstitute the experience* despite *this because I live in a state of distraction* anyway.

JH: But that's the word, *despite*. I wonder if we start to think that instead of *despite*, that we *need* that distraction, that we rely on it, so let's do the performance during the geological event because those are the conditons we need for it, and we start to approach a kind of desired ground.

HW: *Right, a certain kind of duress or resistance?*

JH: An acceptance of it. A reliance on it or celebration of it.

HW: *Yeah, but if a certain kind of culture requires optimal conditions for its reception, and you're saying let's get rid of those elements, let's "celebrate the duress," what I'm saying is the erosion that you're pointing to has already in fact occurred! I'm gonna go to a rock concert and it's like, "Bzzsh ahhhh* [DISTORTED GUITAR IMITATION] *uhhh!!!" Wow, we enjoyed this! The idea of the celebration assumes that one would even comprehend a loss of another thing* [dying laughter].

[CHIRP CONTINUES, SIREN BLARING OUTSIDE]

JH: So we're trying to relive it for ten bucks a head [*laughing*].

HW: *Right, right. It's like, the conditions, going to a stadium or an arena show, whatever enjoyment there is to be had and gotten from this thing, there is already animus to a point. It's not dictated by the idea of what makes me feel comfortable.*

JH: Yeah, so if I feel like my skin is being peeled off during a performance it doesn't matter. I paid for this.

HW: *Right. It's like, can you sit through* both *sides of* Exile on Main Street? *What flavor pill is this? We've already flipped it over to what we listen to, how we listen to, what we're receiving, and to what you're calling "celebration," but we're already celebrating that, we're already doing that in concerts and these other things. And in terms of a hurricane blowing through and incorporating it into the work, it's like, Oh, you mean, SPECTACLE!* [laughing] *We have plenty of that!* [still laughing]

JH: [*laughing*]

[FIRE TRUCK SIREN BLARES, ZOOMS PAST, DOG BARKS, PASSERBY YELLS SOMETHING INAUDIBLE, ALARM CHIRPS]

February 2020, Los Angeles

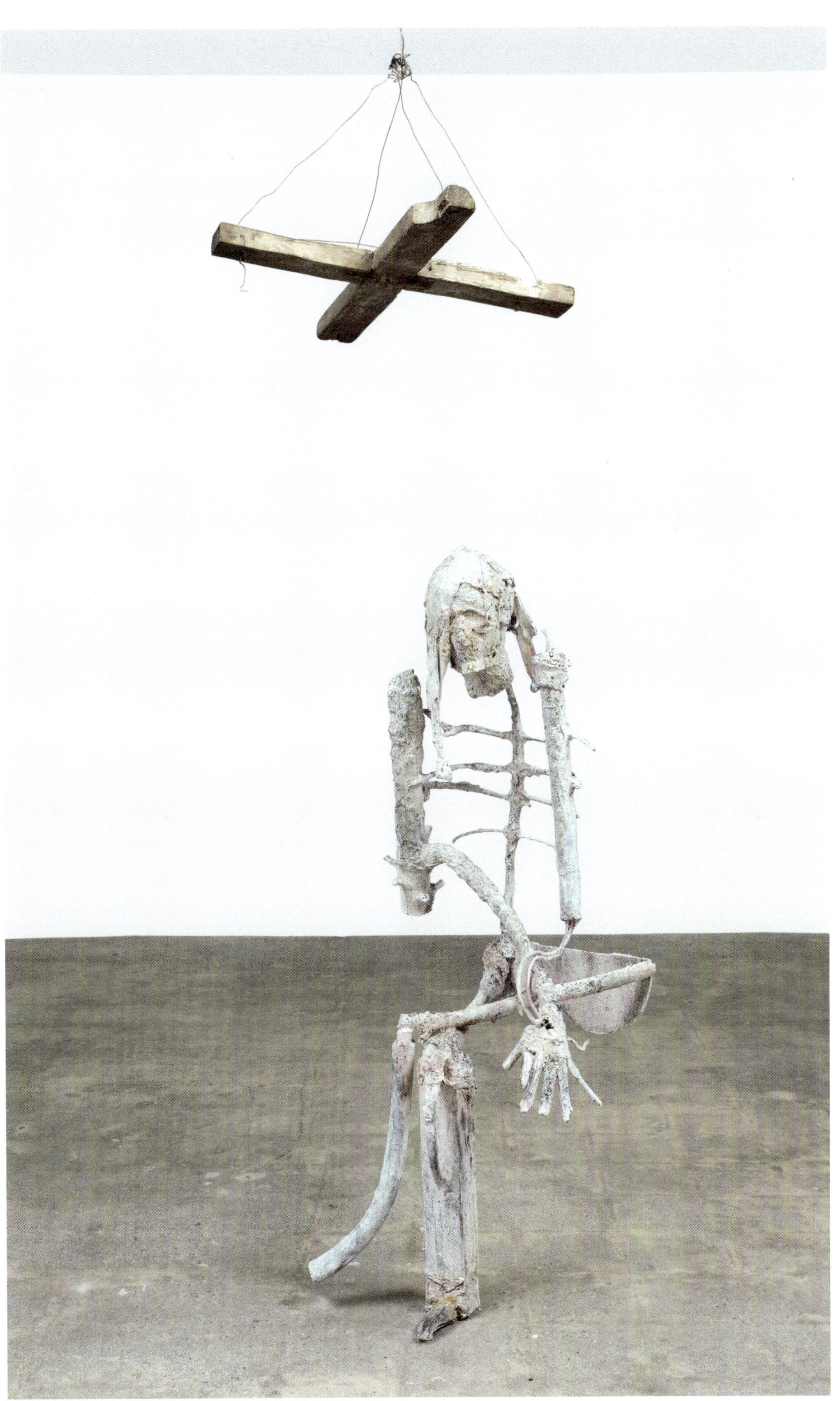

Assisted Living, 2017
Cast bronze, steel slag, steel wire, oil enamel, wax, salt, and brass, figure: 58 × 31 × 29 inches, 147.3 × 78.7 × 73.7 cm;
marionette cross: 31 × 29 × 20 inches, 78.7 × 73.7 × 50.8 cm

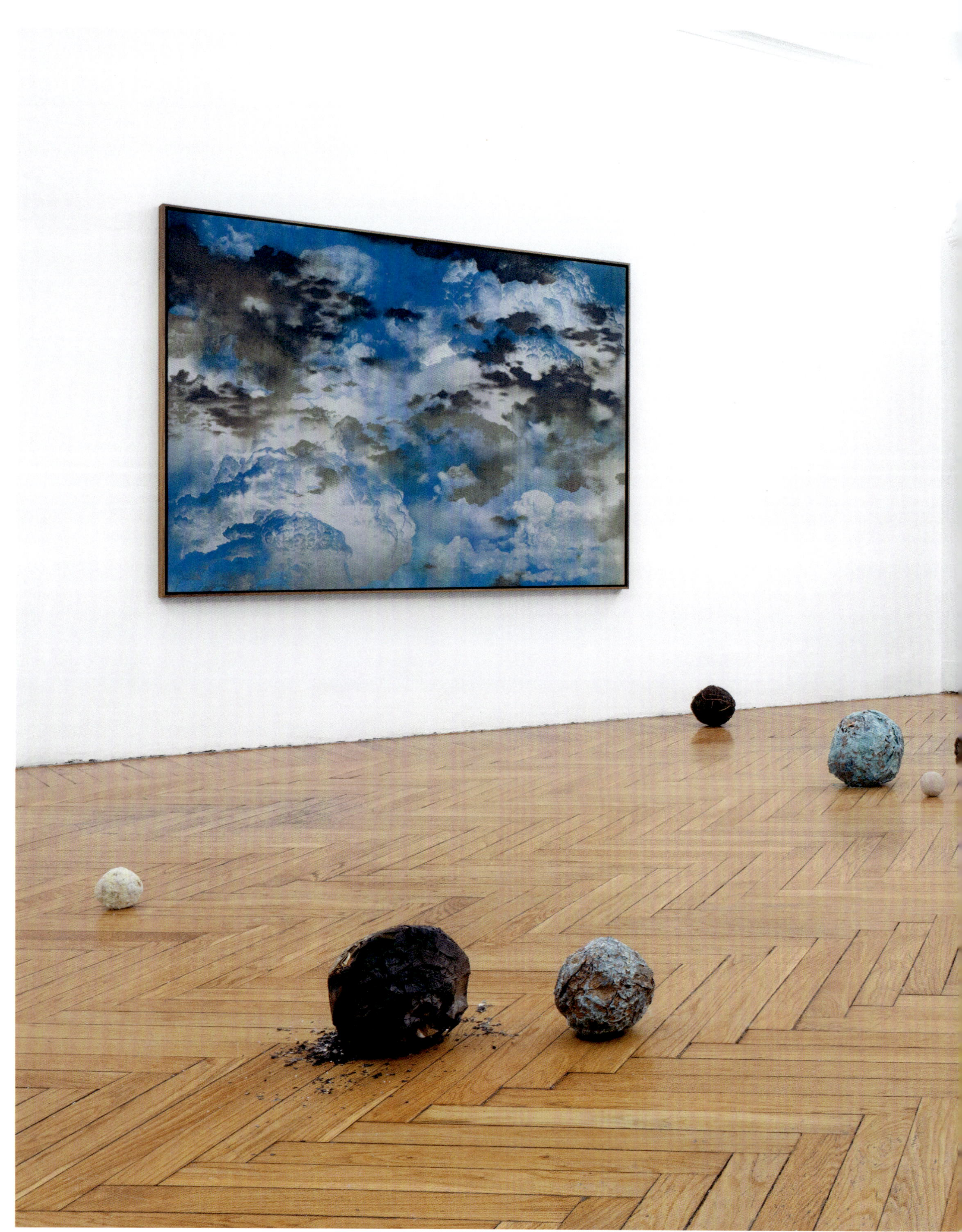

Installation view:
Before Common Era, Federica Schiavo Gallery, Milan, 2019

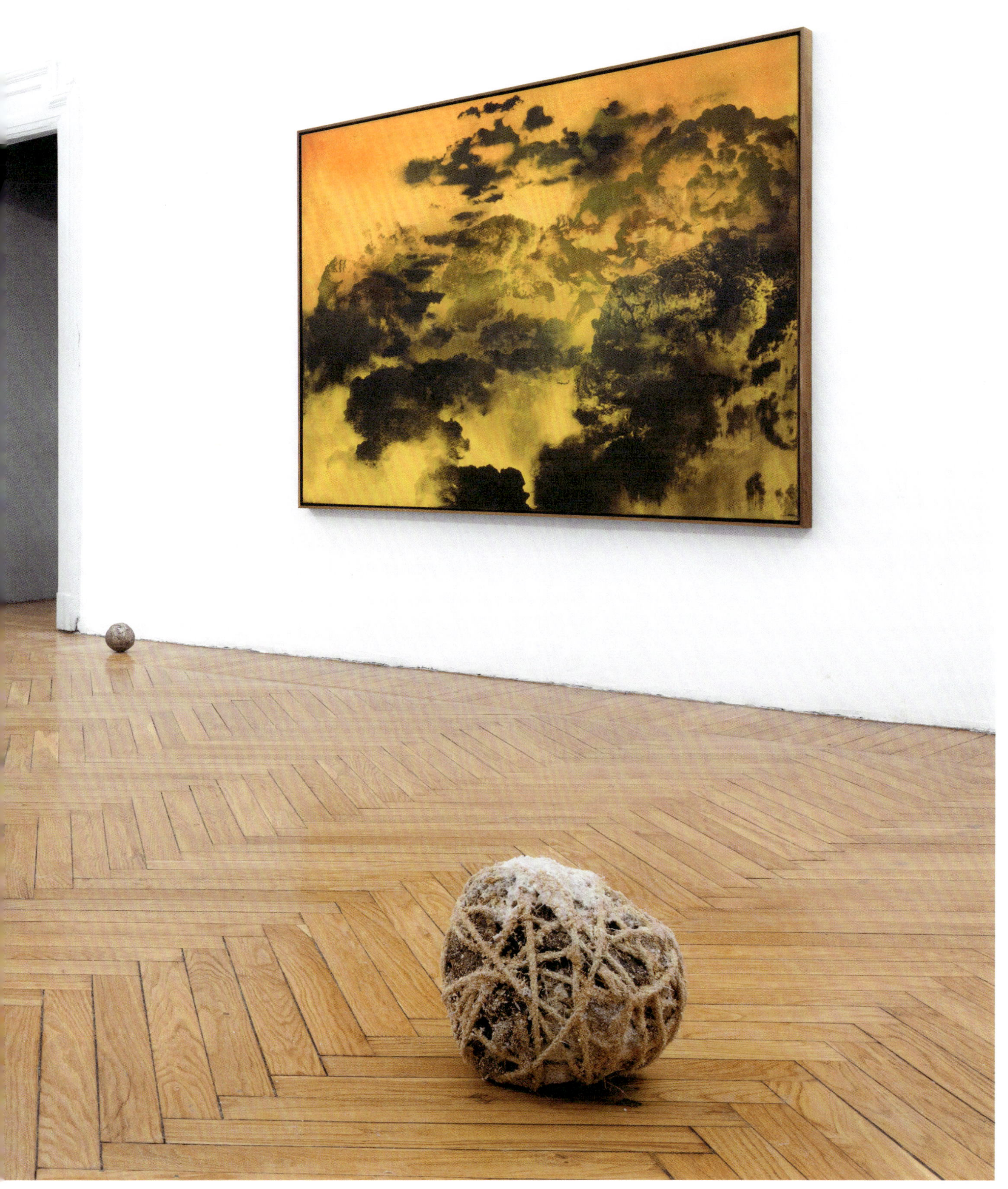

Left to right:
Mother Sky, 2019; *Mother Sky*, 2019; on floor: *Minor Planets*, 2017–19

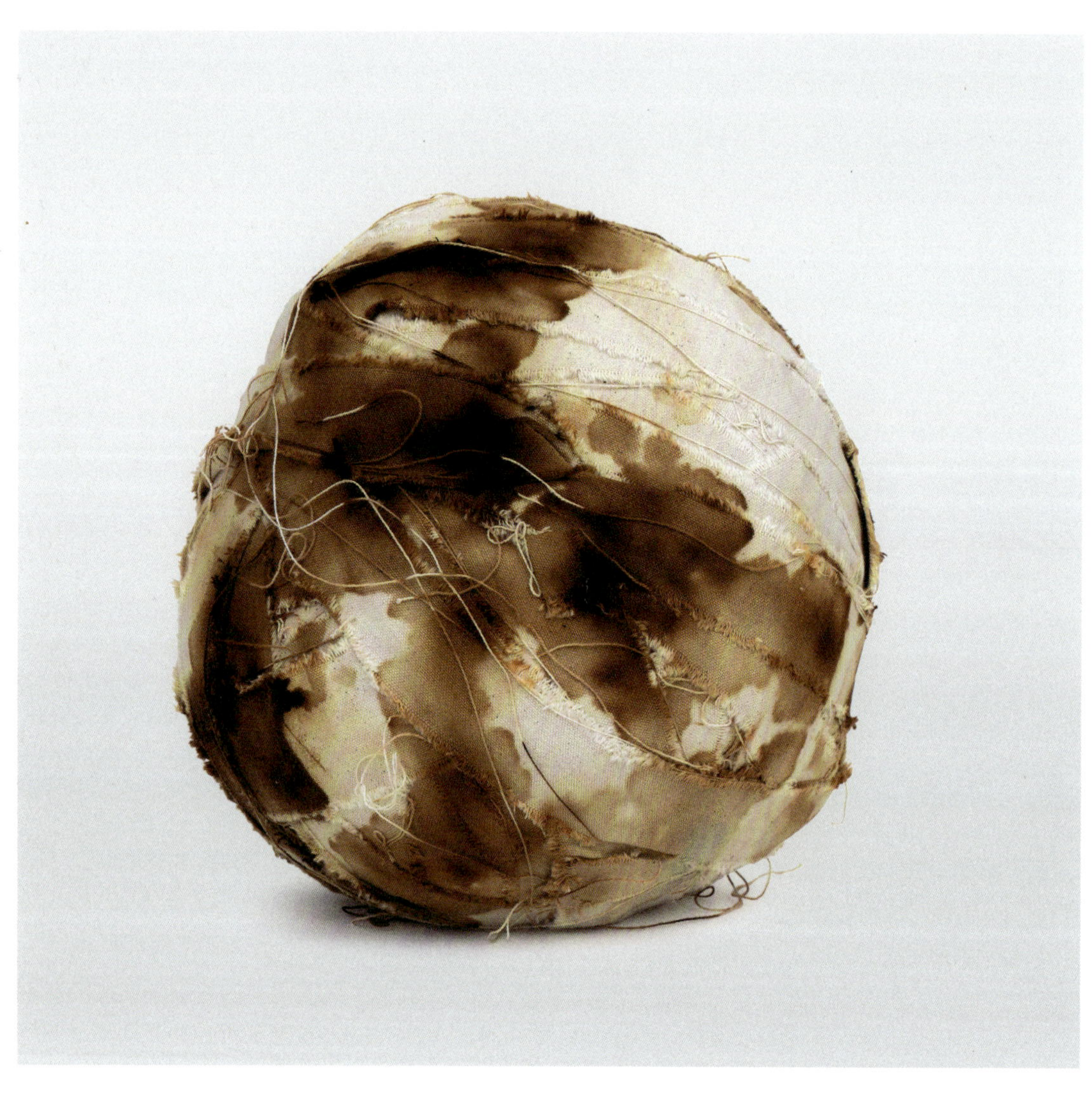

Minor Planet, 2019
Iodine on canvas, 12 inches, 30.5 cm diameter

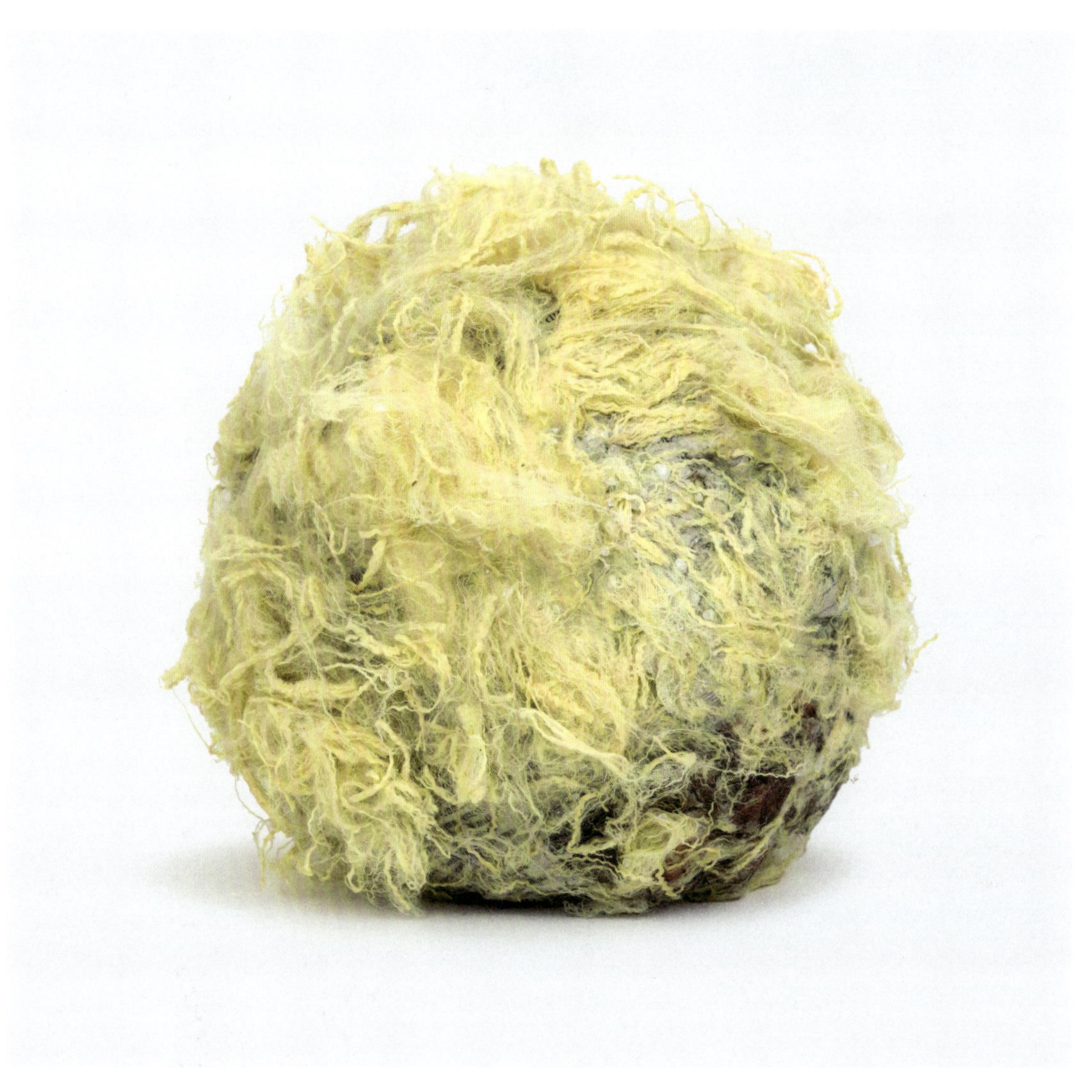

Minor Planet, 2019
Kevlar, steel wire, rope, salt, and glue, 4 inches, 10.2 cm diameter

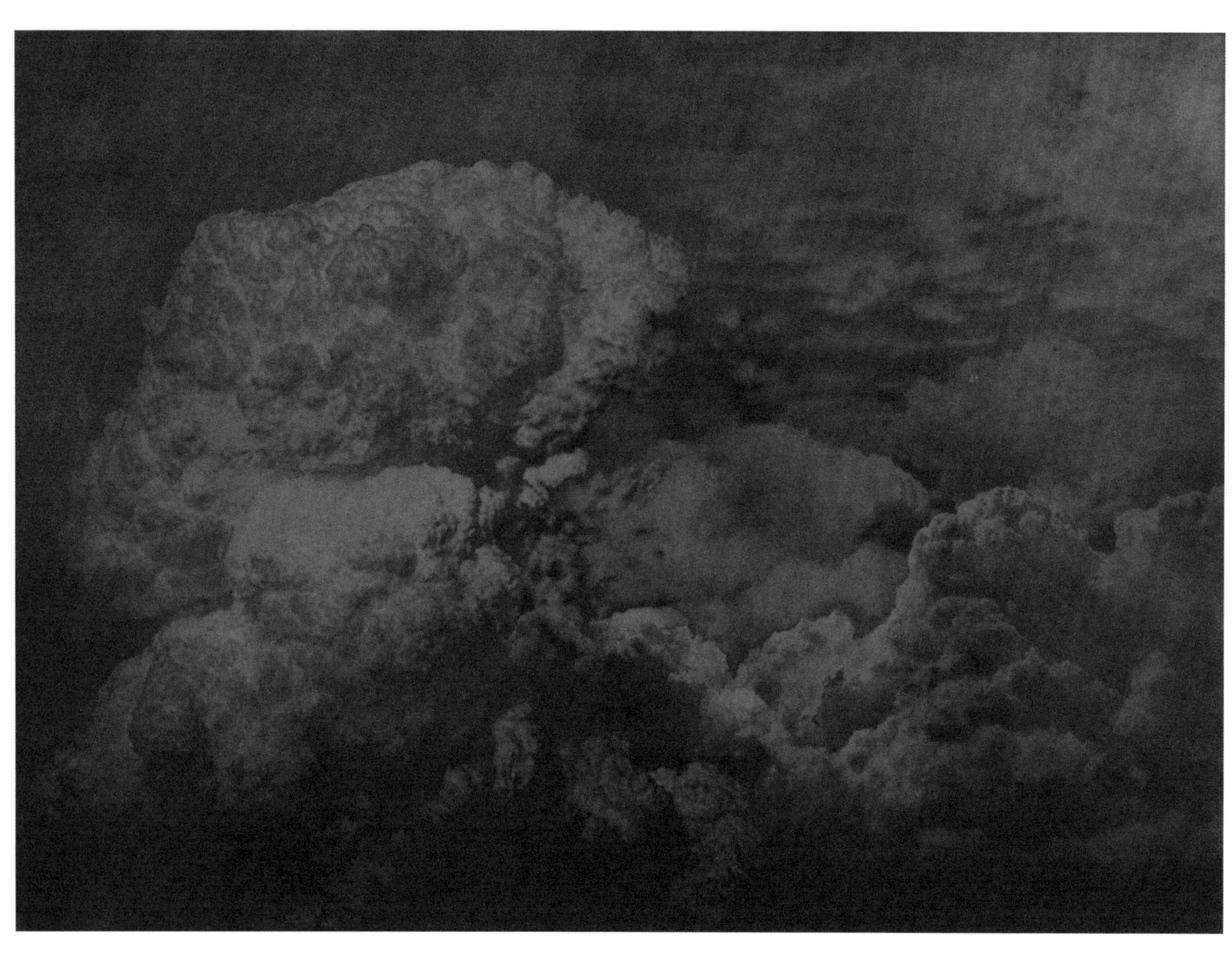

Mother Sky, 2019
Oil on stained canvas, 47 × 65 inches, 119.4 × 165.1 cm

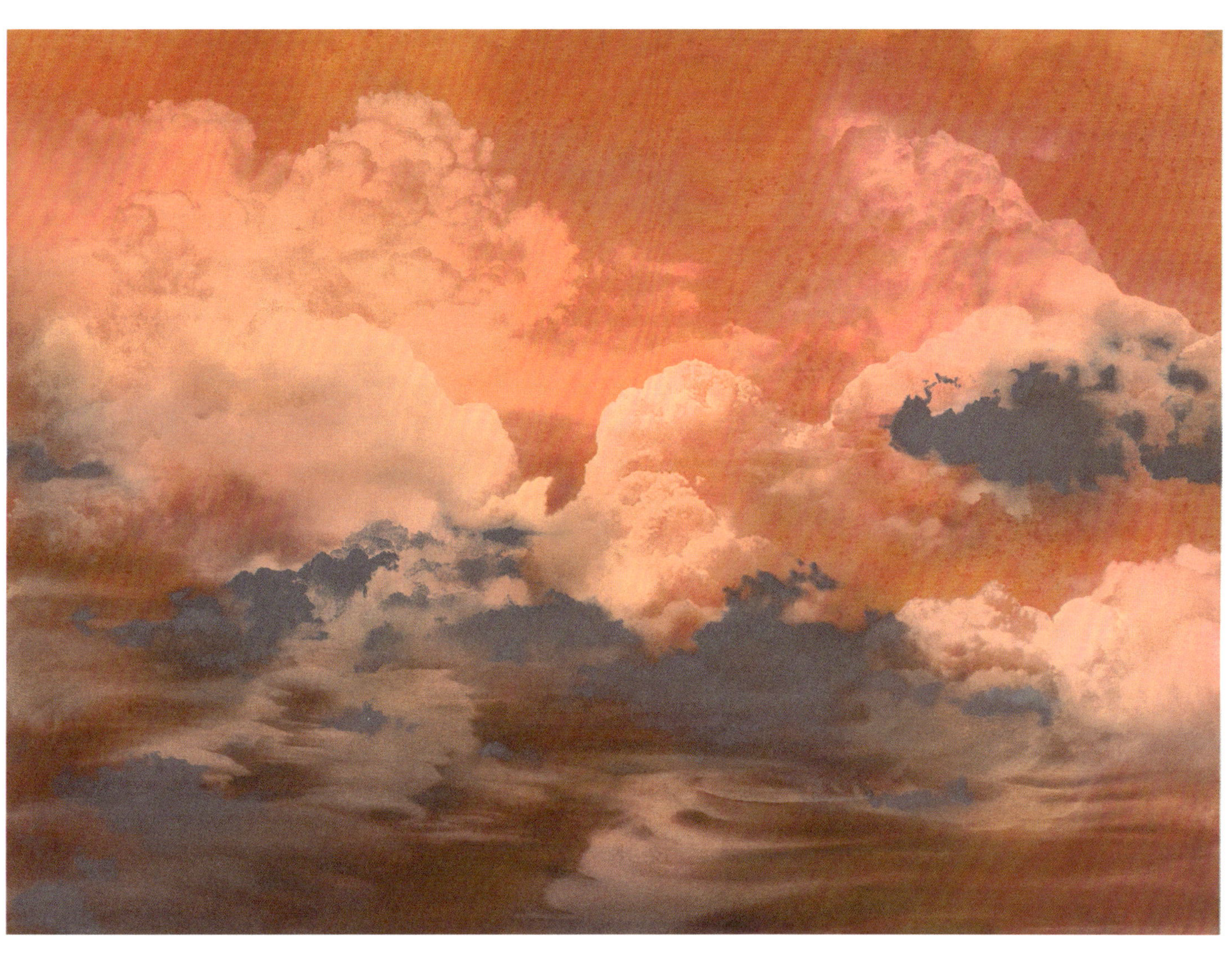

Mother Sky, 2019
Oil on stained canvas, 47 × 65 inches, 119.4 × 165.1 cm

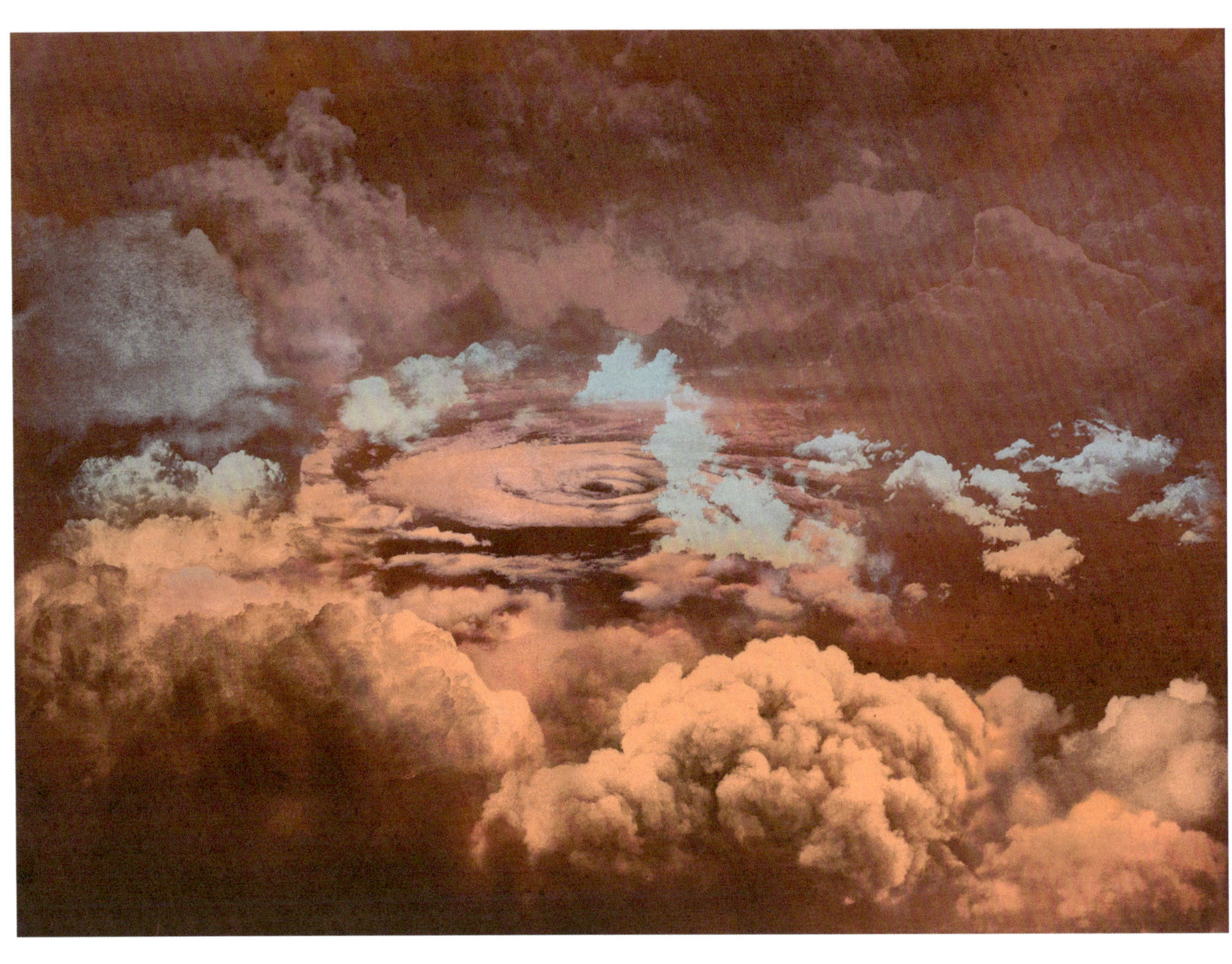

Mother Sky, 2019
Oil on stained canvas, 56 × 75 inches, 142.2 × 190.5 cm

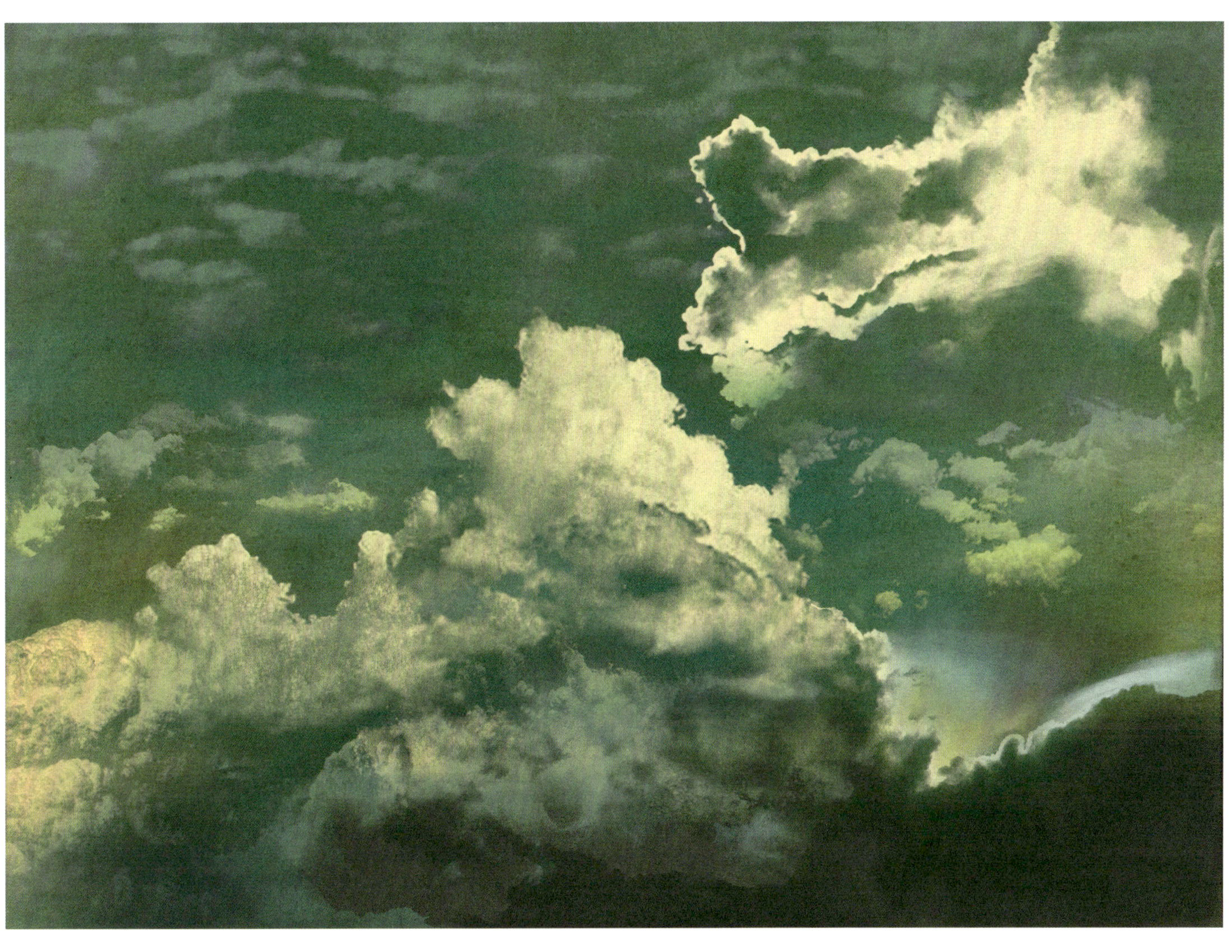

Mother Sky, 2019
Oil on stained canvas, 47 × 65 inches, 119.4 × 165.1 cm

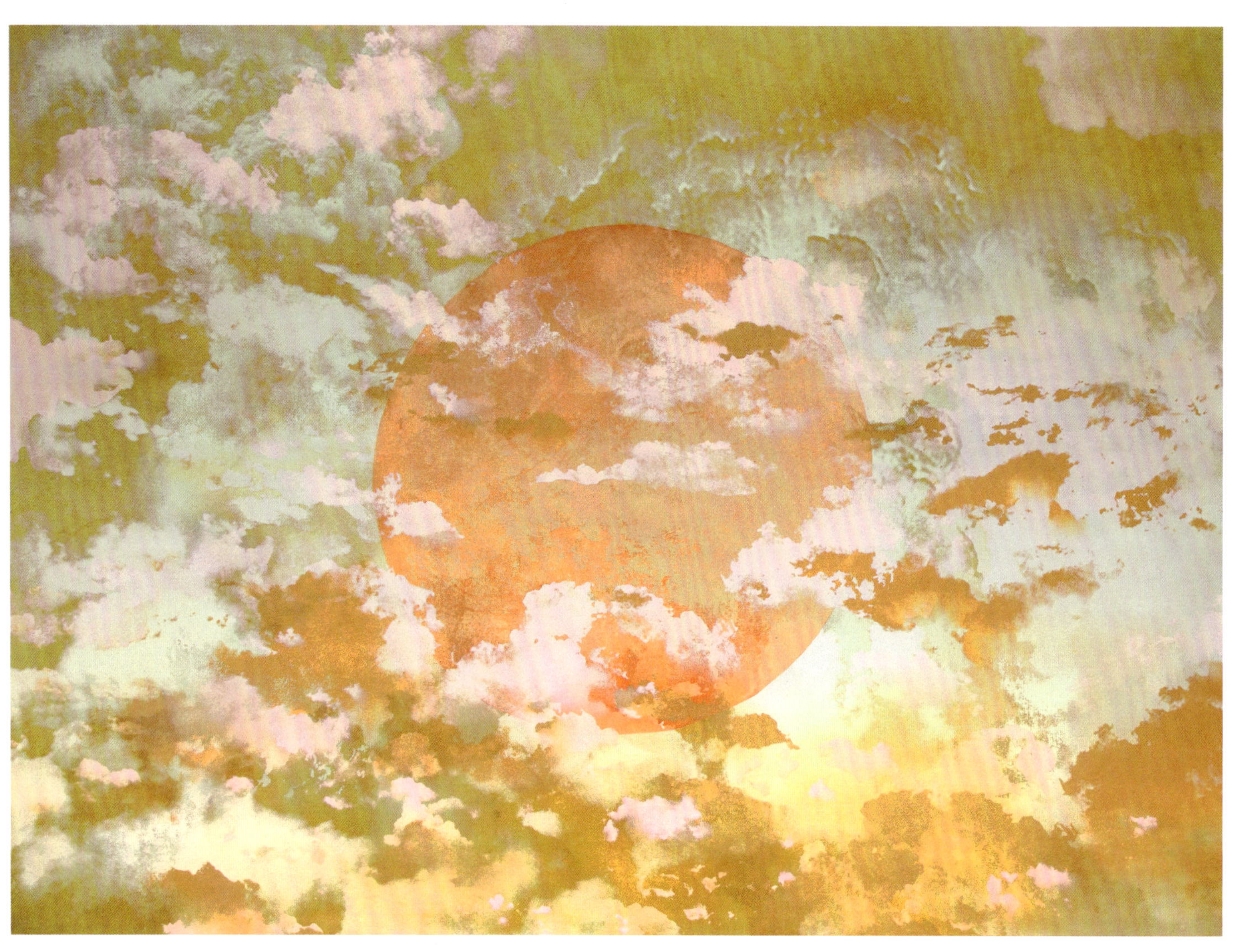

Wanderlust, 2020
Oil on stained canvas, 47 × 65 inches, 119.4 × 165.1 cm

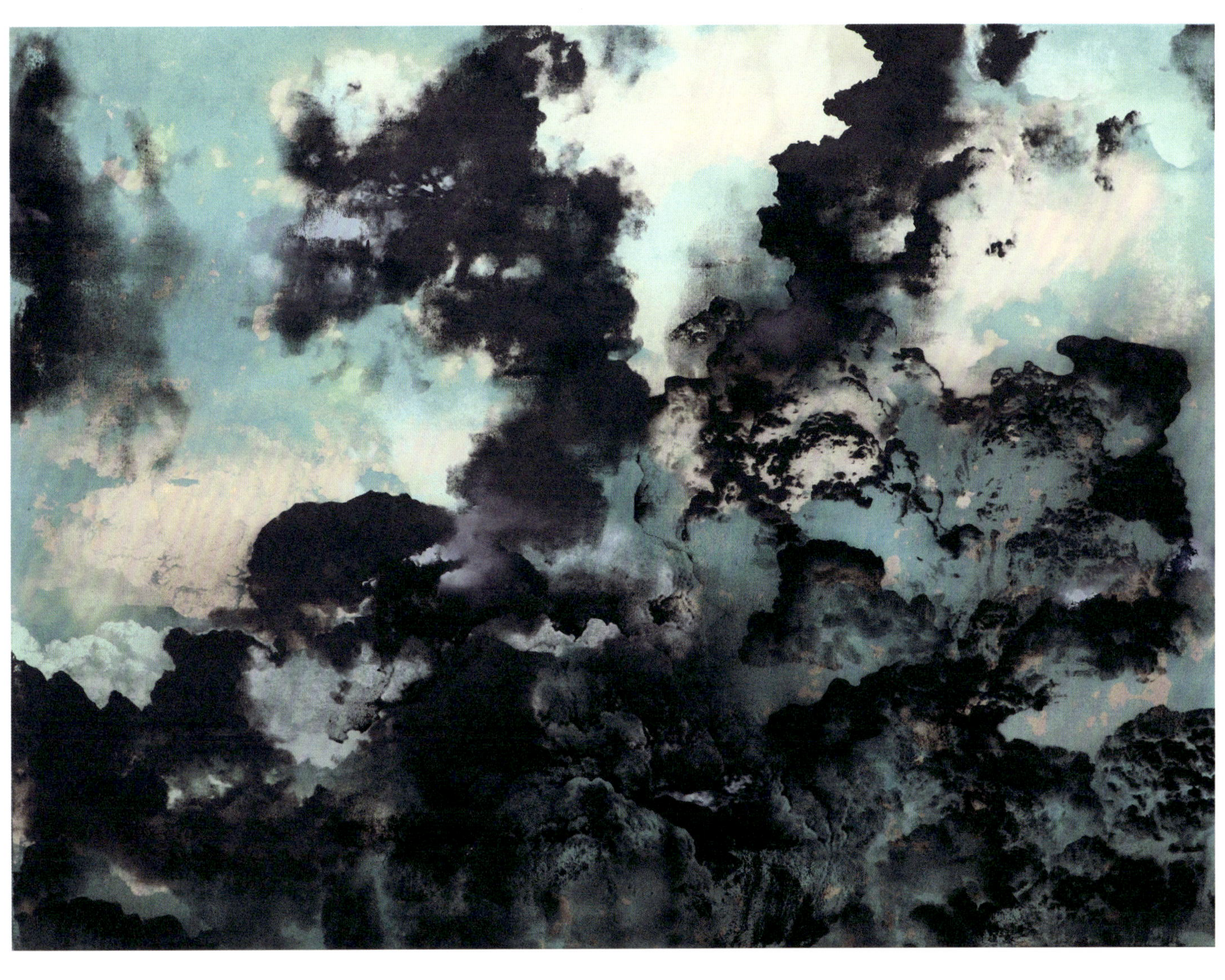

Devil's Sea, 2020
Oil on stained canvas, 56 × 75 inches, 142.2 × 190.5 cm

Following: *Michigan Triangle*, 2020 (detail)
Oil on stained canvas, 47 × 65 inches, 119.4 × 165.1 cm

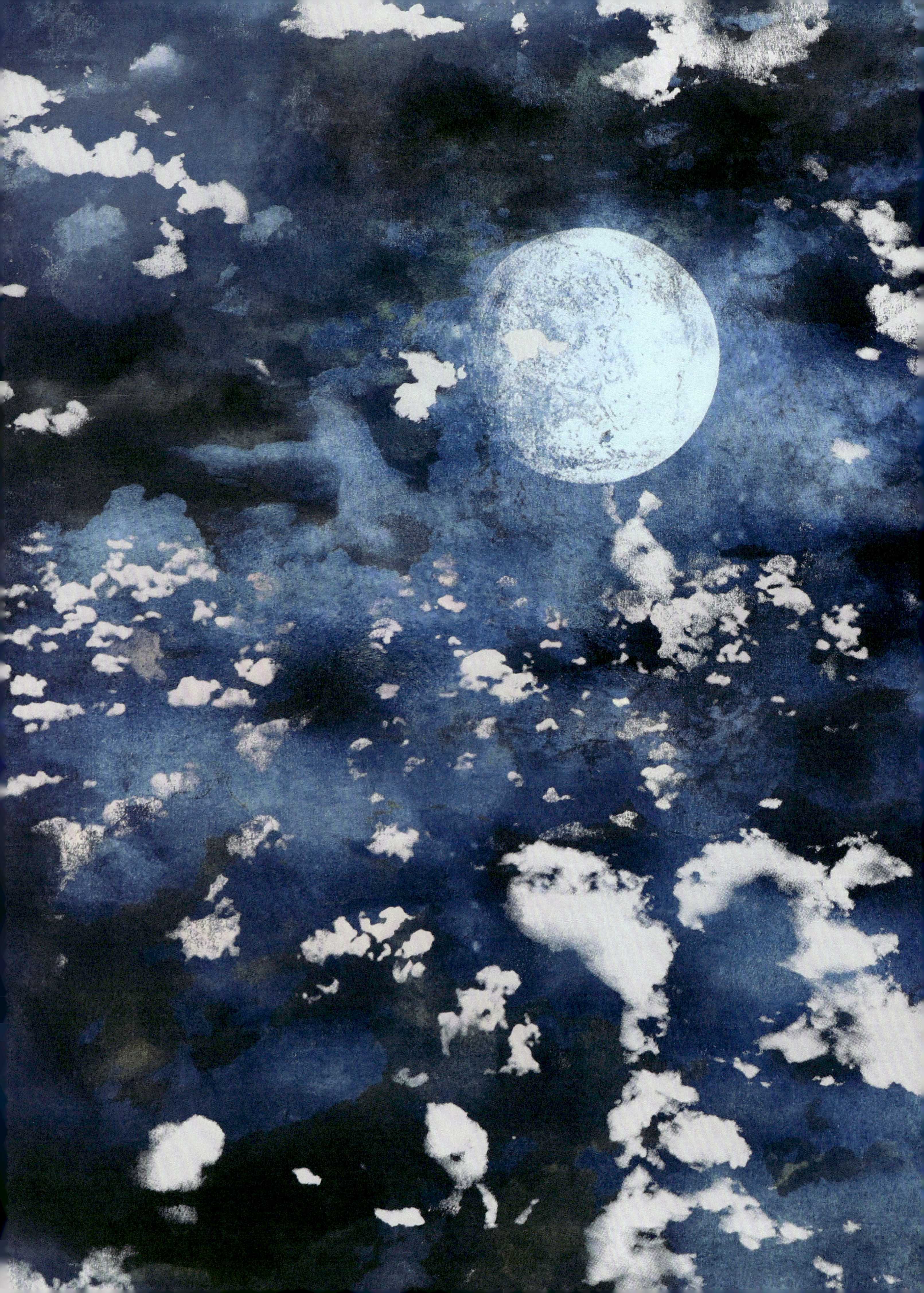

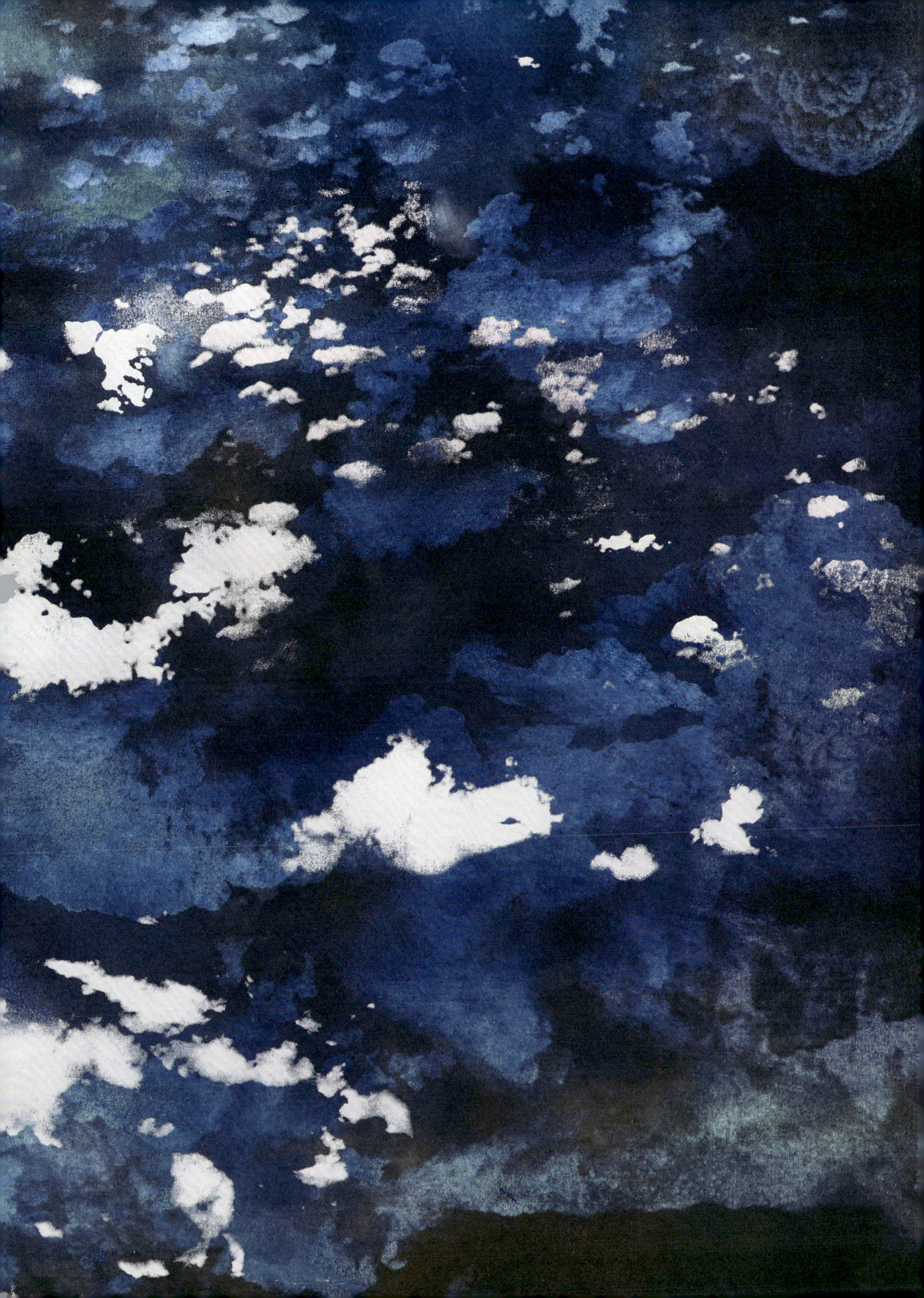

SOLO AND TWO-PERSON EXHIBITIONS

2000
Somewhere Over the Rainbow, Gus Lucky's Gallery, Minneapolis, May 27–June 18, 2000

2002
Jay Heikes and Kirk McCall, curated by John Rasmussen, Midway Contemporary Art, Minneapolis, May 17–June 16, 2002

2003
Kill Yr Idols, curated by Lauri Firstenberg, Artists Space, New York, March 8–May 3, 2003
Kill Yr Idols, Vedanta Gallery, Chicago, February 14–March 15, 2003

2006
The Sixth Retelling, Shane Campbell Gallery, Chicago, November 11–December 20, 2006

2007
Jay Heikes, curated by Jenelle Porter, Institute of Contemporary Art, University of Pennsylvania, Philadelphia, September 7–December 16, 2007. Brochure
Like a Broken Record, Marianne Boesky Gallery, New York, October 13–November 10, 2007

2009
Eroding Rainbow, Schiavo Mazzonis Gallery, Rome, January 28–March 14, 2009. Catalogue

2010
Jay Heikes, Gallería Marta Cervera, Madrid, February 19–March 27, 2010
Inanimate Life, Marianne Boesky Gallery, New York, September 16–October 23, 2010
Alighiero e Boetti: Un'idea Brillante // Jay Heikes: Generational Anxiety, Marianne Boesky Gallery, New York, November 6, 2010–January 15, 2011. Catalogue

2011
The Material Mine, Federica Schiavo Gallery, Rome, April 8–May 12, 2011
Subterranean Isle, Shane Campbell Gallery, Chicago, October 15–November 12, 2011

2012
Buried in the Bright, Aspen Art Museum, Colorado, February 17–May 4, 2012

2013
Walkabout, Marianne Boesky Gallery, New York, October 24–November 30, 2013

2014
Ra, Federica Schiavo Gallery, Rome, May 15–July 2, 2014

2015
Music for Minor Planets, Shane Campbell Gallery, Chicago, April 3–May 23, 2015
Jay Heikes | Dieter Roth, curated by Laura Fried, Reserve Ames, Los Angeles, September 13–December 6, 2015. Catalogue
Necrophiliac, Grimm Gallery, Amsterdam, November 27, 2015–January 16, 2016
Niet voor Kinderen, Highpoint Center for Printmaking, Minneapolis, October 30–November 21, 2015

2016
No future ism, Federica Shiavo Gallery, Milan, September 22–November 11, 2016

2017
Keep Out, Marianne Boesky Gallery, New York, May 5–June 17, 2017
Sailors' Delight, curated by Sarah Lehrer-Graiwer, The Finley, Los Angeles, August 25–November 8, 2017

2018
Jay Heikes / MATRIX 269, curated by Apsara DiQuinzio, UC Berkeley Art Museum & Pacific Film Archive (BAMPFA), February 14–April 29, 2018. Brochure
Quintessence, commission for the Embassy of the United States of America, London

2019
Jay Heikes, curated by Karin Campbell, Joslyn Art Museum, Omaha, June 1–September 8, 2019. Brochure
Before Common Era, Federica Schiavo Gallery, Milan, September 26, 2019–January 18, 2020

SELECTED GROUP EXHIBITIONS

1998
The Enmark Project, Kress Department Store, Savannah, December 11, 1998

2000
Play Dead, Intermedia Arts, Minneapolis, March 23–30, 2000
Celebrity Siblings, 4x Gallery, Portland, Oregon, February–March, 2000

2001
The Program, curated by Pedro Velez, FGA Space, Chicago, March 31–May 31, 2001
Weak Architecture, curated by John Rasmussen, Midway Contemporary Art, Minneapolis, April 20–May 12, 2001
Porn, curated by Pedro Velez, FGA Space at Joymore, Chicago, May 12–31, 2001
Wall to Wall, The Soap Factory, Minneapolis, July 7–August 5, 2001

2002
Watery, Domestic, curated by Hamza Walker, Renaissance Society at the University of Chicago, November 17–December 22, 2002. Brochure
Use Your Illusion, Vedanta Gallery, Chicago, July 26–August 31, 2002

2003
Don't Fail Me Now, TBA Exhibition Space, Chicago, October 10–November 8, 2003
Five Years of the Altoids Curiously Strong Collection, New Museum of Contemporary Art, New York, October 22–November 30, 2003

2004
The Hill Upstairs, Guild & Greyshkul Gallery, New York, March–April 2004
I Am The Resurrection, Locust Projects, Miami, May 8–June 11, 2004
Music/Video, curated by Lydia Yee, The Bronx Museum of the Arts, New York, October–December 2004
Emoticons, Guild & Greyshkul Gallery, New York, November 20–December 18, 2004

2005
Sticks & Stones, Perry Rubenstein Gallery, New York, June 28–August 12, 2005
National Projects 2005: Dianne Frid, Kira Lynn Harris, Mike Cloud, Jay Heikes, and Johannes VanDerBeek, P.S.1 Contemporary Art Center, New York, October 30, 2005–February 3, 2006
All the Pretty Corpses, curated by Hamza Walker, Renaissance Society at the University of Chicago, November 13–December 23, 2005. Brochure

2006
Jay Heikes, Mark Grotjahn, Richard Hawkins, Shane Campbell Gallery, Oak Park, Illinois, January 15–February 15, 2006
Whitney Biennial 2006: Day for Night, curated by Chrissie Iles and Philippe Vergne, Whitney Museum of American Art, New York, March 2–May 28, 2006. Catalogue
The Figs Play Fox Dead, David Kordansky Gallery, Los Angeles, March 24–April 22, 2006

Ordinary Culture: Heikes/Helms/McMillian, curated by Doryun Chong, Walker Art Center, Minneapolis, August 11–November 19, 2006. Brochure

Joe Deutch, Jay Heikes, Chris Moukarbel, Kianja Strobert, Jeffrey Wells, curated by Clarissa Dalrymple, Marianne Boesky Gallery, New York, October 26–November 25, 2006

Modern Primitivism, Shane Campbell Gallery, Chicago, September 16–November 4, 2006

Project Placement, curated by Joseph Del Pesco, Analix Forever, Geneva, December 2006–January 2007

2007

Sympathy for the Devil: Art and Rock and Roll Since 1967, curated by Dominic Molon, Museum of Contemporary Art, Chicago, September 29, 2007–January 6, 2008. Catalogue

Grit and Vigor, curated by Rowley Kennerk, Light & Sie, Dallas, November 15–December 22, 2007

The Office, Tanya Bonakdar Gallery, New York, November 30–December 22, 2007

Looking Back: The White Columns Annual, curated by Clarissa Dalrymple, White Columns, New York, November 16–December 21, 2007

2008

Depositions, curated by Maxwell Graham, Galerie Francesca Pia, Zurich, January 19–March 1, 2008

Martian Museum of Terrestrial Art, curated by Lydia Yee, Barbican Art Gallery, London, March 6–May 18, 2008. Catalogue

2009

On From Here, Guild & Greyshkul, New York, February 5–8, 2009

Ostras Voces Otros Ámbitos, Gallería Marta Cervera, Madrid, June 4–July 18, 2009

Your Gold Teeth II, curated by Todd Levin, Marianne Boesky Gallery, New York, June 19–August 14, 2009

The Secret Life of Objects, curated by John Rasmussen, Midway Contemporary Art, Minneapolis, July 21–September 26, 2009

Event Horizon, curated by Darsie Alexander and Elizabeth Carpenter, Walker Art Center, Minneapolis, November 21, 2009–May 21, 2011

2010

\(Lean), Nicole Klagsbrun Gallery, New York, March 12–April 24, 2010

A Basic Human Impulse, curated by Andrea Bruciati, Galleria Comunale d'Arte Contemporanea di Monfalcone, Gorizia, Italy, May 15–June 27, 2010. Catalogue

Greta Alfaro, Markus Amm, Roe Ethridge, Nuria Fuster, Luis Gordillo, Jay Heikes, Jesús Pedraza, Eileen Quinlan, Tomas Saraceno, Daniel Silvo, Gallería Marta Cervera, Madrid, June 10–July 15, 2010

The Mass Ornament, curated by John Rasmussen, Barbara Gladstone Gallery, New York, June 25–August 13, 2010. Catalogue

2011

dwelling, Marianne Boesky Gallery, New York, February 3–April 2, 2011

Tabula Rasa, Gallería Marta Cervera, Madrid, April 28–June 4, 2011

Dark Room, Night Gallery, Los Angeles, August 8–September 9, 2011

2012

At the Speed of Stone, curated by Anthony Huberman, Marianne Boesky Gallery, New York, March 2–April 14, 2012. Catalogue

Trieste, curated by Jay Heikes, Federica Schiavo Gallery, Rome, March 31–May 26, 2012. Catalogue

Too Old for Toys, Too Young for Boys, curated by Alex Gartenfeld, OHWOW, Los Angeles, June 30–August 31, 2012

2013

Tommy Hartung, Jay Heikes, Alfred Leslie, Sarah Lucas, Luther Price, Brie Ruais & Ryan Sullivan, curated by Clarissa Dalrymple, Xavier Hufkens, Brussels, January 17–February 9, 2013

A Handful of Dust, curated by Laura Fried, Santa Barbara Contemporary Arts Forum, California, January 27–March 24, 2013

Painter Painter, curated by Eric Crosby and Bartholomew Ryan, Walker Art Center, Minneapolis, February 2–October 26, 2013. Brochure

Trieste, curated by Jay Heikes, Marianne Boesky Gallery, New York, March 2–30, 2013. Catalogue

Traces of Life, curated by Ariel Roger-Paris, Wentrup Gallery, Berlin, April 26–May 31, 2013

2014

Trieste, curated by Jay Heikes, Grimm Gallery, Amsterdam, February 1–March 15, 2014. Catalogue

The Ground, curated by Conny Purtill, Adams and Ollman, Portland, Oregon, March 7–April 26, 2014

Another Look at Detroit, curated by Todd Levin, Marianne Boesky Gallery and Marlborough Chelsea, New York, June 26–August 8, 2014

Phantoms in the Dirt, curated by Karsten Lund, Museum of Contemporary Photography, Chicago, July 24–October 5, 2014. Catalogue

2015

Weird Science, Marianne Boesky Gallery, New York, July 9–August 7, 2015

S.Arancio, F.Ardini, S.Deininger, J.Heikes, M.Lauter, K.Pandian, A.Sala, Federica Schiavo Gallery, Rome, September 16–November 12, 2015

Consequences, curated by Jay Heikes, Fondazione Giuliani, Rome, October 10–December 12, 2015. Catalogue

2016

I Talk with the Spirits, curated by Chris Wiley, Marianne Boesky Gallery, New York, June 23–August 2, 2016

Jay Heikes, Todd Norsten, Karthik Pandian, Andrea Sala, Rob Sherwood, Federica Schiavo Gallery, Rome, September 5–October 31, 2016

The Ground, curated by Conny Purtill, Adams and Ollman Gallery, Portland, Oregon, September 16–October 15, 2016

2017

This is a Pipe: Realism and the Found Object in Contemporary Art, Shane Campbell Gallery, Chicago, February 17–March 17, 2018

Hurts to Laugh, curated by Sarah Lehrer-Graiwer, Various Small Fires, Los Angeles, July 8–August 19, 2017

2018

Mother Sky, Boesky West, Aspen, September 1–October 6, 2018

2019

Qui, dove ci incontriamo, Norma Mangione Gallery, Turin, Italy, January 15–March 9, 2019; Federica Schiavo Gallery, Milan, January 23–March 9, 2019; and Galleria Tiziana di Caro, Naples, Italy, January 26–March 9, 2019

I've Been Searching For a Quiet Hole to Bury My Head in for a While, curated by Sophie Weil, Crying Clover, Los Angeles, March 10–April 13, 2019

02.74.75.76, Federica Schiavo Gallery, Milan, March 21–May 11, 2019

2020

Transitional Nature, curated by Katherine Manthorn and Amy Galpin, Patricia & Phillip Frost Art Museum, Miami, January 25–May 17, 2020

BIBLIOGRAPHY

Arnaudo, Luca. "Trieste, una mostra di profondità." Review of *Trieste*, Federica Schiavo Gallery, Rome. *Artribune*, May 27, 2012. https://www.artribune.com/report/2012/05/trieste-una-mostra-di-profondita.

Aspden, Peter. "Shopping with the Tate," *Financial Times Weekend*, London (October 14–15, 2006): 1.

Bailey, Stephanie. "Asia Now, FIAC and Paris Internationale: A walk-through." *Ocula*, October 26, 2018. https://ocula.com/magazine/reports/asia-now-fiac-and-paris-internationale-a-walk.

Barliant, Claire. "Emerging Artists: Jay Heikes," *Modern Painters* (October 2006): 58–60.

Biswas, Allie. "Jay Heikes: 'I've always loved the reminder that the natural world has the upper hand," *Studio International*, June 16, 2017, https://www.studiointernational.com/index.php/jay-heikes-interview-ive-always-loved-the-reminder-that-the-naural-world-has-the-upper-hand.

Capodiferro, Giulia. "Fino all'11.XI.2016 Jay Heikes, *No Future ism*, Federica Schiavo, Milano," *Exibart.com*, November 11, 2016, https://www.exibart.com/milano/fino-all11-xi-2016-jay-heikes-no-future-ism-federica-schiavo-milano.

Chou, Kimberly. "The Serious Joke: The Objects of Jay Heikes," *Art in America*, August 29, 2010, https://www.artnews.com/art-in-america/features/jay-heikes-marianne-boesky-58033.

Conti, Riccardo. "Fino al 14.III.2009 Jay Heikes, Roma, Schiavo Mazzonis," *Exibart.com*, February 13, 2009, https://www.exibart.com/roma/fino-al-14-iii-2009-jay-heikes-roma-schiavo-mazzonis.

D'Agostino, Pietro. "RA. Mostra di Jay Heikes," *New CultFrame*, June 16, 2014, https://www.cultframe.com/2014/06/ra-mostra-di-jay-heikes.

Dafoe, Taylor. "Weird Science," *V Magazine* (2015).

Dault, Julia. "Akimblog: New York City," *Akimbo*, November 7, 2007. No longer online.

Falconer, Morgan. "Last Chance: Morgan Falconer on Jay Heikes at Marianne Boesky, New York," *Saatchiart.com*, November 6, 2007. No longer online.

Fallon, Michael. "Review of *Jay Heikes and Kirk McCall* at Midway Contemporary Art," *Art Papers* 25, no. 5 (September–October 2002): 45.

Farber, Janet. "Stormy Weather." Review of *Jay Heikes*, Joslyn Art Museum, Omaha. *The Reader*, July 11, 2019, https://thereader.com/visual-art/stormy-weather.

Ferrara, Annette. "Goth, all grown up." Review of *All the Pretty Corpses*, Renaissance Society at the University of Chicago. *Time Out Chicago*, December 8–15, 2005.

Gabler, Jay. "Painter Painter," *Artforum*, March 2013, https://www.artforum.com/picks/painter-painter-39750.

González Panizo, Javier. "Jay Heikes en la Galería Marta Cervera," *REVISTA CLAVES DE ARTE*, March 12, 2010. No longer online.

Heikes, Jay. *Consequences*. Rome: CURA.BOOKS, 2016.

Heikes, Jay. *Eroding Rainbow*. New York and Rome: Marianne Boesky Gallery and Federica Schiavo Gallery, 2010.

Heikes, Jay. "Manifesto," *Art in America* 101, no. 2 (February 2013): 40–41.

Jay Heikes. *Trieste*. Rome: Federica Schiavo Gallery; New York: Marianne Boesky Gallery; and Amsterdam: Grimm Gallery, 2014.

Johnson, Ken. "What to See in New York Art Galleries This Week." Review of *I Talk with the Spirits*, Marianne Boesky Gallery, New York. *The New York Times*, July 7, 2016, https://www.nytimes.com/2016/07/08/arts/design/art-galleries-nyc.html.

Kalstrom, Jeff. "Review of 'Wall to Wall' at the Soap Factory," *New Art Examiner* 29, no. 2 (November/December 2001): 97–98.

Labanca, Luca. "L'altra faccia dei diamanti." Review of *The Material Mine*, Federica Schiavo Gallery, Rome. *Artribune*, April 14, 2011, https://www.artribune.com/report/2011/04/l%E2%80%99altra-faccia-dei-diamanti.

Lo, Melissa and Sansone, Valentina. "Sculpture Forever: Contemporary Sculpture (part II)," *Flash Art* 36, no. 231 (July–September, 2003): 100–7.

Menegoi, Simone. Review of *Jay Heikes: No future ism* at Federica Schiavo Gallery, Milan. *Artforum*, January 2017, https://www.artforum.com/print/reviews/201701/jay-heikes-65471.

Milani, Eleonora Milani. Review of *Consequences*, Fondazione Giuliani, Rome. "Sarcasmo e dirordine. Jay Heikes e il tradimento del white cube," *Artribune*, October 12, 2015, https://www.artribune.com/report/2015/10/mostra-collettivo-jay-heikes-fondazione-giuliani-roma.

Miller, Sara Nicole. "Warfare in the Suburbs." Review of *Ordinary Culture: Heikes/Helms/McMillian*, Walker Art Center, Minneapolis. *The Minnesota Daily*, August 9, 2006, https://www.mndaily.com/article/2006/08/warfare-suburbs.

Molina, Óscar Alonso. "Jay Heikes," *Arte y Parte* (2010): 136

Noto, Giorgia. "Escludi il sole, rompi l'incastesimo. Jay Heikes a roma." Review of *Ra*, Federica Schiavo Gallery, Rome. *Artribune*, May 29, 2014, https://www.artribune.com/report/2014/05/escludi-il-sole-rompi-lincantesimo-jay-heikes-a-roma.

Orden, Abraham. "The Windy Apple." Review of *The Sixth Retelling*, Shane Campbell Gallery, Chicago. *Artnet Magazine*, January 24, 2007, http://www.artnet.com/magazineus/reviews/orden/orden1-24-07.asp.

Paghera, Isabella. "Interview with Jay Heikes— Fondazione Giuliani, Rome," *ATP Diary*, October 21, 2015, http://atpdiary.com/jay-heikes-fondazione-giuliani-rome.

Porter, Jenelle. "Jay Heikes." In *Vitamin 3-D: New Perspectives in Sculpture and Installation*. London: Phaidon Press Limited, 2009.

Ryan, Bartholomew. "A Table of Curious Elements: Jay Heikes on Filthy Minds," Walker Art Center. Last modified July 3, 2013. https://walkerart.org/magazine/a-table-of-curious-elements-jay-heikes-on-filthy-minds.

Silvi, Marta. "Critic's Pick: Consequences," *Artforum*, October 10, 2015, https://www.artforum.com/picks/consequences-55753.

Smith, Roberta. "Jay Heikes: 'Inanimate Life,'" *The New York Times*, October 22, 2010, C25.

Smith, Rod. "Of Parrots, Porn and Death Metal," *City Papers*, February 8, 2006, 37, 39.

Stillman, Nick. "Jay Heikes." Review of *Like a Broken Record*, Marianne Boesky Gallery, New York. *Artforum* 45, no. 5 (January 2008): 280–281.

Shaeffer, James. "Visit: Jay Heikes' solo show at Marianne Boesky Gallery," *Kaleidoscope*, November 25, 2013. No longer online.

Vargi, Yasemin. "Interview," *Artspeak.nyc*, May 22, 2017, https://www.artspeak.nyc/home/2017/5/10/jay-heikes.

Velez, Pedro. "Rock n' Raunch." Review of *Use Your Illusion*, Vedanta Gallery, Chicago. *Artnet*, August 27, 2002, http://www.artnet.com/magazine/reviews/velez/velez8-27-02.asp.

Vergne, Philippe. "Jay Heikes." In *ICE CREAM: 10 Curators, 100 Contemporary Artists, 10 Source Artists*. London: Phaidon Press Limited, 2007.

Vozmediano, Elena. "Jay Heikes envuelve el vacío." Review of *Jay Heikes*, Galleria Marta Cervera, Madrid. *El Cultural*, April 9, 2010, 28–29.

Wells, Madeline. "Review: Jay Heikes' Exhibition at BAMPFA Addresses Themes of Alienness and Borders," *East Bay Express*, February 19, 2018, https://www.eastbayexpress.com/CultureSpyBlog/archives/2018/02/19/review-jay-heikes-exhibition-at-bampfa-address-themes-of-alienness-and-borders.

White, Roger. "Jay Heikes at Marianne Boesky," *The Highlights*, November 2007. No longer online.

White, Russ. "Now Showing: Niet Voor Kinderen," *mplsart.com*, November 4, 2015, https://www.mplsart.com/written/2015/11/now-showing-jay-heikes-niet-voor-kinderen.

Williamson, Damien. "Aspen Art Museum opens three new exhibitions." Review of *Buried in the Bright*, Aspen Art Museum. *Aspen Daily News*, February 17, 2012, https://www.aspendailynews.com/aspen-art-museum-opens-three-new-exhibitions/article_3fb7d279-84b9-588f-aba9-02c24410f72e.html.

"Three Things You Should Know About Jay Heikes." *Artsy*, October 16, 2013. https://www.artsy.net/article/editorial-three-things-you-should-know-about-jay.

"Walkabout. Jay Heikes." *Cura Magazine* (November 26, 2013).

AWARDS

Jerome Travel and Study Grant, Jerome Foundation, 2001

Jerome Fellowship, Jerome Foundation, 2001

Bush Fellowship, Bush Foundation, 2007

McKnight Artist Fellowship, McKnight Foundation, 2016

Pollock-Krasner Foundation grant, 2017

Chinati Foundation artist in residence, 2017

PUBLIC COLLECTIONS

Baltimore Museum of Art, Maryland

Hood Museum of Art, Dartmouth College, New Hampshire

Joslyn Art Museum, Omaha

Minneapolis Institute of Art, Minneapolis

Museum of Fine Arts, Boston

Altoids Curiously Strong Collection, New Museum of Contemporary Art, New York

North Dakota Museum of Art, Grand Forks

Walker Art Center, Minneapolis

EDUCATION

B.F.A. University of Michigan, Ann Arbor, Michigan, 1998

M.F.A. Yale University, New Haven, Connecticut, 2005

Born 1975 in Princeton, New Jersey

List of Works Illustrated

Page 25, left to right:

Kill Yr Idols . . . Part III, 2002, digital video transferred to DVD, color, silent, 115:00 minutes

White Light (stills), 2003, tempera, graphite, and marker on photocopy, forty parts, each: 28 ½ × 40 inches, 72.4 × 101.6 cm

Kill Yr Idols . . . Part I, 2003, felt, dimensions variable

Page 32, left to right:

Adam Helms, *Untitled (48 Portraits)*, 2006, ink on Mylar, 124 ½ × 328 inches, 316.2 × 833.1 cm, Walker Art Center, Minneapolis, Gift of Collectors' Council Acquisitions Fund, 2007

Roadgear (Staircase, Severing Box, Beach Ball, Milk Crate, Extension Cord, Frying Pan and Light Bulb, Bocce Ball, Clock, Giant Toblerone, Rain Stick, Duffle Bag Box), 2006, wood, paper, staples, flat black latex, plastic milk crate, cotton, painted extension cord, painted coconuts, string, painted bocce ball, painted rain stick, painted light bulb and cast iron frying pan, dimensions vary

Roadgear (Speaker and Paper), 2006, wood, paper, staples, and flat black latex, dimensions vary

So There's This Pirate . . . Live from Minneapolis, 2006, graphite and sprayed enamel on photocopy, 96 × 216 inches, 243.8 × 548.6 cm

Roadgear (Dildo Walker and Closet), 2006, painted cast bronze, cotton, wood, steel, flat black latex, and casters, walker: 40 × 23 × 12 inches, 101.6 × 58.4 × 30.5 cm; closet: 53 ⅝ × 42 ½ × 9 ⅝ inches, 136.2 × 108 × 24.4 cm

Installation includes acoustical ceiling tiles, dimensions variable

Page 33, left to right:

The Sixth Retelling, 2006, sprayed enamel on photocopy, 132 × 480 inches, 335.3 × 1219 cm

Roadgear (Clock), 2006, wood, paper, staples, coconut, cast bronze coconut, and string, 47 ½ diameter × 5 inches, 120.7 diameter × 12.7 cm

Installation includes acoustical ceiling tiles, dimensions variable

Pages 34–35, left to right:

Left for Dead in New York, 2006, graphite, ink, and sprayed enamel on photocopy, 138 × 360 inches, 350.5 × 914.4 cm

Roadgear (Speaker, Paper, Frying Pan and Lightbulb), 2006, wood, paper, staples, flat black latex, plastic handles, painted lightbulb, and cast iron frying pan, overall: 30 ¾ × 108 × 72 inches, 78.1 × 274.3 × 182.9 cm

Roadgear (Clock), 2006, wood, paper, staples, coconut, cast bronze coconut, and string, 48 diameter × 6 ¼ inches, 121.9 diameter × 15.9 cm

Roadgear (Abstract Sculpture in Severing Box), 2006, wood, painted bronze, and flat black latex, box: 21 × 64 × 29 inches, 53.3 × 162.6 × 73.7 cm; sculpture: 16 × 19 × 12 ½ inches, 40.6 × 48.3 × 31.8 cm

Roadgear (Dildo Walker and Closet), 2006, painted cast bronze, cotton, wood steel, flat black latex, and casters, walker: 40 × 23 × 12 inches, 101.6 × 58.4 × 30.5 cm; closet: 53 ⅝ × 42 ½ × 9 ⅝ inches, 136.2 × 108 × 24.4 cm

Roadgear (Shoebox), 2006, painted shoe box, 7 × 12 × 8 inches, 17.8 × 30.5 × 20.3 cm

Roadgear (Square Staircase), 2006, wood, paper, staples, and flat black latex, 76 × 77 × 18.5 inches, 193 × 195.6 × 47 cm

Installation includes acoustical ceiling tiles, dimensions variable

Page 37, left to right:

I:VIII V, 2007, sprayed enamel on photocopy, overall: 34 × 240 inches, 86.4 × 609.6 cm

Broken Record, 2007, cast bronze, two parts: 121 × 24 ½ × 10 inches, 307.4 × 62.2 × 25.4 cm; 134 × 24 ½ × 10 inches, 340.4 × 62.2 × 25.4 cm

The Rules of Attraction, 2007, iron, bronze, steel, rope, and latex, trap: 32 ½ × 14 × 14 inches, 82.6 × 35.6 × 35.6 cm; cheese: 2 × 3 ½ × 5 inches, 5.1 × 8.9 × 12.7 cm; rope: length variable

Page 39, back to front:

6:30 Today, tomorrow, and the day after that, 2007, wood, string, cast bronze, steel, enamel, latex, cuckoo clock weights, and coconut, 96 diameter × 6 inches, 243.8 diameter × 15.2 cm

The Soft Pillow, 2007, Hydrocal, wood, cast bronze spikes, and enamel, 10 × 84 × 32 inches, 25.4 × 213.4 × 81.3 cm

Pages 40–41, left to right:

6:30 Today, tomorrow, and the day after that, 2007, wood, string, cast bronze, steel, enamel, latex, cuckoo clock weights, and coconut, 96 diameter × 6 inches, 243.8 diameter × 15.2 cm

In the Belly of a Basking Shark, 2007, burlap, foam, dry adhesive, and upholstery tacks, seven panels, overall: 96 × 168 × 2 inches, 243.8 × 426.7 × 5.1 cm

The Soft Pillow, 2007, Hydrocal, wood, cast bronze spikes, and enamel, 10 × 84 × 32 inches, 25.4 × 213.4 × 81.3 cm

The Rules of Attraction, 2007, iron, bronze, steel, rope, and latex, trap: 32 ½ × 14 × 14 inches, 82.6 × 35.6 × 35.6 cm; cheese: 2 × 3 ½ × 5 inches, 5.1 × 8.9 × 12.7 cm; rope: length variable

X:I III I, 2007, sprayed enamel on photocopy, overall: 34 × 200 inches, 86.4 × 508 cm

Pages 46–47, left to right:

A Broken Record Not a Broken Record, 2007, cast bronze, bleached cotton, wood, steel, paper, and latex, 72 ¾ × 105 × 109 inches, 184.8 × 266.7 × 276.9 cm

VI: III II, 2007, sprayed enamel on photocopy, ten parts, overall: 30 × 400 inches, 76.2 × 1,016 cm

Everything All at Once (Channel 4), 2007, sprayed enamel on steel, 32 ½ × 35 inches, 82.6 × 88.9 cm

A Broken Record Not a Broken Record Just a Sound, 2007, cast bronze, bleached cotton, wood, steel, paper, and latex, 92 × 130 × 92 inches, 233.7 × 330.2 × 233.7 cm

Ninth Retelling, 2007, cast bronze, 72 × 15 × 17 inches, 182.9 × 38.1 × 43.2 cm

Pages 48–49, left to right:

The Rules of Attraction, 2007, iron, bronze, steel, rope, and latex, trap: 32 ½ × 14 × 14 inches, 82.6 × 35.6 × 35.6 cm; cheese: 2 × 3 ½ × 5 inches, 5.1 × 8.9 × 12.7 cm; rope: length variable

6:30 Tonight, tomorrow, and the next day, wood, string, cast bronze coconut, steel, cuckoo clock weights, and coconut, 96 diameter × 6 inches, 243.8 diameter × 15.2 cm

The Tomb, 2007, wood, paper, and latex, 16 × 22 × 14 inches, 40.6 × 55.9 × 35.6 cm

Theater of the Mind, 2007, bleached cotton, wood, staples, steel, paper, and latex, 79 × 128 × 23 inches, 200.7 × 325.1 × 58.4 cm

A Broken Record Not a Broken Record Just a Sound, 2007, cast bronze, bleached cotton, wood, steel, paper, and latex, 92 × 130 × 92 inches, 233.7 × 330.2 × 233.7 cm

Ninth Retelling, 2007, cast bronze, 72 × 15 × 17 inches, 182.9 × 38.1 × 43.2 cm

Pages 56–57, left to right:

Sinking Feeling, 2008, cast bronze, iron, and rust, 11 × 29 × 27 inches, 27.9 × 73.7 × 68.6 cm

Caustic Afternoon, 2008, sprayed enamel and rust on steel, 43 × 33 inches, 109.2 × 83.8 cm

Dead Air, 2008, cast bronze, iron, and rust, 18 ¼ × 95 × 29 inches, 46.4 × 241.3 × 73.7 cm

Pages 60–61, left to right:

River's Edge, 2008, cast bronze, iron, and rust, 55 ½ × 112 × 21, 141 × 284.5 × 53.3 cm

Here on Earth, 2008, sprayed enamel and rust on steel, 71 × 28 inches, 180.3 × 71.1 cm

Pages 62–63, left to right:
Molting, 2010, gelatin and metallic pigment,
dimensions variable
Thickly, 2010, dyed porcupine quills, driftwood, and
steel, 74 × 22 × 20 inches, 188 × 55.9 × 50.8 cm
Outside World, 2010, enamel on wood, 18 ¾ × 29 ¼ ×
3 ½ inches, 47.6 × 74.3 × 8.9 cm

Pages 64–65, left to right:
Conversations with a Bitter Pill, 2010, sprayed enamel
and pigment on steel, 62 × 46 inches, 157.5 ×
116.8 cm
Heartless Ascension, 2010, cast bronze, iron, and rust,
99 ½ × 200 × 67 inches, 252.7 × 508 × 170.2 cm
Prickly, 2010, dyed porcupine quills, driftwood,
and steel, 82 ½ × 38 × 21 inches, 209.6 × 96.5 ×
53.3 cm

Pages 88–89, left to right:
Civilian (severed), 2009, hand-dyed palladium print,
48 ¾ × 58 ½ inches, 123.8 × 148.6 cm
Molting, 2010, gelatin and metallic pigment,
dimensions variable
Civilian (poking), 2008, hand-dyed palladium print,
18 × 13 ¾ inches, 45.7 × 34.9 cm

Pages 110–11, left to right:
Ear of Dionysius, 2011, water-based ink, dry pigment,
gesso, wood glue, paper, and expanded aluminum
on wood stretcher, 50 × 38 inches, 127 × 96.5 cm,
Walker Art Center, Minneapolis, Butler Family
Fund, 2012
Mermaid's Hole, 2011, water-based ink, dry pigment,
gesso, wood glue, paper, and expanded aluminum
on wood stretcher, 50 × 38 inches, 127 × 96.5 cm
Moonshine, 2011, water-based ink, dry pigment, gesso,
wood glue, paper, and expanded aluminum on
wood stretcher, 50 × 38 inches, 127 × 96.5 cm
Margin Walker, 2011, water-based ink, dry pigment,
gesso, wood glue, paper, and expanded aluminum
on wood stretcher, 50 × 38 inches, 127 × 96.5 cm
On floor: *Methcathinone Blues*, 2011, raw linen
and copper ore, overall: 6 ½ × 59 × 73 inches,
16.5 × 149.9 × 185.4 cm

Pages 112–13, left to right:
Clowning, 2013, paper, gesso, wood glue, oil based-ink,
and expanded aluminum on wood stretcher,
72 × 48 inches, 182.9 × 121.9 cm
fragment from the Theory of Everything, 2013, wax,
wood, horsehair, ink, and steel wire, 73 ⅝ ×
29 ⅛ × 4 ¾ inches, 187 × 74 × 12 cm
Jessica Jackson Hutchins, *Wedding Present*, 2013,
armchairs, paint, and glazed ceramic, 29 ×
64 × 29 inches, 73.7 × 162.6 × 73.7 cm.
Courtesy of the artist and Marianne Boesky
Gallery, New York
fragment from the Theory of Everything, 2013, wax,
wood, horsehair, ink, and steel wire, 50 × 44 ×
3 inches, 127 × 111.8 × 7.6 cm

Pages 120–21, left to right:
fragment from the Theory of Everything, 2014, wax,
wood, horse hair, ink, and steel wire, 66 ⅞ ×
70 ⅞ × 5 ⅞ inches, 170 × 180 × 15 cm

Desire, 2014, iron cauldron, bronze slag, and cement,
22 × 12 inches diameter, 56 × 30.5 cm diameter

Pages 124–25, left to right:
Self Portrait with Frostbite, 2013, leather, paper, oil-
based ink, and wood, 65 ½ × 15 ⅛ × 2 ¼ inches,
166.4 × 38.4 × 5.7 cm
Storytelling, 2013, cyanotype on linen, 113 × 103 inches,
287 × 261.6 cm

Pages 138–39, left to right:
Conny Purtill, *The Ground: Carl the Eagle*, 2009,
oil, gesso, india ink, and acrylic spray paint on
canvas, 22 × 16 ⅞ inches, 56 × 43 cm
Jay Heikes, Todd Norsten, and Conny Purtill,
Ufficio, 2015, changing room with painting
by Todd Norsten, 78 ¾ × 67 × 58 ½ inches,
200 × 170.2 × 148.6 cm
Gedi Sibony, *Fountain Feet*, 2015, latex, wood,
and cardboard, 50 × 30 ⅜ × 6 ¾ inches,
127 × 77 × 17 cm

Page 144, top, left to right:
Appetite for Destruction, 2015, wood, foam, sand,
wood glue, paper, steel, copper wire, and rubber,
29 × 43 × 34 inches, 73.7 × 109.2 × 86.4 cm
Nostalgia, 2015, chiffon, sand, paper, wood glue,
aluminum wire, and steel slag, three parts:
114 × 31 × 2 inches, 289.6 × 78.7 × 5.1 cm;
117 × 32 × 2 inches, 297.2 × 81.3 × 5.1 cm;
117 × 30 × 2 inches, 297.2 × 76.2 × 5.1 cm
Niet voor Kinderen, 2015, asphaltum on paper,
86 ⅜ × 27 inches, 219.4 × 68.6 cm

Page 144, bottom, left to right:
Daily Rituals (Newday), 2015, collaboration with
Kate Farstad. Digital video transferred to DVD,
color, sound, 27:03 minutes
Welkom, 2015, salt, steel slag, wood glue, paper, glass,
and expanded aluminum, 1 ½ × 20 × 30 inches,
3.8 × 50.8 × 76.2 cm
Zs, 2015, asphaltum on paper, seven parts, each:
43 ¾ × 30 inches, 111 × 76 cm

Pages 150–51, left to right:
Zs, 2016, neoprene, salt, steel slag, copper wire,
and wood glue on wood stretcher, 62 ⅝ × 41 ×
2 ⅜ inches, 159 × 104 × 6 cm
Zs, 2016, fused glass, 15 × 13 × 1 ⅛ inches, 38 ×
33 × 3 cm
Beyond Zebra, 2016, pigmented mortar, burlap, salt,
latex paint, steel, wood glue, steel slag, rubber
hose, and expanded aluminum on wood stretcher,
94 × 74 × 4 inches, 238.8 × 188 × 10.2 cm

Pages 158–59, left to right:
Death Spiral, 2017, copper, wax, aluminum foil, steel,
and steel slag, 216 × 168 × 120 inches, 548.6 ×
426.7 × 304.8 cm
On wall: *Zs*, 2017, paper, dry pigment, oil paint,
glue, and wood glue on wood stretcher, 65 × 46 ×
2 inches, 165.1 × 116.8 × 5.1 cm
Couper l'oeil, 2017, copper, wax, aluminum foil, steel,
steel slag, cast bronze, and iron, 216 × 216 ×
96 inches, 548.6 × 548.6 × 243.8 cm

Minor Planets, 2017, steel slag, wood, wax, wood glue,
paper, wood chips, gladstone ore, cast bronze,
lignum vitae, cast bismuth, aluminum, and copper,
six unique objects, dimensions range from 4 to
14 inches, 10.2 to 35.6 cm diameter
Winter is Coming, 2017, copper, wax, aluminum foil,
steel slag, leather, glue, cast bismuth, and salt,
120 × 192 × 156 inches, 304.8 × 487.7 × 396.2 cm
On wall, rear: *Zs*, 2016, salt, steel wire, ink, canvas,
and foam on wood stretcher, 22 × 17 × 2 inches,
55.9 × 43.2 × 5.1 cm

Pages 164–65, left to right:
Winter is Coming, 2017, copper, wax, aluminum foil,
steel slag, leather, glue, cast bismuth, and salt,
120 × 192 × 156 inches, 304.8 × 487.7 × 396.2 cm
Minor Planets, 2017, steel slag, wood, wood glue,
wax, gladstone ore, cast bronze, lignum vitae,
cast bismuth, paper, wood chips, concrete, glass
beads, ink, and oxidized copper foil, eight unique
objects, ranging from 5 to 14 inches, 12.7 to
35.6 cm diameter
Zs, 2017, ink, copper wire, salt, wood glue, and canvas
on wooden stretcher, 47 × 36 × 2 inches, 119.4 ×
91.4 × 5.1 cm
Zs, 2017, steel slag, salt, glue, pigment, ink, fiberglass,
rubber snakes, copper wire, acorn husks, rocks,
and dirt on wood stretcher, 51 × 38 × 4 inches,
129.5 × 96.5 × 10.2 cm
Couper l'oeil, 2017, copper, wax, aluminum foil, steel,
steel slag, cast bronze, and iron, 216 × 216 ×
96 inches, 548.6 × 548.6 × 243.8 cm
The Devil Has Left My Building, 2015, graphite and
ink on paper, 51 ⅛ × 85 inches, 129.9 × 215.9 cm
The Sports Writer, 2015, graphite and ink on paper,
50 ⅜ × 87 ⅛ inches, 128 × 221.3 cm

Pages 174–75, left to right:
Mother Sky, 2019, oil on stained canvas, 56 × 75 inches,
142.2 × 190.5 cm
Mother Sky, 2019, oil on stained canvas, 56 × 75 inches,
142.2 × 190.5 cm
On floor: *Minor Planets*, 2017–19, Kevlar, salt, paper,
wood glue, oxidized copper foil, wax, copper
wire, cast bronze, lignum vitae, cast bismuth,
fired clay, rope sawdust, niobium, and steel mesh,
fourteen unique objects, ranging from 2 ¾ to
10 ½ inches, 7 to 26.7 cm diameter

Acknowledgments

Jay Heikes

This book only exists because Stephanie Gabriel and Adrian Turner sat me down one afternoon and urged me to take it on. You are both so dedicated and patient. Thank you for convincing me to step back and take a look at what the last twenty years have meant. I am a better artist because of it and will always cherish our ridiculous and profound moments together. An artist can be many things but you reminded me how to be one, without being less than one.

To say this book would not have been possible without the vision of Jenelle Porter and Conny Purtill of Purtill Family Business would be an obvious understatement. I trusted you both to bring this monster to life in book form and our Frankenstein breathes because of a relentless attention to detail and the dream of creating a lasting record worth looking at again and again. The process of making this book has been more profound than I could have ever imagined and there is part of me that wishes we could be frozen in time, huddled together, designing the book just weeks before the pandemic took hold. The sounds of your voices over the course of this last year were a reminder of a time when a laugh wasn't immediately followed by a groan. If the world doesn't end soon, I look forward to the next Purtill Family Experience.

Marianne Boesky. You have always surprised me with your passion and curiosity, so thank you for being curious enough to support from the beginning my romantic dream of an artist's life. Without you this is not possible. Saying thank you almost seems inadequate because I can't express the gratitude through words that would fully capture the scene of joyful crying while hugging you. You are a force of nature that I have been lucky enough to know and be challenged by. Don't ever stop; I know you won't. I also have to thank your incredible team over the years: Kristen Becker, Aniko Berman, Jack Cassou, Sophia Jackson, Peter Kaiser, Rachel Kay, Veronica Levitt, Ricky Manne, Julia Mazur Huet, Elizabeth Miseo, Mary Mitsch, Kai Patricio, Serra Pradhan, Sara Putterman, Ted Riederer, Chris Rodriguez, Bauby Tan, Kory Trolio, Greg Wall, Kelly Woods, Jason Wyche, and Hector Zapata.

The Italians. Someday I will live out my destiny of being with you in my adopted homeland where I can act like a tourist, and as we pass the day without doing much at all I just say all the words I know in Italian: cappuccino, mortadella, nutria, genio, allora! Thank you Federica Schiavo and Chiara Zoppelli for representing me at a time when no gallery in their right mind would have opened a gallery, and for still representing me in an era where no gallery should be open in their right mind. You are, respectively, a lion and a flame that refuse to be silenced or extinguished. To my Italian family—Anna Abbá, Edoardo Baratella, Laura Bellanca, Simone Bellotti, Carla Chiarchiaro, Alessia Cretella, Dario Di Domenico, Ilaria Gianni, Giovanni Giuliani, Valeria Giuliani, Damiana Leoni, Costanza Mazzonis, Andrea Sala, and Alan Santarelli—we will be reunited soon.

The Walker. David Bartley, Bob Brown, Dan Byers, Betsy Carpenter, Sylvia Chivaratanond, Doryun Chong, Eric Crosby, Phil Docken, Richard Flood, Douglas Fogle, Kathy Halbreich, Andria Hickey, Kirk McCall, Jenelle Porter, Conny Purtill, Yasmil Raymond, Bartholomew Ryan, Philippe Vergne, Cameron Wittig. You were all so impressive and left a scar at a time when I understood very little.

The artists, curators, writers and collaborators over the years. Amy Adams, Eric Andersen, Michel Auder, Matt Bakkom, John Ballinger, Claire Barliant, Allie Biswas, Sebastiaan Brandsen, Julie Campbell, Karin Campbell, Shane Campbell, Denis Canakis, Paulina Canakis, Marta Cervera, Leslie Cohan, Bill Cole, Zach Cole, Nathan Coutts, Clarissa Dalrymple, Matthew Day Jackson, Erika de Ixcel, Apsara DiQuinzio, Adrienne Drake, Ronnie Droher, Ben Echeverria, Derek Ernster, Kate Farstad, Lauri Firstenberg, Laura Fried, Isa Gagarin, Maxwell Graham, Joseph Grigely, Jorg Grimm, Adam Helms, Kristen Hileman, Patrick Hill, Lisa Lapinski, Marianne Holtermann, Anthony Huberman, Jessica Jackson Hutchins, Rowley Kennerk, David Kordansky, Marshall LaCount, Wyatt Lasky, Sarah Lehrer-Graiwer, Rhonda Lieberman, Andie Mazarol, Megan McCready, Josiah McElheny, Gregory Miller, Jenny Monick, Jenny Moore, Steve Mose, Todd Norsten, Karthik Pandian, Hirsch Perlman, Melba Price, John Rasmussen, Hannah Reefhuis, Cole Rogers, Jonathon Rosemond, Eric Ruschman, Joe Scanlan, Justin Schaefer, Justin Schlepp, John Schmid, Erin Shirreff, Virginia Shore, Gedi Sibony, Parker Sprout, Michael Stickrod, Jessica Stockholder, Anna Stothart, Bruce Tapola, Johannes VanDerBeek, LaToya Varpness, Pedro Velez, Hamza Walker, Sheila Wagner, Sophie Weil, Rob Weiner, Chris Wiley, Candace Worth, Robyn Wright, Heidi Zuckerman.

And to a family that reminds me there is more to life than the self-absorbed pursuits of an only child: Jen, Claude, and Vita, you are my world and mean everything to me. Pat, Tom, Kindra, Tim, Hazel, Alastair, thank you for making celebrations worth remembering. And mom and dad, thank you for letting me use the extra bedroom as a painting studio. Your never-ending support of my artistic delusions was and is something I'll hold onto eternally.

I love you all.

Jay Heikes is published by Gregory R. Miller & Co. in association with Marianne Boesky Gallery

Gregory R. Miller & Co.
62 Cooper Square, New York, NY 10003
grmandco.com

Marianne Boesky Gallery
509 West 24th Street, New York, NY 10011
marianneboeskygallery.com

Editor: Jenelle Porter
Copyeditor: Lucy Flint
Design: Purtill Family Business
Color separations: Echelon, Santa Monica
Printing: Conti Tipocolor, S.p.A., Florence, Italy

Photography Credits
Susan Alzner: 29, 30, 79; Johanna Arnold: 164; Giorgio Benni: 10 fig. 4, 11 fig. 5, 12 fig. 6, 27, 52–55, 68–75, 137–141; Benjamin Blackwell: 15 fig. 7; Lance Brewer: 178–181; Mario Di Paolo: 56–60; © The Estate of Eva Hesse. Courtesy Hauser & Wirth: 15 fig. 7; Jay Heikes: 78, 126, 182–184; Aaron Igler: 9 fig. 3, 39, 40; Object Studies: 18 fig. 11, 158–160; Gene Pittman: 32, 92–95; Renato Rinaldi, image courtesy of Archivio Merz and Gladstone Gallery, New York and Brussels: 16 fig. 9; Andrea Rossetti: 17 fig. 10, 120–123, 127–128, 150–155, 158, 174–177; Cameron Wittig: 132; Jason Wyche: 15 fig. 8, 20 fig. 12, 36, 37, 46–51, 62–67, 91, 98, 106, 109, 114–119, 124, 135, 149, 152, 156, 157, 160

Cover: *Mother Sky*, 2019 (detail), oil on stained canvas, 47 × 65 inches, 119.4 × 165.1 cm
Inside front and back covers: *Vigilante*, 2020 (detail), oil on stained canvas, 60 × 80 inches, 152.4 × 203.2 cm

Distributed worldwide by:
ARTBOOK | D.A.P.
artbook.com

Library of Congress Control Number:
2020946665

ISBN: 978-1-941366-31-8

Sarah Lehrer-Graiwer is an art writer, curator, and educator in Los Angeles. She is the author of *Lee Lozano: Dropout Piece*, *Joint Dialogue: Lozano, Graham, Kaltenbach*, and *Can't Reach Me There*. She also writes for *Artforum*, *Art in America*, *BOMB*, *CURA*, *Interview*, and *Mousse*, among others, and is the editor of *Pep Talk*, a publication series begun in 2009, which has produced monographic issues on artists and writers. Lehrer-Graiwer has taught at Otis College of Art and Design and the University of Southern California, and currently teaches for the School of the Art Institute of Chicago.

Jenelle Porter is a curator and writer. From 2011–15 she was Senior Curator at the Institute of Contemporary Art/Boston where she organized *Fiber: Sculpture 1960–present*, and several monographic exhibitions. Most recently she organized *Less Is a Bore: Maximalist Art & Design* for the ICA/Boston. From 2005–10, Porter was curator at the Institute of Contemporary Art, Philadelphia. She has held curatorial positions at Artists Space, New York, Walker Art Center, Minneapolis, and Whitney Museum of American Art, New York. Porter has authored numerous books and essays on art and artists.

Philippe Vergne is the Director of the Serralves Museum in Porto, Portugal. From 2014–18 he was Director of The Museum of Contemporary Art, Los Angeles. Prior to his appointment at MOCA, Vergne led the Dia Art Foundation; was Deputy Director and Chief Curator at the Walker Art Center in Minneapolis, where he worked for over a decade organizing more than 25 international exhibitions; and was Director of the Musée d'art Contemporain in Marseille, France.

Hamza Walker is the Director of LAXART, an independent nonprofit art space in Los Angeles. From 1994–2016, he was the Director of Education and Associate Curator at the Renaissance Society at the University of Chicago, a non-collecting museum devoted to contemporary art. In 2017 he co-curated (with Catherine Taft) *Reconstitution*, a group exhibition mounted at LAXART. In 2016 he co-curated (with Aram Moshayedi) *Made in L.A.* at the Hammer Museum, Los Angeles.

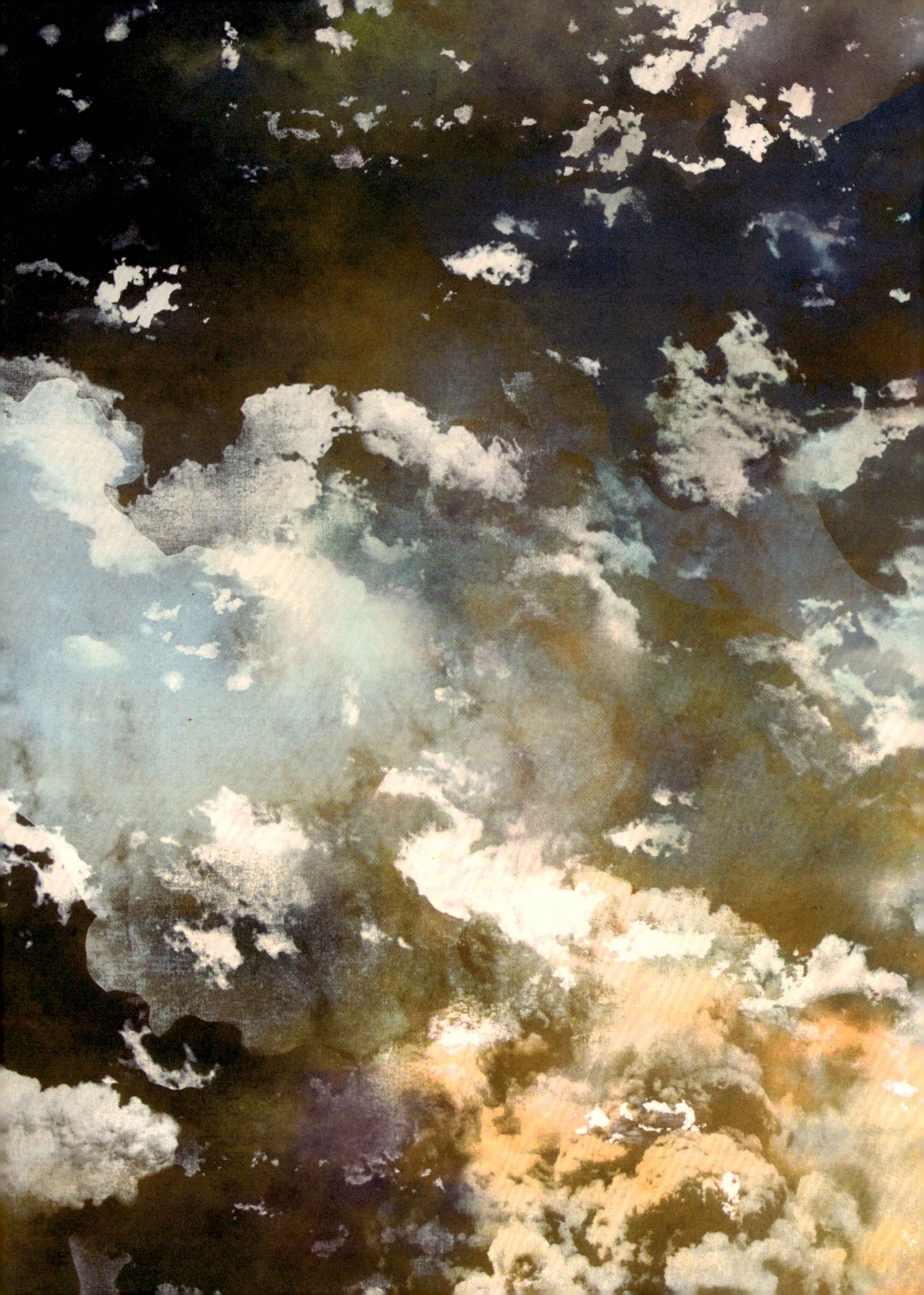